D1783864

Peugeot 504
Owners
Workshop
Manual

John S Mead

Models covered

UK: Peugeot 504 Saloon, Estate and Family Estate with
       1948cc, 2112cc or 2304cc Diesel engine

USA: Peugeot 504 Sedan and Station Wagon with 129
       cu in (2112cc) or 141 cu in (2304cc) Diesel engine

Does not cover petrol (gasoline) engined models

ISBN 0 85696 663 0

ABCDE
FGHIJK
LMNOPQ
RST

HAYNES PUBLISHING GROUP
SPARKFORD YEOVIL SOMERSET ENGLAND
distributed in the USA by
HAYNES PUBLICATIONS INC
861 LAWRENCE DRIVE
NEWBURY PARK
CALIFORNIA 91320
USA

Acknowledgements

Thanks are due to Peugeot Automobiles UK Limited for the supply of technical information and certain illustrations, and to Castrol Limited who supplied lubrication data. The bodywork repair photographs used in this manual were provided by Holt Lloyd Limited, who supply 'Turtle Wax', 'Dupli-Color Holts' and other Holts range products.

The Peugeot 504 LD Saloon used as the project car for this manual was kindly loaned by Mr M W Buckland of Bruton, Somerset.

About this manual

Its aim

The aim of this manual is to help you get the best value from your car. It can do so in several ways. It can help you decide what work must be done (even should you choose to get it done by a garage), provide information on routine maintenance and servicing, and give a logical course of action and diagnosis when random faults occur. However, it is hoped that you will use the manual by tackling the work yourself. On simpler jobs it may even be quicker than booking the car into a garage and going there twice to leave and collect it. Perhaps most important, a lot of money can be saved by avoiding the costs the garage must charge to cover its labour and overheads.

The manual has drawings and descriptions to show the function of the various components so that their layout can be understood. Then the tasks are described and photographed in a step-by-step sequence so that even a novice can do the work.

Its arrangement

The manual is divided into twelve chapters, each covering a logical sub-division of the vehicle. The Chapters are each divided into Sections, numbered with single figures, eg 5; and the Sections into paragraphs (or sub-sections), with decimal numbers following on from the Section they are in, eg 5.1, 5.2, 5.3 etc.

It is freely illustrated, especially in those parts where there is a detailed sequence of operations to be carried out. There are two forms of illustration: figures and photographs. The figures are numbered in sequence with decimal numbers, according to their position in the Chapter – eg Fig. 6.4 is the fourth drawing/illustration in Chapter 6. Photographs carry the same number (either individually or in related groups) as the Section or sub-section to which they relate.

There is an alphabetical index at the back of the manual as well as a contents list at the front. Each Chapter is also preceded by its own individual contents list.

References to the 'left' or 'right' of the vehicle are in the sense of a person in the driver's seat facing forwards.

Unless otherwise stated, nuts and bolts are removed by turning anti-clockwise, and tightened by turning clockwise.

Vehicle manufacturers continually make changes to specifications and recommendations, and these, when notified, are incorporated into our manuals at the earliest opportunity.

Whilst every care is taken to ensure that the information in this manual is correct, no liability can be accepted by the authors or publishers for loss, damage or injury caused by any errors in, or omissions from, the information given.

Introduction to the Peugeot 504 Diesel

Although available in Europe for some time previously, the diesel engined version of the Peugeot 504 Saloon was introduced in the UK and USA in 1974. Current models are available with the choice of three engine sizes, these being 1948cc, 2112cc or 2304cc dependent on market, all of which utilize the highly efficient Ricardo Comet V cylinder head design.

The Peugeot 504 Diesel range comprises three body styles; Saloon, Estate and Family Estate. Apart from the diesel engine, the mechanical and body specifications are similar to the 504 petrol engined models, providing these cars with a standard of trim, finish and luxury seldom found in diesel powered vehicles.

A wide range of options available on various models includes automatic transmission, power assisted steering, air conditioning and (on Estate models) tailgate washers and wipers.

Contents

Peugeot 504 Diesel Saloon (UK spec)

Peugeot 504 Diesel Estate (UK spec)

Peugeot 504 Diesel Sedan (USA spec)

General dimensions and weights

Overall length
Saloon .... 4480 mm (176.3 in)
Estate and Family Estate .... 4803 mm (189.1 in)

Overall width .... 1695 mm (66.7 in)

Overall height
Saloon .... 1460 mm (57.5 in)
Estate and Family Estate .... 1550 mm (61.1 in)

Wheelbase
Saloon .... 2740 mm (107.9 in)
Estate and Family Estate .... 2900 mm (114.1 in)

Front track .... 1420 mm (55.9 in)

Rear track
Saloon .... 1330 mm (52.4 in)
Estate and Family Estate .... 1360 mm (53.5 in)

Turning circle
Saloon .... 10 220 mm (402.3 in)
Estate and Family Estate .... 10 760 mm (423.6 in)

Kerb weight
Saloon .... 1210 kg (2671 lbs)
Family Estate .... 1375 kg (3031 lbs)
Estate .... 1325 kg (2921 lbs)

Use of English

As this book has been written in England, it uses the appropriate English component names, phrases, and spelling. Some of these differ from those used in America. Normally, these cause no difficulty, but to make sure, a glossary is printed below. In ordering spare parts remember the parts list will probably use these words:

English	American	English	American
Aerial	Antenna	Layshaft (of gearbox)	Countershaft
Accelerator	Gas pedal	Leading shoe (of brake)	Primary shoe
Alternator	Generator (AC)	Locks	Latches
Anti-roll bar	Stabiliser or sway bar	Motorway	Freeway, turnpike etc
Battery	Energizer	Number plate	License plate
Bodywork	Sheet metal	Paraffin	Kerosene
Bonnet (engine cover)	Hood	Petrol	Gasoline
Boot lid	Trunk lid	Petrol tank	Gas tank
Boot (luggage compartment)	Trunk	'Pinking'	'Pinging'
Bottom gear	1st gear	Propeller shaft	Driveshaft
Bulkhead	Firewall	Quarter light	Quarter window
Cam follower or tappet	Valve lifter or tappet	Retread	Recap
Carburettor	Carburetor	Reverse	Back-up
Catch	Latch	Rocker cover	Valve cover
Choke/venturi	Barrel	Roof rack	Car-top carrier
Circlip	Snap-ring	Saloon	Sedan
Clearance	Lash	Seized	Frozen
Crownwheel	Ring gear (of differential)	Side indicator lights	Side marker lights
Disc (brake)	Rotor/disk	Side light	Parking light
Drop arm	Pitman arm	Silencer	Muffler
Drop head coupe	Convertible	Spanner	Wrench
Dynamo	Generator (DC)	Sill panel (beneath doors)	Rocker panel
Earth (electrical)	Ground	Split cotter (for valve spring cap)	Lock (for valve spring retainer)
Engineer's blue	Prussian blue	Split pin	Cotter pin
Estate car	Station wagon	Steering arm	Spindle arm
Exhaust manifold	Header	Sump	Oil pan
Fast back (Coupe)	Hard top	Tab washer	Tang; lock
Fault finding/diagnosis	Trouble shooting	Tailgate	Liftgate
Float chamber	Float bowl	Tappet	Valve lifter
Free-play	Lash	Thrust bearing	Throw-out bearing
Freewheel	Coast	Top gear	High
Gudgeon pin	Piston pin or wrist pin	Trackrod (of steering)	Tie-rod (or connecting rod)
Gearchange	Shift	Trailing shoe (of brake)	Secondary shoe
Gearbox	Transmission	Transmission	Whole drive line
Halfshaft	Axleshaft	Tyre	Tire
Handbrake	Parking brake	Van	Panel wagon/van
Hood	Soft top	Vice	Vise
Hot spot	Heat riser	Wheel nut	Lug nut
Indicator	Turn signal	Windscreen	Windshield
Interior light	Dome lamp	Wing/mudguard	Fender

Miscellaneous points

An 'oil seal' is fitted to components lubricated by grease!

A 'damper' is a 'shock absorber', it damps out bouncing, and absorbs shocks of bump impact. Both names are correct, and both are used haphazardly.

Note that British drum brakes are different from the Bendix type that is common in America, so different descriptive names result. The shoe end furthest from the hydraulic wheel cylinder is on a pivot; interconnection between the shoes as on Bendix brakes is most uncommon. Therefore the phrase 'Primary' or 'Secondary' shoe does not apply. A shoe is said to be 'Leading' or 'Trailing'. A 'Leading' shoe is one on which a point on the drum, as it rotates forward, reaches the shoe at the end worked by the hydraulic cylinder before the anchor end. The opposite is a 'Trailing' shoe, and this one has no self servo from the wrapping effect of the rotating drum.

Buying spare parts
and vehicle identification numbers

Buying spare parts

Spare parts are available from many sources, for example: Peugeot garages, other garages and accessory shops, and motor factors. Our advice regarding spare part sources is as follows:

Officially appointed Peugeot garages – This is the best source of parts which are peculiar to your car and are otherwise not generally available (eg complete cylinder heads, internal gearbox components, badges, interior trim etc). It is the only place at which you should buy parts if your car is still under warranty – non-Peugeot components may invalidate the warranty. To be sure of obtaining the correct parts it will always be necessary to give the storeman your car's vehicle identification number, and if possible, to take the 'old' part along for positive identification. Remember that many parts are available on a factory exchange scheme – any parts returned should always be clean! It obviously makes good sense to go straight to the specialists on your car for this type of part for they are best equipped to supply you.

Other garages and accessory shops – These are often very good places to buy materials and components needed for the maintenance of your car (eg oil filters, bulbs, fanbelts, oils and greases, touch-up paint, filler paste, etc). They also sell general accessories, usually have

convenient opening hours, charge lower prices and can often be found not far from home.

Motor factors – Good factors will stock all of the more important components which wear out relatively quickly (eg clutch components, pistons, valves, exhaust systems, brake cylinders/pipes/hoses/seals/shoes and pads etc). Motor factors will often provide new or reconditioned components on a part exchange basis – this can save a considerable amount of money.

Vehicle identification numbers

Although many individual parts, and in some cases sub-assemblies, fit a number of different models, it is dangerous to assume that just because they look the same, they are the same. Differences are not always easy to detect except by serial numbers. Make sure, therefore, that the appropriate identity number for the model or sub-assembly is known and quoted when a spare part is ordered.

The vehicle identification plate is mounted on the right-hand side front inner wing panel and may be seen once the bonnet is open.

The engine number is located on the left-hand side of the cylinder block.

The vehicle identification plate is located on the right-hand inner wing panel

The engine number is located on the left-hand side of the cylinder block

Tools and working facilities

Introduction

A selection of good tools is a fundamental requirement for anyone contemplating the maintenance and repair of a motor vehicle. For the owner who does not possess any, their purchase will prove a considerable expense, offsetting some of the savings made by doing-it-yourself. However, provided that the tools purchased are of good quality, they will last for many years and prove an extremely worthwhile investment.

To help the average owner to decide which tools are needed to carry out the various tasks detailed in this manual, we have compiled three lists of tools under the following headings: *Maintenance and minor repair*, *Repair and overhaul*, and *Special*. The newcomer to practical mechanics should start off with the *Maintenance and minor repair* tool kit and confine himself to the simpler jobs around the vehicle. Then, as his confidence and experience grow, he can undertake more difficult tasks, buying extra tools as, and when, they are needed. In this way, a *Maintenance and minor repair* tool kit can be built-up into a *Repair and overhaul* tool kit over a considerable period of time without any major cash outlays. The experienced do-it-yourselfer will have a tool kit good enough for most repair and overhaul procedures and will add tools from the *Special* category when he feels the expense is justified by the amount of use to which these tools will be put.

It is obviously not possible to cover the subject of tools fully here. For those who wish to learn more about tools and their use there is a book entitled *How to Choose and Use Car Tools* available from the publishers of this manual.

Maintenance and minor repair tool kit

The tools given in this list should be considered as a minimum requirement if routine maintenance, servicing and minor repair operations are to be undertaken. We recommend the purchase of combination spanners (ring one end, open-ended the other); although more expensive than open-ended ones, they do give the advantages of both types of spanner.

Combination spanners - 8 to 20 mm
Adjustable spanner - 9 inch
Engine sump/gearbox/rear axle drain plug key
Set of feeler gauges
Allen keys – 2 to 15 mm
Brake bleed nipple spanner
Screwdriver - 4 in long x $\frac{1}{4}$ in dia (flat blade)
Screwdriver - 4 in long x $\frac{1}{4}$ in dia (cross blade)
Combination pliers - 6 inch
Hacksaw, junior
Tyre pump
Tyre pressure gauge
Grease gun
Oil can
Fine emery cloth (1 sheet)
Wire brush (small)
Funnel (medium size)

Repair and overhaul tool kit

These tools are virtually essential for anyone undertaking any major repairs to a motor vehicle, and are additional to those given in the *Maintenance and minor repair* list. Included in this list is a comprehensive set of sockets. Although these are expensive they will be found invaluable as they are so versatile - particularly if various drives are included in the set. We recommend the $\frac{1}{2}$ in square-drive type, as this can be used with most proprietary torque spanners. If you cannot afford a socket set, even bought piecemeal, then inexpensive tubular box wrenches are a useful alternative.

The tools in this list will occasionally need to be supplemented by tools from the *Special* list.

Sockets (or box spanners) to cover range in previous list
Reversible ratchet drive (for use with sockets)
Extension piece, 10 inch (for use with sockets)
Universal joint (for use with sockets)
Torque wrench (for use with sockets)
'Mole' wrench - 8 inch
Ball pein hammer
Soft-faced hammer, plastic or rubber
Screwdriver - 6 in long x $\frac{5}{16}$ in dia (flat blade)
Screwdriver - 2 in long x $\frac{5}{16}$ in square (flat blade)
Screwdriver - 1$\frac{1}{2}$ in long x $\frac{1}{4}$ in dia (cross blade)
Screwdriver - 3 in long x $\frac{1}{8}$ in dia (electricians)
Pliers - electricians side cutters
Pliers - needle nosed
Pliers - circlip (internal and external)
Cold chisel - $\frac{1}{2}$ inch
Scriber (this can be made by grinding the end of a broken hacksaw blade)
Scraper (this can be made by flattening and sharpening one end of a piece of copper pipe)
Centre punch
Pin punch
Hacksaw
Valve grinding tool
Steel rule/straight-edge
Selection of files
Wire brush (large)
Axle stands
Jack (strong scissor or hydraulic type)

Special tools

The tools in this list are those which are not used regularly, are expensive to buy, or which need to be used in accordance with their manufacturers' instructions. Unless relatively difficult mechanical jobs are undertaken frequently, it will not be economic to buy many of these tools. Where this is the case, you could consider clubbing together with friends (or joining a motorists' club) to make a joint purchase, or borrowing the tools against a deposit from a local garage or tool hire specialist.

The following list contains only those tools and instruments freely available to the public, and not those special tools produced by the vehicle manufacturer specifically for its dealer network. You will find occasional references to these manufacturers' special tools in the text of this manual. Generally, an alternative method of doing the job without the vehicle manufacturers' special tool is given. However, sometimes, there is no alternative to using them. Where this is the case and the relevant tool cannot be bought or borrowed you will have to entrust the work to a franchised garage.

Valve spring compressor
Piston ring compressor
Balljoint separator
Universal hub/bearing puller
Impact screwdriver
Micrometer and/or vernier gauge
Dial gauge
Universal electrical multi-meter

Cylinder compression gauge
Lifting tackle (photo)
Trolley jack
Light with extension lead

Buying tools

For practically all tools, a tool dealer is the best source since he will have a very comprehensive range compared with the average garage or accessory shop. Having said that, accessory shops often offer excellent quality tools at discount prices, so it pays to shop around.

Remember, you don't have to buy the most expensive items on the shelf, but it is always advisable to steer clear of the very cheap tools. There are plenty of good tools around at reasonable prices, so ask the proprietor or manager of the shop for advice before making a purchase.

Care and maintenance of tools

Having purchased a reasonable tool kit, it is necessary to keep the tools in a clean serviceable condition. After use, always wipe off any dirt, grease and metal particles using a clean, dry cloth, before putting the tools away. Never leave them lying around after they have been used. A simple tool rack on the garage or workshop wall, for items such as screwdrivers and pliers is a good idea. Store all normal spanners and sockets in a metal box. Any measuring instruments, gauges, meters, etc, must be carefully stored where they cannot be damaged or become rusty.

Take a little care when tools are used. Hammer heads inevitably become marked and screwdrivers lose the keen edge on their blades from time to time. A little timely attention with emery cloth or a file will soon restore items like this to a good serviceable finish.

Working facilities

Not to be forgotten when discussing tools, is the workshop itself. If anything more than routine maintenance is to be carried out, some form of suitable working area becomes essential.

It is appreciated that many an owner mechanic is forced by circumstances to remove an engine or similar item, without the benefit of a garage or workshop. Having done this, any repairs should always be done under the cover of a roof.

Wherever possible, any dismantling should be done on a clean flat workbench or table at a suitable working height.

Any workbench needs a vice: one with a jaw opening of 4 in (100 mm) is suitable for most jobs. As mentioned previously, some clean dry storage space is also required for tools, as well as the lubricants, cleaning fluids, touch-up paints and so on which become necessary.

Another item which may be required, and which has a much more general usage, is an electric drill with a chuck capacity of at least $\frac{5}{16}$ in (8 mm). This, together with a good range of twist drills, is virtually essential for fitting accessories such as wing mirrors and reversing lights.

Last, but not least, always keep a supply of old newspapers and clean, lint-free rags available, and try to keep any working area as clean as possible.

Jaw gap (in)	Spanner size
0.250	$\frac{1}{4}$ in AF
0.276	7 mm
0.313	$\frac{5}{16}$ in AF
0.315	8 mm
0.344	$\frac{11}{32}$ in AF; $\frac{1}{8}$ in Whitworth
0.354	9 mm
0.375	$\frac{3}{8}$ in AF
0.394	10 mm
0.433	11 mm
0.438	$\frac{7}{16}$ in AF
0.445	$\frac{3}{16}$ in Whitworth; $\frac{1}{4}$ in BSF
0.472	12 mm
0.500	$\frac{1}{2}$ in AF
0.512	13 mm
0.525	$\frac{1}{4}$ in Whitworth; $\frac{5}{16}$ in BSF
0.551	14 mm
0.563	$\frac{9}{16}$ in AF
0.591	15 mm

Jaw gap (in)	Spanner size
0.600	$\frac{5}{16}$ in Whitworth; $\frac{3}{8}$ in BSF
0.625	$\frac{5}{8}$ in AF
0.630	16 mm
0.669	17 mm
0.686	$\frac{11}{16}$ in AF
0.709	18 mm
0.710	$\frac{3}{8}$ in Whitworth, $\frac{7}{16}$ in BSF
0.748	19 mm
0.750	$\frac{3}{4}$ in AF
0.813	$\frac{13}{16}$ in AF
0.820	$\frac{7}{16}$ in Whitworth; $\frac{1}{2}$ in BSF
0.866	22 mm
0.875	$\frac{7}{8}$ in AF
0.920	$\frac{1}{2}$ in Whitworth; $\frac{9}{16}$ in BSF
0.938	$\frac{15}{16}$ in AF
0.945	24 mm
1.000	1 in AF
1.010	$\frac{9}{16}$ in Whitworth; $\frac{5}{8}$ in BSF
1.024	26 mm
1.063	$1\frac{1}{16}$ in AF; 27 mm
1.100	$\frac{5}{8}$ in Whitworth; $\frac{11}{16}$ in BSF
1.125	$1\frac{1}{8}$ in AF
1.181	30 mm
1.200	$\frac{11}{16}$ in Whitworth; $\frac{3}{4}$ in BSF
1.250	$1\frac{1}{4}$ in AF
1.260	32 mm
1.300	$\frac{3}{4}$ in Whitworth; $\frac{7}{8}$ in BSF
1.313	$1\frac{5}{16}$ in AF
1.390	$\frac{13}{16}$ in Whitworth; $\frac{15}{16}$ in BSF
1.417	36 mm
1.438	$1\frac{7}{16}$ in AF
1.480	$\frac{7}{8}$ in Whitworth; 1 in BSF
1.500	$1\frac{1}{2}$ in AF
1.575	40 mm; $\frac{15}{16}$ in Whitworth
1.614	41 mm
1.625	$1\frac{5}{8}$ in AF
1.670	1 in Whitworth; $1\frac{1}{8}$ in BSF
1.688	$1\frac{11}{16}$ in AF
1.811	46 mm
1.813	$1\frac{13}{16}$ in AF
1.860	$1\frac{1}{8}$ in Whitworth; $1\frac{1}{4}$ in BSF
1.875	$1\frac{7}{8}$ in AF
1.969	50 mm
2.000	2 in AF
2.050	$1\frac{1}{4}$ in Whitworth; $1\frac{3}{8}$ in BSF
2.165	55 mm
2.362	60 mm

A Haltrac hoist and gantry in use during a typical engine removal sequence

Jacking and towing

To change a wheel in an emergency, use the jack supplied with the vehicle. Ensure that the roadwheel nuts are slackened before jacking up the car, and make sure that the arm of the jack is fully engaged with the body bracket, and that the base of the jack is standing on a firm level surface. Chock at least one of the wheels remaining in contact with the ground.

The jack supplied with the vehicle is not suitable for use when raising the vehicle for maintenance or repair work. For these operations use a trolley, hydraulic on heavy duty screw type jack, located under the front or rear crossmember, or rear axle casing. Always supplement the jack with axle stands or blocks before working beneath the car.

If your vehicle is being towed, make sure that the tow rope is attached to one of the towing eyes or the front crossmember. If the vehicle is equipped with automatic transmission, ensure that the selector lever is in the 'N' position and do not exceed 30 mph (50 km/h). If towing a car equipped with automatic transmission for a distance greater than 25 miles (40 km), add 1 litre (1.76 pints, 2.1 US pints) of the recommended automatic transmission fluid to the unit.

Vehicle jack in position at the front and rear of the car

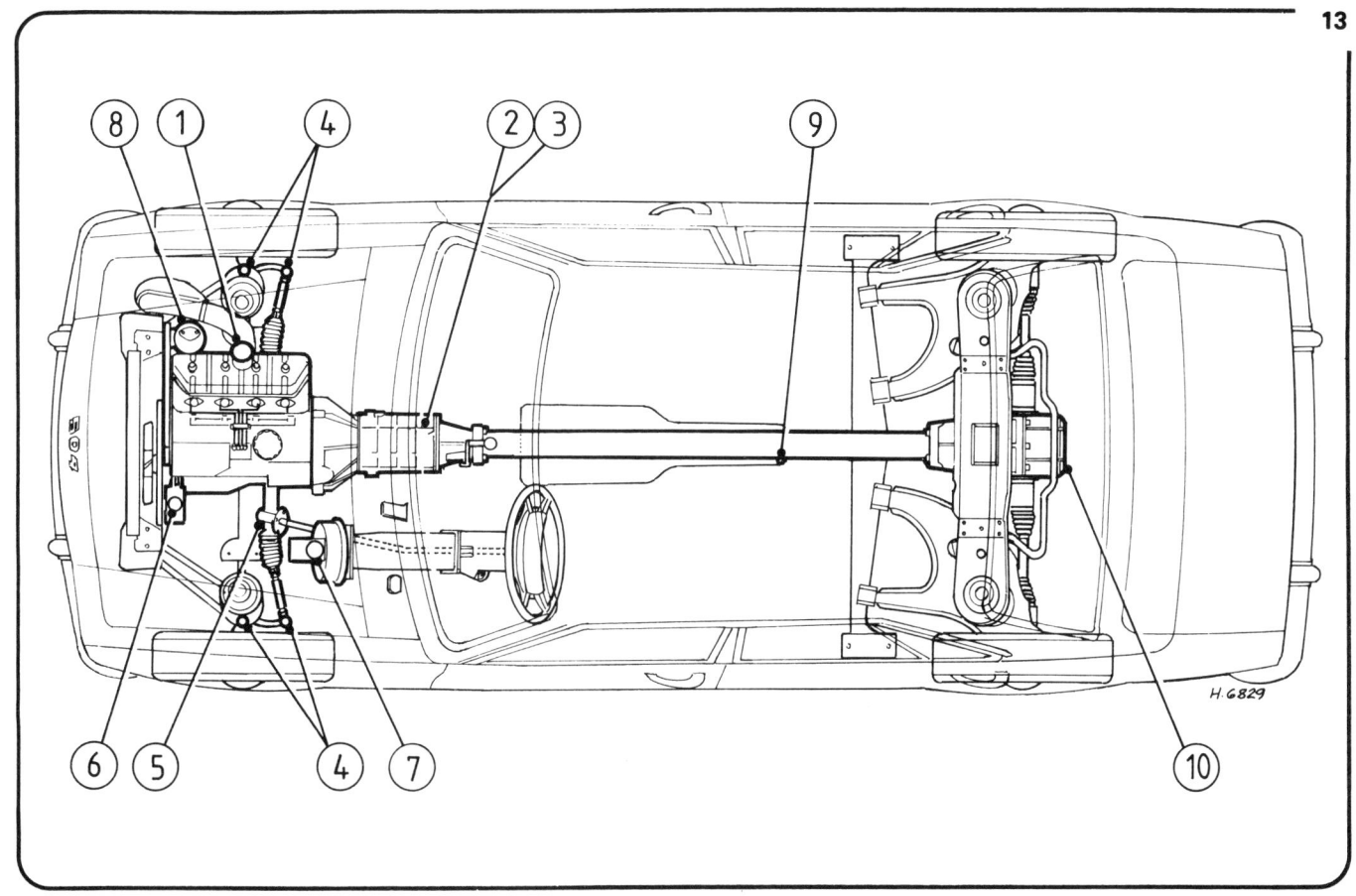

H.6829

Recommended lubricants and fluids

Component or system	Lubricant type or specification	Castrol product
Engine (1)	SAE 20W/50 multigrade engine oil	Castrol GTX
Manual transmission (2)	SAE 20W/50 multigrade engine oil	Castrol GTX
Automatic transmission (3)	Dexron® type automatic transmission fluid	Castrol TQ Dexron
Front suspension/steering balljoint grease nipples (4)	Lithium based multi-purpose grease	Castrol LM Grease
Steering gear rack and pinion (5)	Lithium based multi-purpose grease	Castrol LM Grease
Power assisted steering gear (6)	Dexron® type automatic transmission fluid	Castrol TQ Dexron®
Clutch and brake master cylinder reservoir (7)	Universal hydraulic fluid to specification SAE J1703/DOT 3	Castrol Girling Universal Brake and Clutch Fluid
Vacuum pump (8)	SAE 20W/50 multigrade engine oil	Castrol GTX
Propeller shaft (9)	Lithium based multi-purpose grease	Castrol LM Grease
Differential (10)	SAE 80EP hypoid gear oil	Castrol Hypoy Light
Locks, hinges, pivots etc	General purpose light oil	Castrol Everyman

The above are general recommendations only. Lubrication requirements vary from territory to territory and depend on vehicle usage. If in doubt consult the operator's handbook supplied with the vehicle, or your nearest Peugeot dealer.

Safety First!

Professional motor mechanics are trained in safe working procedures. However enthusiastic you may be about getting on with the job in hand, do take the time to ensure that your safety is not put at risk. A moment's lack of attention can result in an accident, as can failure to observe certain elementary precautions.

There will always be new ways of having accidents, and the following points do not pretend to be a comprehensive list of all dangers; they are intended rather to make you aware of the risks and to encourage a safety-conscious approach to all work you carry out on your vehicle.

Essential DOs and DON'Ts

DON'T rely on a single jack when working underneath the vehicle. Always use reliable additional means of support, such as axle stands, securely placed under a part of the vehicle that you know will not give way.

DON'T attempt to loosen or tighten high-torque nuts (e.g. wheel hub nuts) while the vehicle is on a jack; it may be pulled off.

DON'T start the engine without first ascertaining that the transmission is in neutral (or 'Park' where applicable) and the parking brake applied.

DON'T suddenly remove the filler cap from a hot cooling system – cover it with a cloth and release the pressure gradually first, or you may get scalded by escaping coolant.

DON'T attempt to drain oil until you are sure it has cooled sufficiently to avoid scalding you.

DON'T grasp any part of the engine, exhaust or catalytic converter without first ascertaining that it is sufficiently cool to avoid burning you.

DON'T syphon toxic liquids such as fuel, brake fluid or antifreeze by mouth, or allow them to remain on your skin.

DON'T inhale brake lining dust – it is injurious to health

DON'T allow any spilt oil or grease to remain on the floor – wipe it up straight away, before someone slips on it.

DON'T use ill-fitting spanners or other tools which may slip and cause injury.

DON'T attempt to lift a heavy component which may be beyond your capability – get assistance.

DON'T rush to finish a job, or take unverified short cuts.

DON'T allow children or animals in or around an unattended vehicle.

DO wear eye protection when using power tools such as drill, sander, bench grinder etc, and when working under the vehicle.

DO use a barrier cream on your hands prior to undertaking dirty jobs – it will protect your skin from infection as well as making the dirt easier to remove afterwards; but make sure your hands aren't left slippery.

DO keep loose clothing (cuffs, tie etc) and long hair well out of the way of moving mechanical parts.

DO remove rings, wristwatch etc, before working on the vehicle – especially the electrical system.

DO ensure that any lifting tackle used has a safe working load rating adequate for the job.

DO keep your work area tidy – it is only too easy to fall over articles left lying around.

DO get someone to check periodically that all is well, when working alone on the vehicle.

DO carry out work in a logical sequence and check that everything is correctly assembled and tightened afterwards.

DO remember that your vehicle's safety affects that of yourself and others. If in doubt on any point, get specialist advice.

IF, in spite of following these precautions, you are unfortunate enough to injure yourself, seek medical attention as soon as possible.

Fire

Remember at all times that petrol (gasoline) is highly flammable. Never smoke, or have any kind of naked flame around, when working on the vehicle. But the risk does not end there – a spark caused by an electrical short-circuit, by two metal surfaces contacting each other, or even by static electricity built up in your body under certain conditions, can ignite petrol vapour, which in a confined space is highly explosive.

Always disconnect the battery earth (ground) terminal before working on any part of the fuel system, and never risk spilling fuel on to a hot engine or exhaust.

It is recommended that a fire extinguisher of a type suitable for fuel and electrical fires is kept handy in the garage or workplace at all times. Never try to extinguish a fuel or electrical fire with water.

Fumes

Certain fumes are highly toxic and can quickly cause unconsciousness and even death if inhaled to any extent. Petrol (gasoline) vapour comes into this category, as do the vapours from certain solvents such as trichloroethylene. Any draining or pouring of such volatile fluids should be done in a well ventilated area.

When using cleaning fluids and solvents, read the instructions carefully. Never use materials from unmarked containers – they may give off poisonous vapours.

Never run the engine of a motor vehicle in an enclosed space such as a garage. Exhaust fumes contain carbon monoxide which is extremely poisonous; if you need to run the engine, always do so in the open air or at least have the rear of the vehicle outside the workplace.

If you are fortunate enough to have the use of an inspection pit, never drain or pour petrol, and never run the engine, while the vehicle is standing over it; the fumes, being heavier than air, will concentrate in the pit with possibly lethal results.

The battery

Never cause a spark, or allow a naked light, near the vehicle's battery. It will normally be giving off a certain amount of hydrogen gas, which is highly explosive.

Always disconnect the battery earth (ground) terminal before working on the fuel or electrical systems.

If possible, loosen the filler plugs or cover when charging the battery from an external source. Do not charge at an excessive rate or the battery may burst.

Take care when topping up and when carrying the battery. The acid electrolyte, even when diluted, is very corrosive and should not be allowed to contact the eyes or skin.

If you ever need to prepare electrolyte yourself, always add the acid slowly to the water, and never the other way round. Protect against splashes by wearing rubber gloves and goggles.

Mains electricity

When using an electric power tool, inspection light etc which works from the mains, always ensure that the appliance is correctly connected to its plug and that, where necessary, it is properly earthed (grounded). Do not use such appliances in damp conditions and, again, beware of creating a spark or applying excessive heat in the vicinity of fuel or fuel vapour.

Ignition HT voltage

A severe electric shock can result from touching certain parts of the ignition system, such as the HT leads, when the engine is running or being cranked, particularly if components are damp or the insulation is defective. Where an electronic ignition system is fitted, the HT voltage is much higher and could prove fatal.

Routine maintenance

Maintenance is essential for ensuring safety, and desirable for the purpose of getting the best in terms of performance and economy from your car. Over the years the need for periodic lubrication – oiling, greasing and so on – has been drastically reduced, if not totally eliminated. This has unfortunately tended to lead some owners to think that because no such action is required, components either no longer exist, or will last forever. This is a serious delusion. It follows therefore that the largest initial element of maintenance is visual examination and a general sense of awareness. This may lead to repairs or renewals, but should help to avoid roadside breakdowns. Other neglect results in unreliability, increased running costs, more rapid wear and depreciation of the vehicle in general.

Every 250 miles (400 km) or weekly

Check the tyre pressures (including the spare) and inflate if necessary
Check and top up the engine oil
Check and top up the battery electrolyte level
Check and top up the windscreen and rear window washer reservoirs
Check and top up the cooling system
Check and top up the brake fluid reservoirs
Check the operation of all lights

Every 3000 miles (5000 km)

Drain and refill the engine oil
Renew the oil filter cartridge
Generally check the operation of the brake and clutch hydraulic systems. Inspect all pipes, hoses and unions for leaks
Check the fluid level in the power assisted steering pump reservoir
Check and top up the manual or automatic transmission oil/fluid level
Check and top up the differential oil level
Check and top up the vacuum pump oil level
Inspect the tyres for wear or damage to the tread and side walls and check the pressures (including the spare)
Bleed the water trap fuel filter
Remove dead flies, leaves etc from the radiator fins
Lubricate the following points using a grease gun filled with lithium based general purpose grease:
  (a)   Left and right-hand steering swivels

(b)   Left and right-hand track rod end balljoints
(c)   Propeller shaft centre bearing
(d)   Torque tube spherical bearing (where applicable)
Lubricate all locks and hinges using light oil

Every 6200 miles (10 000 km)

Check the operation and adjustment of the electro-magnetic fan
Check the condition of and adjust all engine drivebelts
Check for wear in all steering and suspension joints and linkages
Check the exhaust system for leaks and security

Every 9500 miles (15 000 km)

Check the front and rear brake pad thickness and rear brake shoe lining thickness (where applicable)

Every 12 500 miles (20 000 km)

Drain and refill the manual transmission oil
Drain and refill the differential oil
Check the driveshaft, steering gear and clutch slave cylinder rubber protectors
Clean the air cleaner element and refill with fresh oil, or renew the element (dry type)
Renew the fuel filter
Check the tightness of the exhaust manifold, vacuum pump and alternator mounting bolts
Adjust the valve clearances
Adjust the engine idling speed
Check the handbrake operation and adjust if necessary
Adjust the rear drum brakes (where applicable)
Check the cooling system and hoses for leaks or deterioration

Every 18 500 miles (30 000 km)

Check the condition of the steering column flexible coupling

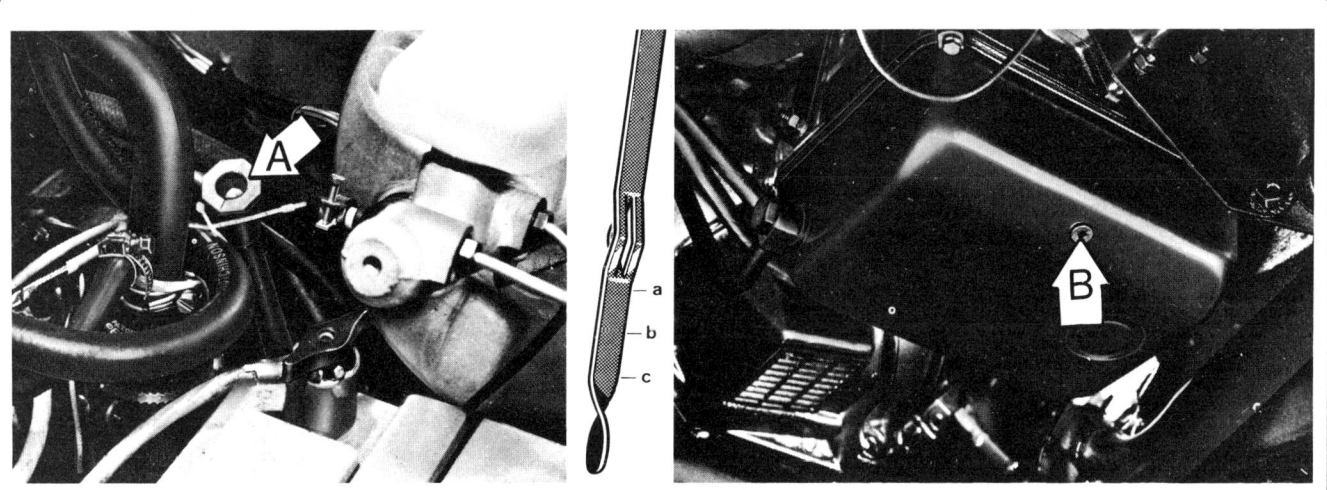

Location of the automatic transmission filler/dipstick (A) and drain plug (B); inset shows dipstick markings – (a) maximum warm, (b) minimum warm or maximum cold, and (c) minimum cold

Every 25 000 miles (40 000 km)

Drain and refill the automatic transmission fluid
Drain and refill the brake and clutch hydraulic fluid and bleed both systems
Check the operation of the automatic transmission kickdown cable

Every 50 000 miles (80 000 km)

Check the shock absorbers for leaks and effectiveness, and renew as necessary
Check the condition of the suspension rubber bushes
Check and adjust the free play of hubs, balljoints and track rod ends

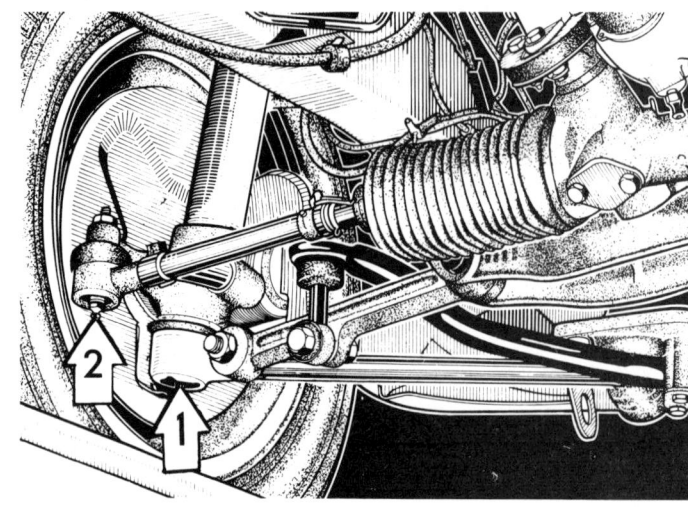

Left-hand lower steering swivel joint (1) and track rod end (2) grease nipples

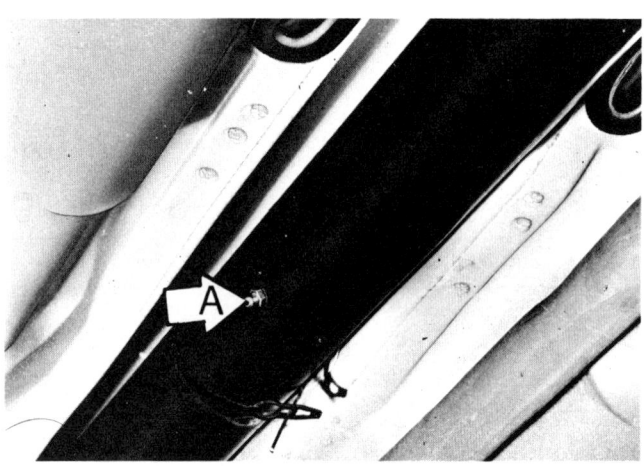
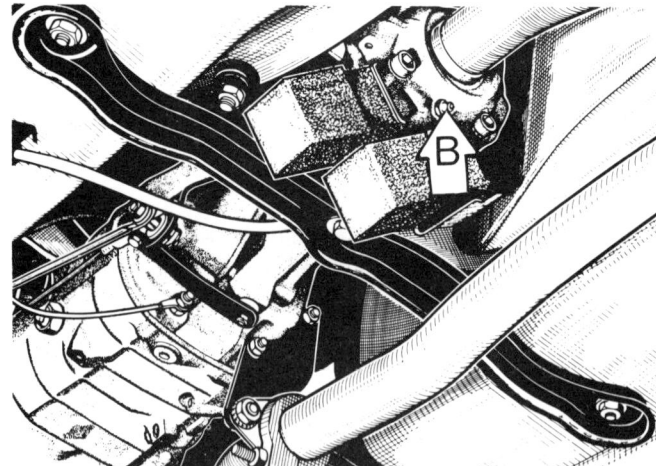

Propeller shaft centre bearing (A) and spherical bearing (B) grease nipples

Checking the engine oil level   Topping up the engine oil   Engine sump drain plug

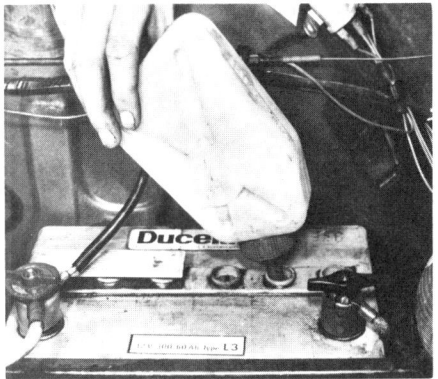

Topping up the battery electrolyte

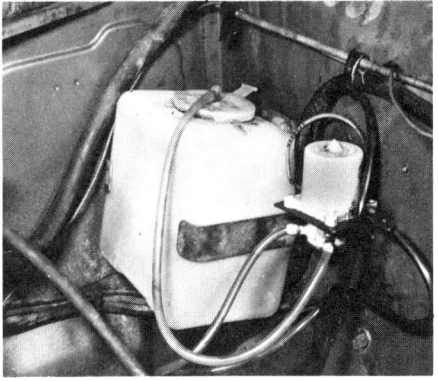

Windscreen washer pump and reservoir

Cooling system and expansion tank filler cap ...

... radiator filler cap ...

... radiator drain tap ...

... and engine drain plug (arrowed)

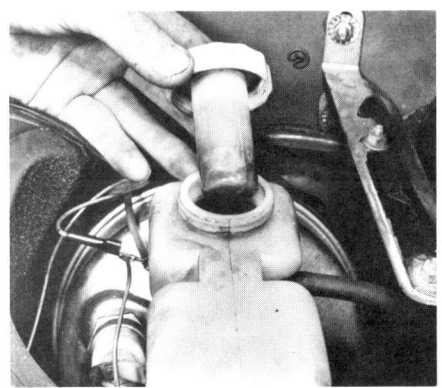

Checking the brake fluid level

The gearbox filler ...

... and drain plugs

Differential filler and drain plugs

Fuel filter and cartridge assembly

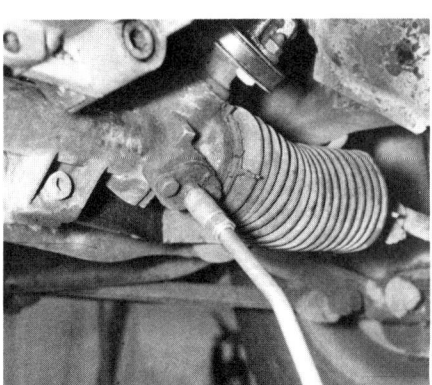

Greasing the steering gear

Fault diagnosis

Introduction

The car owner who does his or her own maintenance according to the recommended schedules should not have to use this section of the manual very often. Modern component reliability is such that, provided those items subject to wear or deterioration are inspected or renewed at the specified intervals, sudden failure is comparatively rare. Faults do not usually just happen as a result of sudden failure, but develop over a period of time. Major mechanical failures in particular are usually preceded by characteristic symptoms over hundreds or even thousands of miles. Those components which do occasionally fail without warning are often small and easily carried in the car.

With any fault finding, the first step is to decide where to begin investigations. Sometimes this is obvious, but on other occasions a little detective work will be necessary. The owner who makes half a dozen haphazard adjustments or replacements may be successful in curing a fault (or its symptoms), but he will be none the wiser if the fault recurs and he may well have spent more time and money than was necessary. A calm and logical approach will be found to be more satisfactory in the long run. Always take into account any warning signs or abnormalities that may have been noticed in the period preceding the fault – power loss, high or low gauge readings, unusual noises or smells, etc – and remember that failure of a component such as a fuse may only be a pointer to some underlying fault.

The pages which follow here are intended to help in cases of failure to start or breakdown on the road. There is also a Fault Diagnosis Section at the end of each Chapter which should be consulted if the preliminary checks prove unfruitful. Whatever the fault, certain basic principles apply. These are as follows:

Verify the fault: This is simply a matter of being sure that you know what the symptoms are before starting work. This is particularly important if you are investigating a fault for someone else who may not have described it very accurately.

Don't overlook the obvious: For example, if the car won't start, is there fuel in the tank? (Don't take anyone else's word on this particular point, and don't trust the fuel gauge either!) If an electrical fault is indicated, look for loose or broken wires before digging out the test gear.

Cure the disease, not the symptom: Substituting a flat battery with a fully charged one will get you off the hard shoulder, but if the underlying cause is not attended to, the new battery will go the same way.

Don't take anything for granted: Particularly, don't forget that a 'new' component may itself be defective (especially if it's been rattling round in the boot for months), and don't leave components out of a fault diagnosis sequence just because they are new or recently fitted. When you do finally diagnose a difficult fault, you'll probably realise that all the evidence was there from the start.

Electrical faults

Electrical faults can be more puzzling that straightforward mechanical failures, but they are no less susceptible to logical analysis if the basic principles of operation are understood. Car electrical wiring exists in extremely unfavourable conditions – heat, vibration and chemical attack – and the first things to look for are loose or corroded connection and broken or chafed wires, especially where the wires pass through holes in the bodywork or are subject to vibration.

All metal-bodied cars in current production have one pole of the battery 'earthed', ie connected to the car bodywork, and in nearly all modern cases it is the negative (-) terminal. The various electrical components – motors, bulb holders etc – are also connected to earth, either by means of a lead or directly by their mountings. Electrical current flows through the component and then back to the battery via the car bodywork. If the component mounting is loose or corroded, or if a good path back to the battery is not available, the circuit will be incomplete and malfunction will result. The engine and/or gearbox are also earthed by means of flexible metal straps to the body or subframe: if these straps are loose or missing, startor, or alternator trouble may result.

Assuming the earth return to be satisfactory, electrical faults will be due either to component malfunction or to defects in the current supply. Individual components are dealt with in Chapter 10. If supply wires are broken or cracked internally this results in an open circuit, and the easiest way to check for this is to bypass the suspect wire tempororarily with a length of wire having a crocodile clip or suitable connector at each end. Alternatively, a 12V test lamp can be used to verify the presence of supply voltage at various points along the wire and the break can be isolated.

If a bare portion of a live wire touches the car bodywork or other earthed metal part the electricity will take the low-resistance path thus formed back to the battery: this is known as a short-circuit. Hopefully a short-circuit will blow a fuse, but otherwise it may cause burning of the insulation (and possibly further short-circuits) or even a fire. This is why it is inadvisable to bypass persistently blowing fuses with silver foil or wire.

Spares and tool kit

Most cars are only supplied with sufficient tools for wheel changing; the *Maintenance and minor repair* tool kit detailed in *Tools and working facilities*, with the addition of a hammer, is probably sufficient for those repairs that most motorists would consider attempting at the roadside. In addition a few items which can be fitted without too much trouble in the event of breakdown should be carried. Experience and available space will modify the list below, but the following may save having to call on professional assistance:

Drivebelt(s) – emergency type may suffice
Spare fuses
Set of principle light bulbs
Tin of radiator sealer and hose bandage
Exhaust bandage
Roll of insulating tape
Length of soft iron wire
Length of electrical flex
Torch or inspection lamp (can double as test lamp)
Battery jump leads
Tow-rope
Litre of engine oil
Sealed can of hydraulic fluid
Emergency windscreen

If spare fuel is carried, a can designed for the purpose should be used to minimise risks of leakage and collision damage. A first aid kit and a warning triangle, whilst not at present compulsory in the UK, are obviously sensible items to carry in addition to the above.

When touring abroad it may be advisable to carry additional spares which, even if you cannot fit them yourself, could save having to wait while parts are obtained. The items below may be worth considering:

Clutch and throttle cables
Cylinder head gasket

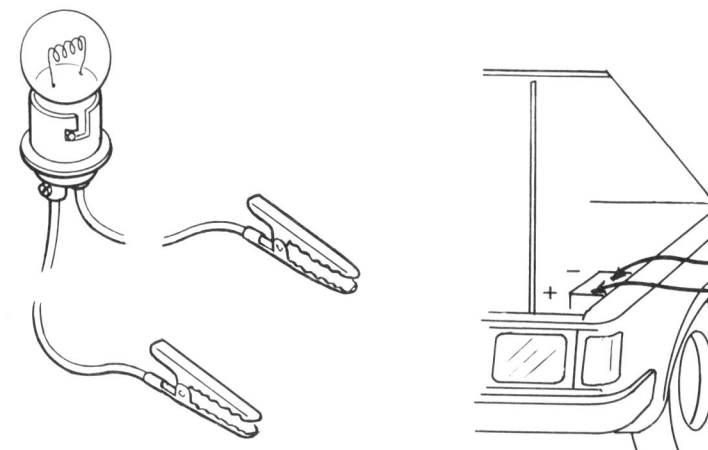

A test lamp is useful for checking electrical continuity

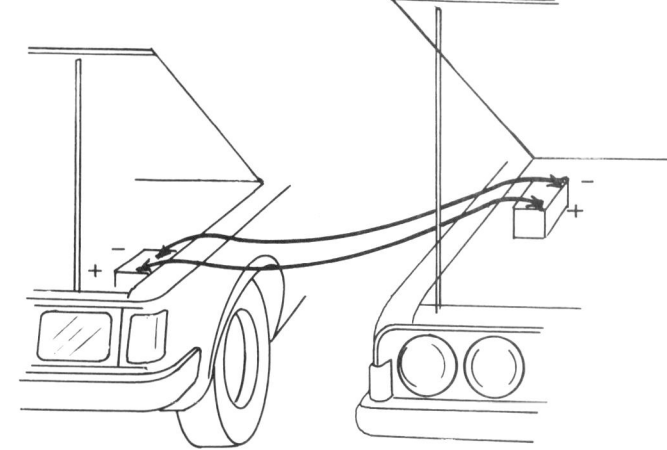

A set of jump leads being used to start the car with the help of the battery of another vehicle

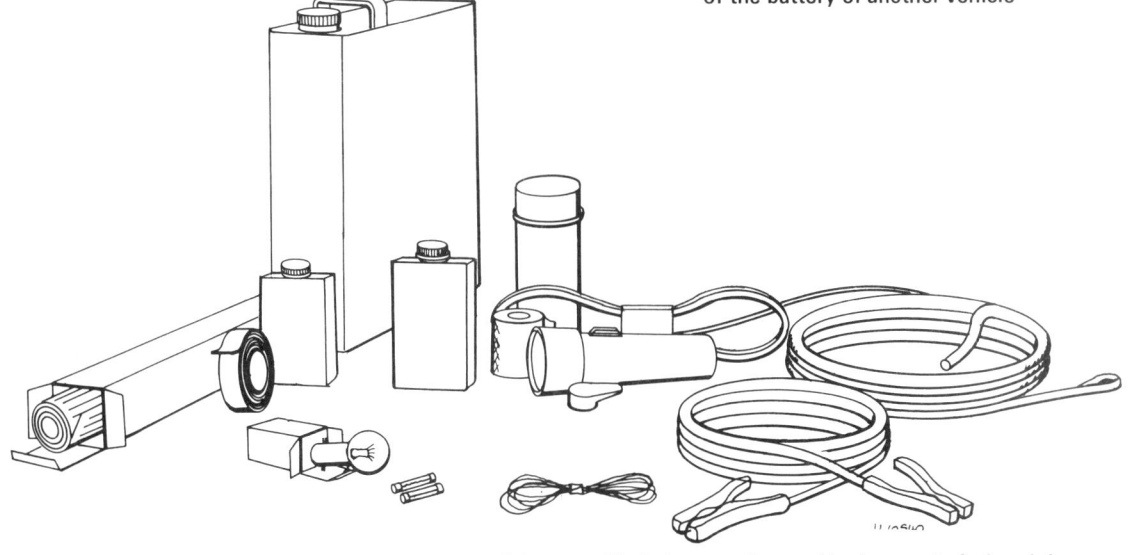

It is always useful to carry a small kit of some of the more likely items to be used in the event of a breakdown

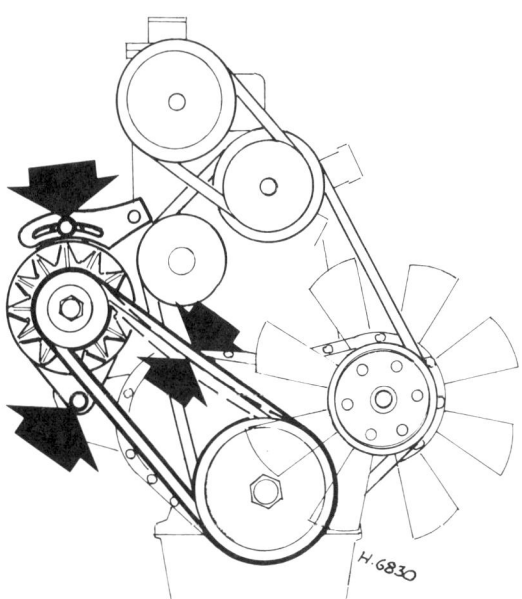

Checking the alternator drivebelt tension

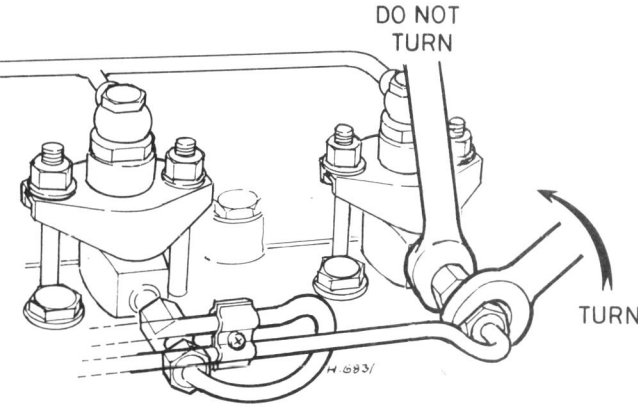

DO NOT TURN

TURN

Slackening a fuel injector feed pipe union to check for faulty operation – see Chapter 3

Alternator brushes
Tyre valve core
Fuel filter cartridge

One of the motoring organisations will be able to advise on availability of fuel etc in foreign countries.

Engine will not start

Engine fails to turn when starter operated
Flat battery (recharge, use jump leads, or push start)
Battery terminals loose or corroded
Battery earth to body defective
Engine earth strap loose or broken
Starter motor (or solenoid) wiring loose or broken
Automatic transmission selector in wrong position, or inhibitor switch faulty
Starter switch faulty
Major mechanical failure (seizure) or long disuse (piston rings rusted to bores)
Starter or solenoid internal fault (see Chapter 10)

Starter motor turns engine slowly
Partially discharged battery (recharge, use jump leads, or push start)
Battery terminals loose or corroded
Battery earth to body defective
Engine earth strap loose
Starter motor (or solenoid) wiring loose
Starter motor internal fault (see Chapter 10)

Starter motor spins without turning engine
Flat battery
Starter motor pinion sticking on sleeve
Flywheel gear teeth damaged or worn
Starter motor mounting bolts loose

Engine turns normally but fails to start
If black smoke is emitted from exhaust:
    Obstruction in air intake system (see Chapter 3)
    Defective injectors (see Chapter 3)
    Incorrect injection pump timing (see Chapter 3)
    Lack of engine compression (see Chapter 1)
If no smoke is emitted from exhaust:
    Fuel tank empty
    Air in fuel system (see Chapter 3)
    Stop control jammed in 'stop' position (see Chapter 3)
    No output from injection pump (see Chapter 3)
    Leak in fuel lines or unions (see Chapter 3)
    Heater plugs inoperative (see Chapter 10)
    Faulty fuel injections (see Chapter 3)

Engine lacks power

Incorrect injection pump timing (see Chapter 3)
Defective fuel injection (see Chapter 3)
Fuel filter clogged (see Chapter 3)
Defective injection pump (see Chapter 3)
Air intake partially blocked (see Chapter 3)
Engine internal fault (see Chapter 1)

Engine overheats

Ignition (no-charge) warning light illuminated
Slack or broken drivebelt – retension or renew (Chapter 10)

Ignition warning light not illuminated
Coolant loss due to internal or external leakage (see Chapter 2)
Thermostat defective
Low oil level
Brakes binding
Radiator blocked externally or internally
Electric cooling fan not operating correctly
Engine waterways clogged

Note: *Do not add cold water to an overheated engine or damage may result*

Low engine oil pressure

Gauge reads low or warning light illuminated with engine running
Oil level low or incorrect grade
Defective gauge or sender unit
Wire to sender unit earthed
Engine overheating
Oil filter clogged or bypass valve defective
Oil pressure relief valve defective
Oil pick-up strainer clogged
Oil pump worn or mountings loose
Worn main or big-end bearings

Note: *Low pressure in a high-mileage engine at tickover is not necessarily a cause for concern. Sudden pressure loss at speed is far more significant. In any event, check the gauge or warning light sender before condeming the engine.*

Engine noises

Thumping noises
Unintentional mechanical contact (eg fan blades)
Worn fan belt
Peripheral component fault (alternator, water pump etc)
Incorrect injection pump timing
Seized injector
Air bubbles in fuel
Worn big-end bearings (regular heavy knocking, perhaps less under load)
Worn main bearings (rumbling and knocking, perhaps worsening under load)
Piston slap (most noticeable when cold)

Whistling or wheezing noises
Leak at fuel injector
Leak at heater plug
Leaking cylinder head gasket

Tapping or rattling noises
Incorrect valve clearances
Worn valve gear
Worn timing chain, tensioner or gears
Broken piston ring

Chapter 1 Engine

Contents

Specifications

General

Type	Four cylinder in-line, ohv
Firing order	1 – 3 – 4 – 2
Bore:	
XD88 engine	88 mm (3.46 in)
XD90 engine	90 mm (3.54 in)
XD2 engine	94 mm (3.70 ln)
Stroke:	
XD88 engine	80 mm (3.14 in)
XD90 engine	83 mm (3.26 in)
XD2 engine	83 mm (3.26 in)
Cubic capacity:	
XD88 engine	1948 cc (119 cu in)
XD90 engine	2112 cc (129 cu in)
XD2 engine	2304 cc (141 cu in)
Compression ratio:	
XD88 engine	21.8 :1
XD90 engine	22.2 : 1
XD2 engine	22.2 : 1

Cylinder block
Material .... Cast iron
Cylinder bore diameter:
  XD88 and XD90 engines .... Renewable matched piston and liner sets
  XD2 engine:
    Grade A .... 94.00 to 94.015 mm (3.700 to 3.701 in)
    Grade B .... 94.015 to 94.030 mm (3.701 to 3.702 in)

Crankshaft
Number of main bearings 5
Main bearing journal diameter .... 54.994 to 55.009 mm (2.165 to 2.166 in)
Main bearing journal undersizes .... 0.3, 0.5 and 0.8 mm (0.012, 0.019 and 0.030 in)
Crankpin diameter .... 49.984 to 50.000 mm (1.967 to 1.968 in)
Crankpin undersizes .... 0.30 mm (0.011 in)
Crankshaft endfloat .... 0.08 to 0.29 mm (0.003 to 0.011 in)
Permissible bearing journal ovality .... 0.030 mm (0.001 in)

Camshaft
Type .... Cast iron
Number of bearings 3
Camshaft journal diameter .... 42 mm (1.653 in)
Camshaft bearing clearance .... 0.05 to 0.11 mm (0.002 to 0.004 in)
Camshaft endfloat .... 0.05 to 0.15 mm (0.002 to 0.005 in)
Type of drive:
  XD88 engine .... Helical gears
  XD90 and XD 2 engine .... Double-row chain

Connecting rods
Type .... Forged steel
Length .... 150 mm ± 0.025 mm (5.90 ± 0.001 in) between centres
Gudgeon pin fit in small-end bush .... Push fit

Pistons
Type .... Aluminium alloy
Number of rings .... 3 compression, 1 oil control (Uflex)
Piston diameter (standard):
  XD88 and XD90 engines .... Matched piston and liner sets
  XD2 engine:
    Grade A .... 93.855 to 93.870 mm (3.695 to 3.696 in)
    Grade B .... 93.870 to 93.885 mm (3.696 to 3.697 in)
Piston clearance in cylinder bore (XD2 engine only):
  Grade A .... 0.13 to 0.16 mm (0.005 to 0.006 in)
  Grade B .... 0.13 to 0.16 mm (0.005 to 0.006 in)
Piston ring width:
  Compression rings .... 2 mm (0.078 in)
  Oil control rings .... 4.5 mm (0.177 in)
Piston ring gap (in bore):
  Compression rings .... 0.30 to 0.45 mm (0.011 to 0.017 in)
  Oil control rings .... Zero gap – ends in contact
Gudgeon pin diameter .... 28 mm (1.102 in)
Gudgeon pin fit in piston .... Push fit

Cylinder head
Type .... Aluminium alloy with Ricardo Comet V swirl chambers
Maximum distortion .... 0.05 mm (0.002 in)
Valve seat angle:
  XD88 and XD90 engine .... 45°
  XD2 engines .... Inlet 60°, exhaust 45°

Valves
Valve head diameter:
  Inlet .... 40.3 to 40.5 mm (1.58 to 1.59 in)
  Exhaust .... 33.3 to 33.5 mm (1.31 to 1.32 in)
Valve stem diameter:
  Inlet .... 8.48 to 8.49 mm (0.333 to 0.334 in)
  Exhaust .... 8.46 to 8.47 in (0.332 to 0.333 in)
Valve face angle:
  XD88 and XD90 engine .... 45°
  XD2 engine .... Inlet 60°, Exhaust 45°
Valve clearance (cold):
  Inlet .... 0.15 mm (0.006 in)   See text
  Exhaust .... 0.25 mm (0.010 in)

Valve timing:
    Inlet opens .... 0° BTDC
    Inlet closes .... 28° ABDC
    Exhaust opens .... 43° BBDC
    Exhaust closes .... 1° ATDC
Valve spring free length:
    Inner .... 35.46 mm (1.396 in)
    Outer .... 38.76 mm (1.525 in)

Oil pump
Type .... Skew gear
Drive .... Helical gear from camshaft

Oil filter
Type .... Full-flow canister type

Sump (lubricant) capacity
XD88 engine .... 4 litres (7 Imp pints, 8.32 US pints)
XD90 engine .... 5 litres (8.8 Imp pints, 10.4 US pints)
XD2 engine .... 5 litres (8.8 Imp pints, 10.4 US pints)

Torque wrench settings

	Nm	lbf ft
Cylinder head bolts (see text):		
Initial:		
XD88 and XD90 engines	40	30
XD2 engine	45	33
Final:		
XD88 and XD90 engines	70	51
XD2 engine	65	47
Rocker shaft central retaining nuts	50	36
Rocker shaft end post retaining bolts	20	15
Big-end bearing cap nuts	60	43
Main bearing cap bolts	100	72
Crankshaft pulley nut	210	152
Flywheel bolts:		
XD88 engine	67	49
XD90 and XD2 engine	78	56
Inlet and exhaust manifold	15	11
Rocker cover	2.0	1.5
Sump	17	10
Camshaft thrust plate	15	11
Timing cover and interface plate	20	15
Oil filter housing	20	15

1 General description

The Peugeot 504 models covered by this manual may be equipped with either the XD88, XD90 or XD2 diesel engine. These engines are all of four cylinder in-line configuration, utilizing pushrod operated overhead valves and have displacements of 1948 cc (119 cu in), 2112 cc (130 cu in) and 2404 cc (141 cu in) respectively.

The cylinder block is of cast iron on all engines, with renewable cylinder liners on the XD88 and XD90 units. On the XD2 engine the cylinder bores are machined directly in the cylinder block.

The crankshaft is supported in the cylinder block by five renewable shell type main bearings, and crankshaft endfloat is controlled by bi-metal thrust washers fitted to the centre main bearing. A statically and dynamically balanced flywheel is secured to the rear of the crankshaft by six bolts.

Forged steel connecting rods are used, having renewable shell type big-end bearings and bronze small-end bushes. The pistons are of aluminium alloy, each having four rings: three compression and one oil control ring.

The camshaft is of cast iron and is mounted laterally in the cylinder block. The camshaft is supported by three bearings, and is driven by helically cut spur gears from the crankshaft in the case of the XD88 engine, and by a double link chain on the XD90 and XD2 engines.

An aluminium alloy cylinder head incorporating 'Ricardo Comet V' swirl chambers is fitted to all engines. The valves are retained in the cylinder head by double springs and split collets, and are operated by rocker arms via pushrods and cam followers from the camshaft.

Lubrication is by a pressure fed oil system incorporating a camshaft driven, gear type oil pump and full-flow canister type oil filter.

2 Major operations possible with engine in place

The following major operations can be carried out with the engine in place in the car. It is recommended, however, that for reasons of cleanliness and accessibility the operations shown with an asterisk are performed with the engine removed:

   (a) *Removal and refitting of the cylinder head and related components*
   (b) *Removal and refitting of the timing cover and timing components*
   (c) *Removal and refitting of the engine mountings*
   (d) *Removal and refitting of the flywheel (gearbox removed)*
 * (e) *Removal and refitting of the sump*
 * (f) *Removal and refitting of the big-end bearings*
 * (g) *Removal and refitting of the piston and connecting rod assemblies (cylinder head removed)*
 * (h) *Removal and refitting of the oil pump*

3 Major operations requiring engine removal

The following operations can only be carried out satisfactorily with the engine removed from the car:

   (a) *Removal and refitting of the camshaft*
   (b) *Removal and refitting of the crankshaft and main bearings*
   (c) *Removal and refitting of the cylinder liners, or reboring the cylinder block*

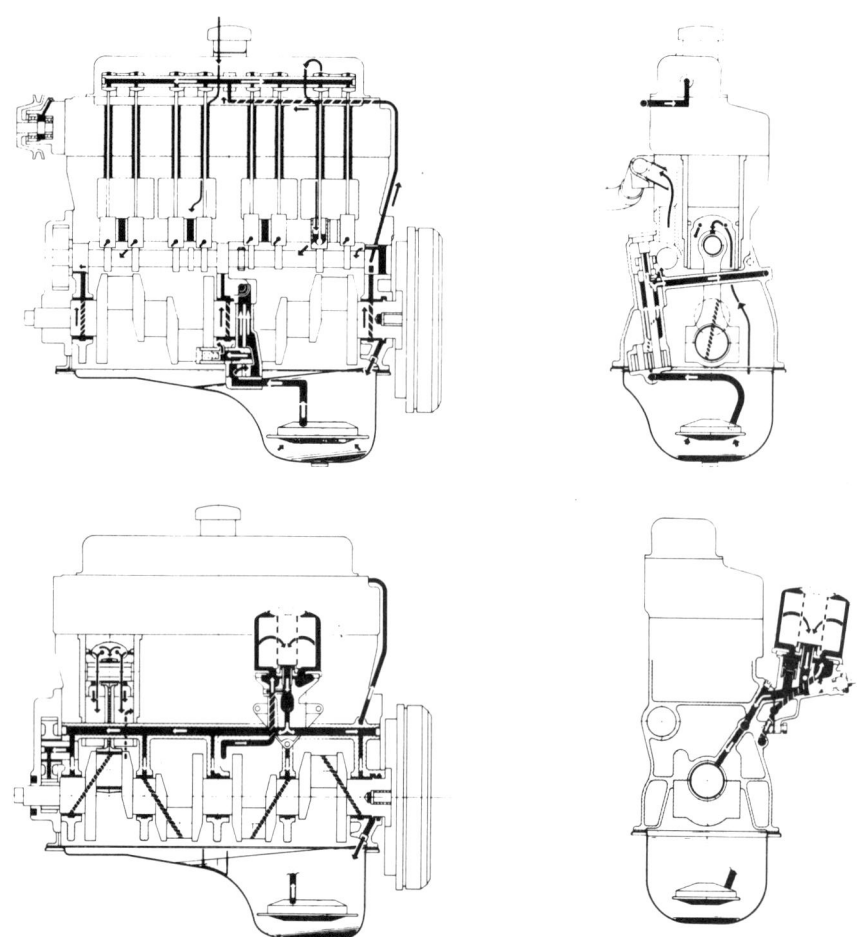

Fig. 1.1 Engine lubrication system – XD88 and XD90 engines (Sec 1)

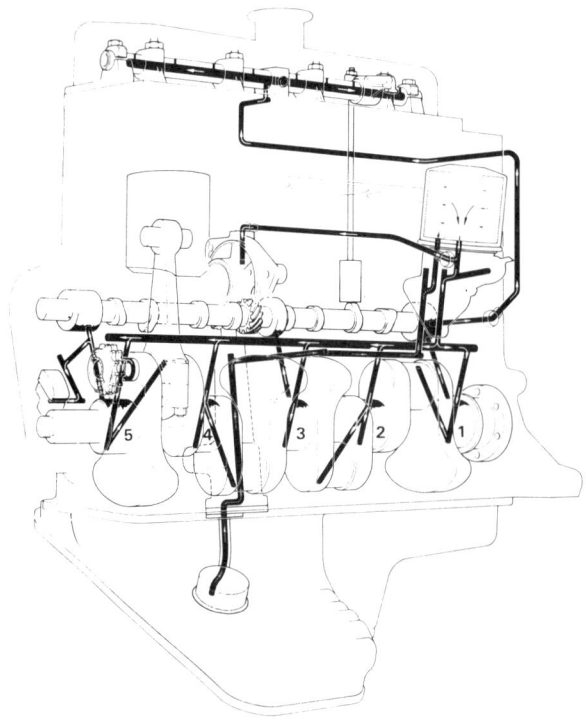

Fig. 1.2 Engine lubrication system – XD2 engine (Sec 1)

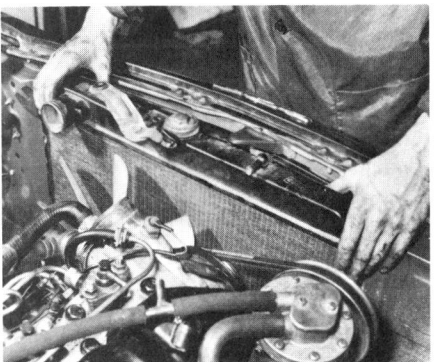

5.5a Lifting out the radiator

5.5b Expansion tank retaining nuts (arrowed) ...

5.5c ... and hose connection

4 Methods of engine removal

The engine may be lifted out either on its own or in unit with the transmission unit. If the engine is to be removed with the transmission still attached, considerable dismantling work must be carried out beneath the car, and in addition a very substantial crane and preferably a ramp or pit will be needed. It is therefore recommended that whenever possible the engine should be removed separately.

5 Engine – removal with manual gearbox or automatic transmission

1 This method of engine removal is rather complex, and it is recommended that you read through the entire Section first, making sure that you have the necessary facilities before beginning the dismantling sequence.

2 Position the a car over a pit or on a ramp, of if these are not available jack up the front and rear of the car and support it on axle stands.
3 Refer to Chapter 12, if necessary, and remove the bonnet.
4 Disconnect the battery terminals, release the battery clamps and remove the battery and its tray.
5 Refer to Chapter 2 and drain the cooling system, then remove the radiator and expansion tank (photos).
6 Refer to Chapter 3 and remove the air cleaner.
7 Slacken the hose clips and remove the hoses from the vacuum pump to vacuum tank and servo unit.
8 Slacken the hose clip and detach the heater hose from the cylinder head.
9 Remove the heater hose support clamp from the rear engine lifting bracket and then detach the two hoses from the water pump. Position the hoses out of the way on the engine compartment bulkhead.
10 Slacken the clip and detach the fuel return hose from the fuel injection pump.

Fig. 1.3 Fuel lines, accelerator cable and electrical connections to be removed from engine (Sec 5)

Fig. 1.4 Heater hose and bracket, heater plug electrical lead and starter solenoid electrical lead locations (Sec 5)

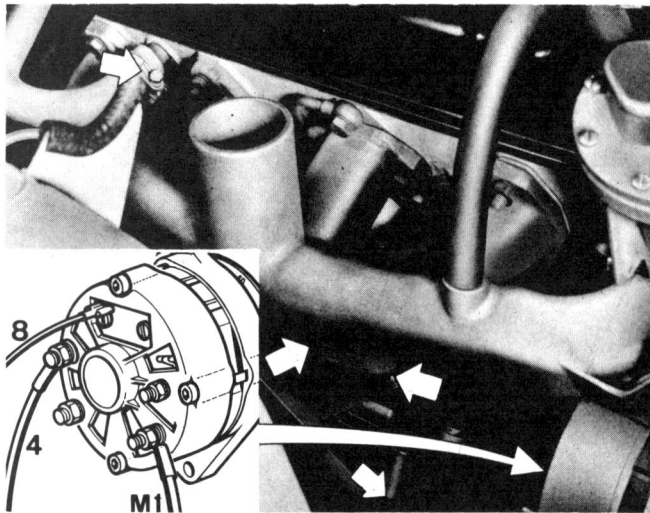

Fig. 1.5 Alternator terminals, cylinder head heater hose and exhaust flange locations (Sec 5)

Fig. 1.6 Components to be disconnected from beneath the car (Sec 5)

1	Clutch slave cylinder	4	Reversing light switch leads
2	Gear selector rods	5	Earth lead
3	Gearchange levers	6	Speedometer cable

5.13a Detach the oil pressure switch lead ...

5.13b ... and heater plug warning light lead

11 Slacken the clip and detach the fuel feed hose from the fuel injection pump banjo union.

12 Undo and remove the cable clamps and detach the control cables from the fuel injection pump.

13 Disconnect the oil pressure switch lead, the temperature transmitter switch lead and the heater plug warning light switch lead (photos).

14 Make a note of the position of the electrical connections at the rear of the alternator and disconnect the leads.

15 Now make a note of the position of the electrical connections at the starter solenoid and disconnect the leads. Position the wiring harness out of the way.

16 Undo the knurled nut and detach the electrical lead to the rear heater plug.

17 If an electromagnetic fan is fitted, disconnect the electrical lead to the fan switch.

18 If the car is equipped with power steering, refer to Chapter 11 and detach the hoses from the pump.

19 Should an air conditioning compressor be fitted, this must not be disconnected, but simply detached from its mountings and tied back out of the way.

20 Undo and remove the nuts securing the exhaust front pipe to the exhaust manifold and allow the system to rest on the crossmember (photo).

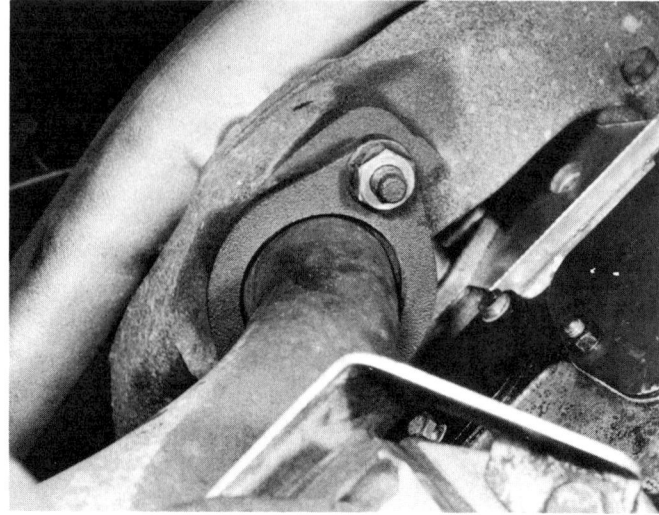

5.20 Exhaust front pipe-to-manifold flange joint

21 Refer to Chapter 7 and remove the propeller shaft and torque tube assembly.

22 Disconnect the earth strap from the rear of the manual gearbox or automatic transmission.

23 Slacken the locknut, remove the grub screw and withdraw the speedometer cable from the gearbox on automatic transmission extension housing. Refit the grub screw once the cable is removed.

24 Disconnect the two electrical leads from the reversing light switch.

25 Disconnect the gearchange linkage ball and socket joints from the operating levers on the manual gearbox.

26 If automatic transmission is fitted, disconnect the selector lever control linkage and the electrical leads from the starter inhibitor switch, after making a note of their positions.

27 To provide further clearance undo and remove the two steering gear retaining bolts, after first removing the locking circlips from the exposed threaded ends of the bolts.

28 Mark the position of the steering column shaft in the collar of the flexible coupling, and then undo and remove the clamp bolt. Lower the steering gear and allow it to hang down without disconnecting the track rod end balljoints.

29 Undo and remove the clutch slave cylinder locking bolt and plate, extract the retaining circlip and slide the cylinder out of its location in the bellhousing. Leave the hydraulic pipe attached and position the cylinder out of the way.

30 If a gearbox or automatic transmission crossmember is fitted, bend back the locktab and undo and remove the centre securing bolt, and then the two side securing nuts and washers. Lift away the crossmember.

31 From inside the car remove the centre console or selector lever gate, and then lift back the carpets over the transmission tunnel.

32 Remove the gear lever and upper linkage, referring to Chapter 6 if necessary.

33 Ensure that the gearbox or automatic transmission is well supported on a sturdy jack and then engage the help of an assistant for the remaining operations.

34 Undo and remove the bolt securing the gearbox or automatic transmission rear support (where fitted) to the centre of the transmission tunnel.

35 Now undo and remove the rear support securing bolts from either side of the transmission tunnel while an assistant holds the nuts from below. The rear support can now be lifted away.

36 Connect suitable lifting gear to the brackets on the engine, positioning it in such a way that it will be possible to achieve a 45° angle of the engine and transmission.

37 Take the weight of the engine and transmission on the crane, and then undo and remove the nut securing the right-hand engine mounting to the crosssmember (photo). Now undo and remove the bolts securing the left-hand engine mounting to the cylinder block and the nut securing the mounting to the crossmember. When the engine is lifted slightly, remove the remaining bolts and lift away the complete mounting.

38 Make a final check that all wires, hoses, cables and components are disconnected from the engine and transmission, and are positioned well clear, where there is no likelihood of damage.

39 Start lifting the engine out, stopping periodically to check that everything is clear. Now raise the engine fully and lift it forward (photo). Have your assistant lift the gearbox or automatic transmission unit over the front grille panel. When everything is clear lower the unit to the ground.

40 Thoroughly wash off the exterior of the engine using a soluble degreaser and jet of water, before commencing the dismantling sequence.

41 The gearbox or automatic transmission can now be removed from the engine as described in Section 7.

---

6 Engine – removal without manual gearbox or automatic transmission

1 Refer to Section 5, and carry out the operations given in paragraphs 3 to 19 inclusive.

2 Undo and remove the two bolts securing the starter motor flange to the bellhousing and the additional bolt, if fitted, securing the starter motor rear support bracket to the cylinder block. Lift off the starter motor.

5.37 Engine mounting-to-crossmember retaining nut

5.39 Lifting out the engine and transmission

Fig. 1.7 Removing the torque converter-to-diaphragm securing bolts (Sec 6)

3   Undo and remove the bolts and lift off the closure plates from the front face of the bellhousing.
4   If automatic transmission is fitted, undo and remove the four bolts securing the torque converter to the diaphragm. Access to these bolts is through the opening in the bellhousing. Rotate the crankshaft a quarter of a turn at a time.
5   Attach suitable lifting gear to the brackets on the engine and just take its weight.
6   Place a jack beneath the gearbox or automatic transmission and in contact with it.
7   Now undo and remove the socket-headed bolts securing the bellhousing to the engine.
8   Undo and remove the nut securing the right-hand engine mounting to the crossmember. Now undo and remove the bolts securing the left-hand engine mounting to the cylinder block and the nut securing the mounting to the crossmember. When the engine is lifted slightly, remove the remaining bolts and lift away the complete mounting.
9   Make a final check that all wires, hoses, cables and components are disconnected from the engine and are positioned well clear, where there is no likelihood of damage.
10 Raise the engine on the crane or lifting gear until the engine mountings are clear, and then pull it forward to disengage the dowels on the bellhousing.
11 Continue pulling the engine forward until the clutch assembly is clear of the gearbox input shaft. Where automatic transmission is fitted make sure that the torque converter remains on the transmission and does not slip forward. If necessary push it back with a screwdriver as the engine is drawn forward.
12 Now carefully lift the engine out of the engine compartment, and when clear lower it to the ground.
13 Thoroughly clean the engine externally using a soluble degreaser and jet of water, before commencing the dismantling sequence.

Fig. 1.8 Removing the bellhousing retaining bolts (Sec 6)

7   Engine – separation from manual gearbox or automatic transmission

1   If the engine has been removed complete with the gearbox or automatic transmission, these units must be removed before engine dismantling can begin.
2   Undo and remove the bolts securing the starter motor flange to the bellhousing and the additional bolt, where fitted, securing the starter motor rear support bracket to the cylinder block. Now lift off the starter motor and closure plate (photo).
3   Undo and remove the bolts securing the closure plates to the bellhousing and lift away the plates (photo).
4   If automatic transmission is fitted undo and remove the four bolts securing the torque converter to the diaphragm. These bolts are accessible through the opening in the bellhousing by turning the crankshaft a quarter of a turn at a time.
5   Undo and remove the bolts securing the bellhousing to the engine.
6   With the help of an assistant withdraw the gearbox or automatic transmission from the rear of the engine. If automatic transmission is fitted ensure that the torque converter stays on the transmission and does not slide forward. If necessary push it back with a screwdriver as the transmission is removed.

7.2 Bellhousing upper ...

8   Engine – dismantling (general)

1   It is best to mount the engine on a dismantling stand, but if this is not available, then stand the engine on a strong bench so as to be at a comfortable working height. Failing this, the engine can be stripped down on the floor.
2   During the dismantling process the greatest care should be taken to keep the exposed parts free of dirt. As an aid to achieving this, it is a sound scheme to thoroughly clean down the outside of the engine, removing all traces of oil and congealed dirt.
3   Use paraffin or a good grease solvent. The latter compound will make the job easier, as, after the solvent has been applied and allowed to stand for a time, a vigorous jet of water will wash off the solvent and all the grease and filth. If the dirt is thick and deeply embedded, work the solvent into it with a stiff paint brush.
4   Finally wipe down the exterior of the engine with a rag, and only then when it is quite clean should the dismantling process begin. As the engine is stripped clean each part in a bath of paraffin.

7.3 ... and lower closure plates

5   Never immerse parts with oilways in paraffin (eg the crankshaft), but to clean wipe down carefully with a paraffin moistened rag. Oilways can be cleaned out with nylon pipe cleaners. If an air line is present all parts can be blown dry and the oilways blown through as an added precaution.

6   Re-use of old engine gaskets is a false economy and can give rise to oil and water leaks, if nothing worse. To avoid the possibility of trouble after the engine has been reassembled, always use new gaskets throughout.

7   Do not throw the old gaskets away as it sometimes happens that an immediate replacement cannot be found, and the old gasket is then very useful as a template. Hang up the old gaskets as they are removed on a suitable hook or nail.

8   When purchasing engine gaskets be particularly careful to state the type of engine fitted. Also take care when obtaining a replacement cylinder head gasket as there are at least three difference types.

9   To strip the engine it is best to work from the top down. The oil sump and suitable wood packing provides a firm base on which the engine can be supported in an upright position. When the stage where the sump must be removed is reached, the engine can be turned on its side and all other work carried out with it in this position.

10 Whenever possible, refit nuts, bolts and washers fingertight from wherever they were removed. This helps to avoid later loss and muddle. If they cannot be refitted then lay them out in such a fashion that it is clear from where they came.

11 It may be that the engine being worked on has one or more modifications that are not shown in the photographs or illustrations. Should this occur make a note of any differences.

9   Ancillary components – removal

1   With the engine removed from the car and thoroughly cleaned, the externally mounted ancillary components should now be removed before major dismantling begins.

2   The following is a suggested sequence of removal; detailed descriptions are to be found in the relevant Chapter of this manual.

   (a) Alternator (Chapter 10)
   (b) Vacuum pump (Chapter 9)
   (c) Water pump (Chapter 2)
   (d) Fan and fan hub (Chapter 2)
   (e) Fuel injection pump (Chapter 3)
   (f) Fuel injectors (Chapter 3)
   (g) Heater plugs (Chapter 10)
   (h) Clutch assembly (Chapter 5)

10 Cylinder head – removal (engine in car)

1   Disconnect the battery earth terminal.

2   Refer to Chapter 3 and remove the air cleaner.

3   Refer to Chapter 9 and remove the vacuum pump.

4   Refer to Chapter 2, drain the cooling system and remove the water pump drivebelt and jockey wheel.

5   Slacken the hose clip and detach the heater hose from the side of the cylinder head.

6   Detach the electrical lead from the heater plug warning light transmitter.

7   Disconnect the electrical lead from the rear heater plug and then remove the heater plugs as described in Chapter 10.

8   Refer to Chapter 3 and remove the fuel injectors.

9   Undo and remove the rocker shaft oil supply pipe banjo unions at the rear of the cylinder block (photo) and at the cylinder head. Lift off the pipe and take care not to lose the two copper washers at each union.

10 Undo and remove the four nuts and lift off the rocker cover and hose bracket.

11 Undo and remove the four nuts and two bolts securing the rocker shaft assembly to the cylinder head and carefully lift the rocker gear off the studs.

12 Now carefully lift out each pushrod, while at the same time twisting it to free the cam follower. Keep the pushrods in order by punching eight holes in a piece of cardboard, numbering the holes and inserting each pushrod as it is removed.

10.9 Rocker shaft oil supply pipe banjo union on cylinder block

Fig. 1.9 Location of the vacuum pump and jockey wheel adjustment and mounting bolts (Sec 10)

Fig. 1.10 Fuel injector fuel line unions and heater plug electrical connection (Sec 10)

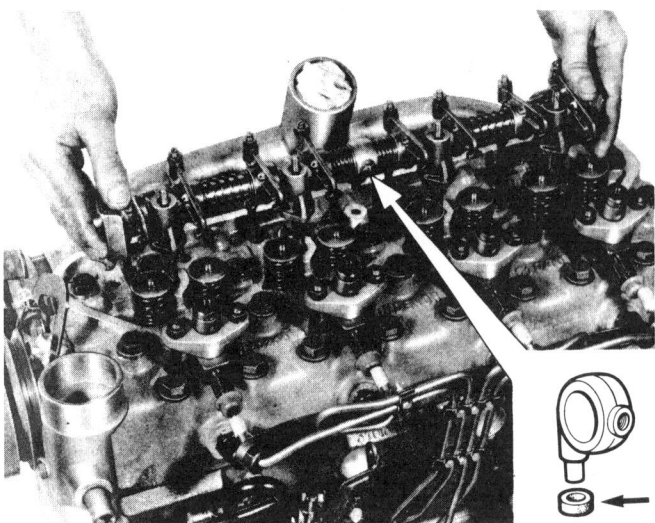

Fig. 1.11 Removal of rocker shaft assembly – note rubber seal on lubrication collar (Sec 10)

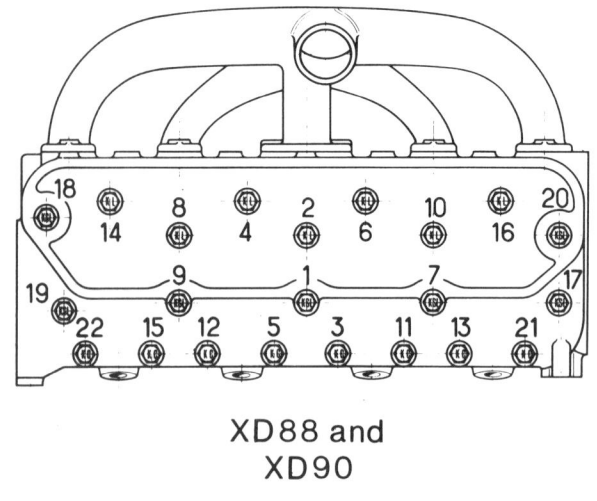

XD88 and XD90

XD 2

13 Undo all the cylinder head retaining bolts half a turn in the reverse order to that shown in Fig. 1.12, and then remove them from the cylinder head.
14 With all the bolts removed lift the cylinder head from the block. If the head is stuck, try to rock it to break the seal. *Under no circumstances try to prise it apart from the cylinder block using a screwdriver or cold chisel,* as damage may be caused to the mating surfaces of the cylinder head and block. If it is extremely stubborn strike the head sharply with a soft-faced mallet until it is free.
15 Now lift of the cylinder head gasket.
16 To stop the cylinder liners moving on the XD88 and XD90 engines, when the cylinder head is removed, clamp them in position using two bolts and flat washers screwed into the cylinder head retaining bolt holes (Fig. 1.13).

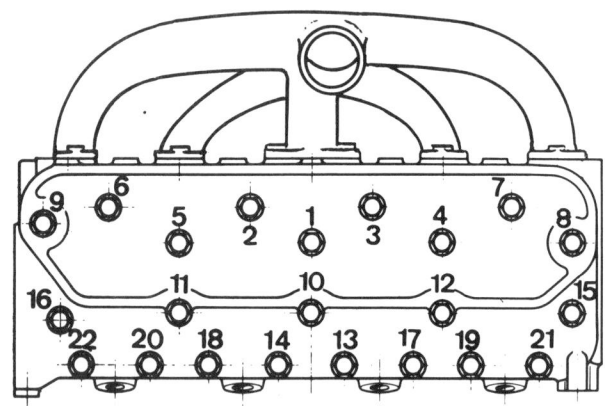

Fig. 1.12 Cylinder head bolt tightening sequence (Secs 10 and 47)

11 Cylinder head: removal (engine on bench)

The procedure for removal of the cylinder head with the engine out of the car is similar to that for removal when the engine is fitted, with the exception of disconnecting the controls and fixtures. Refer to Section 10, and follow paragraphs 9 to 16 inclusive.

12 Cylinder head – dismantling

1 Undo and remove the bolts securing the inlet and exhaust manifolds to the cylinder head and lift off the two manifolds.
2 The valves can be removed from the cylinder head by the following method. Compress each spring in turn with a valve spring compressor until the two halves of the collet can be removed. Release the compressor and lift off the inner and outer springs, the spring cap and spring seat.
3 If, when the valve spring compressor is screwed down, the valve spring cap refuses to free to expose the split collet, do not continue to screw down on the compressor as there is a likelihood of damaging it.
4 Gently tap the top of the tool directly over the valve spring cap with a soft-faced mallet. This will free the cap. To avoid the compressor jumping off the valve spring cap when it is tapped, hold the compressor firmly in one hand.
5 Slide the rubber oil seals off the inlet valve stems and then slide out each valve from its guide.
6 It is essential that the valves are kept in their correct sequence unless they are so badly worn that they are to be renewed. Punch eight holes in a piece of cardboard as was done previously for the pushrods and insert the valves in their correct hole as they are removed.

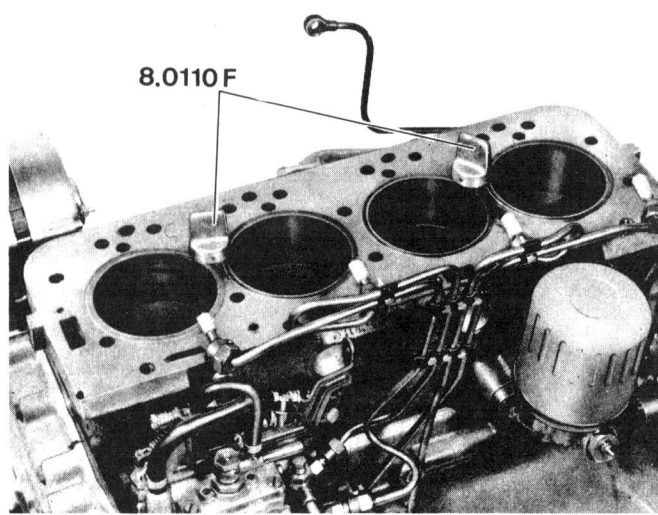

Fig. 1.13 Two Peugeot special tools (bolts and flat washers will do) used to retain the cylinder liners in position (Sec 10)

13 Oil filter and housing – removal

1   The oil filter is of the disposable canister type and is removed by simply unscrewing it from the filter housing. If the filter is tight use a strap wrench or filter removing tool obtainable from most accessory shops.
2   To remove the oil filter housing undo and remove the three retaining bolts and lift off the housing and gasket.

14 Timing cover and timing components – removal

1   Using a large socket and extension bar, undo and remove the crankshaft pulley retaining nut. To stop the crankshaft from turning as the nut is undone, use a large screwdriver engaged with the starter ring gear teeth and in contact with the cylinder block.
2   With the nut removed, ease off the pulley using two levers placed behind the pulley at opposite points to remove it. Once the pulley is off, recover the Woodruff key from the end of the crankshaft and place it somewhere safe, as it is easily lost.
3   Now undo and remove the nuts, plain and socket-headed bolts securing the timing cover to the front of the engine. Lift off the cover and recover the gasket.
4   The removal sequence now varies slightly depending upon whether chain driven or gear driven timing components are fitted.

Engine with chain driven timing components
5   Rotate the crankshaft by means of the flywheel until the copper link in the timing chain is opposite the reference mark on the crankshaft sprocket, and the chain links marked by a line are adjacent to the reference marks on the camshaft and fuel injection pump sprockets.
6   Undo and remove the small bolt from the lower face of the timing chain tensioner. Insert a 3 mm Allen key into the bolt hole and engage the tensioner rod. Turn the Allen key until the tensioner is released.
7   Slacken the idler sprocket retaining nut and then move the sprocket to its slackest position by turning it clockwise.
8   Bend up the locktabs and then undo and remove the three fuel injection pump sprocket retaining bolts.

9   Now lift off the fuel injection pump sprocket, and then remove the timing chain.
10 Undo and remove the chain guide securing bolts and lift off the guide.
11 Undo and remove the two timing chain tensioner securing bolts and lift off the tensioner.
12 Remove the idler sprocket securing nut and lift off the sprocket.
13 The bolts securing the fuel injection pump and sprocket support bearing assembly can now be removed and the bearing assembly withdrawn.
14 Using two levers carefully ease the crankshaft sprocket forward and off the crankshaft. Recover the Woodruff key and put it in a safe place.
15 Do not attempt to remove the camshaft sprocket, as this is removed with the camshaft as described in Section 18.

Engines with gear driven timing components
16 Turn the engine over by means of the flywheel until the timing reference marks on the gears are all opposite each other. Note: *This only occurs once every 22 revolutions of the crankshaft.*
17 The fuel injection pump and its timing gear will already have been removed if the engine dismantling sequence has been closely followed. If the injection pump is still in place, refer to Chapter 3 and remove it at this stage.
18 Using circlip pliers extract the idler gear retaining circlip. Lift off the thrust washers followed by the gear.
19 The crankshaft pinion gear can now be removed using two levers to ease it off the front of the crankshaft. Recover the Woodruff key and put it in a safe place.
20 Do not attempt to remove the camshaft gear as this is removed with the camshaft as described in Section 18.

15 Flywheel – removal

1   Using a screwdriver or small chisel, knock back the locking tabs and then undo and remove the six flywheel retaining bolts. Lock the flywheel with a screwdriver engaged with the ring gear to stop it turning.

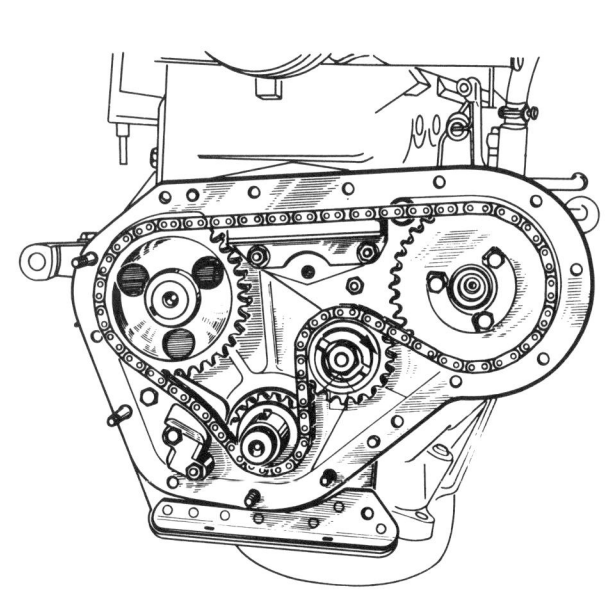

Fig. 1.14 Layout of chain driven timing gear and tensioner (Sec 14)

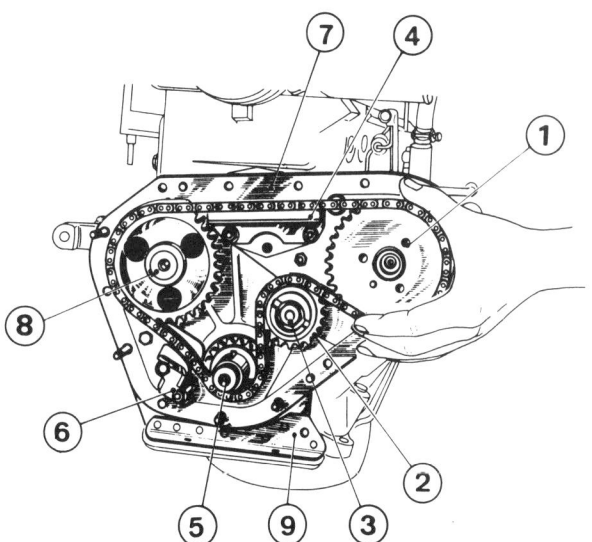

Fig. 1.15 Chain driven timing component removal (Sec 14)

1	Fuel injection pump sprocket	6	Timing chain tensioner
2	Idler sprocket	7	Front interface plate
3	Retaining nut	8	Camshaft sprocket
4	Chain guide	9	Interface plate flange
5	Crankshaft sprocket		

2   With the bolts removed, lift off the locking plate and suitably mark
the relationship of the flywheel to the crankshaft flange as a guide to
refitment.
3   Now lift off the flywheel.

16 Sump – removal

1   If this operation is being carried out with the engine in the car, first
jack up the front of the car and support it on stands. Remove the drain
plug and allow the engine oil to drain into a suitable container.
2   Undo and remove the sump securing bolts and lift off the sump. If
it is stuck, tap it carefully with a soft-faced mallet to break the gasket
seal.

17 Oil pump – removal

1   Undo and remove the large socket-headed thrust plug from the
right-hand side of the cylinder block, taking care not to lose any shims
that may be fitted under the plug.
2   Now undo and remove the domed nut located just below the
previously removed thrust plug.
3   With the domed nut removed the oil pump retaining grub screw
will be exposed. Unscrew the grub screw and then slide the oil pump
down and out from beneath the crankcase.

18 Camshaft and cam followers – removal

1   Begin by removing the nuts that secure the two side covers to the
right-hand side of the cylinder block. Now lift off the two side covers
and recover the gaskets.
2   Lift out each cam follower in turn from its bore and keep the cam
followers in their correct order of removal.
3   Undo and remove the two camshaft thrust plate securing bolts,
which are accessible using a socket through the two holes in the
camshaft gear or sprocket. Now carefully withdraw the camshaft from
the front of the engine, taking care not to damage the camshaft
bearings as the camshaft passes through them. **Note:** *On later XD2
engines the camshaft thrust plate is omitted and the camshaft is
retained by the engine front interface plate, which must be removed
first.*
4   Undo and remove the remaining nuts securing the interface plate
to the cylinder block and lift it off complete with gasket.
5   The camshaft on later model XD2 engines can now be withdrawn.

19 Pistons and connecting rods – removal

1   The pistons and connecting rods can be removed with the engine
still in the car or with the engine on the bench.
2   With the cylinder head and sump removed, undo and remove the
big-end cap retaining nuts.
3   Remove the big-end caps one at a time, taking care to keep them
in the right order and the correct way round. Also ensure that the shell
bearings are kept with their correct connecting rods and caps unless
they are to be renewed.
4   It is a good idea to mark the side face of each rod and cap with
identification marks using a centre punch and light hammer, unless
they are already marked. Use a single dot for No 1 connecting rod and
cap, two dots from No 2, and so on. This will ensure there is no mix-
up on reassembly, as it is very important that the caps are refitted to
the connecting rods from which they are removed.
5   If the big-end caps are difficult to remove they may be gently
tapped with a soft-faced mallet.
6   To remove the shell bearings, press the bearing opposite the
groove in both the connecting rod and the connecting rod caps and the
bearings will slide out easily.
7   Push the connecting rod upwards, tapping gently with a block of
wood until the piston emerges from the top of the cylinder bore. Now
lift the piston and connecting rod assembly out of its cylinder and keep
it in the correct order for refitment in the same bore (photo).

19.7 Connecting rod, cap, nuts and big-end bearing shells

20 Crankshaft and main bearings – removal

1   Mark the main bearing caps and cylinder block faces to ensure
that the caps are refitted the correct way round and in the correct
order.
2   Undo and remove the bolts securing the five main bearing caps to
the cylinder block.
3   Tap the caps lightly using a soft-faced mallet to free them, and
then lift off each cap and the bottom half of each bearing shell. Take
care to keep the bearing shells in the right caps.
4   When removing the centre bearing cap recover the two semi-
circular thrust washers from either side of the cap. Lay the thrust
washers together with the cap.
5   Now carefully lift out the crankshaft. Remove the upper halves of
the main bearing shells and lay them with their respective lower halves
and bearing caps. Recover also the remaining two thrust washers from
the centre main bearing.

21 Engine components – examination for wear

When the engine has been stripped down and all parts properly
cleaned, decisions have to be made as to what needs renewal, and the
following Sections tell the examiner what to look for. In any borderline
case it is always best to decide in favour of a new part. Even if a part
may still be serviceable its life will have been reduced by wear and the
degree of trouble needed to renew it in the future must be taken into
consideration. However, these things are relative and it depends on
whether a quick 'survival' job is being done or whether the car as a
whole is being regarded as having many thousands of miles of useful
and economical life remaining.

22 Oil pump – examination and renovation

1   Undo and remove the four bolts securing the oil pump pick-up
strainer assembly and oil pump cover to the pump body. Lift off the
pick-up strainer and the cover (photo).
2   Slide the oil pump driveshaft and gear out of the base of the pump
and then lift out the two pump gears (photo).
3   Extract the split pin from the side of the pump body while at the
same time holding the oil pressure relief valve in place with a
screwdriver. Now carefully release the pressure relief valve plunger,
spring and cap (photo).
4   With the pump dismantled and the parts laid out for inspection,
check first the pump body for any signs of scoring or wear on the
internal walls. Refit the driveshaft to the pump body and check for
excessive side-to-side movement of the shaft.
5   Closely examine the teeth of the pump gears for pitting, scoring or

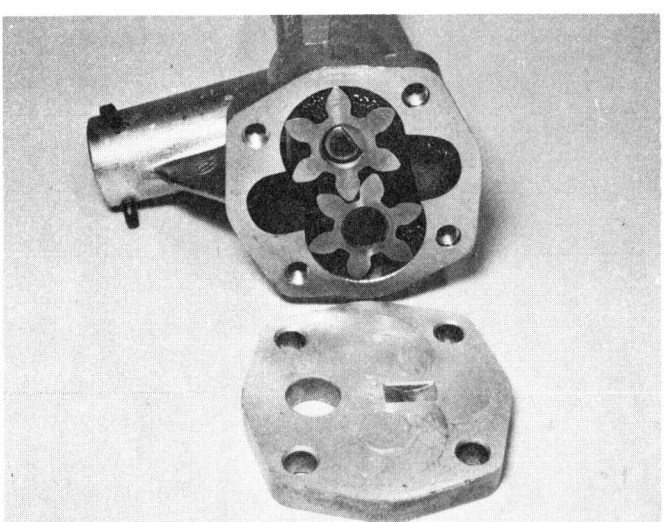

22.1 Removal of the oil pump cover

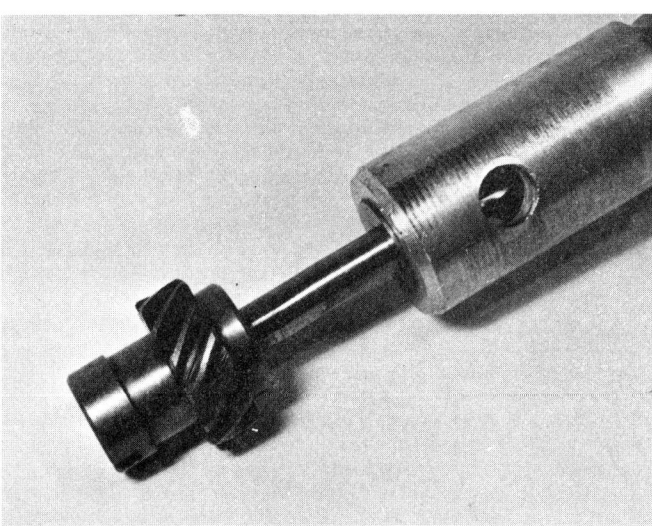

22.2 Withdrawing the oil pump driveshaft

22.3a Extract the retaining split pin ...

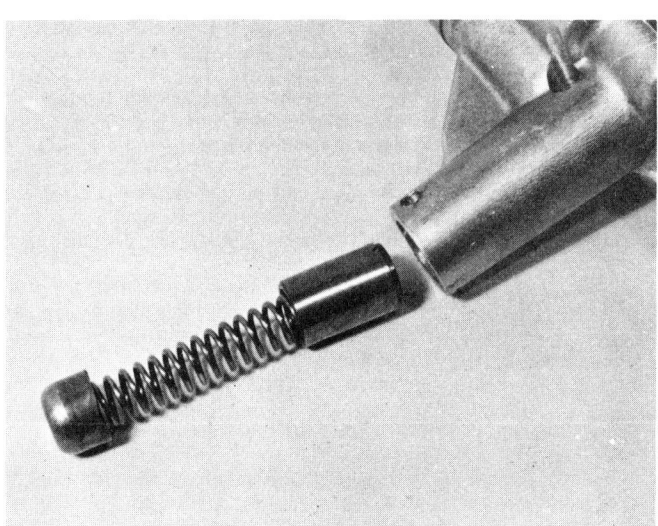

22.3b ... and lift out the oil pressure relief valve assembly

wear ridges. Refit the gears to the pump and check for any side-to-side movement or excessive backlash of the gears.

6   Check the oil pump cover for wear ridges or grooving caused by excessive endfloat of the gears.

7   Finally, inspect the oil pressure relief valve for wear and ensure that it is free to move in its bore without sticking. Check also that the relief spring is sound with no signs of distortion or weakening of the coils.

8   If any of the oil pump components were found to be worn, scored or in any way suspect, the pump should be renewed. Generally speaking if the engine has covered a high mileage and is being reconditioned or overhauled, it is advisable to renew the pump as a matter of course.

9   If, however, the oil pump components are in a satisfactory condition, the pump should be reassembled using the reverse sequence to removal. Thoroughly lubricate all the parts in engine oil during assembly and fill the pumping chambers around the gears with engine oil before refitting the oil pump cover and pick-up strainer assembly.

23 Crankshaft main and big-end bearings – examination and renovation

1   Look at the main bearing journals and the crankpins, and if there

are any scratches or score marks then the crankshaft will need regrinding. Such conditions will nearly always be accompanied by similar deterioration in the matching bearing shells.

2   Each bearing journal should also be round and can be checked with a micrometer or caliper gauge around the periphery at several points. Compare the figures obtained with those given in the Specifications at the beginning of this Chapter. If the crankshaft journals are excessively oval, the crankshaft will have to be reground.

3   A Peugeot garage or motor engineering specialist will be able to decide to what extent regrinding is necessary and also supply the special undersize shell bearings to match whatever may need grinding off.

4   Before taking the crankshaft for regrinding, check also the cylinder bores and pistons, as it may be advantageous to have the whole engine done together.

24 Crankshaft main and big-end bearing shells – examination and renovation

1   With careful servicing and regular oil and filter changes, bearings will last for a very long time, but they can still fail for unforeseen reasons. With big-end bearings the indication is a regular rhythmic knocking from the crankcase. The frequency depends on engine speed and is particularly noticeable when the engine is under load. This

symptom is accompanied by a fall in oil pressure, although this is not normally noticeable unless an oil pressure gauge is fitted. Main bearing failure is usually indicated by serious vibration, particularly at higher engine revolutions, accompanied by a more significant drop in oil pressure and a 'rumbling' noise.

2   Bearing shells in good condition have bearing surfaces with a smooth, even matt silver/grey colour all over. Worn bearings will show patches of a different colour when the bearing metal has worn away and exposed the underlay. Damaged bearings will be pitted or scored. It is always well worthwhile fitting new shells as their cost is relatively low. If the crankshaft is in good condition it is merely a question of obtaining another set of standard size. A reground crankshaft will need new bearing shells as a matter of course.

25 Cylinder block and crankcase – examination and renovation

1   A new cylinder is perfectly round and the walls parallel throughout its length. The action of the piston tends to wear the walls at right-angles to the gudgeon pin due to side thrust. This wear takes place principally on that section of the cylinder swept by the piston rings.

2   It is possible to get an indication of bore wear by removing the cylinder head with the engine still in the car. With the piston down in the bore first signs of wear can be seen and felt just below the top of the bore where the top piston ring reaches and there will be a noticeable lip. If there is no lip it is fairly reasonable to expect that bore wear is not severe and any lack of compression or excessive oil consumption is due to worn or broken piston rings or pistons (see the next Section).

3   If it is possible to obtain a bore-measuring micrometer, measure the bore in the thrust plane below the lip and again at the bottom of the cylinder in the same plane. If the difference is greater than 0.006 in (0.15 mm), it will be necessary in the case of the XD88 and XD90 engines to fit new cylinder liners and matching piston assemblies. Similarly, a greater than 0.003 in (0.08 mm) difference in measurement across the bore indicates ovality and calls for the same treatment.

4   Any bore which is significantly scratched or scored will need renewing. This symptom usually indicates that the piston or rings are damaged. In the event of only one cylinder being in need of liner renewal, it is considered best for a complete set of four to be fitted.

5   Renewal of the liners is not a difficult job provided that a good puller is available to remove the old ones. If the crankshaft is undergoing regrinding, it is a good idea to let the same firm renew the liners, and renovate and reassemble the crankshaft and pistons to the block. A reputable firm normally gives a guarantee for such work.

6   In the case of the XD2 engine the cylinder bores are machined directly in the cylinder block, and liners are not fitted. Should the cylinder bores of this engine be worn, scored or oval, the cylinder may be rebored and oversize pistons fitted. Again this work must be carried

Fig. 1.16 Matching piston and cylinder liner assemblies as fitted to XD88 and XD90 engines (Sec 25)

out by a specialist firm who will decide how much metal must be ground off the cylinder bores, and will supply a set of oversize pistons and piston rings to suit.

7   If new standard size pistons and/or rings are being fitted and the cylinder have not been rebored or had new liners fitted, it is essential to slightly roughen the hard glaze on the sides of the bores with fine emery so the new piston rings will have a chance to bed in properly. The top piston ring will also have to be of the 'stepped' type to avoid fouling the unworn ridge at the top of the cylinder bore.

8   Examine the crankcase for cracks and leaking core plugs. To renew a core plug, drill a hole in its centre and tap a thread in it. Screw in a bolt and, using a distance piece, tighten the bolt and extract the core plug. When fitting the new plug, smear its outer edge with gasket cement.

9   Probe oil galleries and waterways with a piece of wire or nylon pipe cleaners to make sure that they are quite clear.

26 Piston/connecting rod assemblies – examination and renovation

1   Using a pair of circlip pliers, remove the circlips from the piston and slide out the gudgeon pin from the piston and connecting rod small-end bearing (photos). If the gudgeon pin is a tight fit, immerse

26.1a Removing the circlips ...

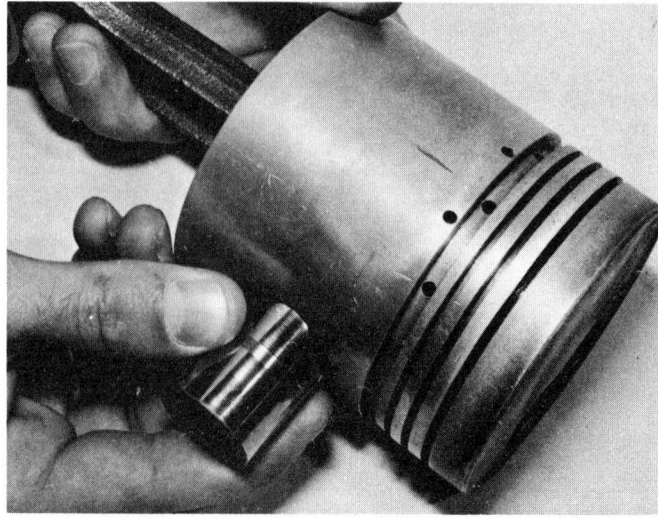

26.1b ... and gudgeon pin from the piston

the piston in hot water. The gudgeon pin should then slide out quite easily. Mark the connecting rod in relation to the piston so that it may be refitted in exactly the same way.

2   To remove the piston rings, slide them carefully over the top of the piston, taking care not to scratch the aluminium alloy of the piston. Never slide them off the bottom of the piston skirt. It is very easy to break piston rings if they are pulled off roughly, so this operation should be done with extreme caution. It is helpful to use an old feeler gauge to facilitate their removal as follows.

3   Lift one end of the piston ring to be removed out of its groove and insert the end of the feeler gauge under it.

4   Turn the feeler gauge slowly round the piston; as the ring comes out of its groove it rests on the land above. It can then be eased off the piston with the feeler gauge stopping it from slipping into any empty grooves, if it is any but the top piston ring that is being removed.

5   Piston ring wear can be checked by first removing the rings from the pistons as described previously. Place each ring in the cylinder bores individually from the top and push them down the bores approximately 1.5 inches (38 mm) with the head of a piston, so that they rest square in the cylinder. Then measure the gap at the ends of the rings with a feeler gauge. If the gap exceeds the figures given in the Specifications the rings will need renewal.

6   The grooves in which the rings locate in the piston can also become enlarged in use. If the clearance between ring and piston in the piston ring groove is other than minimal, the piston and rings must be renewed.

7   Examine the connecting rods carefully. They are not subject to wear, but in extreme cases such as partial engine seizure they could be distorted. Such conditions may be visually apparent, but if doubt exists they should be changed or checked for alignment by engine reconditioning specialists. If new gudgeon pin bushes are required, this job should also be entrusted to a specialist as the new bushes have to be reamed to fit the gudgeon pins.

8   If new pistons are being fitted they will be supplied with the rings already assembled. If new rings are to be fitted to existing pistons, follow the manufacturers fitting instructions supplied with the rings. Note that when fitting new standard size pistons and/or rings to partially worn cylinders, the top ring will need to be of the 'stepped' type to avoid fouling the unworn ridge at the top of the cylinder bore.

9   Refitting the piston to the connecting rod in the reverse sequence to removal, ensuring that the two components are refitted the same way as noted during dismantling.

27 Camshaft and camshaft bearings – examination and renovation

1   The camshaft bearing bushes should be examined for signs of scoring and pitting. If they need renewal they will have to be dealt with professionally as, although it may be relatively easy to remove the old bushes, the correct fitting of new ones requires special tools. If they are not fitted evenly and square they will wear in a very short time. See your Peugeot garage or local engineering specialist for this work.

2   The camshaft itself may show signs of wear on the bearing journals, cam lobes or the skew gear. The main decision to take is what degree of wear justifies renewal, which is costly. Any signs of scoring or damage to the bearing journals cannot be remedied by regrinding. Renewal of the whole camshaft is the only solution. Similarly, excessive wear on the skew gear which can be seen where the oil pump driveshaft teeth mesh will mean renewal of the whole camshaft.

3   The cam lobes themselves may show signs of ridging or pitting on the high points. If ridging is light then it may be possible to smooth it out with fine emery. The cam lobes however, are surface hardened, and once this is penetrated wear will be very rapid thereafter.

28 Cam followers – examination

The faces of the cam followers which bear on the camshaft should show no signs of pitting, scoring or other forms or wear. Thoroughly clean them out, removing all traces of sludge. It is most unlikely that the sides of the tappets will prove worn, but if they are a very loose fit in their bores and can be rocked readily, then they should be exchanged for new units. It is very unusual to find any wear in the

tappets, and any wear present is likely to occur only at very high mileages.

29 Timing components – examination and renovation

Engine with chain drive timing components

1   Carefully examine the teeth of the crankshaft, camshaft, fuel injection pump and idler gear sprockets.

2   Each tooth forms an inverted 'V' with the sprocket periphery, and if worn the side of each tooth (ie one side of the inverted 'V') will be concave when compared with the other. If any sign of wear is present the sprockets must be renewed.

3   Should the camshaft sprocket be worn, the use of a press will be required to remove and refit the sprocket. When refitting heat the pinion in well-heated oil and then press it on the camshaft until the specified clearance exists between the sprocket and thrust plate.

4   If any of the timing sprockets are to be renewed it will also be necessary to replace the crankshaft sprocket with one having three dots on its front face directly opposite the Woodruff keyway. It will then also be necessary, upon reassembling the engine, to check the valve timing as described in Section 49.

5   Examine the links of the chain for side slackness, and renew the chain if any slackness is noticeable when compared with a new chain. It is a sensible precaution to renew the chain at about 30 000 miles (48 000 km) and at a lesser mileage if the engine is stripped down for a major overhaul. The actual rollers on a very badly worn chain may be slightly grooved.

6   Carefully inspect the timing chain tensioner thrust pad, and if it is badly grooved it must be renewed. Also check that the plunger is free to move in and out with no signs of sticking.

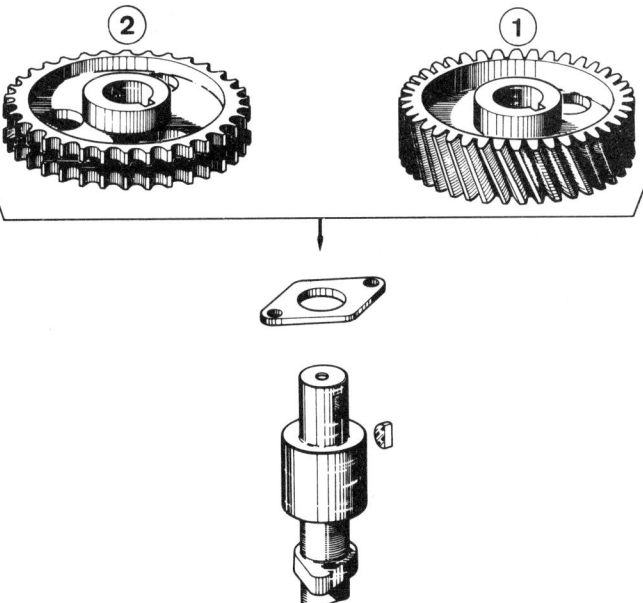

Fig. 1.17 Assembly sequence of timing gear (1) or sprocket (2) to camshaft (Sec 29)

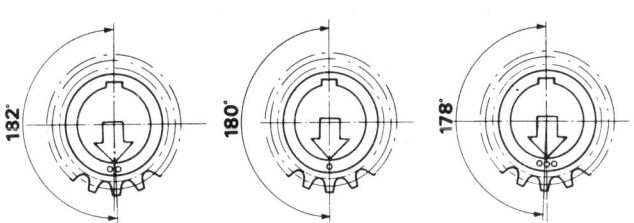

Fig. 1.18 The three crankshaft sprocket types are identified by dots on their front faces (Sec 29)

29.8 Checking the clearance between the camshaft thrust plate and gear

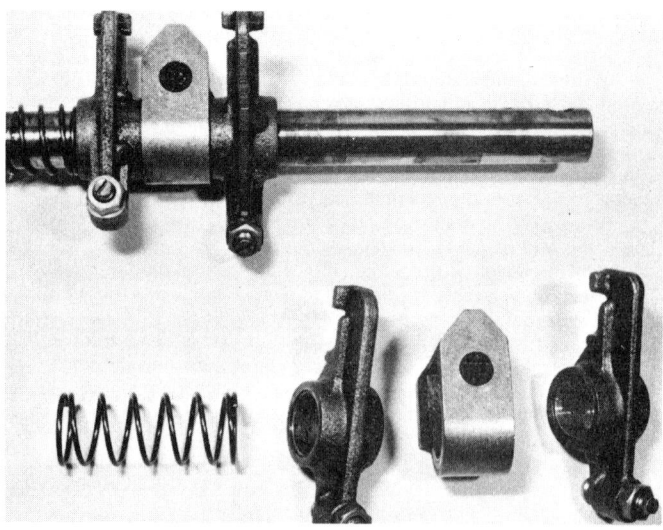

30.1 Dismantling the rocker shaft assembly

Engines with gear driven timing components

7   On engines equipped with gear driven timing, these components are very robust and it is unlikely that any wear will have taken place. Check, however, that the teeth are sound with no signs of chipping or pitting that would indicate a breakdown of the surface hardening.
8   Renew any gears that show signs of wear, referring to paragraph 3 of this Section if the camshaft gear requires renewal (photo).

30 Rockers and rocker shaft – examination and renovation

1   Lift out the end post retaining bolt and then slide the end post, rockers, springs and pedestals off the rocker shaft, noting their positioning and keeping them in order as they are removed (photo).
2   The lubrication collar on the centre of the shaft can be removed after withdrawing the locating bolt.
3   Check the shaft for straightness by rolling it on the bench. It is most unlikely that it will be bent, but if it is then a judicious attempt must be made to straighten it. If this is not successful a new shaft must be obtained. The surface of the shaft must be free from any worn ridges caused by the rocker arms. If any wear is evident renew the shaft. Wear is only likely to have occurred if the rocker shaft oil holes have become blocked.
4   Check the rocker arms for wear of the rocker bushes, for wear at the rocker arm face which bears on the valve stem, and for wear of the adjusting ball-ended screws. Wear in the rocker arm bush can be checked by gripping the rocker arm tip and holding the rocker arm in place on the shaft, noting if there is any lateral rocker arm shake. If shake is present, and the arms are very loose on the shaft, a new bush or rocker arm must be fitted.

Fig. 1.19 Dismantling the rocker shaft assembly (Sec 30)

5   Check the tip of the rocker arm where it bears on the valve head for cracking or serious wear of the case hardening. If none is present, re-use the rocker arm. Check the lower half of the ball on the end of the rocker arm adjusting screw. On high mileage engines, wear on the ball and top of the pushrod is easily noted by the unworn 'pip' which fits in the small central oil hole on the ball. The larger this 'pip' the more wear has taken place to both the ball and the pushrod. Check the pushrods for straightness by rolling them on the bench. Renew any that are bent.

31 Flywheel – examination and renovation

1   Examine the clutch disc mating surface of the flywheel. If this is deeply grooved or scored the flywheel must be renewed.
2   If the teeth on the starter ring gear are badly worn or some are missing, then it will be necessary to remove the ring gear. The old ring can be removed from the flywheel by cutting a notch between two teeth with a hacksaw and then splitting it with a cold chisel. Take suitable precautions to avoid flying fragments, paying particular attention to protection of the eyes. Note which way round the ring gear is fitted!
3   To fit a new ring gear requires heating the ring to 400°F (204°C). This can be done by polishing four equally spaced sections of the gear, laying it on a suitable heat resistant surface (such as fire bricks) and heating it evenly with a blow torch or lamp until the polished areas turn a light yellow tinge. *Do not overheat*, or the hard wearing properties will be lost. When hot enough place the gear in position quickly, tapping it home if necessary, and let it cool naturally without quenching in any way.

32 Cylinder head and piston crowns – decarbonising

1   With the cylinder head off, carefully remove with a wire brush and blunt scraper all traces of carbon deposits from the combustion spaces and the ports. The valve heads, stems and valve guides should also be freed from any carbon deposits. Wash the combustion spaces and ports down with petrol and scrape the cylinder head surface free of any foreign matter with the side of a steel rule, or a similar surface.
2   Clean the pistons and top of the cylinder bores. If the pistons are still in the block, then it is essential that great care is taken to ensure that no carbon gets into the cylinder bores, as this could scratch the cylinder walls or cause damage to the pistons and rings. To ensure this does not happen, first turn the crankshaft so that two of the pistons are at the top of their bores. Stuff rag into the other two bores, or seal them off with paper and masking tape. The waterways should also be covered with small pieces of masking tape to prevent particles of carbon entering the cooling system and damaging the water pump.
3   There are two schools of thought as to how much carbon should

be removed from the piston crown. One school recommends that a ring of carbon should be left around the edge of the piston and on the cylinder bore wall as an aid to low oil consumption. Although this is probably true for old engines with worn bores, on newer engines the thought of the second school can be applied, which is that for effective decarbonisation, all traces of carbon should be removed. If all traces of carbon are to be removed, press a little grease into the gap between the cylinder walls and the two pistons which are to be worked on. With a blunt scraper, carefully scrape away the carbon from the piston crown, taking great care not to scratch the aluminium. Also scrape away the carbon from the surrounding lip of the cylinder wall. When all carbon has been removed, scrape away all the grease which will now be contaminated with carbon particles, taking care not to press any into the bores. To assist prevention of carbon build-up, the piston crown can be polished with a metal polish. Remove the rags or masking tape from the other two cylinders, and turn the crankshaft so that the two pistons which were at the bottom are now at the top. Place rag or masking tape in the cylinders which have been decarbonised and proceed as just described.

4   If a ring of carbon is going to be left round the piston, then this can be helped by inserting an old piston ring into the top of the bore to rest on the piston and ensure that carbon is not accidentally removed.

5   Check that there are no particles of carbon in the cylinder bores. Decarbonising is now complete.

33 Valves and valve seats – examination and renovation

1   Examine the heads of the valves for pitting and burning, especially the heads of the exhaust valves. The valve seats should be examined at the same time. If the pitting on valve and seat is very slight, the marks can be removed by grinding the seats and valves together with fine grinding paste. Where bad pitting has occurred to the valve seats, it will be necessary to recut them and fit new valves. If the valve seats are so worn that they cannot be recut, then it will be necessary to fit new valve seat inserts. These latter two jobs should be entrusted to the local Peugeot garage or engineering works. In practice, it is very seldom that the seats are so badly worn that they require renewal. Normally, it is the exhaust valve that is too badly worn for refitting, and the owner can easily purchase a new set of valves and match them to the seats by valve grinding.

2   Valve grinding is carried out as follows: Smear a trace of fine carborundum paste on the seat face and apply a suction grinder tool to the valve head. With semi-rotary motion, grind the valve head to its seat, lifting the valve occasionally to redistribute the grinding paste. When a smooth unbroken ring of light grey matt finish is produced, on both valve and valve seat faces, the grinding operation is completed.

3   Scrape away all carbon from the valve head and the valve stem. Carefully clean away every trace of grinding compound, taking care to leave none in the ports or in the valve guides. Clean the valves and valve seats with a paraffin soaked rag, then with a clean rag, and finally, if an air line is available, blow the valves, valve guides and valve ports clean.

34 Valve guides and swirl chambers – inspection

1   Examine the valve guides internally for wear. If the valves are a very loose fit in the guides and there is the slightest suspicion of lateral rocking using a new valve, then the guide will have to be reamed and oversize valves fitted. This is a job best left to the local Peugeot garage.

2   Check the swirl chambers for security of fit, excessive cracking and distortion. Small cracks may be evident around the fuel outlet, but these are acceptable and will not affect the operation of the engine. It is not normally necessary to remove the swirl chambers from the cylinder head unless there are obvious signs of damage. If this is the case this work also should be entrusted to your Peugeot garage.

35 Sump – inspection

Wash out the oil sump in petrol and wipe dry. Inspect the exterior for signs of damage or excessive rust. If evident, a new oil sump must be obtained. To ensure an oil tight joint, scrape away all traces of the old gasket from the cylinder block mating face.

36 Engine – reassembly (general)

To ensure maximum life with minimum trouble from a rebuilt engine, not only must everything be correctly assembled, but everything must be spotlessly clean, all the oilways must be clear, locking washers and spring washers must always be fitted where indicated, and all bearing and other working surfaces must be thoroughly lubricated during assembly.

Before assembly begins, renew any bolts or studs the threads of which are in any way damaged, and whenever possible use new washers.

In addition to the normal range of good quality socket spanners and general tools which are essential, the following must be available before assembly begins:

(a)   Complete set of new gaskets
(b)   Supply of clean rag
(c)   Clean oil can full of engine oil
(d)   Torque wrench
(e)   All new parts as necessary

One point worth noting is that there are two types of cylinder head gasket available for the XD2 engine. The correct gasket to be fitted is determined by the amount of protrusion above the mating face of the cylinder block. It will therefore be necessary to assemble the crankshaft, pistons and connecting rods to enable a measurement of piston protrusion to be taken before obtaining the cylinder head gasket.

The engine shown in the photographs is the XD88 type and differs in minor ways from the other two diesel engines used in this Peugeot range. Provided that care is taken to note any differences between the text and the actual engine being worked on during dismantling, no problems will arise.

37 Crankshaft, oil seals and main bearings – refitting

1   Ensure that the crankcase is thoroughly clean and that all oilways are clear. A thin twist drill or nylon pipe cleaner is useful for cleaning them out. If possible blow them out with compressed air.

2   Treat the crankshaft in the same fashion and then inject engine oil into the crankshaft oilways.

3   Commence the work of rebuilding the engine by fitting the two composite half oil seals into the grooves adjacent to the crankcase rear main bearing journal and rear main bearing cap (photo).

4   Ensure that the seal is pushed fully home into its groove but without excessively compressing it. A wooden dowel or hammer handle is useful for carefully rolling the seal into position (photo). After fitting cut the seal ends so that they are perfectly flush with the mating surfaces of the crankcase and bearing cap.

5   Now wipe the main bearing shell locations in the crankcase with a soft non-fluffy rag.

6   Fit the five upper halves of the main bearing shells into their locations in the crankcase ensuring that the notches on the shells engage with the slots in the crankcase (photo).

7   Apply a little grease to the two thrust washer halves and position them either side of the crankcase centre main bearing journal. Note that the dimpled side faces the crankshaft (photo).

8   Thoroughly lubricate the five main bearing shells and then carefully lower the crankshaft into position (photo).

9   Fit the main bearing shell lower halves to each main bearing cap and then lay them out beside the crankcase (photo).

10   Apply a little grease to the remaining two thrust washers and then position them on the centre main bearing cap, dimpled side toward the crankshaft (photo).

11   Thoroughly lubricate the crankshaft centre main bearing journal and then fit the centre main bearing cap to the crankcase. **Note:** *The notches on the crankcase and bearing cap that accept the tags on the bearing shells must be on the same side (photo).*

12   Refit the centre main bearing cap retaining bolts and progressively tighten them to half their specified torque wrench setting.

13   Move the crankshaft as far as it will go to the rear and then, using feeler gauges, measure the clearance between the thrust washers and the side of the crankshaft journal (photo). This is the crankshaft endfloat, and if it is outside the limits shown in the Specifications, oversize thrust washers must be fitted.

37.3 Crankshaft half oil seal in position in main bearing cap

37.4 Using a wooden dowel to ease the half oil seal into its crankcase location

37.6 Fitting the upper half rear main bearing shell to the crankcase

37.7 The thrust washers must be fitted with the dimpled side toward the crankshaft

37.8 Lowering the crankshaft into position

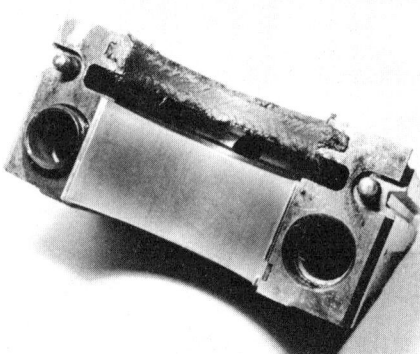

37.9 Main bearing shell correctly positioned in cap

37.10 Positioning the remaining two thrust washers on the centre main bearing cap

37.11 Installing the centre main bearing cap

37.13 Checking crankshaft endfloat

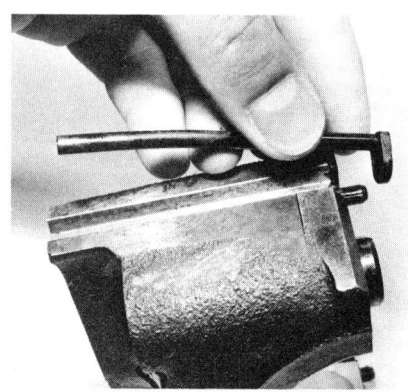

37.14a Position the rear main bearing cap lateral oil seals in their grooves ...

37.14b ... ensuring that the head of the seal engages with the dowel pin

37.15 Hold the seals in place when refitting the rear main bearing cap

37.17 Using a torque wrench to tighten the main bearing cap retaining bolts

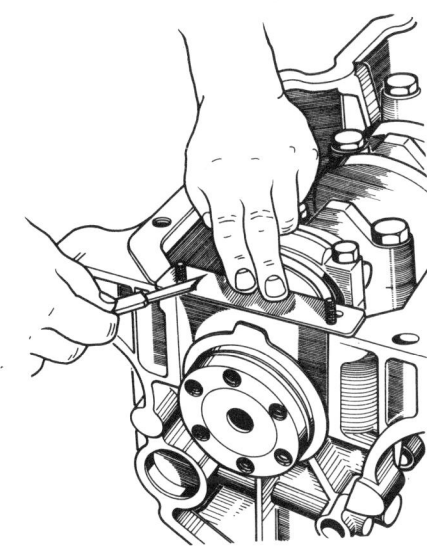

Fig. 1.13 Trimming the protruding edges of the main bearing cap lateral oil seals (Sec 37)

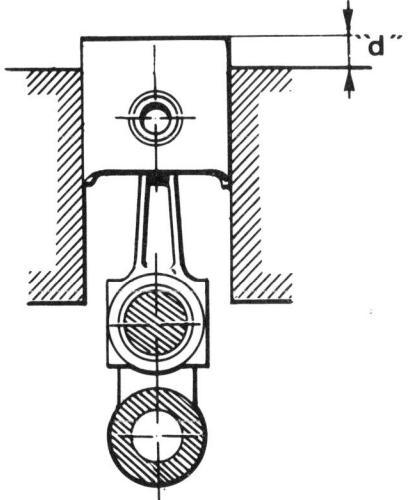

Fig. 1.21 Checking piston protrusion above cylinder block face (Sec 39)

d = amount of protrusion

14 The rear main bearing cap lateral oil seals can now be installed. Position the seals in the groove on either side of the cap, ensuring that the head of the seal engages with the dowel pin on the cap (photo).
15 Smear a little grease on the seals, lubricate the crankshaft rear journal, and then carefully lower the rear main bearing cap into position. Ease the cap and seals down by hand, holding the seals in place with your fingers (photo). When the cap is fully home refit the retaining bolts tightened to half the specified torque wrench setting.
16 Fit the remaining main bearing caps, tightening the retaining bolts to half the specified torque wrench setting only at this stage.
17 Now fully tighten the retaining bolts of each main bearing cap in turn to the specified torque wrench setting (photo). Check that the crankshaft is free to turn after tightening each cap. Should it be excessively stiff to turn, or possess high spots, a most careful inspection must be made with a micrometer, preferably by a qualified mechanic to get to the root of the trouble. It is very seldom that problems of this nature will be experienced when fitting the crankshaft.
18 After fully tightening all the main bearing bolts, trim off the protruding ends of the lateral oil seals using a sharp knife so that 0.5 mm (0.01 in) is left protruding.

38 Cylinder liners – refitting

1 As stated previously, it is best if the cylinder liners fitted to the XD88 and XD90 engines are renewed by your Peugeot garage or engineering works. It is possible for this work to be carried out by an enthusiast but a dial indicator gauge must be available.
2 With the cylinder block liner locations very clean, first fit the liners without their seals. Remember, do not mix up the pistons and liners as they are matched pairs.
3 Using a dial indicator gauge, check that the liner head (top) protrusion does not exceed 0.07 mm (0.003 in). If it does, remove and look for dirt or other causes.
4 Remove the liners again, fit new seals and refit the liners.
5 Temporarily retain the liners in position with bolts and large washers screwed into the cylinder head mating face.

39 Pistons and connecting rods – refitting

1 The piston complete with connecting rods can now be fitted to the cylinder bores in the following manner.
2 First place the big-end bearing shells in position on the connecting rods and caps, with the notches on the bearing shells engaged in the groove of the rod and cap.
3 Wipe the cylinder bores clean with a non-fluffy rag and then liberally lubricate them with engine oil.
4 Position the piston rings so that their gaps are 120° apart from each other and then lubricate the pistons and piston rings.
5 Insert one of the connecting rod and piston assemblies into the top of the cylinder bore, ensuring that it is the correct assembly for that cylinder and that it is positioned the correct way round (the cutaway portion on the piston crown toward the right-hand side of the cylinder block) (photo).
6 Before pushing the piston fully into its bore, compress the piston rings using a piston ring compressor (photo), and then tap the piston firmly into the cylinder bore using a block of wood against the centre of the piston crown.
7 With the crankshaft journal at its lowest point, continue pushing the piston down the bore until the connecting rod and bearing shell are firmly seated on the crankshaft journal.
8 Lubricate the crankshaft journal and then assemble the big-end bearing cap and shell onto the connecting rod, with the notches on the shells on adjacent sides (photo).
9 Refit the retaining nuts and tighten them to the torque figure given in the Specifications (photo).
10 Repeat the foregoing operations on the remaining three piston and connecting rod assemblies.
11 As mentioned previously, when working on the XD2 engine it is necessary to measure the amount of piston protrusion above the top of the cylinder block in order to determine the correct cylinder head gasket thickness. With the piston and connecting rods all installed, proceed as follows:
12 Rotate the crankshaft until one of the pistons is at its TDC position.

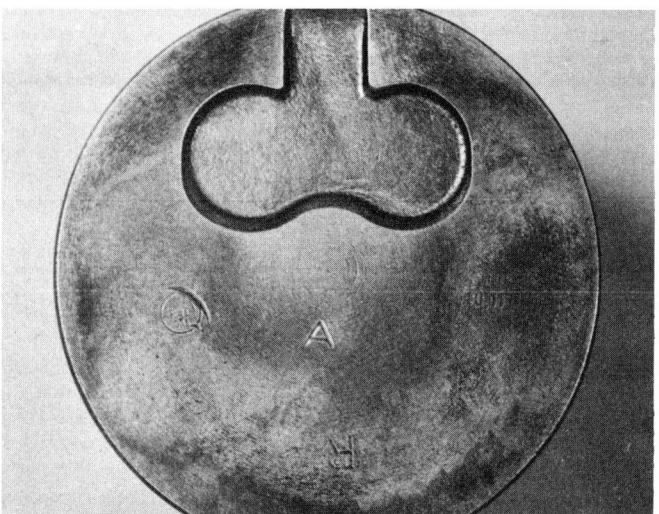

39.5 When refitting piston/connecting rod assemblies, the cutaway portion on the piston must be toward the right-hand side of the cylinder block

39.6 Piston ring compressor in position

39.8 Fitting the big-end cap to the connecting rod

39.9 Using a torque wrench to tighten the big-end cap retaining nuts

13 Using a dial indicator or the probe of a vernier caliper, measure the amount by which the piston protrudes above the top of the cylinder block mating face.

14 If this dimension is less than or equal to 0.84 mm (0.033 in), a cylinder head gasket having a compressed thickness of 1.48 mm (0.058 in) must be used. This gasket is identified by two notches in the identification tab.

15 If the dimension is greater than 0.84 mm (0.033 in), a gasket having a compressed thickness of 1.60 mm (0.062 in) must be used. This gasket is identified by three notches in the identification tab.

40 Camshaft and cam followers – refitting

1 Wipe the front face of the cylinder block with a non-fluffy rag and then place a new gasket in position (photo).

2 Make sure that the mating surface of the front interface plate is clean and free of any traces of old gasket.

3 Now position the interface plate on the front of the engine and secure it in position using only the bolts which are not also used for securing the timing cover (photo).

4 Wipe the camshaft and camshaft bearings clean and then liberally lubricate them with engine oil.

5 Carefully insert the camshaft into the cylinder block, taking care not to damage the bearing surfaces with the sharp edges of the cam lobes (photo).

6 Refit the two bolts to the camshaft thrust plate and tighten them to the specified torque wrench settings (photo). Note: *On later XD2 engines the camshaft is retained by a lip on the interface plate and the thrust plate is omitted.*

7 With the camshaft in place, lubricate the cam follower bores with engine oil and insert each cam follower into its correct bore (photo).

8 Using new side cover gaskets lightly smeared with gasket compound, refit the two side covers and securing nuts (photo).

41 Oil pump – refitting

1 Position the oil pump so that the grub screw locating hole is toward the side of the engine (photo) and then slide the oil pump into position in the crankcase.

2 Push the oil pump fully home until the drive gear meshes with the gear on the camshaft, and the locating hole on the pump body is visibly in line with the grub screw hole on the side of the cylinder block.

3 Using a small Allen key, screw the grub screw into position making sure that it engages with the pump (photo).

4 Now refit the domed locknut to the grub screw (photo).

5 Install the retaining/thrust plug and shims and fully tighten the plug (photo).

40.1 Place a new gasket on the front of the cylinder block ...

40.3 ... and then refit the front interface plate

40.5 Insert the camshaft ...

40.6 ... and refit the thrust plate retaining bolts

40.7 Insert the cam followers into their original bores ...

40.8 ... then refit the side covers with new gaskets

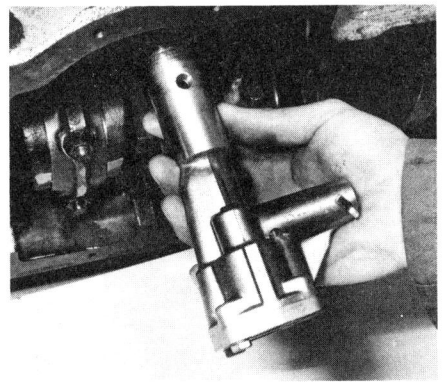

41.1 Install the oil pump with the locating hole facing the side of the engine

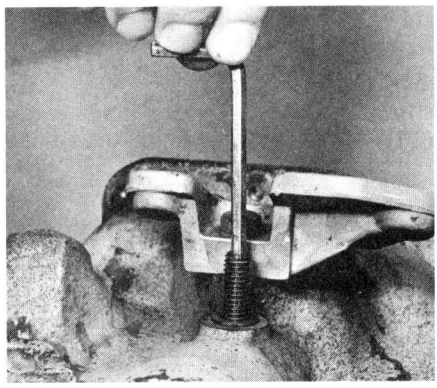

41.3 Screw in the grub screw to retain the oil pump ...

41.4 ... then refit the domed locknut

41.5 Refitting the retaining/thrust plug and shims

42.2 With a new gasket in position ...

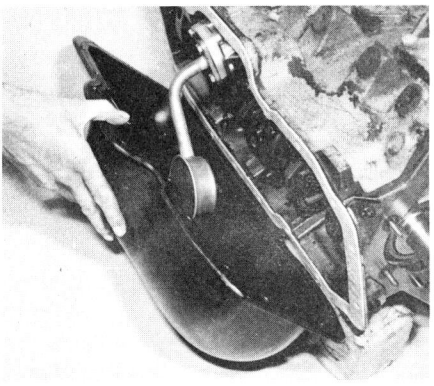

42.3 ... refit the sump

42 Sump – refitting

1   Ensure that the mating surfaces of the sump and crankcase are clean and free from any traces of old gasket material.
2   Coat both sides of a new sump gasket with jointing compound and place the gasket in position on the crankcase (photo).
3   Place the sump in position and refit the retaining bolts. Tighten the bolts progressively, and in a diagonal sequence to avoid distortion, to the specified torque wrench setting (photo).

43 Flywheel – refitting

1   Place the flywheel in position on the rear of the crankshaft and line up the marks made during removal.
2   Using a new locking plate, refit the flywheel retaining bolts and tighten them to the specified torque wrench setting (photo).
3   Now bend over the tabs to lock the retaining bolts (photo).

44 Timing components – refitting

Engines with chain drive timing components

1   Rotate the crankshaft until Nos 1 and 4 pistons are at their TDC position.
2   Refit the Woodruff key to the crankshaft and then slide on the crankshaft sprocket.
3   Refit the fuel injection pump and sprocket support bearing assembly to the front interface plate and secure with the retaining bolts.
4   Refit the idler sprocket and retaining bolt, but do not tighten the bolt at this stage. Turn the idler sprocket to its minimum adjustment position. Now fit the timing chain. When refitting the timing chain around the gearwheels, the copper link in the chain must be adjacent to the reference marks on the crankshaft sprocket, and the chain links marked by a line must be adjacent to the reference marks on the camshaft and fuel injection pump sprockets.
5   By trial and error alter the position of the chain, camshaft and fuel

43.2 Tighten the flywheel retaining bolts to the specified torque ...

43.3 ... and bend over the locking tabs

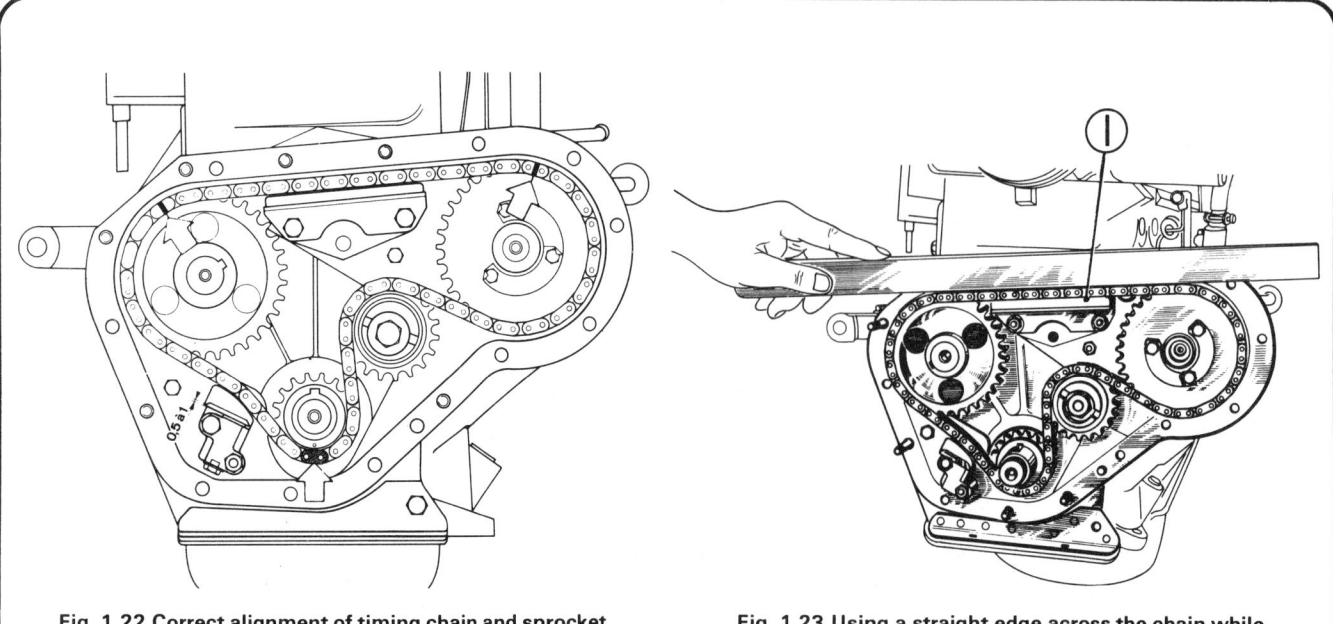

Fig. 1.22 Correct alignment of timing chain and sprocket reference marks (Sec 44)

Fig. 1.23 Using a straight edge across the chain while tightening the chain guide (1) retaining bolts (Sec 44)

44.11a Ensure that the Woodruff key is in place ...

44.11b ... and slide on the crankshaft gear

44.12 Fuel injection pump and gear in position

44.13a Refit the idler gear ...

44.13b ... ensuring that the timing marks (arrowed) on all four gears are in line

44.14 Idler gear thrust washer and circlip refitted

45.4 Refit the timing cover ...

45.5 ... followed by the crankshaft pulley

45.7 ... and then tighten the retaining nut

46.2 Oil seal in position on the valve stem

46.3 Refit valve springs and spring retainer ...

46.4 ... then compress the spring and insert the two split collets

injection pump sprockets until all the reference marks are in line. Refit the chain tensioner assembly and then the chain guide. Do not fully tighten the chain guide bolts at this stage.

6 Now turn the idler sprocket eccentric anti-clockwise, thus tensioning the chain slightly, until the clearance between the chain tensioner pad and its housing is between 0.5 and 1 mm (0.02 and 0.04 in). With the idler sprocket in this position fully tighten the retaining bolt.

7 Using an Allen key engaged with the timing chain tensioner rod, turn the key to the right until the pad is just in contact with the chain. Now remove the Allen key and refit the small bolt and washer.

8 Place a straight edge along the run of the chain between the camshaft and fuel injection pump sprockets. Move the chain guide until it is in contact with the chain and then tighten the retaining bolts.

9 If any of the timing components have been renewed, it will be necessary to check the valve timing, as described in Section 49, upon completion of engine reassembly. It will also be necessary to have the fuel injection pump timing checked, and if necessary reset, by a Peugeot garage after the engine has been initially started and run for a short while (see Chapter 3).

Engines with gear driven timing components

10 Rotate the crankshaft until Nos 1 and 4 pistons are at the TDC position.

11 Refit the Woodruff key to the crankshaft and then slide on the crankshaft gear with the raised centre boss toward the engine (photos).

12 Place the fuel injection pump complete with drive gear in position and secure it with the lower rear mounting bolt only at this stage (photo).

13 Now turn the camshaft and fuel injection pump gears as necessary, and then slide on the idler gear so that when fitted the timing marks on all four gears are in line (photo).

14 Refit the thrust washer and circlip to the idler gear (photo).

15 If any of the timing gears have been renewed, it will be necessary to have the fuel injection pump timing checked, and if necessary reset, by your Peugeot garage after the engine has been initially started and run for a short while (see Chapter 3).

45 Timing cover – refitting

Note: *If working on engines with chain driven timing, and any of the timing components have been renewed, do not refit the timing cover at this stage. Continue with the engine reassembly sequence and then refit the timing cover after checking, and if necessary correcting the valve timing as described in Section 49.*

1 Ensure that the mating surfaces of the timing cover and front interface plate are clean and free from any traces of old gasket.

2 Smear some gasket compound onto both faces of a new timing cover gasket and then position the gasket on the timing cover.

3 Insert the crankshaft pulley Woodruff key into the slot in the crankshaft.

4 Position the timing cover on the front of the engine and refit the retaining bolts, finger tight only at this stage (photo). **Note:** *Where gear driven timing components are employed, the fuel injection pump intermediate mounting flange retaining bolts also secure the timing cover.*

5 Lubricate the oil seal in the front of the timing cover and then slide the crankshaft pulley onto the front of the crankshaft (photo).

6 Now fully tighten the timing cover retaining bolts, progressively and in a diagonal sequence to avoid distortion.

7 Refit the pulley retaining nut to the front of the crankshaft and tighten to the specified torque wrench setting (photo). Lock the flywheel ring gear with a screwdriver to prevent the crankshaft from turning.

46 Cylinder head – reassembly

1 With the cylinder head on its side, lubricate the valve stems and refit the valves to their correct guides.

2 Refit the lower valve spring retainer and then slide on the valve stem oil seal (photo).

3 Position the inner and outer valve springs and upper spring retainer over the valve stem (photo).

4 Using a valve spring compressor, compress the springs and then refit the split collets (photo). A trace of grease will help to hold them in position on the valve stem until the spring compressor is released.

5 Release the valve spring compressor and check that the collets are correctly in position. Give the top of the valve stem a few taps with a soft-faced mallet to fully settle the collets and springs.

47 Cylinder head – refitting

1 The next step is to thoroughly clean the faces of the block and cylinder head to remove all traces of old cylinder head gasket or jointing compound. Clean out the retaining bolt holes with a piece of wire and rag. Run the bolts up and down to make sure that they are all free and that the threads are clean. Finally wipe over the block and cylinder head faces with a petrol moistened rag.

2 Remove the bolts and washers (where applicable) that were previously screwed into the top face of the cylinder block to retain the liners.

3 Place the cylinder head gasket in position on the top face of the block with the larger crimped area toward the block face (photo). Do not use any jointing compound on the gasket unless advised to do so on the gasket manufacturer's instructions.

4 Carefully lower the cylinder head onto the cylinder block (photo).

5 Insert all the retaining bolts and plain washers, noting the three different lengths.

6 The bolts must now be tightened using the sequence shown in Fig. 1.12. Tighten each bolt in turn to the initial torque wrench setting shown in the Specifications, then back it off a quarter of a turn before tightening to the final specified setting.

7 Insert each pushrod into the hole from which it was originally removed. Make sure that the pushrod end seats correctly in the cam follower (photo).

8 Carefully lower the rocker shaft assembly onto the studs of the cylinder head (photo). Ensure that the lubrication collar in the centre of the shaft seats correctly into its oil feed hole, with a new seal fitted (photo).

9 Secure the rocker shaft assembly with the nuts and end post retaining bolts (photo). As the nuts and bolts are tightened, make sure that the ball end of each rocker arm is sitting snugly in the pushrod cup, and is not trapped or dislodged to one side. Finally tighten the rocker shaft assembly to the specified torque wrench setting.

10 Refit the inlet and exhaust manifolds and the rocker gear oil supply pipe, using new copper washers on each side of the banjo union (photo).

11 Adjust the valve clearances as described in the following Section and then, if the engine is in the car, reconnect the remaining components using the reverse sequence to removal.

48 Valve clearances – adjustment

1 The valve adjustments should be made with the engine cold. The importance of correct rocker arm/valve stem clearances, cannot be overstressed as they vitally affect the performance of the engine. If the clearances are set too open, the efficiency of the engine is reduced as the valves open late and close earlier than was intended. If, on the other hand, the clearances are set too close there is a danger that the valve stems will expand upon heating or not allow the valves to close properly, which will cause burning of the valve head and seat, and possibly warping. If the engine is in the car, access to the rockers is gained by removing the rocker cover.

2 It is important that the clearance is set when the cam follower of the valve being adjusted is on the heel of the cam, (ie opposite the peak).

3 The correct sequence for adjusting the valves is shown in Fig. 1.24. Note that No 1 cylinder is at the rear nearest the flywheel. A valve is fully open when the valve stem end of its rocker arm is observed to be at its lowest point of travel.

4 If the valve clearances are being initially adjusted after engine or cylinder head overhaul they should be set to the following:

Inlet	*0.25 mm (0.010 in)*
Exhaust	*0.35 mm (0.013 in)*

5 After the engine has been run for the first 600 miles (1000 km),

47.3 With the cylinder head gasket in position ...

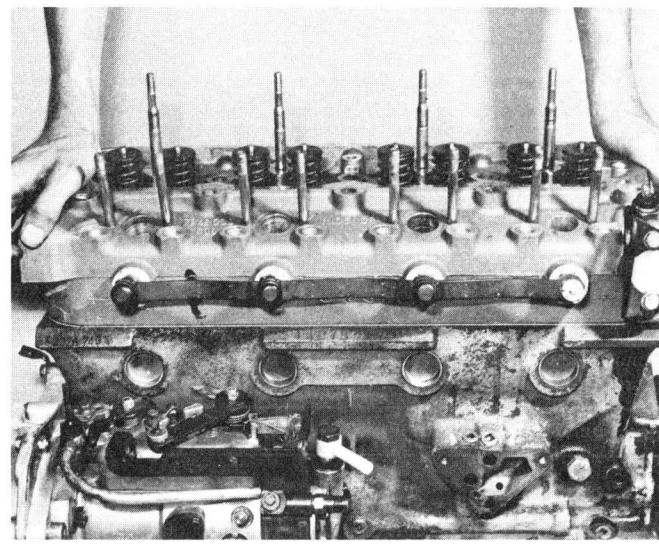

47.4 ... carefully lower the cylinder head onto the cylinder block

47.7 Insert the pushrods into their original locations ...

47.8a ... and then lower the rocker shaft assembly onto the studs

47.8b Make sure that the lubrication collar seats correctly into the oil feed hole ...

47.9 ... and then refit the retaining bolts and nuts

47.10 Rocker gear oil supply pipe banjo union at cylinder head

48.6 Adjusting the valve clearances

and whenever the clearances are rechecked in service, the correct setting is:

Inlet	*0.15 mm (0.006 in)*
Exhaust	*0.25 mm (0.010 in)*

6   Working from the rear of the engine the correct clearance is obtained by slackening the hexagon locknut with a spanner while holding the ball pin against rotation with a screwdriver. Then, still pressing down with the screwdriver, insert a feeler gauge in the gap between the valve stem and the rocker arm and adjust the ball pin until the feeler gauge will just move in and out without nipping (photo). Then, still holding the ball pin in the correct positions, tighten the locknut.

7   When the clearances have all been set, refit the rocker cover using a new gasket and secure with the four nuts. Note the hose steady bracket is fitted to the forwardmost retaining stud.

To adjust rockers	fully open the valve
● 3 ⊗ 4	⊗ 1
● 4 ⊗ 2	⊗ 3
● 2 ⊗ 1	⊗ 4
● 1 ⊗ 3	⊗ 2

INLET ●
EXHAUST ⊗

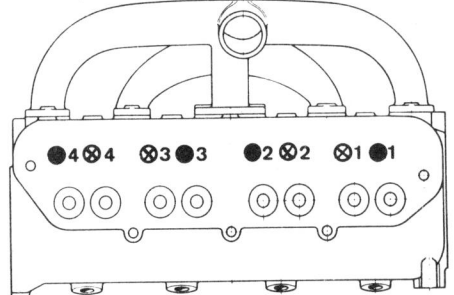

●4 ⊗4   ⊗3 ●3   ●2 ⊗2   ⊗1 ●1

Fig. 1.24 Valve clearance adjustment sequence (Sec 48)

49 Valve timing (chain driven timing gear) – checking and adjusting

1   Whenever any of the timing components on engines having chain driven timing gear are renewed, the following check must be made before starting the engine to ensure that the valve timing is correct.

2   Adjust the valve clearances using the sequence shown in Fig. 1.24 to the following settings:

	XD88/90 engines	**XD2 engines**
Inlet	*0.015 mm (0.006 in)*	*0.25 mm (0.010 in)*
Exhaust	*0.25 mm (0.010 in)*	*0.35 mm (0.013 in)*

3   Insert a 0.40 mm (0.015 in) thick feeler gauge between each inlet valve stem and rocker in turn, and then rotate the crankshaft by hand two complete revolutions. Check that there is no contact between the valve and piston at the point when the valve is fully open.

4   Should contact occur the crankshaft sprocket, which will have three reference dots adjacent to one of the teeth on the front face, must be replaced by a sprocket having only one reference dot (Fig. 1.8).

5   After completing the checks and making any necessary alteration, reset the valve clearances as described in Section 48.

50 Oil filter and housing – refitting

1   Ensure that the mating surfaces of the filter housing and cylinder block are clean with all traces of old gasket removed.

2   Apply a trace of jointing compound to both sides of a new gasket and position it on the filter housing.

3   Refit the oil filter housing to the cylinder block (photo) and secure it in place with the three retaining bolts.

4   To refit the oil filter, first smear a trace of engine oil around the rubber sealing ring at the base of the filter.

5   Screw the filter onto the filter housing and tighten it *by hand only*. Do not use any tools to tighten the filter further.

6   With the engine running, check closely for any leaks.

51 Engine mountings – removal and refitting

1   The two engine mountings located on each side of the cylinder block each consist of three parts; a mounting bracket bolted to the cylinder block, the actual rubber engine mounting block, and a safety bracket. Normally the only component that will need renewal due to wear is the rubber mounting block.

2   If the engine is in the car, position a jack beneath the sump, with an interposed block of wood to spread the load. Now jack up the engine slightly until the weight of the engine is off the mountings.

3   Undo and remove the nut securing the rubber mounting block to the crossmember, and then the bolts securing the mounting block and safety bracket to the mounting bracket. On some engines the crossmember makes access to some of the bolts difficult, and it may be necessary to remove the mounting bracket bolts and lift the mounting off as an assembly, separating the three components after removal from the car (photo).

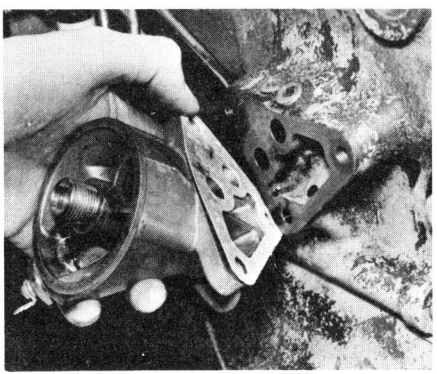

50.3 Refitting the oil filter housing

51.3 Removing the engine mounting assembly from the car

51.4 Removing the rubber mounting block from the bracket

4   If the engine is out of the car removal is much simpler and a visual inspection will show the easiest method of removal (photo).
5   Refitting the engine mountings is in all cases the reverse of the removal procedures.

52 Ancillary components – refitting

1   This is a reversal of the removal sequence given in Section 9 of this Chapter.
2   Always use new gaskets when refitting previously removed components, and refer to the appropriate Chapter of this manual for the full installation instructions for the component concerned.

53 Engine – refitting without manual gearbox or automatic transmission

1   The sequence for refitting is basically the reverse to that of removal, and should present no particular problems. However the following additional notes should be of assistance.
2   With the engine suitably suspended over the engine compartment, carefully lower it until the centre of the flywheel is in line with the gearbox input shaft or torque converter. Move the engine rearwards, ensuring that with the manual gearbox, the input shaft enters the clutch assembly in a straight line and not an angle. It may be necessary to turn the crankshaft by means of the front pulley slightly to allow the splines of the clutch disc to align with those on the input shaft.
3   Reconnect the gearbox or automatic transmission to the engine. Where automatic transmission is fitted it will be necessary to rotate the torque converter and crankshaft to align the converter and diaphragm bolt holes and allow the bolts to be fitted.
4   Whenever possible use new hose clips, and if necessary renew any suspect hoses.
5   Reconnect all electrical connections, controls, cables and pipes.
6   Check that the drain taps or plugs are closed and refill the cooling system with coolant, and the engine with the correct grade of engine oil.

54 Engine – refitting with manual gearbox or automatic transmission

1   The sequence for refitting is basically the reverse to that of removal and should present no particular problems. The following additional points should be noted.

2   As the gearbox or automatic transmission will be attached to the engine before refitting, it will be necessary to lower the unit into the engine compartment at a steep angle. Assuming the car to be jacked up and supported on stands, or over a pit or hoist as in the removal operation, it may be necessary to support the engine on jacks when it is in position in the engine compartment and change the position of the lifting gear. This will make the final positioning of the power unit easier as it will not be at such a steep angle.
3   With the engine in position refer to Section 53, paragraphs 4 to 6 inclusive.
4   Do not forget to refill the gearbox or automatic transmission with the correct grade and quantity of lubricant.

55 Engine – initial start-up after major overhaul or repair

1   With the engine refitted to the car, make a visual check to see that everything has been reconnected and that no loose rags or tools have been left within the engine compartment.
2   Make sure that the battery is fully charged and that all coolant and lubricants are fully replenished. Prime the fuel system as described in Chapter 3.
3   The engine should start after the fuel priming operation.
4   As the engine fires and runs keep it going at a fast idle only (no faster) and allow it to reach normal working temperature.
5   As the engine warms up there will be odd smells and some smoke from parts getting hot and burning off oil deposits. The signs to look for are leaks of water or oil, which will be obvious if serious. Check also the exhaust pipe and manifold connections as these do not always find their exact gas tight position until the heat and vibration have acted on them – it is almost certain that they will need tightening further. This should be done, of course, with the engine stopped.
6   When normal operating temperature has been reached, stop the engine and adjust the engine idle speed as described in Chapter 3.
7   Stop the engine and wait a few minutes to see if any coolant or lubricant is dripping out when the engine is stationary.
8   Road test the car to check that the engine is giving the necessary smoothness and power. Do not race the engine – if new bearings and/or pistons have been fitted it should be treated as a new engine and run in at a reduced speed for the first 1000 miles (1600 km).
9   After the car has been driven for approximately 30 miles (50 km), allow the engine to cool down for a minimum of 6 hours and then retighten the cylinder head bolts using basically the procedure described in Section 47. Each bolt should be slackened in turn, in the correct sequence, a quarter of a turn and then retighened to the final specified torque wrench setting. Do not forget to recheck the valve clearances afterwards. This operation must be carried out again after approximately 600 miles (1000 km).

56 Fault diagnosis – engine

Symptom	Reason(s)
Engine will not rotate when attempting to start	Battery discharged Loose battery connections Faulty starter motor or solenoid Earth strap broken or disconnected Fault in starting circuit wiring
Engine rotates but will not start, and emits black smoke	Fuel injection pump timing incorrect Fuel injectors faulty Lack of engine compression Obstruction in air intake system
Engine rotates but will not start, and emits white smoke	Cylinder head gasket leaking Cylinder head, cylinder block or liners cracked
Engine rotates but will not start, with no smoke emission	Fuel tank empty Air in fuel system Leak in fuel liner or unions Heater plugs inoperative Stop control jammed in stop position Fuel injection pump faulty Fuel injection faulty
Engine lacks power	Air intake system choked Fuel injection pump timing incorrect Fuel filter blocked Defective fuel injector Engine worn internally
Low oil pressure	Oil level too low Oil pressure warning light transmitter faulty Faulty or worn oil pump Oil pressure relif valve sticking engine bearings and internal components worn
Thumping noises from engine	Fuel injector faulty Fuel injection pump timing incorrect Air in fuel system or leaks in fuel lines Incorrect valve timing Broken internal component
Whistling or whispering noises from engine	Defective cylinder head gasket Leak at heater plug Leak at full injector seating Poor seating of inlet on exhaust valves Leak at manifold joint faces

Chapter 2 Cooling system

Contents

Specifications

System type .... Pressurised, assisted by pump and fan

Thermostat
Type .... Bellows
Location .... Radiator top hose
Opening temperature:
    Standard .... 69° to 72°C (156° to 162°F)
    Cold climates .... 81° to 84°C (178° to 183°F)

Radiator
Type .... Copper web, sealed system, with expansion tank
Filler cap pressure .... 0.8 bar (12 lbf/in^2)

Water pump
Type .... Centrifugal

Fan
Type .... Fixed or electromagnetic self-engaging/disengaging
Fan engages .... 81° to 83.5°C (178° to 182°F)
Fan disengages .... 69.5° to 67°C (157° to 152.5°F)
Electromagnetic winding current .... 0.7 to 0.9 amps at 12 volts
Hub air gap setting .... 0.35 to 0.40 mm (0.014 to 0.016 in)

Cooling system capacity (including heater) .... 10 litres (17.6 pints, 20.8 US pints)

Torque wrench settings

	Nm	lbf ft
Fan hub retaining nut	35	25
Water pump pulley retaining nut	35	25
Electromagnetic fan switch	40	29

1 General description

The engine cooling water is circulated by the thermo-syphon principle with assistance from an impeller-type water pump. The system is designed to operate under pressure, which effectively increases the boiling point of the cooling water and allows the engine to operate at higher, more efficient temperatures. The pressure in the system is controlled by the filler cap situated on the radiator expansion tank.

The system comprises a radiator, expansion tank, water pump, thermostat, fan and associated hoses. There is one drain plug located on the right-hand side of the cylinder block, towards the rear, and another at the bottom of the radiator.

The system functions in the following manner: Cold water from the bottom of the radiator circulates up the lower radiator hose to the water pump, where it is pumped around the water passages in the cylinder block, cooling the cylinders and (indirectly) the pistons. The water then travels up into the cylinder head and circulates around the combustion chambers and valve seats. When the engine has reached its normal operating temperature, the coolant travels out of the cylinder head, past the now open thermostat and into the radiator header tank. The water travels down the radiator core, where it is rapidly cooled by the rush of air created by both the motion of the vehicle and the rotation of the fan blades. The water, now much cooler, reaches the bottom of the radiator where the cycle is repeated.

When the engine is cold the thermostat remains closed, stopping the cycle of coolant from engine to radiator and allowing the same

Fig. 2.1 Radiator expansion tank and filler neck (arrowed) (Sec 2)

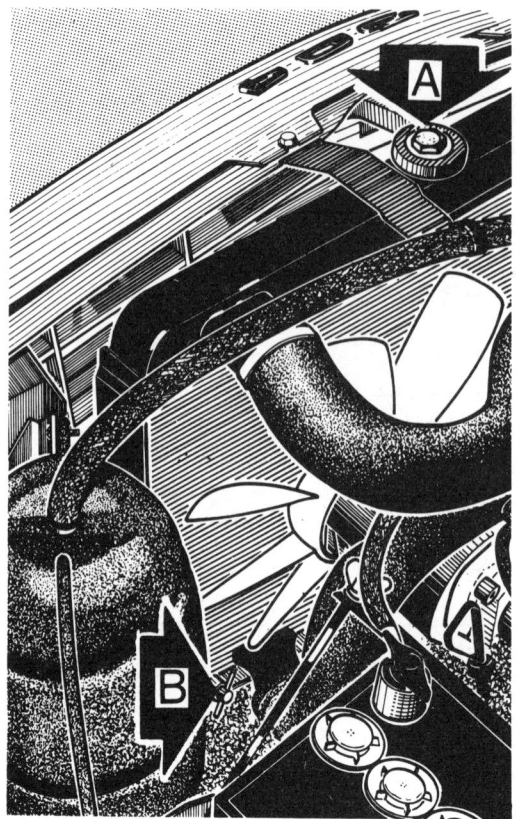

Fig. 2.2 Radiator header tank filler cap (A) and drain tap (B)
(Sec 2)

cooling water to recirculate around the engine. Only when the correct coolant temperature has been reached does the thermostat begin to open and allow the coolant to return to the radiator.

As the coolant expands with heat, the displaced water travels up the overflow pipe into the expansion tank situated above the engine. When the engine is stopped and the water is cooling, contraction takes place and the coolant return to the radiator header tank. In this way the radiator is kept completely filled with coolant at all times.

The fan pulley incorporates an electromagnetic drive which is only energised when the cooling water is hot. By this means the fan is only driven when it is really needed, with a consequent reduction in noise and power consumption.

2 Cooling system – draining

1   If the engine is cold remove the filler cap from the expansion tank by turning the cap anti-clockwise. If the engine is hot, then turn the filler cap very slightly until pressure in the system has had time to be released. Use a rag over the cap to protect your hand from escaping steam. If, with the engine very hot, the cap is released suddenly, the rapid drop in pressure can result in the water boiling. When the pressure is released the cap can be removed.
2   Unscrew the radiator cap from the top of the radiator header tank.
3   If antifreeze is used in the cooling system, have a bowl ready, having a capacity of at least 21 pints (11 litres), to contain the coolant for re-use.
4   Set the heater control to the maximum heat position and then open the drain plug located on the underside of the radiator bottom tank.
5   When the radiator has drained, open the chain plug located toward the rear right-hand side of the cylinder block.
6   When the coolant has finished draining, probe the drain plug orifices with a short piece of wire to dislodge any particles of rust or sediment which may be causing a blockage.

3 Cooling system – flushing

1   In time the cooling system will gradually lose its efficiency as the radiator becomes choked with rust, scale deposits from the water, and other sediment. To clean the system out, remove the radiator filler cap and drain plug, and leave water running into the filler cap neck for ten to fifteen minutes.
2   In very bad cases the radiator should be reverse flushed. This can be done with the radiator in position. The bottom hose should be detached from the radiator and a hose with a suitable tapered adaptor placed in the radiator bottom hose union. Water under pressure is then

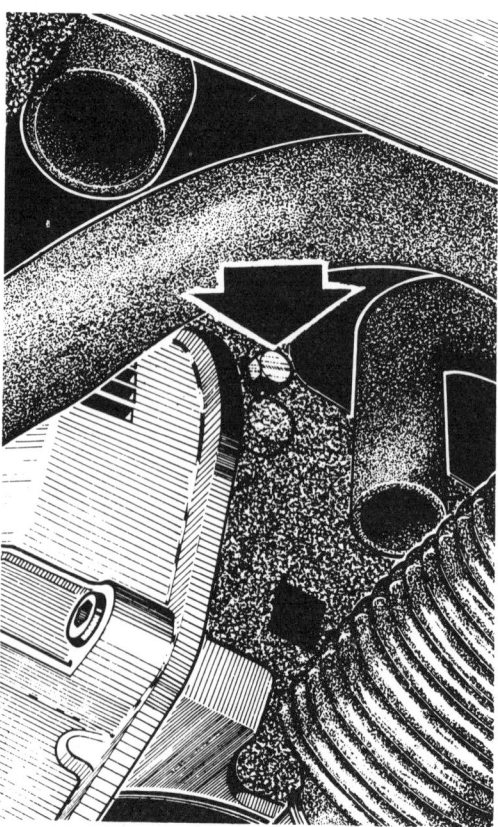

Fig. 2.3 The engine drain plug (arrowed) located at the rear right-hand side of the cylinder block (Sec 2)

forced through the radiator and out of the top tank filler cap neck.

3   It is recommended that some polythene sheeting is placed over the engine to stop water finding its way into the electrical system.

4   The hose should now be removed and placed in the radiator filler cap neck, and the radiator washed out in the usual manner.

4   Cooling system – filling

1   Refit and tighten the cylinder block and radiator drain plugs.

2   Ensure that the heater control is set to the maximum heat position to prevent air locks, and then fill the radiator slowly with water. The best type of water to use in the cooling system is rain water, which should be used whenever possible. **Note:** *In winter months refer to Section 12, and add the appropriate quantity of antifreeze to suit local climatic conditions.*

3   When the radiator is full, refit the filler cap and then fill the expansion tank up to the 'MAXI' mark.

4   Refit the expansion tank filler cap and start the engine, allowing it

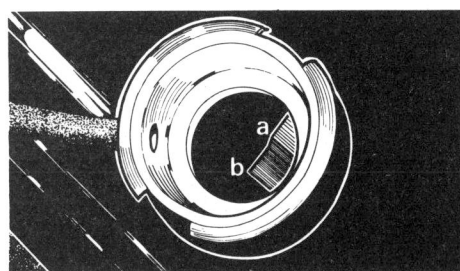

Fig. 2.4 Radiator expansion tank 'MAXI' (a) and 'MINI' (b) levels (Sec 4)

to idle until the radiator header tank reaches normal operating temperature.

5   Run the engine at a fast idle for a few more minutes and then switch off. Recheck the level in the expansion tank, taking the precautions detailed in Section 2, and top up if necessary.

6   Recheck the expansion tank level again the next time the car is driven.

5   Radiator – removal and refitting

1   Refer to Section 2 and drain the cooling system.

2   Slacken the hose clips securing the radiator top and bottom hoses, and the expansion tank hose to the radiator, and remove the hoses (photos).

3   Slacken the two clips securing the top and bottom hoses to the water pump and cylinder head outlet unions. Carefully remove the two hoses. Note that the thermostat is fitted into the top hose.

4   Disconnect the electrical connections from the fan cut-in switch located in the radiator bottom tank (photo).

5   Undo and remove the nuts and bolts securing the radiator upper mounting bracket to the body and radiator top tank and then remove the bracket (photo).

6   From under the front of the car undo and remove the nuts and washers from each of the two radiator lower mountings (photo). It may be necessary to hold the square-headed mounting bolts from above to prevent them turning as the nuts are removed.

7   The radiator can now be lifted upwards and out of the engine compartment. Very little clearance exists between the fan and the front body panel, and it may be necessary to turn the radiator on its side as it is lifted out. Take great care not to damage the fragile matrix on the fan blades as the radiator is removed (photo).

8   Refitting the radiator is the reverse sequence to removal.

9   With the radiator installed refill the cooling system as described in Section 4.

5.2a Radiator top hose ...

5.2b ... and bottom hose connections

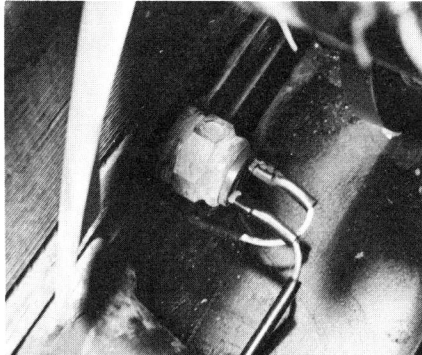

5.4 Electromagnetic fan cut-in switch electrical connections

5.5 Radiator upper mounting bracket ...

5.6 ... and lower rubber mounting blocks and locknut

5.7 Removing the radiator

6 Radiator – cleaning and servicing

1 With the radiator removed from the car, clean the exterior thoroughly by hosing down the matrix with a strong jet of water. This will remove road dirt, dead insects etc that may be trapped between the cooling fins. Clean out the inside of the radiator by flushing as described in Section 3.

2 Repair any leaks by soldering or with a suitable sealing compound.

3 Inspect the hoses for cracks, internal and external deterioration and damage caused by over-tightening of the hose clips. Renew any suspect hoses.

4 Examine the hose clips and renew them if they are rusted or distorted.

7 Water pump – removal and refitting

1 Disconnect the battery earth terminal.

2 Refer to Section 2 and drain the cooling system.

3 Refer to Section 5 and remove the radiator.

4 Slacken the bolt securing the vacuum pump adjusting arm to the mounting bolt and nut and move the pump toward the engine.

5 Lift off the vacuum pump drivebelt and then move the pump away from the engine as far as the elongted slot in the adjusting arm will allow.

6 Slacken the two bolts securing the jockey wheel to the water pump.

7 Move the jockey wheel in toward the centre of the engine and lift the drivebelt off the jockey wheel, water pump and fan pulleys.

8 Disconnect the electrical lead from the temperature gauge transmitter on the water pump (photo).

9 Slacken the hose clips and remove the radiator and heater hoses from the water pump (photo).

10 Undo and remove the water pump pulley retaining locknut and then slide off the pulley (photo). To stop the pulley turning as the nut is undone, use an old fanbelt wrapped around the pulley, and with its free end inserted in a tube or pipe of suitable diameter. Use a screwdriver, inserted through the loop of the belt that protrudes from the end of the tube, to tension the belt. With a little manipulation the 'V' of the belt will grip the sides of the pulley sufficiently to stop rotation.

11 Now remove the previously slackened jockey wheel retaining bolts and lift off the jockey wheel and its bracket.

12 Undo and remove the water pump retaining bolts and lift off the pump (photo). If it is stuck, tap it carefully on the side of the body with a soft-faced mallet.

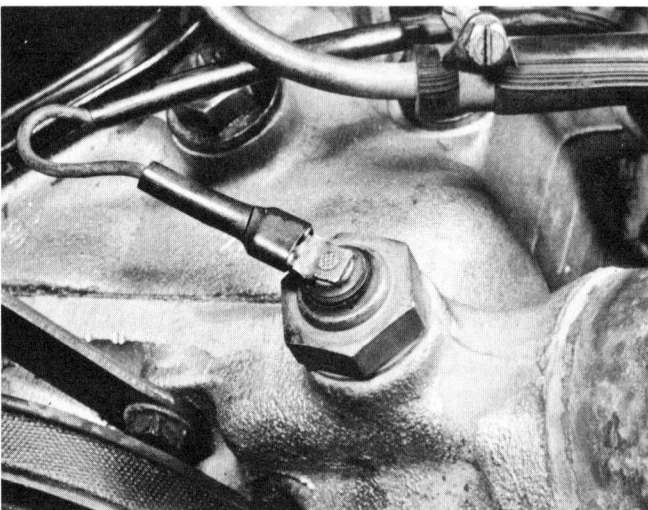

7.8 Temperature gauge transmitter and electrical connection

7.9 Radiator and heater hose connection at water pump

7.10 Water pump pulley and locknut

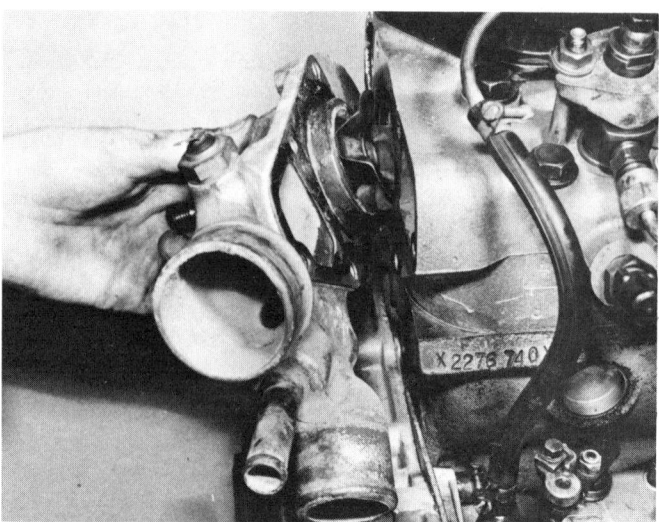

7.12 Lifting off the water pump

9.2 Location of thermostat in radiator top hose

10.1 Arrangement of the engine ancillary component drive belts

13 Refitting the water pump is the reverse sequence to removal, bearing in mind the following points:

(a) Ensure that the mating surfaces of the water pump and cylinder head are clean and free from all traces of old gasket

(b) Use a new gasket coated on both sides with sealing compound

(c) Adjust the fanbelt tension as described in Section 10, and the vacuum pump belt as described in Chapter 9

(d) Refill the cooling system as described in Section 4

8 Water pump – overhaul

1 Water pump failure is indicated by leaks, noisy operation and/or excessive slackness of the pump spindle.
2 The dismantling and overhaul of the water pump is considerably involved and requires the use of a number of special tools and a press. It is therefore recommended that in the event of water pump failure, an exchange reconditioned unit should be purchased from your Peugeot dealer.

9 Thermostat – removal, testing and refitting

1 Partially drain the cooling system, as described in Section 2.
2 Slacken the two upper hose clips and carefully remove the top hose. The thermostat is located in the outlet connection from the water pump (photo).
3 Carefully remove the thermostat from its location, noting which way round it is fitted.
4 Test the thermostat for correct functioning by suspending it on a string in a saucepan of cold water together with a thermometer. Make sure the thermostat or thermometer do not touch the sides or bottom of the saucepan.
5 Heat the water and note the temperature at which the thermostat begins to open. Compare the figure with those given in the Specifications at the beginning of this Chapter. Continue heating to check that the thermostat opens fully.
6 Allow the thermostat to cool down and ensure that the valve is fully closed when cold.
7 If the thermostat does not fully open in boiling water, or does not close down as the water cools, then it must be discarded and a new one fitted. Should the thermostat be stuck open when cold, this will usually be apparent when removing it from the water pump outlet.
8 Refitting the thermostat is the reverse sequence is removal.

10 Fanbelt – removal, refitting and adjustment

1 A minimum of three V-belts are used on Peugeot diesel engines to drive the engine ancillary components (photo). If power steering or air conditioning accessories are fitted, additional belts are used to drive these units. To gain access to the fanbelt, all other belts must be first removed.
2 Begin by removing the power steering or air conditioning belts (if fitted) by slackening the adjusting and mounting bolts and then lifting the belts off the pulleys.
3 Remove the alternator drivebelt as described in Chapter 10, and the vacuum pump drivebelt as described in Chapter 9.
4 Slacken the two bolts securing the fanbelt jockey wheel to the water pump and move the jockey wheel toward the centre of the engine.
5 The fanbelt can now be lifted off the four pulleys and removed from the engine.
6 Refitting the fanbelt in the reverse sequence to removal. Tension the fanbelt by means of the jockey wheel until it is possible to deflect the belt by 12.7 mm (0.5 in), using light finger pressure at a point midway between the water pump and fan pulleys.

11 Fan and fan hub – removal and refitting

Note: *The Peugeot models covered by this manual may be fitted with either a fixed fan or a self-engaging/disengaging electromagnetic fan.*

Models with fixed fan
1 Remove the fanbelt as described in Section 10.
2 To provide easier access remove the radiator as described in Section 5.
3 Undo and remove the bolts securing the fan and fan pulley to the hub spindle and lift away the fan.
4 Refitting the fan is the reverse sequence to removal.

Models with electromagnetic fan
5 Remove the fanbelt as described in Section 10.
6 To provide easier access remove the radiator as described in Section 5.
7 The fan is secured to the fan hub by three nuts and flat washers. These must not be confused with the three hub air gap adjusting nuts which are identified by their hexagon headed studs (photo). Having identified the correct three nuts they may now be undone and the fan lifted off.
8 To remove the fan hub, undo and remove the locknut securing the hub assembly to the spindle. To stop the hub turning as the nut is undone, wrap an old fanbelt around the hub pulley and insert its free end into a tube or pipe of suitable diameter and length. Use a screwdriver, inserted through the loop of the belt that protrudes from the end of the tube to tension the belt. With a little manipulation the 'V' of the belt will grip the sides of the pulley sufficiently to stop rotation (photo).

11.7 The three fan retaining nuts (arrowed)

11.8 Locking the fan hub with an old fanbelt and tube to aid removal of the retaining nut

11.9 Withdrawing the fan hub

11.10a Lift up the wire retaining clip ...

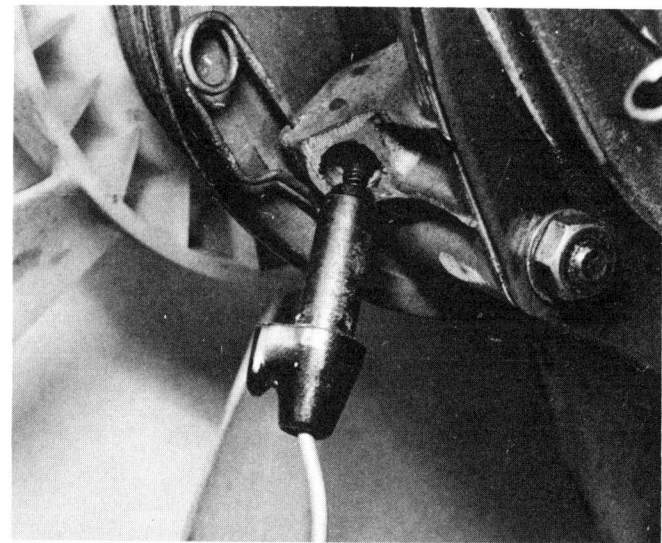

11.10b ... and slide out the contact brush holder

11.12 Checking the fan hub air gap setting

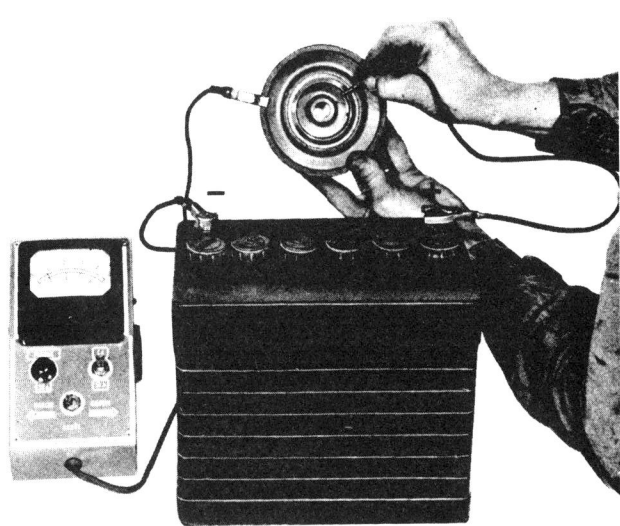

Fig. 2.5 Checking the electromagnet in the fan pulley (Sec 11)

9 With the locknut removed the fan hub and then the pulley may be withdrawn from the spindle (photo).
10 If necessary the carbon brush that actuates the fan may be removed from its location by lifting up the retaining spring clip and sliding out the brush and holder assembly (photo). To check the winding of the electromagnet in the fan pulley, connect a 12 volt battery and ammeter in the manner shown in Fig. 2.5 but to avoid dismantling put the carbon brush back in the holder temporarily and connect the lead from the positive terminal of the battery to the brush. **Do not** attempt to push a wire or probe through the brush holder direct onto the slip ring. You may scratch or burn it. The winding current should be as given in the Specifications. A higher reading

indicates a partial or complete short circuit, whilst a lower or zero reading denotes a break in the winding.
11 Refitting the fan and hub assembly is the reverse sequence to removal. When assembled the air gap between the hub and pulley should be checked as follows:
12 Place a feeler gauge blade equal to the air gap setting between the hub and pulley (photo) and check the clearance at three equidistant points. If necessary adjust the clearance by means of the three adjusting screws and locknuts on the front face of the hub.

12 Antifreeze mixture

1 Where temperatures are likely to drop below freezing point (0°C, 32°F), the cooling system must be adequately protected by the addition of antifreeze. It is still possible for the water to freeze in the radiator with the engine running in very cold conditions – particularly if the engine cooling is being adequately dealt with by the heater radiator. The thermostat will remain closed and the coolant in the radiator will not circulate. It is therefore necessary to partially drain the cooling system and add an adequate amount of Peugeot special diesel antifreeze to the cooling water.
2 The table below gives the amount of antifreeze and the degree of pretection:

Commences to freeze		Amount of antifreeze
°C	°F	
-6°	21°	4 pints (2.2 litres, 4.8 US pints)
-14°	7°	6 pints (3.4 litres, 7.2 US pints)
-21°	-6°	8 pints (4.5 litres, 9.6 US pints)
-30°	-22°	10 pints (5.6 litres, 12 US pints)
-37°	-35°	12 pints (6.7 litres, 14.4 US pints)

3 Add the required quantity of antifreeze to the radiator and then top up with water in the normal way. Remember to add a small quantity of antifreeze to the expansion tank before topping up to the 'MAXI' mark.
4 Never use antifreeze in the windscreen washer reservoir as it will cause damage to the paintwork.

13 Fault diagnosis – cooling system

Symptom	Reason(s)
Overheating	Insufficient water in cooling system Fanbelt slipping (accompanied by a shrieking noise on rapid engine acceleration) Radiator core blocked or radiator grille restricted Bottom water hose collapsed, impeding flow Thermostat not opening properly Electromagnetic fan inoperative Incorrect fuel injection pump timing Blown cylinder head gasket (water/steam being forced down the radiator overflow pipe under pressure) Engine not yet run-in Brakes binding
Cool running	Thermostat jammed open Incorrect thermostat fitted allowing premature opening of valve Thermostat missing
Loss of cooling water	Loose clips on water hose Top, bottom or bypass water hoses perished and leaking Radiator core leaking Radiator pressure cap spring worn or seal ineffective Blown cylinder head gasket (pressure in system forcing water/steam down overflow pipe) Cylinder wall or head cracked

Chapter 3 Fuel system

Contents

Specifications

Air cleaner
Type .... Oil bath or renewable dry cartridge

Fuel filter
Type .... Purflux or CAV renewable cartridge

Fuel injection pump
Type .... Bosch or CAV Roto-Diesel
Injection order 1-3-4-2

Fuel injectors
Type .... Bosch or CAV

Fuel tank capacity
Saloon .... 56 litres (12.3 Imp gal, 14.6 US gal)
Estate and Family Estate .... 60 litres (13.2 Imp gal, 15.6 US gal

Torque wrench settings

	Nm	lbf ft
Fuel injector securing nuts	15	11

1 General description

The fuel system on the Peugeot 504 Diesel comprises a fuel tank, fuel filter, injection pump and four fuel injectors.

Clean fuel is essential for the efficient operation of the fuel injection pump, and for this reason a renewable cartridge type fuel filter is incorporated in the system. As well as removing foreign matter, the filter also separates any large droplets of water which may be present in the fuel. The water is collected in a glass bowl beneath the filter cartridge and must be drained off as part of the routine maintenance operations.

The system operates in the following manner; The injection pump draws fuel from the tank, through the filter and then supplies it in finely controlled amounts, depending on engine demand, to the appropriate injector. The fuel then enters the combustion chamber as a fine spray. Air is also drawn into the cylinders via the air filter and intake manifold to form the correct air/fuel ratio necessary for combustion.

Due to the complex nature of the fuel injection pump and the need for specialist knowledge and equipment, no attempt should be made to overhaul the ignition pump or injectors. If these units give trouble they should be renewed or overhauled by your Peugeot dealer or diesel injection specialist.

2 Air cleaner – removal, servicing and refitting

1   The air cleaner fitted to Peugeot diesel models may be either the renewable dry element cartridge type, or the oil bath and wire mesh variety. It is essential to service it at the intervals stated in the Routine Maintenance section at the beginning of this manual, especially when operating in dusty conditions.
2   To service the air cleaner, it is necessary to remove the complete assembly from the vehicle.
3   Slacken the retaining clip and remove the air intake hose from the air cleaner body.
4   Undo and remove the nuts and flat washer securing the air cleaner to its rubber mounting blocks and withdraw the unit from the engine compartment.
5   With the air cleaner on the bench, spring back the retaining clips and lift off the upper body.
6   If a dry element cartridge is fitted, lift out and discard the old cartridge and thoroughly clean the inside of the air cleaner. Refit a new cartridge and reassemble the air cleaner.
7   If the unit is the oil bath type, lift out the the wire mesh element and wash it thoroughly in paraffin or clean diesel fuel. Empty the old oil from the air cleaner and wash this unit thoroughly as well. Fill the

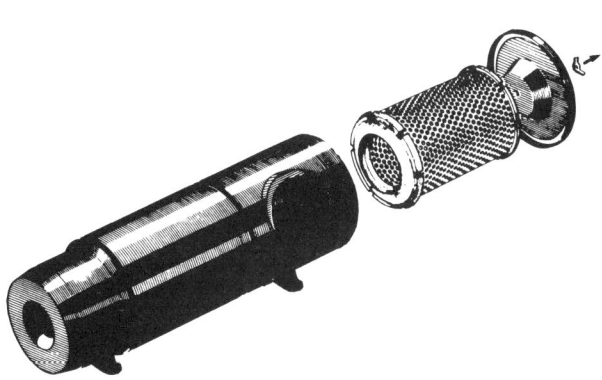

Fig. 3.1 Dry element type air cleaner assembly (Sec 2)

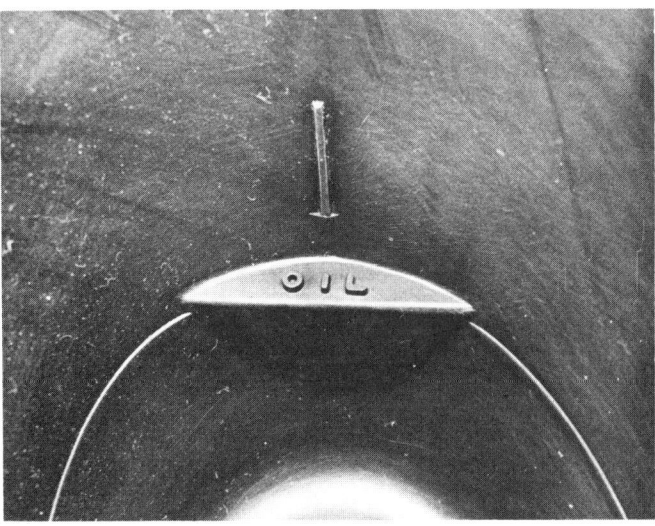

2.7 Air cleaner oil filling level

lower air cleaner body with engine oil up to the 'OIL' level (photo). Refit the element and reassemble the air cleaner.

8   Refit the complete air cleaner assembly to the car using the reverse sequence to removal.

3   Fuel filter – maintenance

1   At the intervals stated in the Routine Maintenance section at the beginning of this manual, the fuel present in the transparent filter bowl should be checked for cleanliness, and if any traces of water are evident in the fuel, the filter should be bled as described below.

2   The fuel system may be fitted with either a Purflux or Roto-Diesel filter. The illustrations show the differences between the two units and it is important to identify the type fitted, as there are slight variations in the bleeding procedure.

Purflux type

3   Loosen the needlevalve and then operate the priming lever until all the water has drained and clean fuel emerges from the drain tube.

4   Tighten the needle valve while still operating the priming lever.

5   Now loosen the air bleed screw and operate the lever again until resistance is felt. Tighten the air bleed screw.

Roto-Diesel type

6   Unscrew the feed pipe union, the priming plunger, the bleed screw and the drain tap.

7   Operate the priming plunger until all the water has drained and then tighten the drain tap and the feed pipe union.

8   Continue pumping until fuel free from air bubbles flows through the bleed screw.

9   Now tighten the bleed screw and the priming plunger.

4   Fuel filter cartridge – removal and refitting

1   To remove the filter cartridge, undo and remove the filter bowl retaining bolt and washers, and then lift off the bowl followed by the cartridge. **Note:** *On Purflux filters the retaining bolt is located below the bowl, and on Roto-Diesel filters the bolt is positioned above, behind the priming lever.*

2   Thoroughly clean the filter bowl and discard the old element.

3   Carefully inspect the sealing rings and renew if worn.

4   To refit a new filter, place it in position on the filter housing and then refit the filter bowl and retaining bolt.

5   The fuel system must now be primed as described in Section 5.

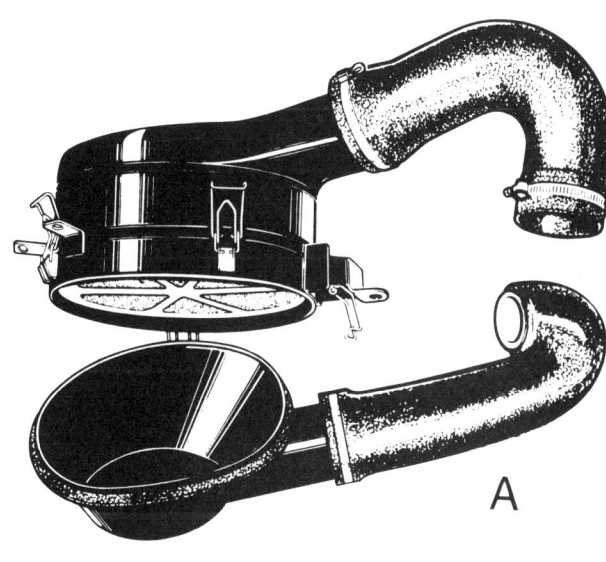

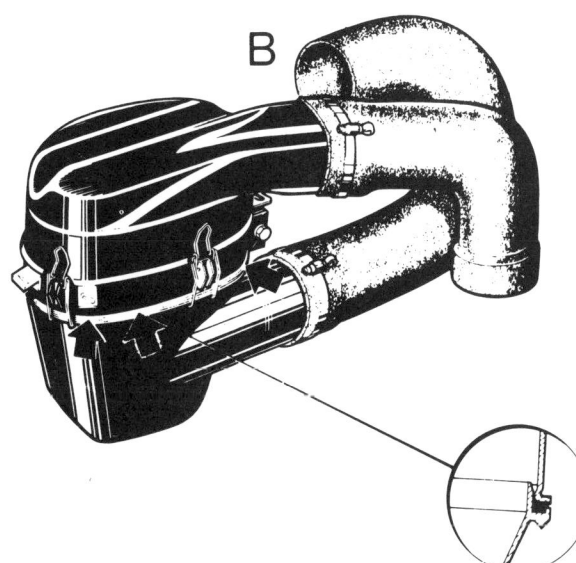

Fig. 3.2 Oil bath type air cleaner assembly (Sec 2)

A   Removing upper body

B   Assembled air cleaner – inset shows   correct positioning of seal at joint arrowed

5   Fuel system – priming

1   If for any reason the vehicle has been allowed to run out of fuel,

A

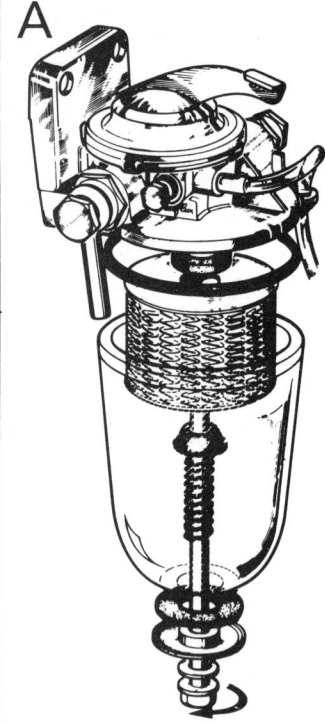

B

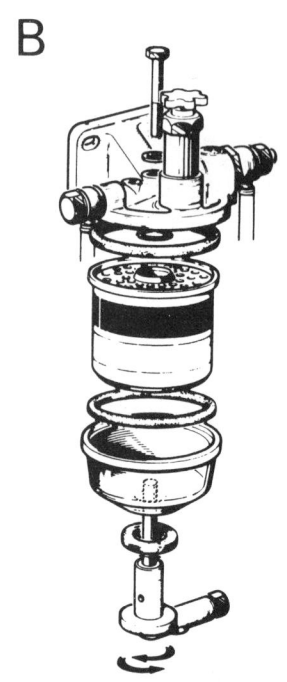

Fig. 3.3 Purflux (A) and Roto-Diesel (B)
fuel filters (Sec 3)

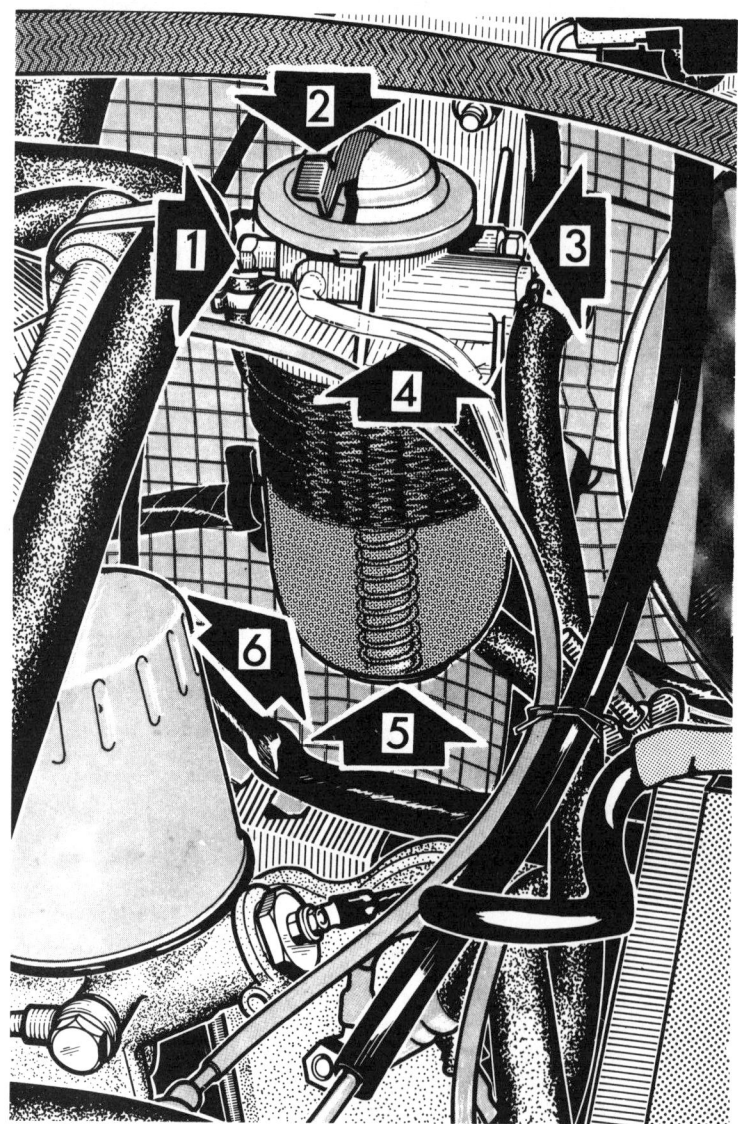

Fig. 3.4 Purflex filter components (Sec 3)

1	Needle valve	4	Drain tube
2	Primary lever	5	Retaining screw
3	Air bleed screw	6	Filter bowl

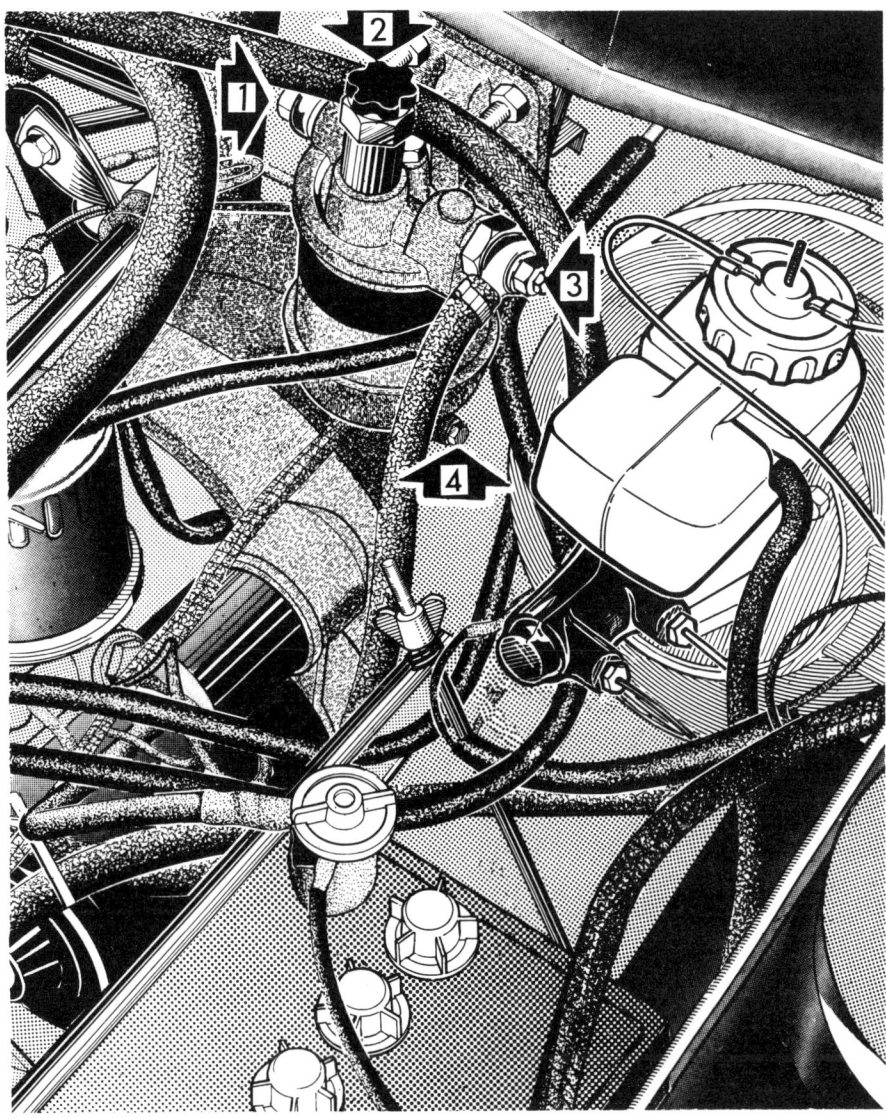

Fig. 3.5 Roto-Diesel filter components (Sec 3)

1 Fuel feed pipe union	2 Primary plunger	3 Bleed screw	4 Drain tap

or if the fuel lines, injection pump or filter have been removed, it will be necessary to eliminate all the air from the system before attempting to start the engine. If only the filter bowl and filter has been removed, follow paragraphs 2 to 6 inclusive. If the fuel system has been completely emptied, carry out the full priming procedure.

2   At the fuel filter, slacken the needle valve (Purflex filter) or the bleed screw (Roto-Diesel filter).

3   Operate the priming plunger until fuel free from air bubbles flows from the drain tube or bleed screw (photo).

4   Tighten the needle valve or bleed screw while still operating the priming plunger.

5   If a Purflex filter is fitted, slacken the air bleed screw and operate the priming plunger until resistance is felt. Now tighten the bleed screw.

6   Start the engine in the normal way and carefully check for any fuel leaks.

7   If the fuel system has been completely drained, or if the engine will not start after carrying out the procedure in paragraphs 2 to 6, repeat paragraphs 2 to 6 inclusive and then proceed as follows.

Bosch EP/VM equipment

8   Slacken the bleed screw on the injection pump and operate the priming plunger until fuel free from air bubbles flows through the bleed screw.

9   Tighten the bleed screw while still operating the priming plunger.

5.3 Bleeding the Roto-Diesel fuel filter

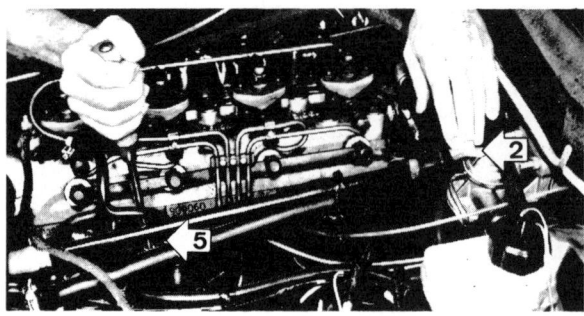

Fig. 3.6 Priming the Bosch EP/VM injection pump (Sec 5)

2   *Priming lever*   5   *Injection pump bleed screw*

10 Start the engine in the normal way and check carefully for any fuel leaks.

Bosch EP/VAC equipment

11 Operate the priming plunger lever approximately 30 to 40 pumps.
12 Turn the starter switch to the 'on' position ensuring that the stop control is released.
13 If fitted, turn the fast idling control knob to the fast idle position.
14 Engage the starter for 10 to 15 seconds, then switch off.
15 Where applicable turn the key to the 'pre-heat' position until the warning light is extinguished.
16 Now start the engine and check for any fuel leaks.

Roto-Diesel equipment

17 Slacken the two bleed screws on the injection pump and the fuel line unions at the injectors (photos).
18 Operate the priming plunger until fuel free from air bubbles flows through the bleed screw nearest the front of the engine. Now tighten the bleed screw and the primary plunger (photo).
19 Have an assistant operate the starter while keeping the accelerator pedal fully depressed. While the engine is cranking, tighten the remaining bleed screw on the injection pump when fuel free from air bubbles emerges (photo).

5.17a Slacken the two bleed screws on the fuel injection pump (arrowed) ...

5.17b ... and the fuel line unions at the injectors (arrowed)

5.18 Fuel emerging from the bleed screw

5.19 Tighten the bleed screw with the engine cranking

20 With the starter still engaged, tighten the injector fuel line unions as soon as fuel emerges.
21 If the engine has now started by this time, turn the key to the 'pre-heat' position until the warning light is extinguished.
22 Now start the engine and carefully check for any fuel leaks.

6 Fuel injection pump – removal and refitting

1 For efficient running of a diesel engine, accurate fuel injection pump timing is essential. Providing the procedures listed below are strictly followed, it will be possible to remove the fuel injection pump and refit it in its original position. This will be acceptable assuming the timing was correct before removal and the original pump is being refitted. If the pump is to be replaced by a new or reconditioned unit, a number of Peugeot special tools will be required to accurately set the pump timing prior to fitting. It is therefore recommended that this work be entrusted to your Peugeot dealer.
2 The Peugeot 504 diesel engine may be fitted with either a Bosch or CAV Roto-Diesel type fuel injection pump. The removal and refitting procedures are similar and any differences will be stated where necessary.
3 Disconnect the battery terminals, release the battery retaining clamp and then remove the battery and its tray.
4 Refer to Chapter 1 and remove the timing cover from the front of the engine.
5 Disconnect the stop control cable (where fitted), the accelerator cable and the fast idle cable from their connections on the injection pump (photo).
6 Slacken the hose clips and remove the fuel injector return system hose and the fuel inlet and outlet couplings from the injection pump (photos).
7 Undo and remove the union nuts and lift off the complete fuel injector fuel pipe assembly.
8 It is now necessary to rotate the crankshaft until the timing marks on the timing gears or sprockets are aligned. To reduce the engine compression and enable the crankshaft to be turned more easily, remove the heater plugs from the cylinder head as described in Chapter 10. To enable the crankshaft to be turned, temporarily refit the crankshaft pulley.

Engines with chain driven timing components
9 Turn the crankshaft until the copper link in the chain is opposite the timing mark on the crankshaft sprocket, and the chain links marked by a line are opposite the camshaft and injection pump sprocket timing marks.
10 Using a small centre punch, accurately mark the relationship of the injection pump flange to the bearing support, and also the pump shaft to the timing sprocket.
Note: *It is most important that these marks are made accurately, otherwise the injection pump timing will be lost when the unit is removed.*
11 Undo and remove the bolts securing the pump rear support to the cylinder block and the pump flange to the bearing support. Move the pump rearwards and lift it off the engine.

Engines with gear driven timing components
12 Turn the crankshaft until the dots on the timing gears are all adjacent. **Note**: *This only occurs once every 22 revolutions of the crankshaft.*
13 Using a small centre punch, accurately mark the relationship of the injection pump flange to the intermediate mounting flange, and intermediate mounting flange to the timing gear housing. **Note**: *It is most important that these marks are made accurately, otherwise the injection pump timing will be lost when the unit is removed.*
14 Undo and remove the bolts securing the pump rear support to the cylinder block (photo), and the pump intermediate flange to the timing gear housing. Now withdraw the pump complete with timing gear by moving it rearwards and pivoting it toward the engine.

All engines
15 Refitting the fuel injection pump is the reverse sequence to removal, bearing in mind the following points:

(a) *Before fitting the pump check that the position of the*

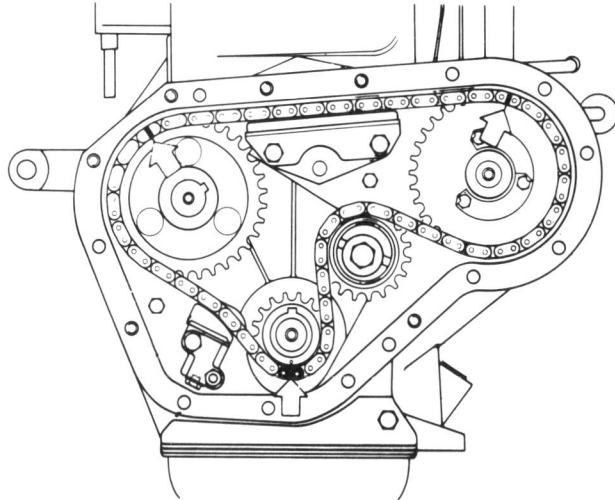

Fig. 3.7 Correct alignment of timing marks and chain (arrowed) prior to fuel injection pump removal (Sec 6)

Fig. 3.8 Correct alignment of marks on timing gears (circled) prior to fuel injection pump removal (Sec 6)

Fig. 3.9 Removing the Bosch EP/VM fuel injection pump (Sec 6)

6.5 The stop control cable (A), accelerator cable (B) and fast idle cable (C) on the Roto-Diesel injection pump

6.6a Fuel injector return system hose ...

6.6b ... fuel inlet hose ...

6.6c ... and outlet hose connections on Roto-Diesel fuel injection pump

6.14 Fuel injection pump rear support mountings

crankshaft has not been inadvertently moved and that the timing marks are still in line

(b) Ensure that the pump is fitted with the previously-made reference marks aligned

(c) Refit the timing cover as described in Chapter 1

(d) When the pump is installed, prime the fuel system as described in Section 5

(e) Adjust the injection pump idle speed settings as described in the following Section

7 Fuel injection pump – adjustments

Bosch EP/VM injection pump

1   Two adjustments are possible on the EP/VM unit. These are to the idle speed and fast idle speed. Certain export models are equipped with a deferred injection accumulator fitted to the rear of the injection pump, and adjustment procedures for this unit are also given.

2   Run the engine until normal operating temperature is reached and then stop the engine.

3   Disconnect the accelerator cable from the accelerator arm on the injection pump.

4   Unscrew the locknut, and screw in the fast idle stop screw a few turns.

5   Slacken the locknut at the front of the idle speed adjustment rod, while preventing the rod from turning with a spanner.
6   Start the engine and adjust the idle speed by turning the adjustment rod until the slowest possible engine speed consistent with even running is obtained (approximately 730 rpm).
7   Hold the adjustment rod in this position and tighten the locknut.
8   Now unscrew the fast idle adjustment screw until the engine speed just starts to increase.
9   Screw in the fast idle adjustment screw one complete turn and then tighten the locknut.
10 Switch off the engine and refit the accelerator cable, ensuring that the accelerator arm on the injection pump moves through its full travel when the accelerator pedal is fully depressed.
11 With the fast idle control on the dashboard in the minimum position, check that the cable clamp is positioned against the slide on the
injection pump with the minimum of free play.
12 If a deferred injection accumulator is fitted to the injection pump this device should be adjusted as follows:
13 Ensure that the fast idling control on the dashboard is set at its minimum position.
14 Disconnect the link rod from the ball socket on the accumulator lever.
15 Move the accumulator lever as far as it will go in the fully open position, ie the direction in which it moves when the accelerator arm on the injection pump is closed (minimum engine speed).
16 Start the engine and adjust the idling speed as described in paragraphs 2 to 7 inclusive.
17 Move the accumulator lever slowly towards the closed position until the engine speed just increases and there is an appreciable increase in engine noise.
18 Hold the accumulator lever in this position and then reconnect and adjust the link rod so that the injection pump accelerator arm is 1 mm (0.03 in) away from the idling stop.

Bosch EP/VAC injection pump
19 On the EP/VAC unit the idling speed and deferred injection accumulator control link rod are adjusted as follows:
20 Start the engine and allow it to reach normal operating temperature.
21 Ensure that the fast idle control on the dashboard is set to its minimum position.
22 Slacken the two locknuts on the deferred injection accumulator link rod and then disconnect the link rod at the accumulator end.
23 Move the accumulator control lever to the fully open position, ie direction in which it moves when the accelerator arm on the injection pump is closed (minimum engine speed).
24 Now move the idling speed stop screw until the slowest possible engine speed consistent with even running is obtained (approximately 730 rpm).
25 Move the accumulator control lever slowly towards the closed position until the engine speed just increases and there is an appreciable increase in engine noise.
26 Hold the accumulator control lever in this position, adjust the length of the link rod to suit and then reconnect the link rod to the accumulator control lever.
27 Now turn the threaded adjustable part of the link rod one complete turn to reduce the length of the link rod by approximately 2 mm (0.07 in). Tighten the two link rod lock nuts.

CAV Roto-Diesel injection pump
28 On the Roto-Diesel injection pump the idle speed and deceleration speed control are adjusted as follows:
29 Slacken the locknut and unscrew the deceleration screw until it protrudes by 13 to 14 mm (0.51 to 0.55 in) from the front of the injection pump cover (photo).
30 Start the engine and allow it to reach normal operating temperature.
31 Ensure that the fast idle control on the dashboard is set to its minimum position.
32 Now slacken the idle speed control locknut and turn the stop screw until the slowest possible engine speed consistent with even running is obtained. If necessary, release the accelerator cable clamp until the accelerator arm makes contact with the stop.
33 Tighten the idle speed control locknut and accelerator cable clamp (if previously released).

Fig. 3.10 Adjusting the Bosch EP/VM fuel injection pump (Sec 7)

  1   Fast idle stop screw   3   Idle speed adjustment
  2   Adjustment rod locknut   rod
                                   4   Accelerator lever

Fig. 3.11 Adjust the Bosch EP/VM deferred injection accumulator lever (a) as shown until engine speed increases (Sec 7)

7.29 Fuel injection pump deceleration screw

Fig. 3.12 Bosch EP/VAC fuel injection pump and deferred
injection accumulator (Sec 7)

1	Idle speed stop screw	6	Deferred injection
2	Accelerator arm		accumulator
3	Link rod	7	Accumulator control lever
4	Locknuts	8	'Stop' lever
5	Link adjusting rod		

Fig. 3.13 Link rod locknuts (arrowed) slackened and link rod
disconnected (Sec 7)

Fig. 3.14 Accumulator control lever (a) moved to fully open
position (Sec 7)

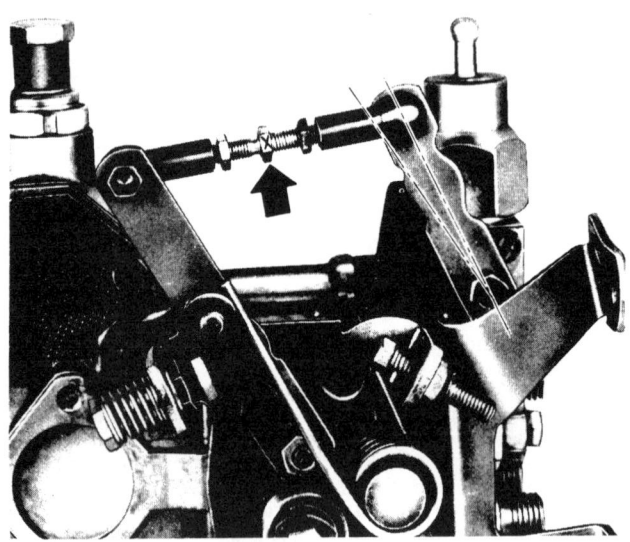

Fig. 3.15 Adjusting accumulator link rod to suit control lever using
threaded adjuster (arrowed) (Sec 7)

Fig. 3.16 Adjusting the Roto-Diesel fuel injection pump (Sec 7)

1	Deceleration screw	3	Idle speed control
2	Locknut		locknut
		4	Idle speed stop screw

34 Screw in the deceleration screw until the engine speed just starts
to increase.
35 Accelerate the engine to maximum speed and allow it to return to
idle. If the engine stalls, screw in the deceleration screw a further $\frac{1}{4}$
turn. Repeat this operation until the engine can be accelerated to
maximum speed and returned to idle without stalling.
36 Tighten the deceleration screw locknut.

8   Fuel injection pump timing – adjustment

For complete combustion of the diesel fuel and optimum engine
performance a finely controlled amount of fuel must be supplied by the
fuel injection pump to the injector of each cylinder when the piston
reaches a pre-determined point before TDC on the compression stroke.
The position of the crankshaft (in degrees) when the injection pump
starts to deliver the fuel is known as the injection pump timing setting.
If the timing is incorrect the engine will exhibit various symptoms such
as emission of smoke, lack of power, knocking noises etc. It follows,
therefore, that whenever the fuel injection pump has been removed, or
if any of the timing components such as chain, sprockets or gears are
renewed, the timing should be checked and if necessary reset.

Adjustment of the injection pump timing is a complete operation requiring specialist knowledge and instruments, and this work should be entrusted to your Peugeot dealer. However, once the adjustment has been carried out the settings should not alter, and further attention will not be necessary unless the injection pump or timing components are disturbed again.

9 Fuel injectors – testing on engine

1   It is not recommended that any attempt be made to dismantle or repair a fuel injector, as this requires specialist knowledge and equipment and is outside the scope of the home mechanic. The best policy is to renew a faulty injector or have it reconditioned by a diesel injection specialist.
2   Should an injector be suspect, the following test may be used to determine whether an injector is the cause of rough running and loss of power.
3   Assuming the engine internal components and cylinder compression pressures to be satisfactory, start the engine and allow it to idle until normal operating temperature is obtained.
4   Now slacken the fuel feed pipe union on each injector in turn and note any variation in engine speed. Repeat this test again with the engine running at a fast idle.
5   If the injector is operating correctly there will be a distinct reduction in engine speed accompanied by obvious roughness. If the injector is faulty there will be very little difference in engine speed when the union is slackened.
6   Having isolated the faulty injector using the above procedure, it may now be removed for renewal or reconditioning as described in Section 10.

10 Fuel injectors – removal and refitting

1   Undo and remove the union nut and withdraw the fuel feed pipe from the front of the injector.
2   Undo and remove the return pipe banjo union from the top of the injector, taking care not to lose the copper washers.
3   Undo and remove the nuts and washers securing the injector holder to the studs on the cylinder head. Lift off the holder (photo).
4   Carefully lift out the injector from its location in the cylinder head and recover the sealing washer. **Note:** *Handle the injectors with care, as there is a small needle valve protruding from the base of each injector which is easily damaged.*
5   Refitting is the reverse sequence to removal, bearing in mind the following points:

   (a) *Always use new sealing washers when refitting an injector (photo)*
   (b) *Tighten the injector holder retaining bolts to the specified torque wrench setting*
   (c) *Prime the fuel system as described in Section 5*

11 Fuel tank – removal and refitting

1   As it is not possible to drain the tank prior to removal, the following operations should only be carried out when the tank is as near empty as possible.
2   Jack up the rear of the car and support it on axle stands.
3   Disconnect the battery earth terminal.
4   Remove the access plate from inside the luggage compartment and disconnect the electrical lead to the fuel gauge tank unit.
5   From under the car disconnect the main fuel pipe union, the filler neck and any vent pipes that may be fitted to the fuel tank (photo).
6   Support the tank on a jack and interposed block of wood, and then undo and remove the bolts securing the tank to the underbody (photo).
7   Carefully lower the tank to the ground, releasing any connections that may have been inaccessible with the tank installed.
8   Refitting is the reverse sequence to removal. It will be necessary to prime the fuel system when the tank is refitted as described in Section 5.

Fig. 3.17 Fuel injector fuel feed and fuel return pipes (Sec 10)

10.3 Fuel injector holder retaining nuts and washers

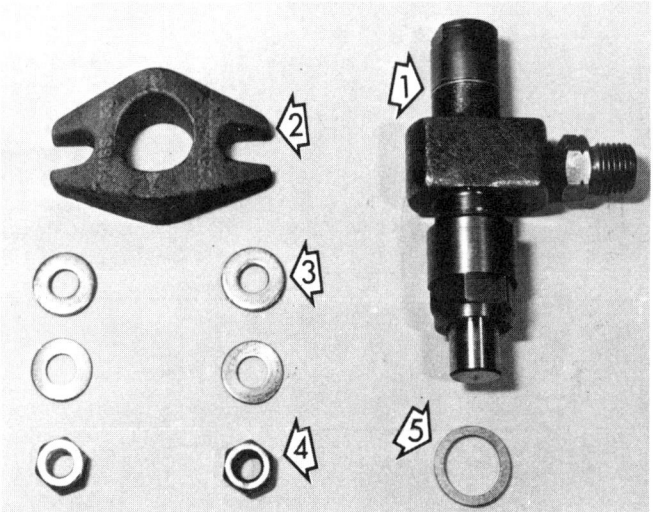

10.5 Fuel injector assembly
1   Injector
2   Injector holder
3   Dished washers
4   Retaining nuts
5   Sealing washer

11.5 Fuel tank feed and vent pipes

11.6 Fuel tank rear mounting (saloon models)

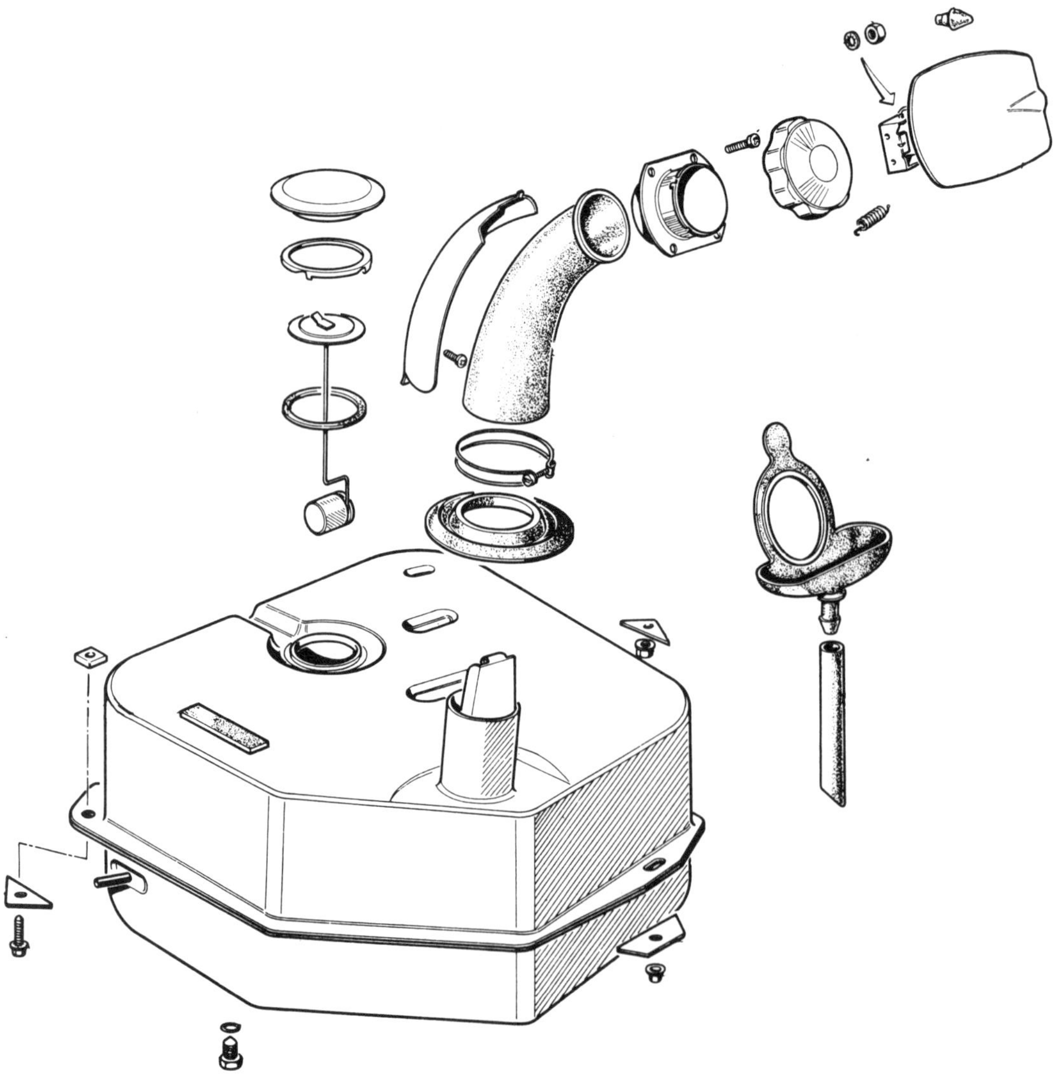

Fig. 3.18 Fuel tank assembly (saloon models) (Sec 11)

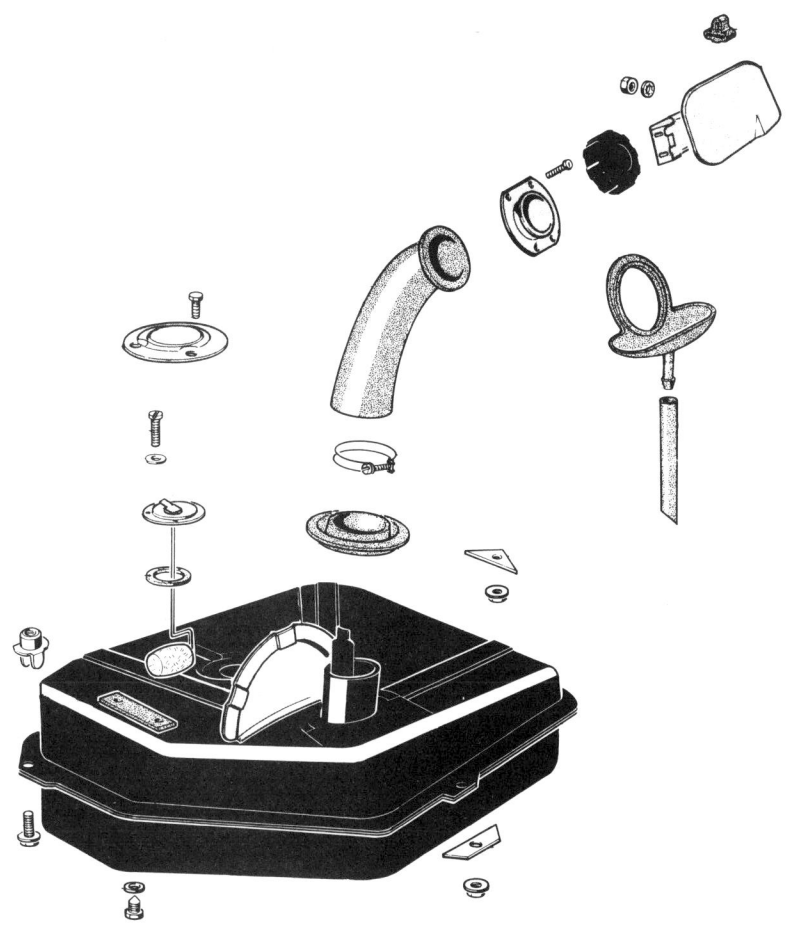

Fig. 3.19 Fuel tank assembly (saloon models – alternative type) (Sec 11)

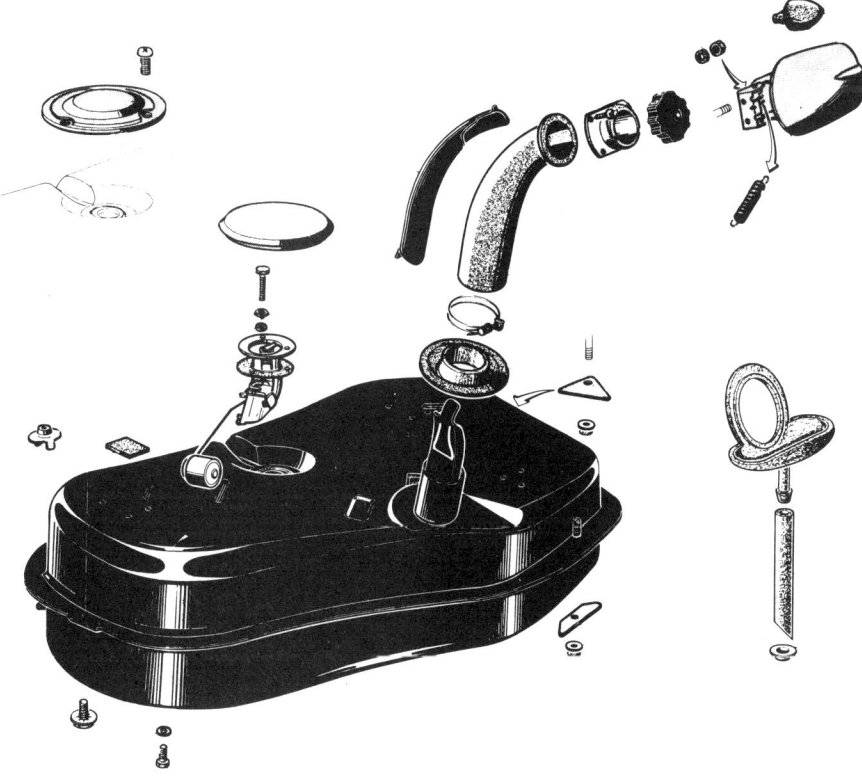

Fig. 3.20 Fuel tank assembly (Estate and Family Estate models) (Sec 11)

12 Accelerator cable – removal and refitting

1   Unscrew the bolt locking the inner cable to the clamp assembly located on the acceleratorer arm of the fuel injection pump.
2   Detach the outer cable from its support at the fuel injection pump end.
3   Working inside the car push the small cup down into the main cup using a small screwdriver, and ease the large cup off the end of the pedal control rod.
4   Carefully remove the cable from the car.
5   Before fitting a new cable assembly, lubricate the inner cable with engine oil. Do not use grease as it will cause the cable to stiffen especially in cold weather.
6   Refitting the accelerator cable is the reverse sequence to removal. Ensure that maximum accelerator arm travel exists when the accelerator pedal is fully depressed, and that the arm returns to its stop when the pedal is released.

13 Accelerator pedal – removal and refitting

1   To remove the pedal footrest, undo and remove the two securing screws located at the floor end.
2   Detach the footrest from the pedal control rod.
3   To remove the pedal control rod, detach the inner cable from the control rod, as described in Section 12, paragraph 3.
4   Release the spring clip located at the end of the shaft and draw off the control rod.
5   Refitting the accelerator pedal is the reverse sequence to removal. Lubricate the pivot with a little engine oil.

14 Stop and fast idle control cables – removal and refitting

1   Where a stop cable and fast idle control cable are fitted, their attachments at the fuel injection pump are the same as described previously for the accelerator cable.
2   The method of attachment of the cables at the stop control lever or starter switch, and at the fast idle control knob, will vary according to model but will be obvious upon inspection. Access to the cables is from under the dashboard or at the starter switch after removal of the steering column shroud.
3   When refitting the stop cable, make sure that there is 1 to 2 mm (0.03 to 0.07 in) of cable free travel before the stop control lever on the fuel injection pump is activated.

15 Fault diagnosis – fuel system

Symptom	Reason(s)
Engine difficult to start, with emission of black smoke	Defective injectors Fuel injection pump timing incorrect Obstruction in air intake system *See also Chapter 1, 'Fault Diagnosis – engine'*
Engine difficult to start, with no emission of smoke	Fuel tank empty Heater plugs inoperative No fuel output from injection pump Fuel system unprimed 'Stop' control jammed in stop position Fuel filter clogged Air leak in fuel lines
Erratic slow running or stalling	Fuel injection pump idle adjustments incorrect Fuel injection pump timing incorrect Faulty fuel injection pump Worn fuel injectors
Lack of engine power	Fuel injection pump timing incorrect Deferred injection accumulator out of adjustment (where fitted) Air intake partially blocked Faulty fuel injection pump Faulty fuel injector/s Fuel filter clogged *See also Chapter 1, 'Fault diagnosis – engine'*
Engine emits excessive smoke on acceleration	Fuel injection pump timing incorrect Worn fuel injectors Faulty fuel injection pump Engine worn internally

Chapter 4 Exhaust system

Contents

1 General description and maintenance

The exhaust system fitted to the diesel engined Peugeot 504 comprises a front pipe bolted to the exhaust manifold and one or more intermediate pipe and silencer assemblies, depending on vehicle type, leading into a rear silencer and tailpipe. All the sections are connected by overlap joints and clamps, and are detachable separately. The complete system is suspended from the underside of the body by a system of metal brackets and flexible rubber mounting straps or blocks.

The exhaust system should be examined periodically for corrosion or damage. If any defects are found, the affected section of pipe or silencer should be renewed.

When working on any part of the exhaust system always ensure that the vehicle is jacked up and firmly supported on stands with adequate working room underneath.

Due to the exposed nature of the system and the considerable changes in temperature that the components are subject to, the retaining nuts and bolts on the clamps and mounting brackets will become corroded very quickly (photo). It is advisable when dismantling any part of the system or its mountings to apply liberal amounts of penetrating oil to the fastenings, and allow it to soak for a few hours before proceeding. This will save considerable time and frustration later and make the work a lot easier.

2 Front pipe – removal and refitting

1 Undo and remove the two nuts and spring washers securing the front pipe flange joint to the exhaust manifold (photo).

1.1 Effects of water, road grit and temperature extremes on exhaust mountings

2.1 Exhaust front pipe-to-manifold flange joint

2   Slacken the clamp bolt securing the other end of the front pipe to the silencer (photo).
3   Undo and remove the bolts securing any additional support brackets that may be fitted depending on model (photo).
4   Pull the front pipe down out of the exhaust manifold and move it forward, turning it from side to side at the same time until it disengages from the intermediate silencer.
5   Refitting the front pipe in the reverse sequence to removal. Always use a new gasket on the flange joint between front pipe and exhaust manifold. Ensure that adequate clearance exists between the exhaust system and the body or suspension components before fully tightening the clamp and mounting bolts.

3   Intermediate pipe and silencer – removal and refitting

1   Remove the exhaust front pipe as described in the previous Section.
2   Slacken the clamp securing the intermediate pipe or silencer to the tailpipe (photo).
3   Undo and remove the nuts and bolts securing the mountings and support brackets to the intermediate pipe.
4   Slide the pipe forward while at the same time twisting it from side to side until it disengages from the tailpipe.
5   Refitting is the reverse sequence to removal. Ensure that there is adequate clearance between the exhaust system and the body or suspension components before tightening the clamp and mounting bolts.

4   Rear silencer and tailpipe – removal and refitting

1   The layout of the rear silencer and tailpipe varies slightly according to model type, but the removal method will be fairly obvious on inspection.
2   Slacken the clamp securing the tailpipe to the intermediate pipe.
3   Undo and remove all mounting nuts and bolts, and any support brackets that may be fitted.
4   Move the tailpipe rearwards while at the same time twisting it from side to side until it disengages from the intermediate pipe.
5   Refitting is the reverse sequence to removal. Ensure that there is adequate clearance between the exhaust system and the body or suspension components before tightening the clamp and mounting bolts.

5   Exhaust mountings – removal and refitting

1   Undo and remove the nuts and bolts securing the mounting to the exhaust system or bracket and the underbody.
2   Lift off the complete mounting from the car.
3   Carefully examine the mounting for cracks or distortion of the rubber, or in the case of the rubber mounting blocks, for separation of the metal backing. If worn or damaged it must be renewed. Check also the condition of the support brackets, where these are used, for cracks, distortion or elongation of the bolt holes. Renew where necessary.
4   Check the exhaust clamps for corrosion or distortion, and the nuts and bolts for damaged threads.
5   Refitting the exhaust mountings is the reverse sequence to removal.

6   Exhaust manifold – removal and refitting

1   Undo and remove the two nuts and spring washers securing the front pipe flange joint to the manifold.
2   Undo and remove the four bolts and spring washers securing the exhaust manifold to the cylinder head. Lower the manifold until it is clear of the inlet manifold and then lift it away.
3   Refitting is the reverse sequence to removal, ensuring that all mating surfaces are perfectly clean and new gaskets are used where applicable.

2.2 Exhaust front pipe-to-silencer joint

2.3 Front pipe support bracket attached to rear of gearbox

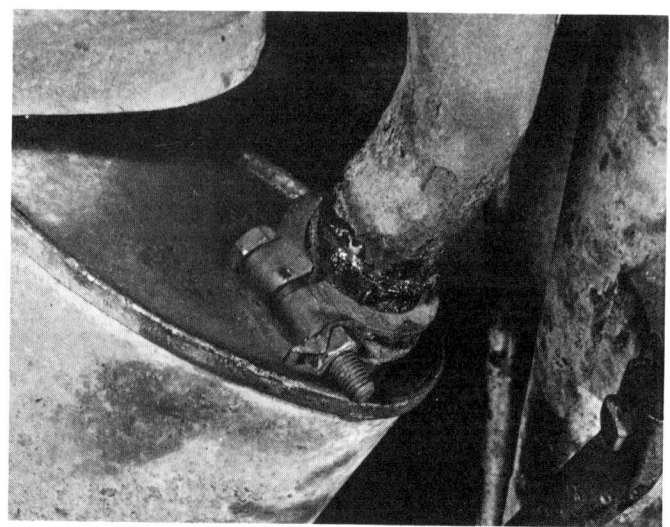

3.2 Intermediate silencer mounting clamp

71

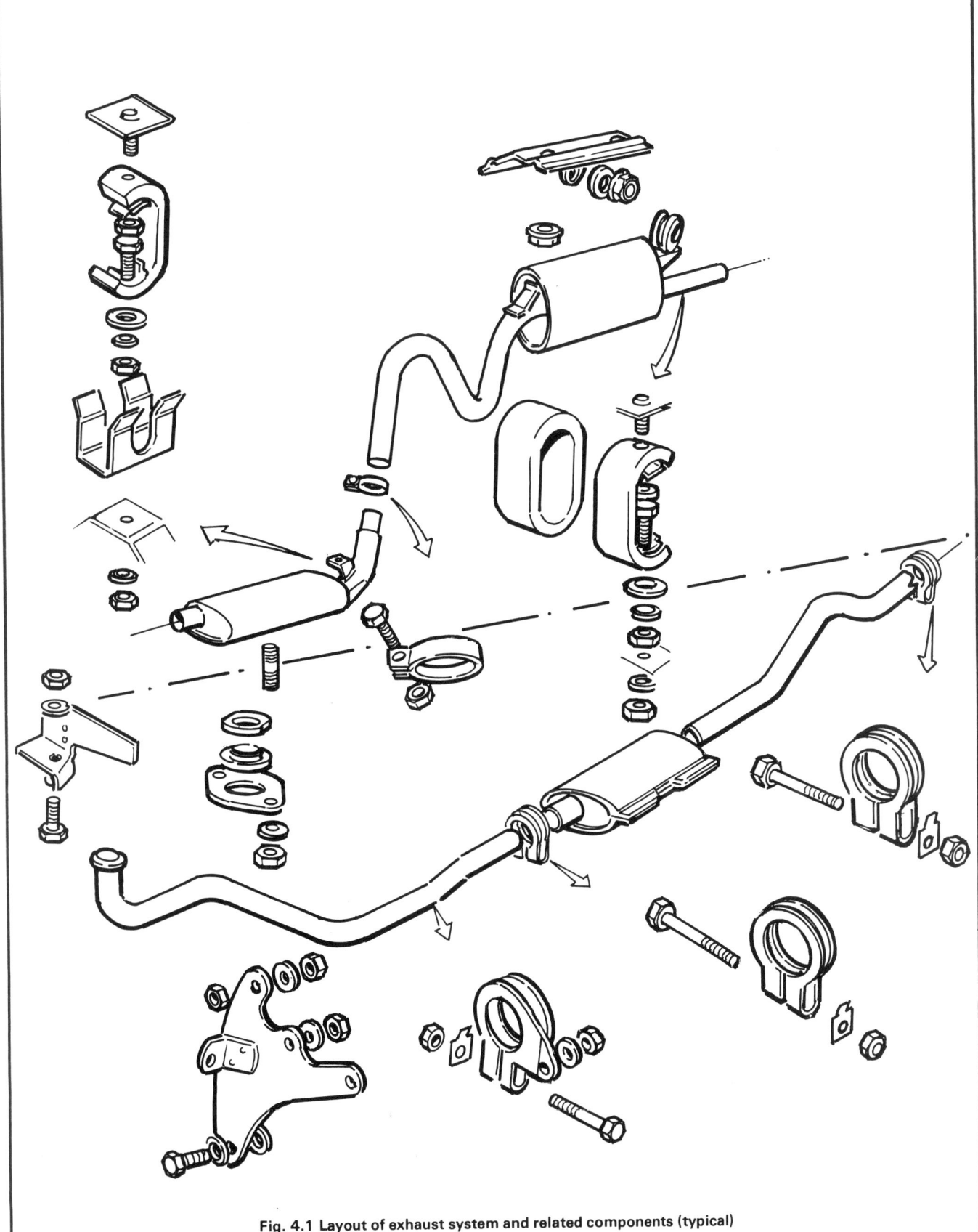

Fig. 4.1 Layout of exhaust system and related components (typical)

Chapter 5 Clutch

Contents

Specifications

Type .... Diaphragm spring, single dry plate, hydraulic operation

Driven plate
Lining diameter:
    Outer .... 215 mm (8.46 in)
    Inner .... 145 mm (5.70 in)
Lining thickness:
    New .... 8.4 mm (0.32 in)
    After compression (new) .... 8.0 mm (0.31 in)

Pressure plate
Diaphragm spring rating .... 420 kgf (928 lbf)

Master cylinder
Bore diameter .... 19.05 mm (0.75 in)

Slave cylinder
Bore diameter .... 28.6 mm (1.125 in)

Release bearing
Type .... Thrust, ball bearing race

Torque wrench setting

	Nm	lbf ft
Cover assembly securing bolts	15	11

1 General description

The Peugeot 504 Diesel models covered by this manual are equipped with a hydraulically-operated diaphragm spring clutch assembly. The clutch comprises a steel cover, which is bolted and dowelled to the rear face of the flywheel, and contains the pressure plate and clutch disc or driven plate.

The pressure plate, diaphragm spring and release plate are all attached to the clutch assembly cover. The clutch disc is free to slide along the splined gearbox first motion shaft and is held in position between the flywheel and pressure plate by the pressure of the diaphragm spring. Friction lining material is rivetted to the clutch disc, which has a spring-cushioned hub to absorb transmission shocks and to help ensure a smooth take off.

The clutch master cylinder is mounted on the engine compartment bulkhead and is connected to the pendant-type clutch pedal by a short pushrod. Hydraulic fluid for both the clutch and brake hydraulic system is supplied from a common reservoir mounted on the brake master cylinder. Depressing the clutch pedal moves the piston in the master cylinder forwards, so forcing hydraulic fluid through the clutch hydraulic pipe to the slave cylinder. The piston in the slave cylinder moves forwards on the entry of the fluid and actuates the release arm by means of a short pushrod. The opposite end of the release arm is forked and is located behind the release bearing.

As this pivoted clutch release arm moves backwards, it bears against the release bearing, pushing it forward to bear against the release plate, so moving the centre of the diaphragm spring inwards. The spring is sandwiched between two annular rings which act as fulcrum points as the centre of the spring is pushed out, so moving the

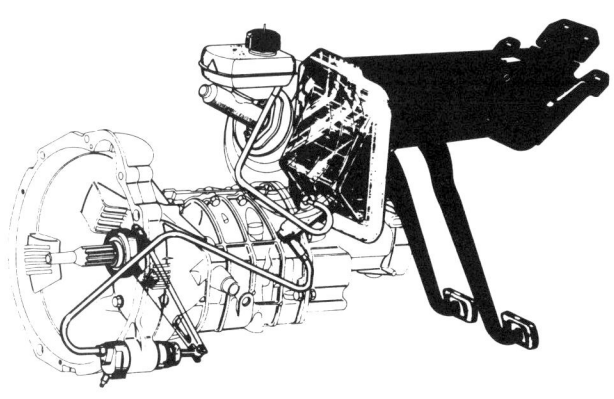

Fig. 5.1. Layout of the clutch operating system (Sec 1)

pressure plate backwards and disengaging the pressure plate from the clutch disc.

When the clutch pedal is released, the diaphragm spring forces the pressure plate into contact with the friction linings on the clutch disc, and at the same time pushes the clutch disc a fraction of an inch forwards on its splines so engaging the clutch disc with the flywheel. The clutch disc is now firmly sandwiched between the pressure plate and the flywheel so the drive is taken up.

As the friction linings on the clutch disc wear, the pressure plate automatically moves closer to the disc to compensate. There is therefore no need to periodically adjust the clutch.

2 Clutch hydraulic system – bleeding

Note: *If any of the clutch hydraulic components have been removed or disconnected, or if the fluid level in the master cylinder reservoir has been allowed to fall appreciably, air will inevitably have been introduced into the system. In order for the clutch to function satisfactorily, all this air must be removed.*

1   It is not possible to bleed the clutch system in the conventional way, as this must be carried out by 'reverse feed'. Hydraulic fluid under pressure is forced through the bleed nipple until the complete system is full and the fluid level in the reservoir is up to the full mark.

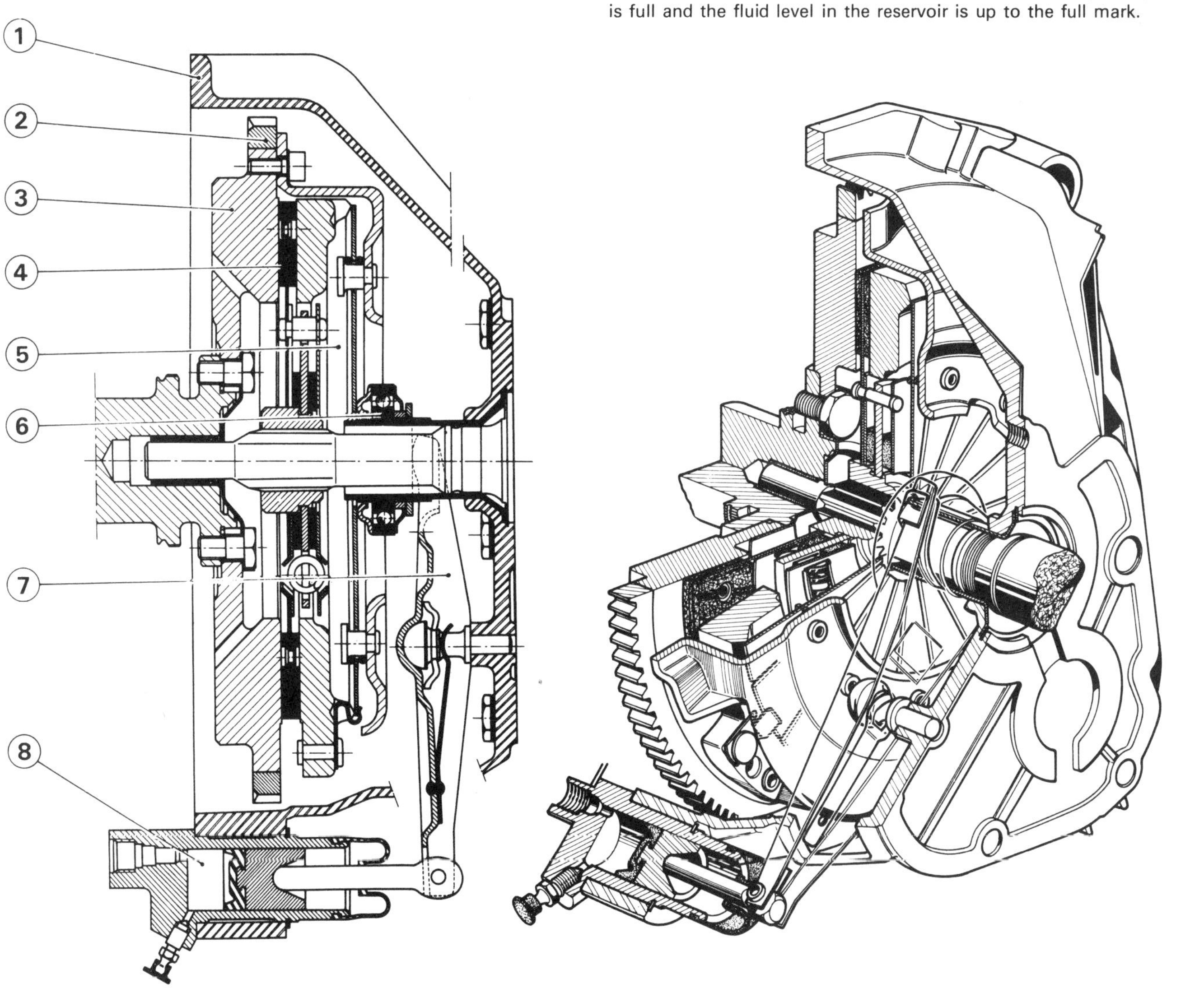

Fig. 5.2 Sectional views of the clutch assembly (Sec 1)

1 Bellhousing	3 Flywheel	5 Pressure plate	7 Release fork
2 Starter ring gear	4 Clutch disc	6 Release bearing	8 Slave cylinder

2   Special equipment is used by Peugeot garages to bleed the clutch, and under normal conditions it will be better to take the car to the garage for the work to be completed, even if this means towing the car.

3   In an emergency, the following method may be used, but extreme care must be taken not to draw air-contaminated fluid into the brake hydraulic system.   .

4   Obtain a length of rubber or plastic tubing long enough to reach the left-hand brake caliper from the clutch slave cylinder. Fill the tubing with fresh hydraulic fluid and connect it up to both bleed nipples.

5   Loosen both nipples $\frac{1}{4}$ of a turn each and have an assistant slowly depress the footbrake pedal. Remove the brake/clutch fluid reservoir cap and continue to force fluid into the system until bubbles cease to surface; then tighten the nipples.

6   Top-up the fluid in the reservoir if necessary then check the operation of the clutch and brakes. If air has been drawn into the braking system it will be necessary to bleed the system as described in Chapter 9. Remove the bleed tube from the nipples.

3   Clutch – removal and refitting

1   Access to the clutch assembly is rather difficult on Peugeot 504 Diesel models; the recommended and easiest method is to remove the engine first as described in Chapter 1. The reason for this is that the rigid torque tube connecting the gearbox to the differential must be disconnected to allow the gearbox to be removed. To do this it is necessary to move the differential rearwards on models fitted with independent rear suspension, or remove the axle completely on models equipped with a solid 'banjo' type rear axle. Both of these operations can be rather long and involved, requiring considerable dismantling, whereas removal of the engine is relatively straight-forward by comparison.

2   With the engine removed from the car, first mark the clutch assembly in relation to the flywheel. Remove the clutch assembly by undoing the six socket-headed bolts securing the clutch cover to the rear face of the flywheel. Undo the bolts in a diagonal sequence, half a turn at a time to prevent distortion of the cover flange and also to prevent the cover flange binding on the dowels and suddenly flying out.

3   With the bolts removed, lift the clutch cover assembly off the locating dowels. The driven plate or clutch disc will fall out at this stage as it is not attached to either the clutch cover assembly or the flywheel. Carefully make a note of which way round it is fitted.

4   It is important that no oil or grease is allowed to come into contact with the clutch disc friction linings or the pressure plate and flywheel faces. It is advisable to handle the parts with clean hands and to wipe down the pressure plate and flywheel faces with a clean dry rag before inspection or refitting commences.

5   To refit the clutch assembly begin by placing the clutch disc against the flywheel with the raised portion of the hub containing the cushioning springs facing away from the flywheel (photo).

6   Position the clutch cover, according to the alignment marks made previously, over the locating dowels (photo) and refit the six socket-headed bolts. Tighten the bolts finger tight so that the clutch disc is gripped but can still be moved.

7   The clutch disc must now be centralised, so that when the engine and gearbox are mated, the gearbox first motion shaft will pass through the splines in the centre of the hub and engage with the spigot bearing in the end of the crankshaft.

8   Centralisation can be carried out quite easily by inserting a round bar or long screwdriver through the splined hub of the clutch disc so that the end of the bar rests in the spigot bearing. Moving the bar sideways or up and down will move the clutch disc in whichever direction is necessary to achieve centralisation.

9   Centralisation is easily judged by removing the bar and viewing the clutch disc hub in relation to the spigot bearing and the hole in the centre of the diaphragm spring. When the clutch disc hub appears exactly in the centre, all is correct (photo). Alternatively, if an old first motion shaft or similar clutch centralising tool can be borrowed this will eliminate all the guesswork, as it will fit the spigot bearing and clutch disc hub exactly, obviating the need for visual alignment.

10 With the disc correctly centralised, tighten the clutch cover bolts firmly in a diagonal sequence half a turn at a time to ensure that the cover is pulled down evenly and without distortion of the flange.

2.3 Clutch slave cylinder bleed nipple (arrowed)

Fig. 5.3 Removing the clutch cover (Sec 3)

Fig.5.4 Using a torque wrench to tighten the clutch cover securing bolts (Sec 3)

3.5 Refitting the clutch disc ...

3.6 ... and clutch cover

3.9 Clutch disc correctly centralised in relation to the spigot bearing and diaphragm spring

5.6 Refitting the clutch release fork rubber cup

5.7a Using a screwdriver to lift the backing spring while fitting the release fork

5.7b Correct engagement of the backing spring on the ball head

Finally tighten the bolts to the torque wrench setting given in the Specifications.

11 Mate the engine to the gearbox, this being a direct reversal of the procedure decided upon for removal. Bleed the hydraulic system (if necessary) and check the clutch for correct operation.

4 Clutch – inspection

1 Examine the clutch disc friction linings for wear, and loose or broken springs and rivets. The linings must be proud of the rivets and light in appearance, with the material structure visible. If the linings are dark in appearance, further investigation is necessary as this is a sign of oil contamination, caused by oil leaking past the crankshaft rear oil seal or gearbox first motion shaft oil seal.

2 Check the faces of the flywheel and pressure plate for signs of grooving or deep scoring. If apparent the flywheel and pressure plate must be machined until smooth, or preferably renewed. If the pressure plate is cracked or split or if any of the diaphragm spring fingers are distorted, loose, or broken, the cover assembly must be renewed.

3 Place the clutch disc on the gearbox first motion shaft and check that it is free to slide up and down the splines without binding.

4 Check the release bearing for smoothness of operation. There should be no harshness or slackness in it. Check that it spins freely with no sign of roughness from the bearing.

5 Should either the release bearing, clutch disc or clutch cover assembly require renewal, practical experience has shown that whenever possible all three units should be renewed together. Renewal of individual clutch components separately can often cause judder, squeal and a general roughness of the clutch, as new components do not easily bed into old ones. However, cost is a major consideration and it is left to the owner's discretion as to which course of action he chooses.

5 Clutch release bearing and fork assembly – removal and refitting

1 To gain access to the release bearing and fork assembly it is necessary to remove the engine (see Section 3, paragraph 1).

2 Whilst inspecting the clutch assembly, it is worthwhile checking the release bearing assembly. The bearing assembly can be detached without removing the clutch fork.

3 Release the bearing retaining clip and rotate in an anti-clockwise direction.

4 If the bearing is worn or shows signs of overheating it should be renewed.

5 The clutch release fork can be removed by working inside the housing and removing the rubber cup and fork thrust ball.

6 To reassemble, pack the rubber cup with a little grease and slide the release fork from the inside towards the outside of the clutch housing (photo).

7 It will be beneficial to use a screwdriver to lift the clutch release fork backing spring whilst engaging the fork on the ball head: The spring should be backed against the rubber cup (photo).

8 Smear the guide sleeve with a little high melting point grease and engage the new bearing by positioning the retaining jaw towards the starter motor housing.

9 Engage the thrust bearing with the clutch release fork, and lock by rotating the bearing clockwise and refitting the retaining clip.

6 Clutch master cylinder – removal and refitting

1 Disconnect the hydraulic fluid supply pipe from the clutch master cylinder and then plug the end of the pipe to prevent further fluid loss.

2 Unscrew the pipe that connects the clutch slave cylinder to the master cylinder at the master cylinder union. Tape over the end of the pipe to prevent dirt ingress.

3 From inside the car disconnect the master cylinder pushrod from the clutch pedal.

4 Undo and remove the two nuts (or bolts) and washers securing the master cylinder to the bulkhead. Lift away the master cylinder.

5 Refitting the master cylinder is the reverse sequence to removal. On completion of the installation, bleed the clutch hydraulic system as described in Section 2.

7 Clutch master cylinder – dismantling, examination and reassembly

1 To dismantle the master cylinder use a pair of circlip pliers to release the circlip retaining piston stop washer.

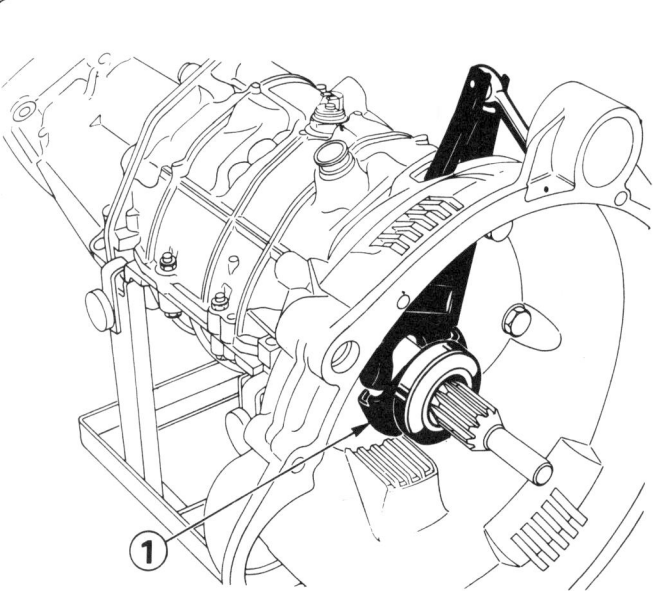

Fig. 5.5 Clutch release bearing assembly (1) removed after turning anti-clockwise (Sec 5)

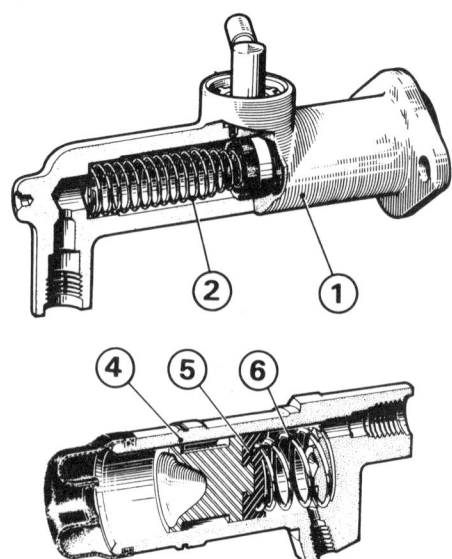

Fig. 5.6 Sectional views of the clutch master cylinder and slave cylinder (Secs 7 and 9)

1	Master cylinder body	5	Cup seal
2	Spring	6	Spring
4	Slave cylinder body		

2 Carefully remove the piston stop washer from the cylinder bore, followed by the piston assembly, main and secondary cups and return springs.

3 If they prove stubborn, carefully use a foot pump or air jet on the hydraulic pipe connection and this should move the internal parts, but do take care as they will fly out. Place a cloth pad over the end to catch the parts.

4 Note which way round the primary and secondary cups are fitted.

5 Thoroughly clean the parts in hydraulic fluid or methylated spirit. After drying the items inspect the cups for signs of distortion, swelling, splitting or hardening, although it is recommended new rubber cups are always fitted after dismantling as a matter of course.

6 Inspect the bore and piston for signs of deep scoring marks which, if evident, means a new cylinder should be fitted. Make sure all drillings are clear by poking gently with a piece of thin wire.

7 As the parts are refitted to the cylinder bore, make sure that they are thoroughly wetted with clean hydraulic fluid.

8 Fit the secondary cup onto the piston making sure it is the correct way round.

9 Refit all parts in the reverse order to removal. Make sure that the lips of the cups do not roll over as they enter the bore.

10 Finally refit the circlip and ensure that it is fully seated.

11 The master cylinder is now ready for refitting to the car.

8 Clutch slave cylinder – removal and refitting

1 Jack up the front of the car and support it on axle stands.

2 From under the car disconnect the hydraulic fluid pipe from the union on the slave cylinder and allow the fluid to drain into a suitable container. Tape over or plug the end of the pipe when the fluid has drained to prevent dirt ingress.

3 Undo and remove the two socket-headed bolts (photo) securing the steering gear to the front suspension crossmember. **Note**: *Certain models have a small retaining spring clip at the threaded end of the steering gear retaining bolts. If fitted these must be removed first (photo).* Now ease the steering gear down until sufficient clearance exists to enable the slave cylinder to be withdrawn. Take care not to strain the steering column shaft and flexible coupling unduly.

4 Undo and remove the bolt and slave cylinder retaining plate from the front face of the bellhousing (photo).

5 Using circlip pliers remove the slave cylinder retaining circlip (photo). Now slide the slave cylinder forward toward the front of the car and out of its location in the bellhousing.

6 Refitting the slave cylinder in the reverse sequence to removal, noting that the bleed nipple faces downward when the cylinder is installed.

8.3a Steering gear retaining bolts ...

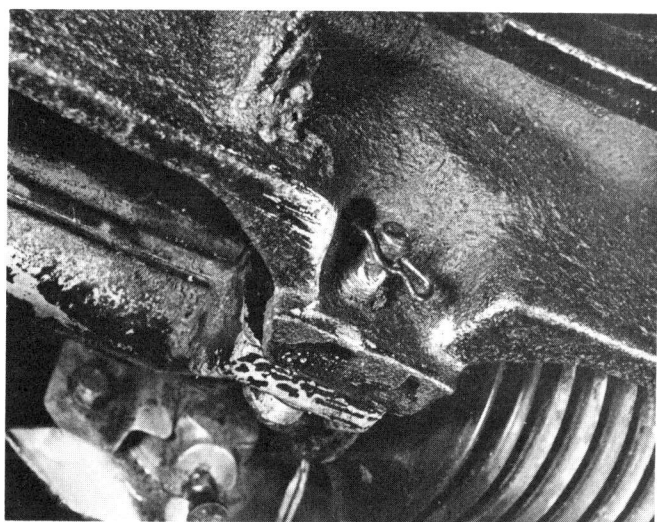
8.3b ... and the retaining spring clips

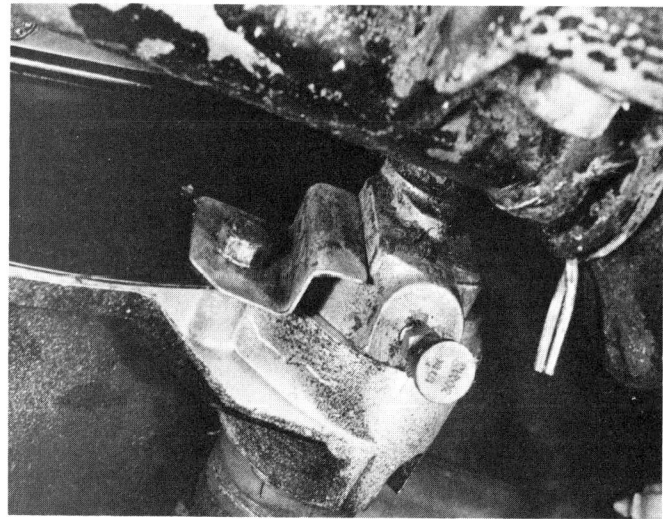
8.4 Slave cylinder retaining plate

8.5 Removing the retaining circlip

7   On completion of reassembly bleed the clutch hydraulic system as described in Section 2.

9   Clutch slave cylinder – dismantling, examination and reassembly

1   Clean the outside of the slave cylinder before dismantling.
2   Pull off the rubber dust cover, and by shaking hard, the piston and cup assembly should come out of the cylinder bore.
3   If they prove stubborn, carefully use a foot pump or air jet on the hydraulic pipe connection, and this should remove the internal parts, but do take care as they will fly out. Place a cloth pad over the end to catch the parts.
4   Note which way round the cup is fitted.
5   Wash all internal parts with either brake fluid or methylated spirit and dry using a non-fluffy rag.
6   Inspect the bore and piston for signs of deep scoring which, if evident, means a new cylinder should be fitted.
7   Carefully examine the rubber components for signs of swelling, distortion, splitting, hardening or other wear, although it is recommended new rubber parts are always fitted after dismantling.
8   All parts should be reassembled, wetted with clean hydraulic fluid.
9   Fit the cup to the piston the correct way round and insert the piston into the bore. Take care not to roll the lip of the cup.
10 Pack the dust cover with a little rubber grease and fit over the end of the slave cylinder body, engaging the lips over the groove in the body.

10 Clutch hydraulic pipe – removal and refitting

1   Jack up the front of the car and support it on axle stands.
2   From under the car unscrew the union nut and withdraw the pipe from the slave cylinder. Allow the hydraulic fluid to drain into a suitable container.
3   Working in the engine compartment, unscrew the union nut at the other end of the pipe and withdraw the pipe from the master cylinder.
4   Detach the pipe from the retaining clips on the body (where fitted) and then remove the hydraulic pipe from the car. Plug the unions in the master cylinder and slave cylinder to prevent dirt ingress.
5   Refitting the hydraulic pipe is the reverse sequence to removal. On completion it will be necessary to bleed the clutch hydraulic system as described in Section 2.
6   If the fluid supply pipe between the reservoir and master cylinder is to be removed, the same general comments apply. However, take care when detaching the union from the master cylinder.

11 Clutch pedal – removal and refitting

The clutch pedal is mounted on the same pedal bracket as that used for the brake pedal. Should it be necessary to remove the clutch pedal, refer to Chapter 9 for further information.

12 Fault diagnosis – clutch

Symptom	Reason(s)
Clutch pedal appears spongy, accompanied by harsh engagement of gears	Air in hydraulic system Leaks in fluid pipe or unions Bulging in flexible hose Faulty master cylinder
Hydraulic system will not maintain pressure (vehicle creeps forward with pedal fully depressed)	Faulty seals in master and/or slave cylinder Leaking hydraulic pipe, hose or union
Clutch will not fully disengage	Driven plate sticking on input shaft Driven plate sticking to flywheel due to oil contamination Broken pressure plate springs
Clutch slip (engine speed increases with no increase in road speed)	Clutch driven plate badly worn Pressure plate faulty Oil or grease contamination of friction linings
Clutch judder	Oil or grease contamination of friction materials Worn or loose engine or gearbox mountings Excess run-out of flywheel Excess wear of clutch assembly Faulty release mechanism
Squeal or rumble when depressing clutch pedal	Worn or faulty release bearing Worn or broken pressure plate springs

Chapter 6 Manual gearbox and automatic transmission

Contents

Specifications

Manual gearbox

Gearbox series BA7

Gearbox type .... Four forward gears (all synchromesh) and one reverse gear

Gear ratios

First	3.663 : 1
Second	2.169 : 1
Third	1.409 : 1
Fourth	1.000 : 1
Reverse	3.747 : 1

Input shaft

Endfloat adjustment shims:
- Outer diameter .... 42.00 mm (1.653 in)
- Inner diameter .... 37.20 mm (1.464 in)
- Shim thickness range .... 0.15 to 0.35 mm (0.006 to 0.014 in) in increments of 0.05 mm (0.002 in)

Layshaft

Endfloat adjustment shims:
- Outer diameter .... 28.00 mm (1.102 in)
- Inner diameter .... 21.60 mm (0.850 in)
- Shim thickness range .... 2.25 to 3.40 mm (0.085 to 0.134 in) in increments of 0.05 mm (0.002 in)

Mainshaft

Endfloat adjustment shims:
- Outer diameter .... 46.00 mm (1.811 in)
- Inner diameter .... 35.20 mm (1.386 in)
- Shim thickness range .... 0.15, 0.20, 0.25 and 0.50 mm (0.006, 0.008, 0.010 and 0.020 in)

Reverse idler gear shaft

- Diameter .... 20.00 mm (0.787 in)
- Length .... 90.00 mm (3.543 in)

Lubricant capacity .... 1.15 litres (2.1 Imp pints, 2.3 US pints)

Automatic transmission

Type .... ZF-3HP-12, three-speed epicyclic gear trains with three-element torque converters

Gear ratios
Torque converter ratio .... 2.29 : 1
Mechanical reduction ratios:
    First 0.391
    Second 0.658
    Third 1.000
    Reverse 0.500

Fluid capacity (maximum) .... 5.2 litres (9.2 Imp pints, 11.2 US pints)

Torque wrench settings

	Nm	lbf ft
Manual gearbox		
Gearbox drain plug	28	20
Bellhousing to engine	60	43
Gearbox filler plug	28	20
Bellhousing to gearbox	28	20
Gearbox casing halves nuts and bolts	10	7
Gearbox backing plate screw	10	7
Rear housing nuts and bolts	15	11
Mainshaft universal joint	15	11
Reverse pinion nut	55	40
Detent ball and spring plug	10	7
Reverse light switch:		
Copper body	12	9
Steel body	28	20
Automatic transmission		
Diaphragm securing bolts	23	17
Oil sump	10	7

1 General description (manual gearbox)

The gearbox fitted to the Peugeot models covered by this manual is equipped with four forward gears and one reverse gear. All forward gears are engaged through cone type synchromesh units to obtain smooth, silent gearchanges.

The external positions of the gear selector levers vary slightly depending on whether the car is equipped with independent rear suspension or a 'banjo' type solid rear axle. A universal joint is also fitted to the end of the gearbox mainshaft on models equipped with a solid rear axle. The gearbox internal components, however, are identical for all models.

The gearbox is of die-cast aluminium with detachable bellhousing and tail extension housing. The split case construction makes dismantling a simple matter, and provided that the layout and operation of the gearbox is understood, no problems should arise.

It should be appreciated that although the assembly looks as one complete unit, in fact the input and output ends are completely independent of each other. This must be so, because the engine drives the input end whilst the output end drives the propeller shaft. The input shaft is sometimes referred to as the driveshaft and the output shaft as the mainshaft.

The input shaft assembly carries a single gear which is integral with the shaft. The gear drives the layshaft, which carries four gears which are integral with the shaft and a fifth gear – the reverse pinion – which is splined to it. The gear on the input shaft is always in mesh with its opposite number on the layshaft and both rotate when the engine is running whether a gear has been selected or not.

The remaining gears integral with the layshaft drive their opposite numbers on the mainshaft. The exception however, is the reverse pinion which, although in mesh with the mainshaft, does not drive the mainshaft gear directly, but is coupled to it through an intermediate gear when reverse is selected. Selecting a forward speed is a matter of locking the appropriate gear on the mainshaft assembly to the mainshaft (output gear) itself. In the case of the fourth gear the mainshaft is locked directly to the input shaft.

This locking is achieved by moving a splined sleeve which forms part of the synchroniser assembly so that it simultaneously engages with the synchronising hub, which is locked to the output shaft and a corresponding hub on the selected gear.

2 Gearbox (manual) – removal

1 The gearbox is not very easy to remove, and this involves a considerable amount of dismantling that must be carried out underneath the car.
2 The procedure for removing the gearbox varies according to model, and it is recommended that you read through the entire Section first to familiarise yourself with the work involved before commencing the removal operation.
3 One other point that needs special mention: when the gearbox is detached from the engine, be sure never to let its weight hang on the input shaft. This can lead to distortion in the shaft or in the clutch, which will cause judder or other clutch or gearbox trouble.
4 From inside the engine compartment, disconnect the battery terminals and then remove the battery and its tray.
5 Refer to Chapter 2 and drain the cooling system. When the cooling system has drained remove the radiator, then remove the expansion tank and its mounting brackets.
6 Refer to Chapter 10 and remove the starter motor.
7 Disconnect the electrical lead to the heater plugs and lift the wiring harness out of the way.
8 Refer to Chapter 3 and remove the air cleaner assembly.
9 Jack up the front and rear of the car and securely support it on stands or sturdy blocks. Ensure that there is sufficient working clearance underneath the car. Drain the gearbox oil into a suitable container.
10 Refer to Chapter 7 and remove the torque tube and propeller shaft assembly.
11 Undo and remove the bolt securing the earth strap to the rear of the gearbox (photo).
12 Remove the two reversing light electrical leads from the switch on the side of the gearbox.
13 Slacken the locknut and undo and remove the grubscrew securing the speedometer cable to the gearbox. Now lift out the speedometer cable.

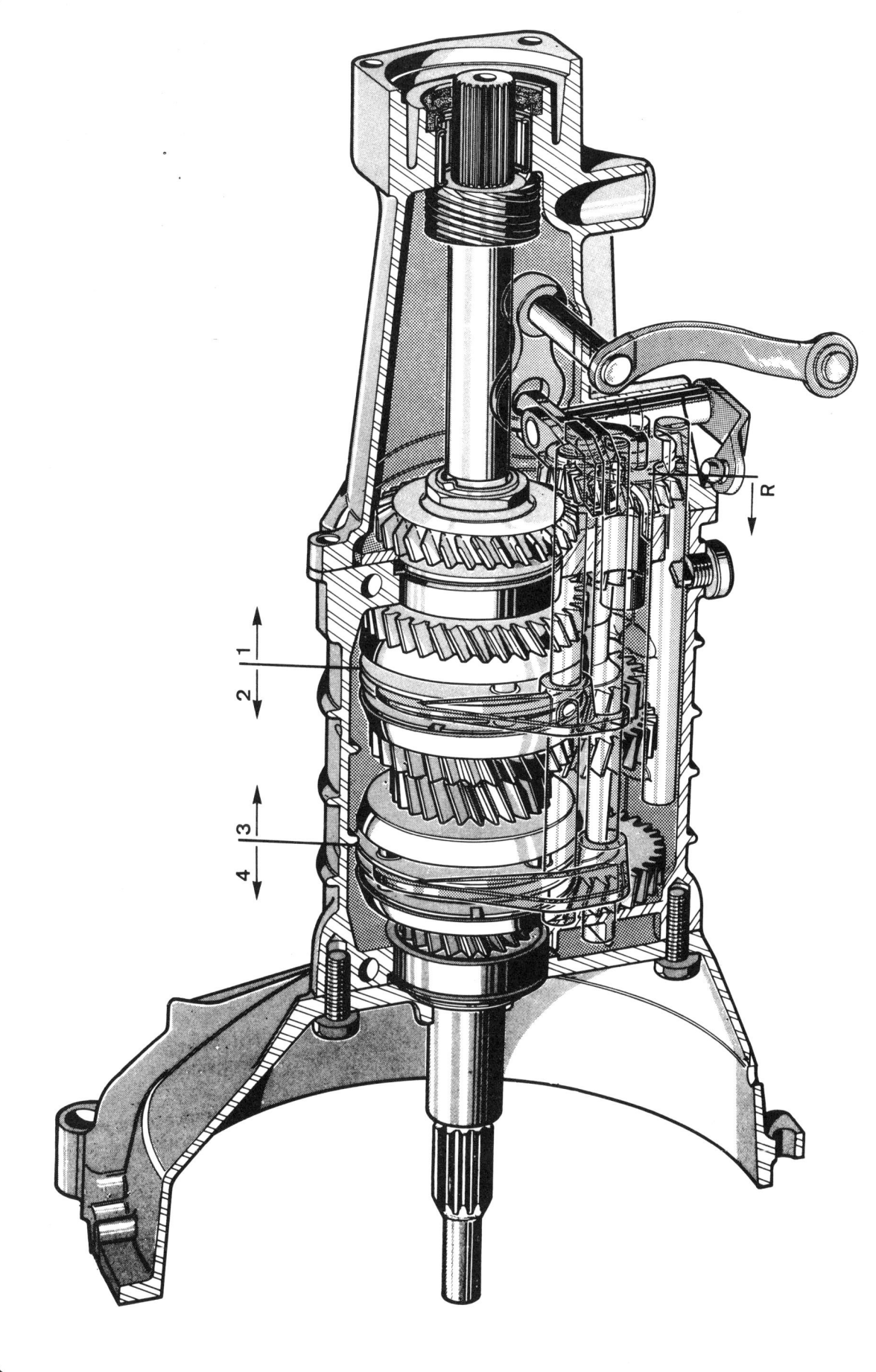

Fig. 6.1 Manual gearbox showing gear movement (Sec 1)

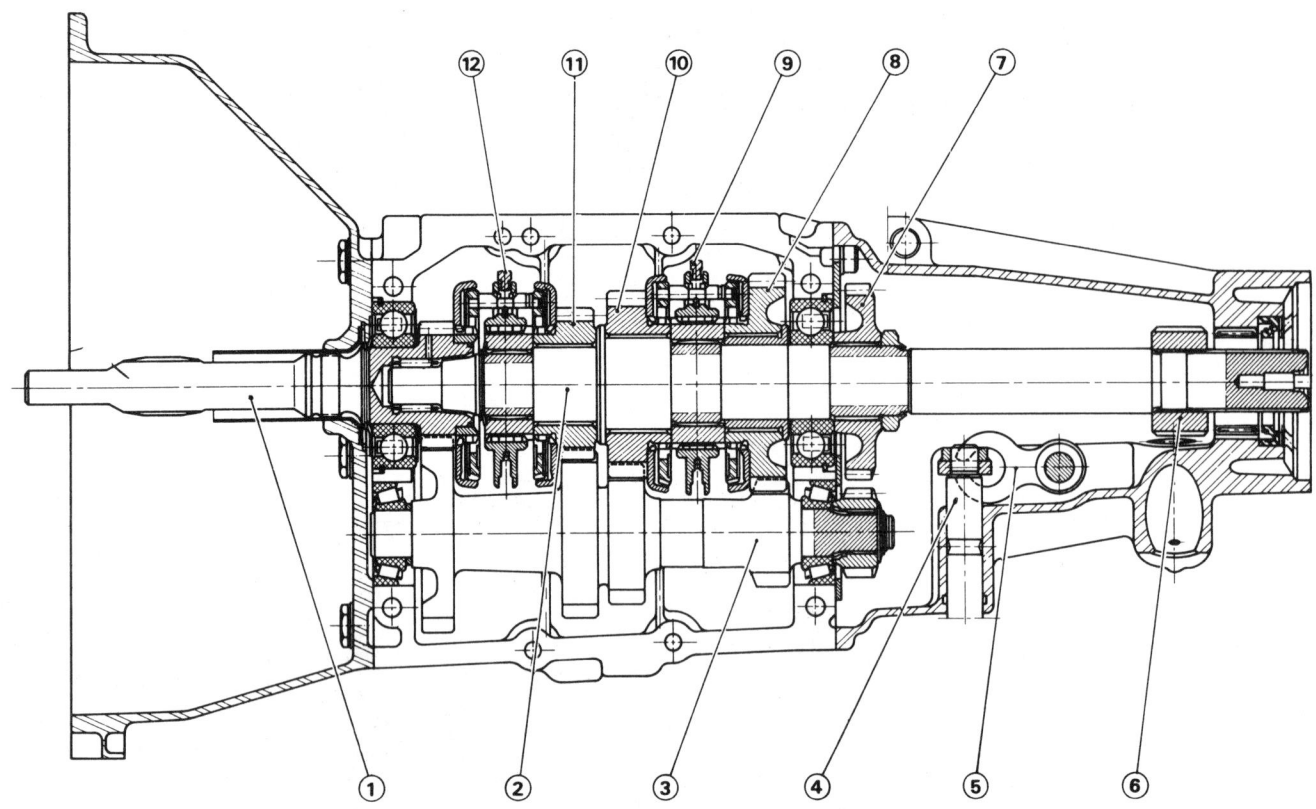

Fig. 6.2 Sectional view of manual gearbox (Sec 1)

1 Input shaft	4 Gearbox control	7 Reverse gear pinion	10 2nd gear pinion
2 Mainshaft	5 Gear selector control	8 1st gear pinion	11 3rd gear pinion
3 Layshaft	6 Speedometer drive gear	9 1st/2nd synchromesh cones	12 3rd/4th synchromesh cones

14 Disconnect the gear lever operating rods by first removing the linkage retaining clips and washer, and then prising the socket joints off the balls on the levers (photo).

15 Undo and remove the bolt securing the clutch slave cylinder locking plate and lift off the plate.

16 Extract the circlip and slide the slave cylinder out of its location in the bellhousing (photo). Allow it to hang by its fluid hose.

17 Extract the circlips from the protruding ends of the steering rack and pinion gear retaining bolts.

18 Undo and remove the two steering gear retaining bolts (photo).

19 Undo and remove the clamp bolt securing the steering column shaft to the flexible coupling (photo). Disengage the shaft from the coupling and lower the steering gear without disconnecting the track rod end balljoints.

20 From inside the car unscrew the gear lever knob and then lift away the carpet over the transmission tunnel. **Note:** *If a centre console is fitted, refer to Chapter 12 and remove the console first.*

21 Undo and remove the screws securing the gear lever rubber boot retaining plate to the tunnel and withdraw the boot and plate (photo).

22 Now undo and remove the transverse pivot bolt securing the gear lever to the linkage on top of the gearbox. Carefully lift out the gearlever complete with operating rod (photo).

23 It is now necessary to seek the help of an assistant for the remainder of the removal sequence.

24 On models having a 'banjo' type solid rear axle, position a jack beneath the gearbox and in contact with it.

25 Undo and remove the bolt securing the crossmember to the gearbox, and the nuts and washers securing the crossmember to the body. Lift off the crossmember (photo).

26 From inside the car undo and remove the bolt securing the gearbox rear support to the top of the transmission tunnel. Now remove the remaining rear support mounting nuts from below, while the bolts are held, to prevent them from turning, from above. Lift away the rear support.

Fig. 6.3 Withdrawing the gearbox from the engine (Sec 2)

27 Position suitable lifting tackle around the front of the engine or engaged with the front engine lifting bracket.

28 Undo and remove the three socket-headed bolts securing the gearbox bellhousing to the engine.

29 Undo and remove the retaining bolts and lift off the closure plates from the bellhousing flange (photo).

30 From under the car, carefully lower the jack supporting the weight

2.11 Gearbox earth strap

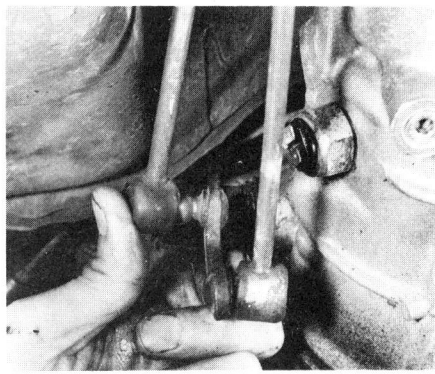

2.14 Detaching the gear lever operating rod socket joints

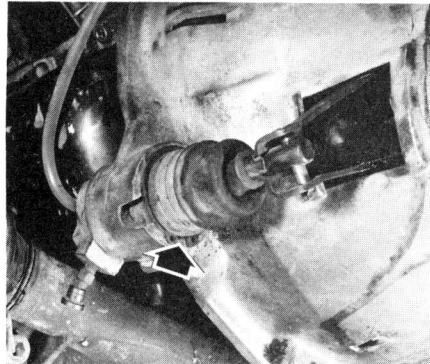

2.16 Clutch slave cylinder retaining circlip (arrowed)

2.18 Steering gear retaining bolts (arrowed) ...

2.19 ... and flexible coupling clamp bolt (arrowed)

2.21 Gear lever rubber boot, retaining plate, and screws

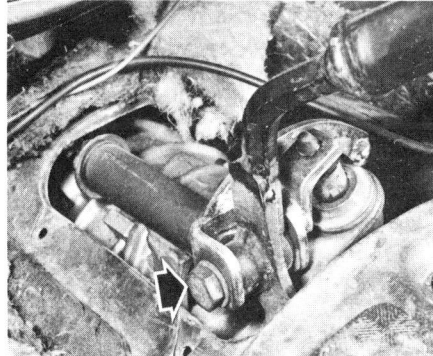

2.22 Gear lever transverse pivot bolt (arrowed)

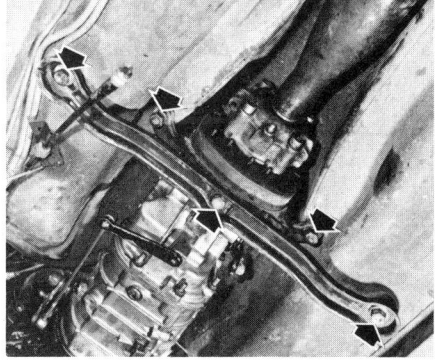

2.25 Gearbox crossmember mountings (arrowed)

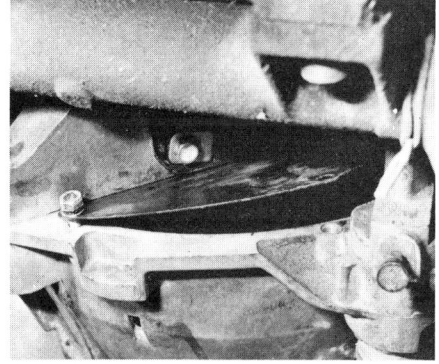

2.29 Removing the bellhousing lower closure plate

of the gearbox while at the same time holding the gearbox in position on the engine.

31 Now, using the lifting tackle raise the front of the engine, taking care not to allow the cylinder head to come into contact with the voltage regulator cover on the bulkhead.

32 When sufficient clearance exists, rotate the gearbox a quarter of a turn anti-clockwise and then withdraw the gearbox rearwards off the engine.

33 Lower the gearbox to the ground and slide it out from under the car.

3 Gearbox (manual) – refitting

1 Refitting the gearbox is basically the reverse of the removal procedure, but there are several points which should be noted.

2 Be sure that the clutch thrust bearing is correctly fitted. It should be offered to the clutch release fork with the retaining tag pointing to the starter motor housing, and then turned clockwise so that this tag hooks over the release fork.

3 The guide sleeve of the bearing and the part of the input shaft bearing retainer over which it runs should be smeared with molybdenum disulphide grease before the bearing is fitted.

4 Assuming the engine has been left hoisted or jacked up in the position it was in during gearbox removal, refitting of the gearbox is straightforward, the only point to watch being the engagement of the input shaft with the clutch disc on the flywheel. This is a matter of alignment of the mating splines.

5 Once the input shaft has been engaged with the clutch disc, the dowels on the housing will make it easy to align the gearbox to the engine and secure it with the three socket-headed bolts.

6 Carry out the remainder of the refitting operations using the reverse sequence to removal. Observe the correct torque wrench setting when tightening all fastenings, and remember to refill the gearbox with oil when installation is complete.

4 Gear lever and external linkage (manual gearbox) – overhaul

1   Overhaul of the gearchange mechanism consists of checking the various bushes and linkages for wear or damage, greasing them and renewing them as necessary. Unless there has been gross neglect or the car has covered a high mileage, it is unlikely that renewal will be necessary.
2   Should excessive play at the gearlever develop or difficulty be experienced when selecting gear, carry out the following checks.
3   Observe the movement of the external linkage from below while an assistant moves the gear lever inside the car.
4   If any wear is apparent at the ball and socket joints or the pivot bushes, renew the components as necessary.
5   Now adjust the control rods to obtain full travel of the linkages consistent with gear lever movement.

5 Gearbox (manual) – dismantling

1   With the gearbox removed from the car, thoroughly wash off the exterior of the casing using paraffin or a soluble degreaser.
2   Place the unit on a firm bench or table and commence dismantling by removing the speedometer drive socket. To do this slacken the locknut and then undo and remove the grub screw.
3   Withdraw the clutch release bearing and operating lever from the bellhousing (photo). Now undo and remove the bellhousing retaining bolts and lift away the housing (photo).
4   If a universal joint is fitted to the rear of the mainshaft, undo and remove the retaining bolt using a socket and extension inserted through the centre of the yoke. Now lift off the universal joint (photos).
5   Set the control lever to the neutral position and pull the selector lever fully to the rear. Undo and remove the seven fixing bolts and remove the rear housing. Tap it gently with a soft-faced hammer if it is difficult to part, as it is dowelled to the rear of the gearbox main casing (photo).
6   Note the exact position of the speedometer pinion on the mainshaft and, using a universal puller, draw off the pinion (photo).
7   Undo the large nut that secures the reverse pinion to the mainshaft (photo). If it is difficult to move try using two thin screwdrivers gently wedged between the reverse pinion and the bearing locking plate.
8   Slide the reverse pinion off the mainshaft, noting which way round it is fitted (photo).
9   Undo and remove the bearing locking plate securing bolts and lift off the bearing locking plate (photos).
10 Undo and remove the bolts securing the two halves of the gearbox main casing. From the photo note which half is on the table. Lift away the top half of the casing (photo).

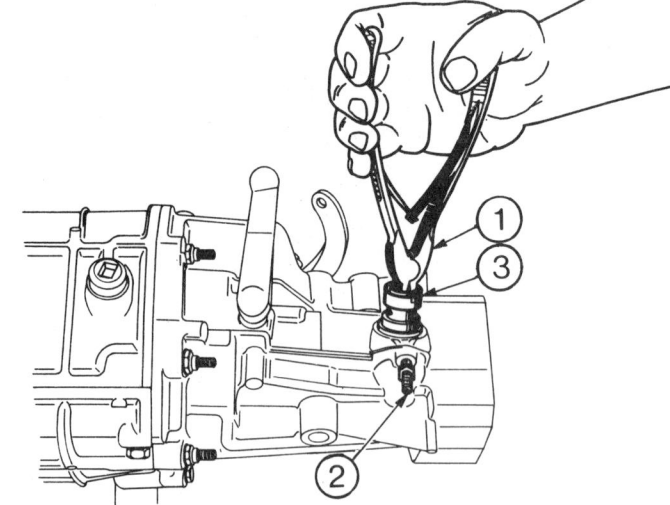

Fig. 6.4 Removing the speedometer drive socket (Sec 5)

1   Circlip pliers   3   Speedometer drive socket
2   Grub screw

5.3a Removal of the clutch release bearing and operating lever

5.3b Removing the bellhousing

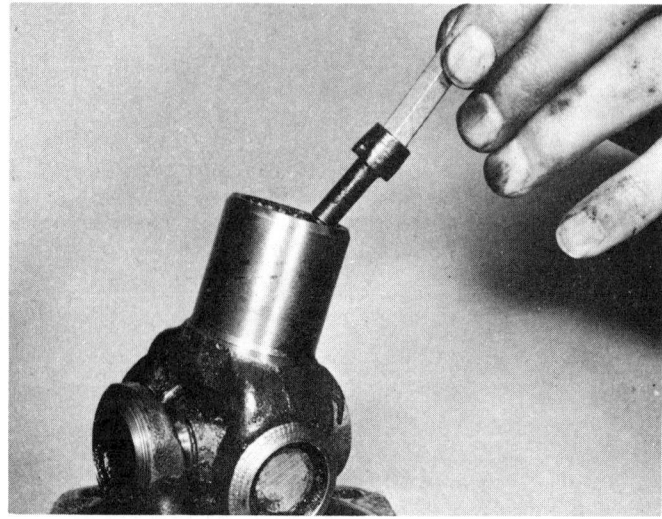

5.4a Undo and remove the socket-headed bolt ...

5.4b ... and lift off the universal joint

5.5 Removing the rear housing

5.6 Drawing off the speedometer pinion

5.7 The nut that secures the reverse pinion on the mainshaft

5.8 Sliding off the reverse pinion

5.9a Removing the bearing locking plate retaining screws ...

5.9b ... and withdrawing the locking plate

5.10 Parting the two halves of the gearbox main casing

5.11a The gear train layout

5.11b Lifting out layshaft assembly ...

5.11c ... followed by the input shaft and mainshaft assemblies

6.1 Separating input shaft from mainshaft

6.3 Removing the snap-ring from the end of the mainshaft

6.4 Sliding off 3rd/4th speed synchroniser

6.5 Lifting away 3rd/4th speed hub

6.7 Withdrawing the mainshaft rear bearing

6.8 Sliding off the 1st speed spacer bushing, bearing and 1st speed pinion

6.9 Removal of the 1st/2nd speed synchroniser

11 Now carefully lift out the layshaft gear assembly, the input shaft assembly and mainshaft assembly (photos).

12 The gearbox itself may now be considered to be dismantled, and it now remains for the various sub-assemblies to be attended to, as determined by a thorough inspection for wear or damage.

6 Mainshaft (manual gearbox) – dismantling

1 To part the input shaft from the mainshaft, first slide the third/fourth speed synchroniser as far as it will go into the third speed synchroniser cone and simply pull apart (photo).

2 It is important that when the synchronisers are reassembled after having been taken apart, the hubs and sliders should go back in exactly the same position as they were found to be in on removal. Before dismantling, mark the various components if there is to be any doubt. The other thing to be certain of is that the various shims are put back exactly where they came from. They take up manufacturing tolerances and their number and thickness varies with individual gearboxes.

3 Start dismantling the mainshaft by marking the third/fourth speed sliding gear and hub. Using a pair of circlip pliers, release and then remove the snap-ring and spring washer from the end of the mainshaft (photo).

4 Slide the third/fourth speed synchroniser assembly from mainshaft (photo).

5 Lift off the third/fourth speed synchroniser assembly hub and gearwheel (photo).

6 Should by chance the reverse pinion and retaining nut still be in position on the rear end of the mainshaft, these must be removed. Hold the reverse gear between soft faces in a large bench vice and unscrew the nut. Slide off the reverse pinion.

7 It is now necessary to remove the rear bearing. For this ideally a press is necessary, but it can be done by judicious levering. Note which way the circlip in the outer track is positioned (photo).

8 Recover any shims from behind the bearing and then slide off the first speed spacer bushing, needle bearing cage and first speed pinion (photo).

9 Remove the first/second speed synchroniser without parting the sliding gear from the hub (photo).

10 Slide the second speed gear from the mainshaft.

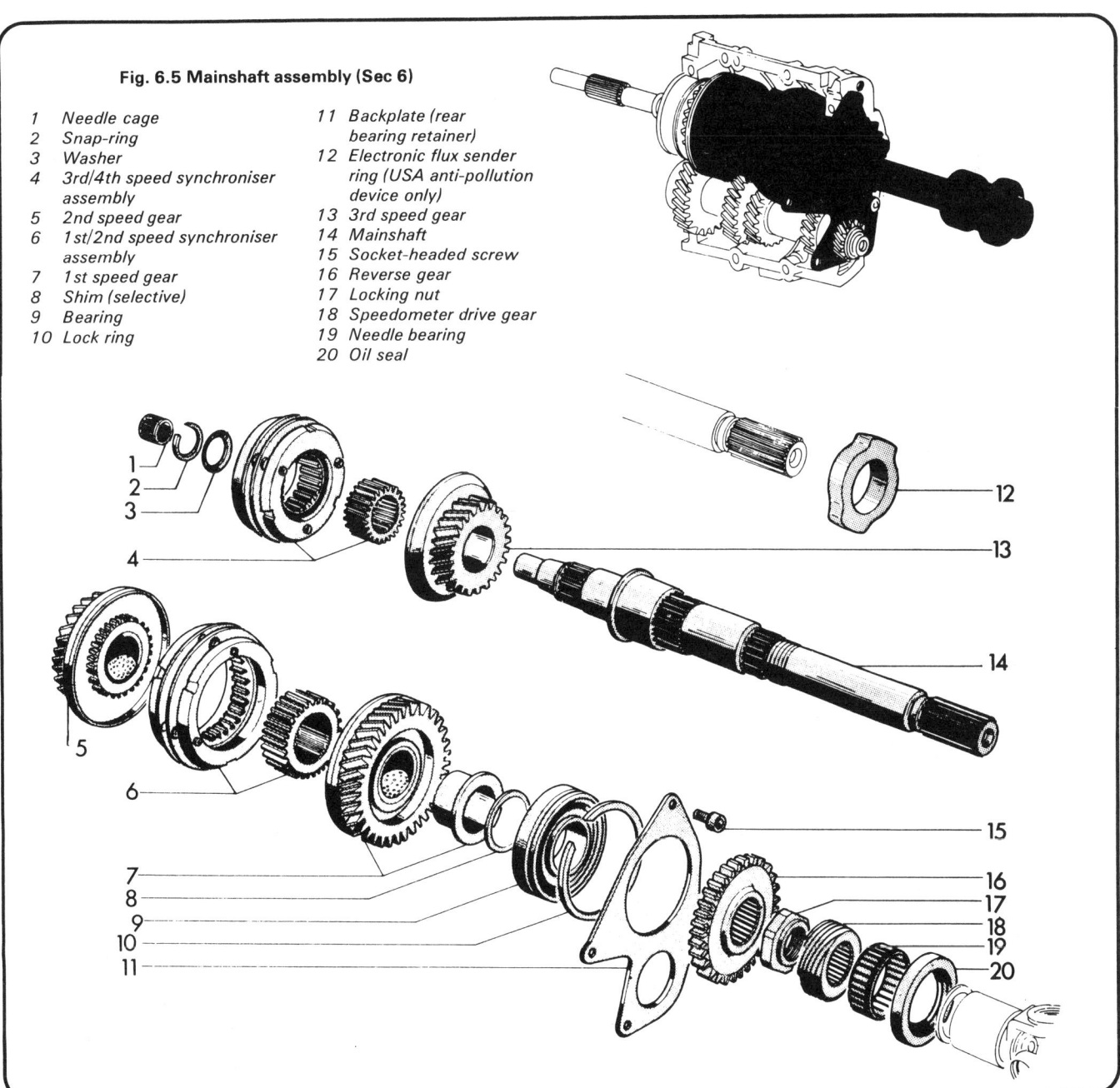

Fig. 6.5 Mainshaft assembly (Sec 6)

1 Needle cage
2 Snap-ring
3 Washer
4 3rd/4th speed synchroniser assembly
5 2nd speed gear
6 1st/2nd speed synchroniser assembly
7 1st speed gear
8 Shim (selective)
9 Bearing
10 Lock ring
11 Backplate (rear bearing retainer)
12 Electronic flux sender ring (USA anti-pollution device only)
13 3rd speed gear
14 Mainshaft
15 Socket-headed screw
16 Reverse gear
17 Locking nut
18 Speedometer drive gear
19 Needle bearing
20 Oil seal

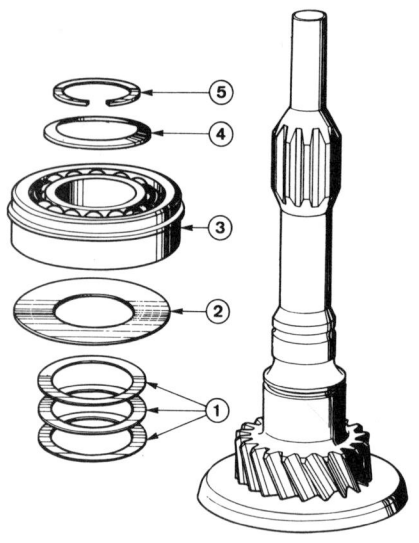

Fig. 6.6 Input shaft assembly (Sec 7)

1	Shim	4	Dished washer
2	Deflector washer	5	Snap-ring
3	Ball-race		

7 Input shaft assembly (manual gearbox) – dismantling

1   First recover the needle bearing from the end of the input shaft.
2   Using a pair of circlip pliers, release the snap-ring and then remove, followed by the dished washer underneath it.
3   Support the bearing between soft faces in a large bench vice and drive the input shaft assembly through the bearing using a soft-faced hammer.
4   Recover any shim from behind the bearing.

8 Selector and interlock mechanism (manual gearbox) – dismantling

1   The selector forks are fixed to their respective shafts by spring pins, which are easily drifted out. In all cases use a suitable diameter parallel pin punch. The simplest order of operation is:

 (a) Put first/second gearshaft in second gear position (ie as far forward as it will go)
 (b) Drive out pin from first/second gear shifting fork
 (c) Return shaft to neutral position
 (d) Put third/fourth speed shaft in fourth gear position (ie as far forward as it will go)
 (e) Remove pin from third/fourth gear shifting fork

2   Withdraw the third/fourth gear selector shaft from the gearbox casing, watching for the locking needle which is located in a hole about half way along it. Put the locking needle in a safe place. The locating ball which engages with notches at the end of this shaft will probably have come out and be rolling about inside the housing.

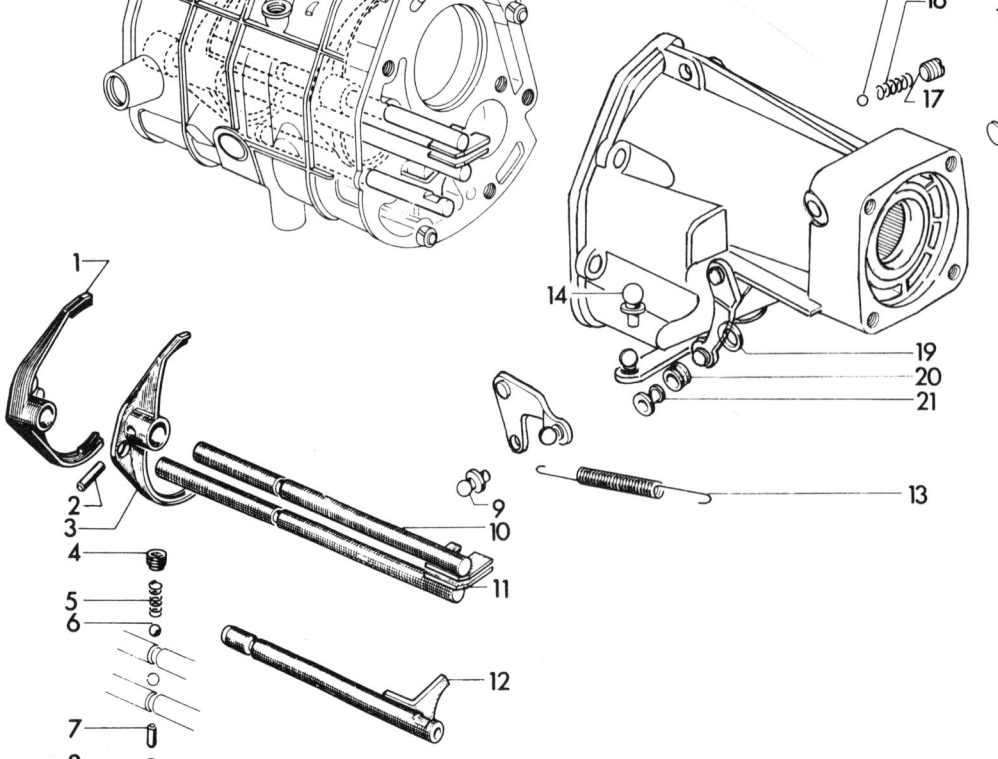

Fig. 6.7 Gearbox selector mechanism (Sec 8)

1	3rd/4th speed selector	7	Needle	12	Reverse selector	17	Plug
2	Pin	8	Finger	13	Spring	18	Expansion plug
3	1st/2nd speed selector	9	Ball head	14	Ball head	19	Washer
4	Plug	10	1st/2nd shaft	15	Ball	20	Rubber bush
5	Spring	11	3rd/4th shaft	16	Spring	21	Eyelet
6	Ball						

Recover the ball and hook out the spring. Note in some early models the arrangement is somewhat different, the spring and ball being retained by a plug.

3 Remove the plugs on either side of the housing which retain the locking springs and balls for the other two selector rods. Hook out the springs, and with luck the balls will shake out quite easily. If for any reason they do not, temporarily refit the retainer plugs.

4 Pull out the two selector rods, sliding the reverse idler pinion off its spindle as the reverse rod comes out.

5 Remove the retaining plugs again and poke out the retaining balls if not already removed. Also recover the locking ball and locking finger which lie between the selectors. By now the following should have been recovered:

    (a)   *Three locking springs*
    (b)   *Four balls*
    (c)   *One locking finger*

6 The reverse shaft can be removed by drifting out the pin which holds it in and driving the shaft towards the inside of the housing.

9 Gearbox (manual) – inspection and overhaul

1 If the gearbox has been stripped becuase of some obvious fault, such as failure to stay in the selected gear, difficulty in engaging gear or the sort of noise which can no longer be ignored, the cause of the fault is usually pretty obvious. A not so obvious cause of noise and trouble is bearing wear, which it is well worthwhile to nip in the bud by renewing the bearings concerned before things get to such a state that a shaft has to be renewed.

2 If movement in the bearings exists when they are still well lubricated, it is a fair assumption that when dry movement will be even worse. Give them a good wash in paraffin and a final rinse in white spirit. Examine them for signs of wear such as scoring, blueing or excessive play. If there is any doubt they should be renewed.

3 If the cones of a synchroniser are obviously worn or heavily scored, or if the synchroniser teeth which engage with the gear pinions have a battered look, the synchroniser should be renewed. Replacement synchronisers come complete with the synchroniser hub and care should be taken to see that the hub belonging to a particular synchroniser remains with it, and that its position relative to the synchroniser does not get altered (ie the hub does not get turned over relative to the synchroniser).

4 Examine the teeth of all gears for signs of uneven or excessive wear and chipping. If the gear is in a bad state have a good look at the gear it engages with – this may have to be renewed as well.

5 All gears should be a good running fit on the shaft with no sign of rocking. The synchronising hubs should not be a sloppy fit on the shaft splines.

6 Examine the selector rods and forks for damage, wear of distortion. Renew any item that is doubtful.

7 Examine the control levers in the rear housing for wear or damage. If any defect is found, this will be expensive because the levers are not detachable from the rear housing and the whole housing has to be renewed. The ball heads or adjustable joints connecting these levers to the link rods of the gearchange mechanism can, however be renewed.

8 Peugeot recommend that when the gearbox is overhauled parallelism of the front and rear faces of the clutch housing should be checked. Fig. 6.8 shows this being done. This is a very simple matter if a surface table and dial gauge are to hand. If the surfaces are not parallel the input shaft to the gearbox will not be properly aligned with the crankshaft. This can lead to excessive wear in the gearbox bearings, particularly the front bearing which supports the input shaft. If bearing wear is excessive take the housing to the local Peugeot garage or a local engineering works and get them to check it. Peugeot recommend that if the lack of parallelism exceeds 0.0039 inch (0.10 mm) the housing should be renewed. However, to save unnecesary expense if there is a small lack of parallelism up to say 0.012 in (0.30 mm) careful matching should be carried out.

9 Renewal of a worn guide sleeve is shown in Fig. 6.9. The sleeve is held in position by a snap-ring which can be levered out with a screwdriver. Fig. 6.10 shows the sleeve being pressed out, but if a piece of wood is held over it, it should be possible to tap it out with a soft-faced hammer. When fitting a new one, be very careful not to distort it. Fig. 6.9 shows the use of a special Peugeot tool but no doubt

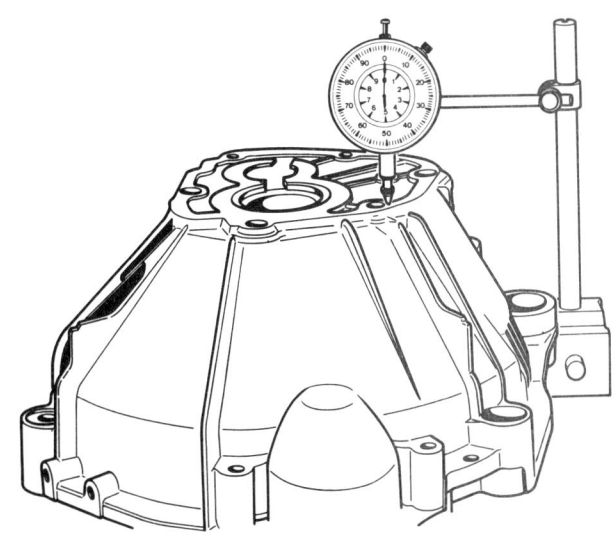

Fig. 6.8 Ideal method of checking clutch housing surfaces for parallelism (Sec 9)

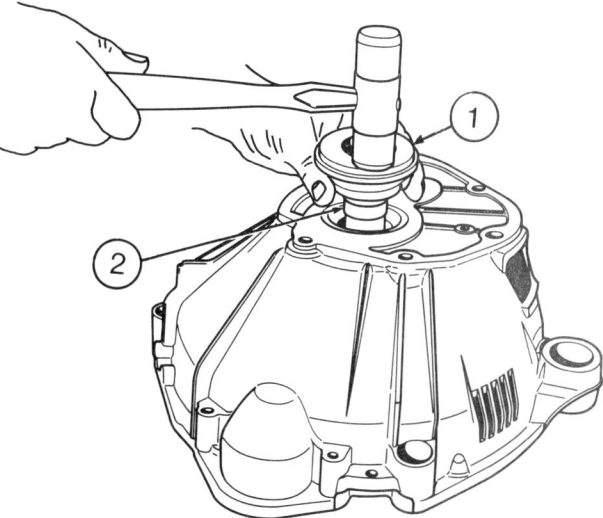

Fig. 6.9 Fitting a new guide sleeve (Sec 9)

1   Suitable drift   2   Guide sleeve

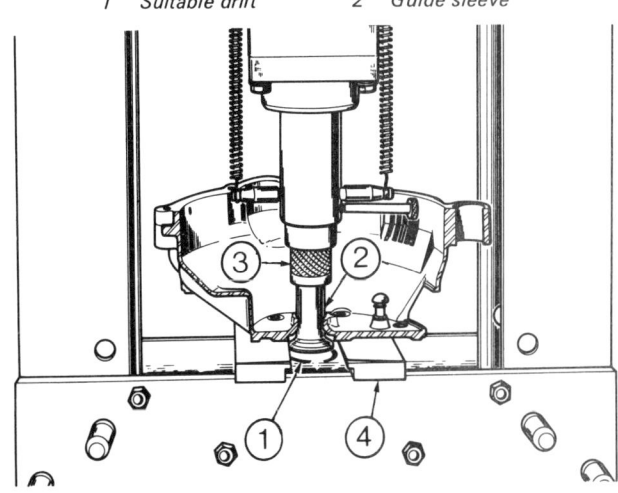

Fig. 6.10 Guide sleeve removal (Sec 9)

1   Snap-ring   3   Drift
2   Guide sleeve   4   Supports

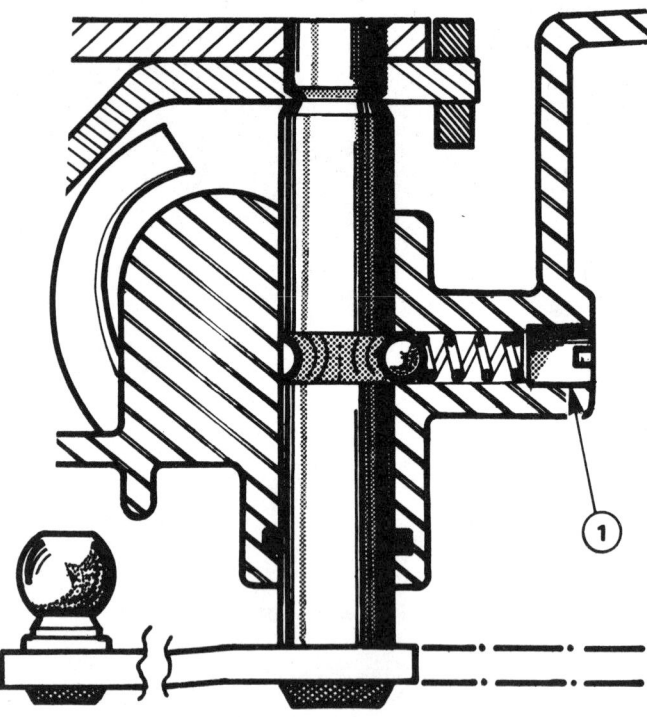

Fig. 6.11 Sectional view of neutral ball lock (Sec 9)

1   Plug

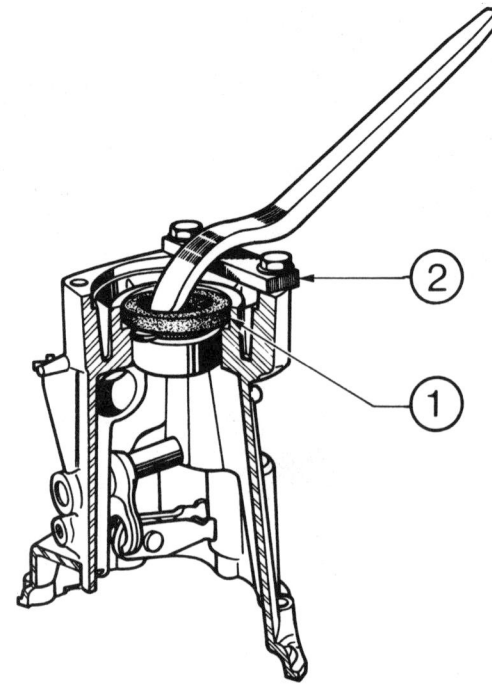

Fig. 6.12 Removing rear housing oil seal (Sec 9)

1   Oil seal   2   Fulcrum for lever

a substitute can be found. Be careful to drive the sleeve in straight and avoid hitting it directly with the soft-faced hammer. Use a new snapping-ring to hold it in position.

10 Turning now to the rear housing, it has already been stated that the gear control levers cannot be detached from it, and that the housing must be renewed if these are worn or defective. Remove the plug retaining the locking ball and spring for the selector lever, take out the ball and spring, and check that they are in good condition. Give the plug and the recess a good clean, smear the ball and spring with oil, put them back and screw in the plug, smearing its threads with a suitable sealing compound. The plug should be screwed flush with the housing and then locked into position by two punch marks.

11 The rear bearing and oil seal should be renewed every time the gearbox is dismantled. Fig. 6.12 shows the oil seal being removed. Notice the safety bar secured to the housing to protect the mating surface.

12 The needle bearing can be drifted out with a suitable diameter drift and hammer. Be careful when doing this that the surface at the other end of the housing is not damaged. Stand it on some cardboard. The replacement rear bearing is fitted with the engraved face turned outwards (ie upwards). Here again, a suitable drift can be used to fit the new bearing. The end of the bearing should be level with the shoulder in the housing. Lubricate the bearing well before inserting it. The same applies to the oil seal which sits on top of the bearing which should be pressed in as far as it will go.

---

10 Mainshaft universal joint (manual gearbox) – inspection and overhaul

1   On models equipped with a 'banjo' type solid rear axle, the universal joint fitted to the end of the gearbox mainshaft should be inspected for wear as follows:

2   Clamp one of the universal joint yokes in a vice and then attempt to turn the other yoke back and forth by hand. Check for excessive free play of the joint that would indicate wear of the needle roller bearings or the universal joint spider.

3   As the universal joint operates within the confines of the torque tube and is therefore protected from the adverse effects of water and

road grit, it is unlikely that any wear will be detectable. If, however, the joint does show signs of wear a new bearing and spider overhaul kit should be obtained from your Peugeot dealer.

4   To dismantle the universal joint, first extract the four bearing cup retaining circlips.

5   Grip one of the yokes of the universal joint in a vice with jaws protected so that bearing cups on the gripped yoke are in a vertical plane.

6   Using a hammer and drift of suitable diameter, tap the uppermost bearing cap until the lower cup protrudes from the yoke by approximately 3 mm (0.125 in).

7   The exposed lower bearing cup can now be withdrawn from the yoke using a self-gripping wrench or by gripping the cup in a vice and twisting the yoke until it is free.

8   Now support the yoke in a vice again with the bearing cup that was trapped originally facing downward.

9   Tap the now exposed spider downwards until the cup protrudes and then remove the cup as previously described.

10 The yoke can now be lifted off the spider and the remaining two bearing cups removed using the above procedure.

11 With the universal joint dismantled, thoroughly clean the two yokes and remove any burrs from the bearing surfaces with a small file.

12 Begin reassembly by removing the four bearing cups from the new universal joint assembly.

13 Liberally smear general purpose grease to the inside of the cups to retain the needle rollers in position during reassembly.

14 Support one of the yokes in a vice and insert the spider. Place a bearing cup squarely on the yoke and engage the spider partially to keep the needle rollers in position. Now tap the bearing cap fully into the yoke and refit a new circlip.

15 Turn the yoke over and install the other bearing cup in the same fashion.

16 Repeat this procedure for the second yoke and remaining two bearing cups.

---

11 Gearbox (manual) – initial reassembly

1   Although the split case construction makes reassembly a fairly

11.2 Reverse selector engaged with reverse pinion

11.3 Installing reverse pinion shaft roll pin

11.4 Inserting ball into locking passage ...

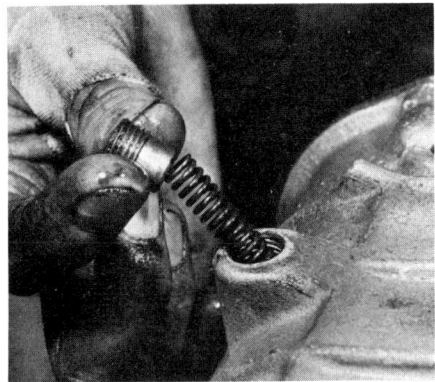

11.5 ... followed by spring and plug

11.6 Inserting the locking finger

11.7 Sliding in 3rd/4th gearchange fork shaft

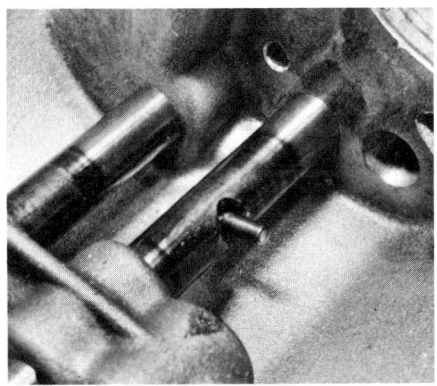

11.8 Locking needle in position in 3rd/4th gearchange fork shaft

11.9 The 1st/2nd gearchange fork in position

11.10 Inserting spring into casing web hole

11.11 ... followed by the ball bearing

11.12 Fitting the 3rd/4th gearchange fork roll pin

11.13 Inserting the 1st/2nd gearchange fork shaft

11.14 Inserting the last ball bearing ...

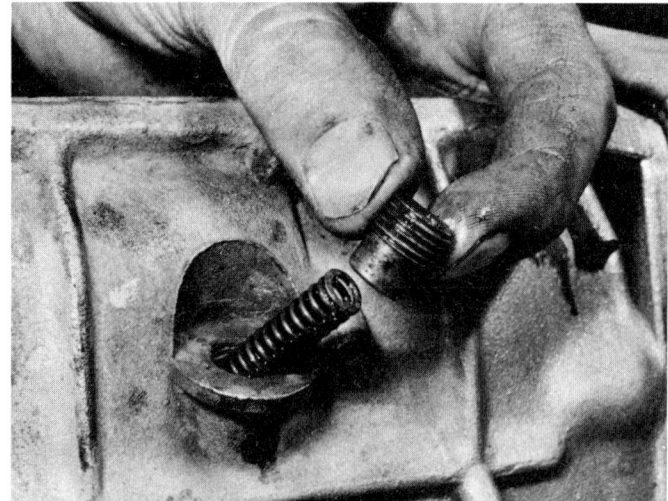

11.15 ... followed by the spring and plug

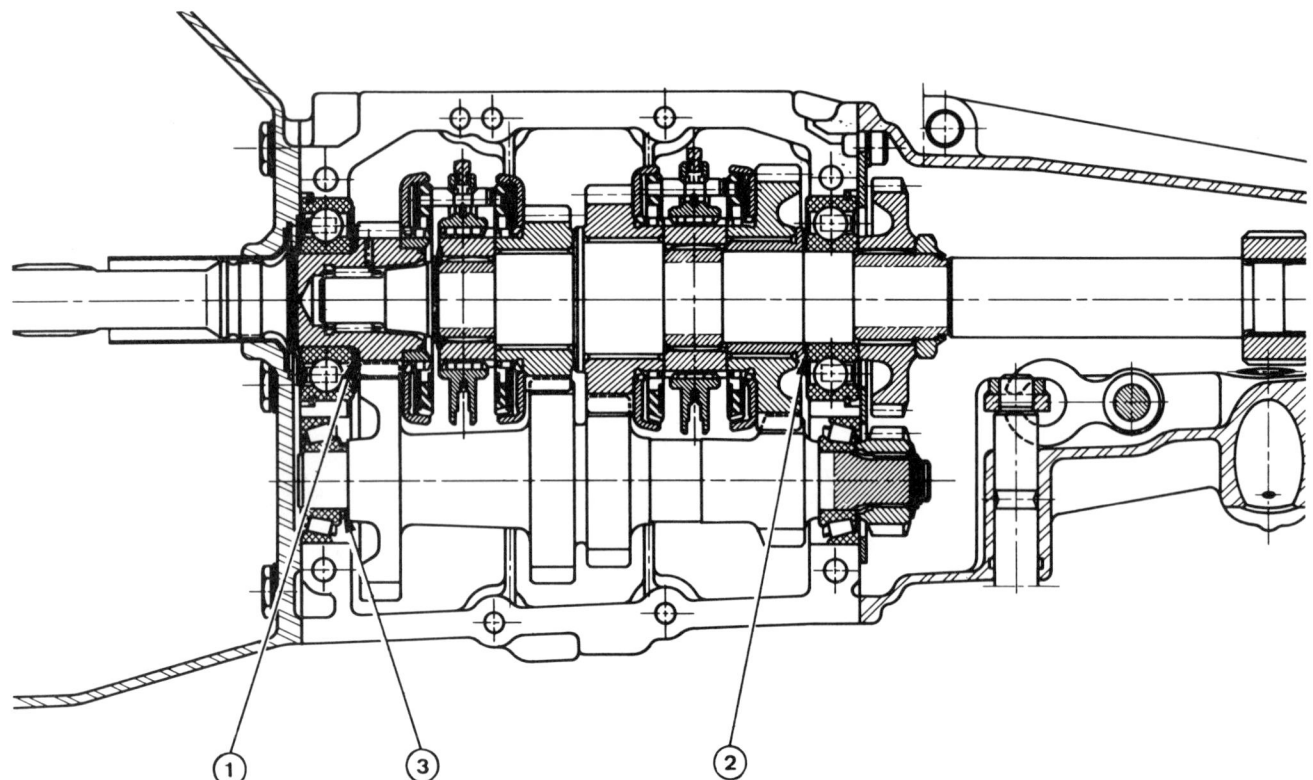

Fig. 6.13 Gearbox adjustment points (Sec 11)

1   *4th gear synchroniser cone
    position*

2   *2nd gear sychrnoniser cone
    position*

3   *Layshaft selective shim*

simple matter, a certain amount of engineering judgement and common sense is called for, and it is recommended that the whole of this Section be thoroughly read before work commences. As discovered during dismantling, both the input shaft and the mainshaft assemblies incorporate adjusting shims which are individually chosen for each gearbox. The function of these shims is to ensure that the synchromesh hubs are correctly positioned. The layshaft also carries adjusting shims which control the distance between the layshaft bearings. These bearings, being taper roller bearings, should be 'preloaded' on assembly; that is, they should be squeezed slightly when the gearbox is assembled. Determination of the shim thickness is very easy if all the correct gauges and a dial depth indicator are

available, but these gauges (issued to Peugeot garages by the manufacturers) may well be difficult to come by. However, more often than not they can be done without.

2   Reassembly starts with the refitting of the reverse pinion. First assemble the reverse pinion shaft with the roll pin hole is alignment with the hole in the casing web. Also slide on the reverse pinion and the reverse shift fork assembly, the latter two parts in engagement (photo).

3   Insert the roll pin into the hole in the casing web and tap fully home (photo).

4   Insert the ball into the locking passage leading to the shift rod (photo)

5   Follow this with the spring, and having smeared the threads of the plug with a little sealing compound, tighten the plug to the specified torque wrench setting (photo).
6   Draw out the reverse shift fork until the neutral position is felt and then insert the third/fourth and reverse locking finger. This must pass through the reverse shift rod (photo).
7   Insert the third/fourth gearchange fork shaft until the hole in the centre is well into the casing, and then slide on the third/fourth gearchange fork (photo).
8   Smear the locking needle with a little grease and insert it into the hole in the third/fourth gearchange fork shaft (photo).
9   Do not forget that the third/fourth gearchange fork shaft passes through the first/second gearchange fork, so this must be placed in the casing before the shaft is pushed through the centre web of the casing half (photo).
10   Insert the spring into the casing web hole (photo).
11   Now follow with the ball bearing. Push the bearing down with a small screwdriver and ease the shaft into position (photo).
12   Line up the holes in the third/fourth gearchange fork and shaft, and lock with a roll pin (photo).
13   Insert the first/second gearchange fork shaft, line up the holes in the fork and shaft and lock with a roll pin (photo).
14   Move the selector shafts to the neutral position and then insert the last ball bearing into the hole in the side of the casing (photo).
15   Now follow this with the spring and plug. The same comments as in paragraph 5 apply (photo).
16   The description given in this Section is applicable to most gearboxes, but should any deviations have been noted during dismantling then obviously they will have to be taken into account during reassembly.

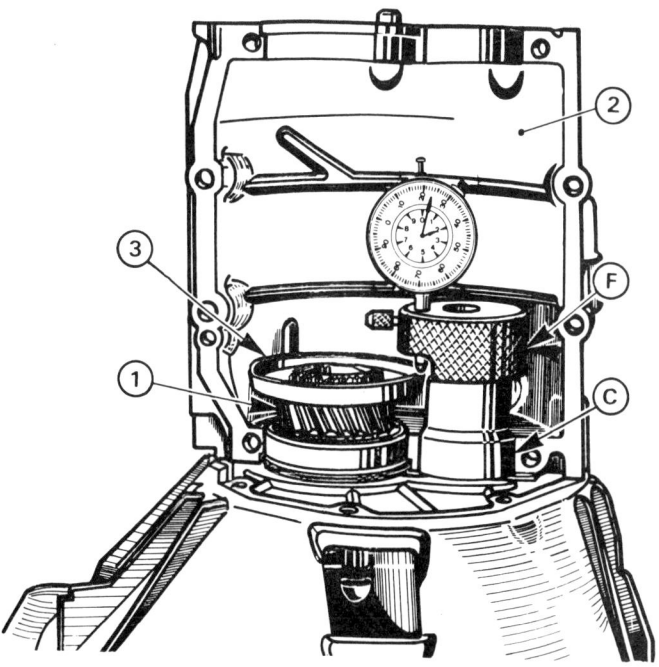

Fig. 6.14 Input shaft shim thickness measurement (Sec 12)

1	Input shaft	C	Gauge
2	RH housing	F	Support
3	Synchroniser cone		

---

12 Input shaft (manual gearbox) – assembly and shim selection

1   The only reason for dismantling the input shaft is usually to fit a new ball bearing assembly or, if the input shaft is being renewed and the old bearing is in excellent condition, then the fitting of a new shaft to an old bearing.
2   During dismantling it was probably found that there were some shims behind the bearing and these should be transferred to the new assembly. There are special gauges to determine any change in shim thickness required, and these are at the local Peugeot garage! However, from experience, although it is desirable to reassemble all parts 'according to the book', it has been found that without using these gauges the job can still be done, and in most cases a reasonable result obtained. For those with the necessary equipment however, full information is given.
3   As shown in Fig. 6.13 the input shaft assembly includes shims between the bearing and gear head. These shims determine the distance between the fourth gear synchronizer cone and the end of the case. The thicker the shims, the further away from the case the synchronize will be.
4   Fig. 6.14 shows how the shim thickness is determined when the special gauges are available. The object is to ensure that the edge of the synchronizer cone is exactly the same height above the end of the case as the gauge 'C'. The adjustment is carried out with the shaft and gauge fitted into the right-hand half of the gearbox case which is assembled to the clutch housing – be sure to tighten the assembling bolts to the correct torque wrench setting.
5   The shaft is assembled first of all without any shims and without the old deflector washer between the bearing and drive pinion. Be sure that the bearing is the correct way round (ie the groove with the lock ring in it should be furthermost from the drive pinion).
6   This being done, set up the dial indicator in its support resting on the gauge, as shown in Fig. 6.14. Rotate the input shaft and set the indicator to zero at the average high spot found for one complete revolution of the input shaft.
7   Move the dial indicator gauge support until the indicator rests on the gauge surface as in Fig. 6.14. The clearance found is the total shim and washer thickness to be inserted between the drive pinion and the bearing. The measured value should be rounded off to the nearest 0.05 mm. For example an indicator reading of 0.58 mm is taken as 0.60 mm and the shims selected accordingly. Shims are available in thicknesses of 0.15 mm, 0.20 mm, 0.25 mm, 0.30 mm and 0.35 mm. The total shim thickness must include the thickness of the deflector washer which is 0.15 mm, so in this case choose two shims, one of

0.20 mm and one of 0.25 mm to bring the total thickness of shims and washer to 0.60 mm.
8   This is the 'official way' of selecting shim thickness, for those lucky enough to have access to the gauges.
9   The purpose of this shimming is to take up tolerances in the machining of the gearbox casing and the input shaft.
10   Clearly, if neither the shaft nor the gearbox casing has to be renewed the same shims can be used. If the bearing alone is renewed, but the shaft itself shows no signs of wear such as might be caused by a seized bearing moving on the shaft, it is reasonable to assume that the original shims will be satisfactory.
11   If for any reason, the case has to be renewed but the shaft assembly is satisfactory, assemble the shaft complete with its shims and fit it into the old half casing as described in paragraphs 2 and 3, and with whatever equipment is available measure the distance between the synchronizing cone face and the case. Bear in mind that this distance should be within 0.02 mm. This being done, repeat the process using the corresponding half of the new case (**Note**: *if one half of the case requires renewal both halves must be renewed as they are a matched pair)* and measure the distance. If the difference between the two distances exceeds 0.05 mm, alter the shim size to make this difference as small as possible.
12   If the input shaft is being renewed, reassemble the bearing and shims on the original shaft and measure the distance between the edge of the synchromesh cone and the back of the bearing. Now repeat the process exactly with the new shaft. If the difference between the measured distances exceeds 0.05 mm alter the shim sizes until the measurement obtained with the new shaft is, as nearly as possible, the same as that obtained with the old shaft.
13   It will be seen that measurements must be made accurately, and it is the difference between two measurements which is important rather than the absolute value of either of them. If necessary use spacing blocks of unknown thickness but always use them the same way round. It is only when damage or wear is involved that problems arise, because the original thickness will not be known. In this case the correct gauges will be necessary, and if not to hand it may be best to place the gearbox in the hands of the local Peugeot garage.

13 Mainshaft (manual gearbox) – shim size selection

1   The purpose of the shims on the mainshaft is to ensure that the second gear synchronizer cone is accurately placed relative to the gearbox casing. The 'officially' recommended setting up procedure is almost identical with that described for the input shaft, except that a longer gauge is used and the dial indicator is positioned on the case, not on the gauge itself.

2   The right-hand half of the gearbox casing should be fixed to the clutch housing exactly as described in Section 12, and the input shaft correctly assembled. Then fit the following parts:

Mainshaft second gear pinion
1st/2nd gear synchronizer hub
1st gear pinion spacer
Bearing
New snap ring (fitted to bearing)

Press the bearing fully home until it bottoms against the first gear pinion spacer.

3   Assemble the needle cage into the input shaft end and insert the mainshaft spigot. Place the whole assembly in the right-hand half casing and position the gauge as shown in Fig. 6.15 but with the probe on the top of the gauge.

4   Set the dial indicator gauge to zero when its finger is touching the top of the gauge.

5   Put the indicator finger in contact with the upper edge of the second gear synchronizer cone and obtain the mean reading for this as the input shaft is rotated. Because there are no shims on the mainshaft assembly, the second gear synchronizer cone will be slightly above the gauge surface and the indicator gauge will show by how much. Round off this reading to the nearest 0.05 mm. For example, if the indicator reads 0.47 mm, call this 0.45 mm and use shims of 0.20 mm and 0.25 mm for the pack, and prepare a shim pack of the appropriate thickness. Shims are available in the following thicknesses; 0.15 mm, 0.20 mm, 0.25 mm and 0.50 mm.

14 Layshaft (manual gearbox) – shim size selection

1   The purpose of the layshaft shims is to preload the taper roller bearings on the ends of the layshaft. 'Preloading' means ensuring that they are 'squeezed' slightly when the gearbox is assembled, this being achieved by choosing the correct spacing between them on the shaft. It is important when selecting the shims that everything is properly lined up, hence the somewhat elaborate procedure outlined in this Section.

2   Start by installing the layshaft, equipped with its bearing assemblies in the left-hand housing (see Fig. 6.16).

3   Secure the right-hand housing with the four housing bolts and hand-tighten. Next fix the rear plate with the four socket-headed screws and again hand-tighten.

4   Support the gearbox as rigidly as possible on the bench with the front part facing upwards. Push down on the layshaft front bearing with a suitable piece of tubing so bedding the bearings well down onto the shaft.

5   Secure the clutch housing to the gearbox housing with the four bolts and hand-tighten. Now tighten all bolts and socket-headed screws to the specified torque wrench setting. Then remove the clutch housing and check that the half housings are not out-of-flush by more than 0.02 mm. For this a dial indicator gauge is best, but feeler gauges and a straight edge can be used. If the housings are too far out of line, go through the procedure described in this paragraph again.

6   Because there are no shims on the layshaft, the outer race of the front bearing will now be slightly below the level of the front face of the housing. Measure this distance using a dial indicator gauge or feeler gauges and a straight edge. This distance should not vary by more than 0.02 mm, and if it does try straightening the bearing by gentle tapping. If this tapping causes the layshaft to bind, slacken off the two nearest housing fixing bolts and then retighten. Round off this reading to the nearest 0.05 mm and add 0.10 mm for the preload. For example: depth below housing 2.52 mm, add preload 0.10 mm, total 2.62 mm. Round off to 2.60 mm. This should be the thickness of the shim. Shims are available in thicknesses between 2.25 and 3.40 mm, in increments of 0.05 mm.

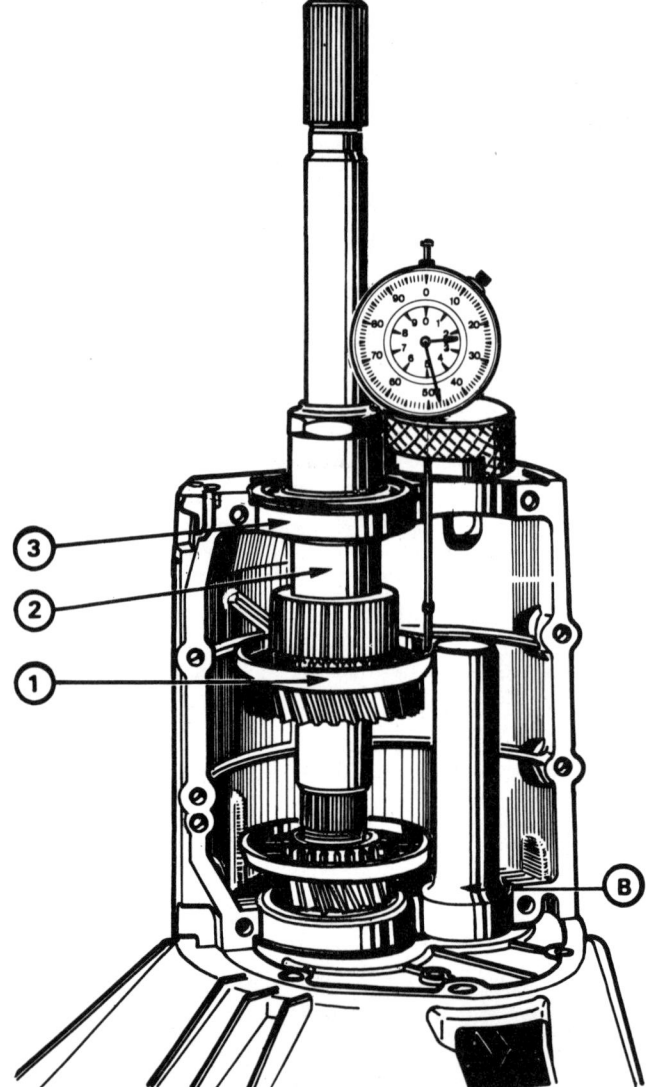

Fig. 6.15 Mainshaft shim size selection (Sec 13)

1	2nd gear synchroniser cone	3	Rear bearing
2	1st gear pinion bushing	B	Gauge

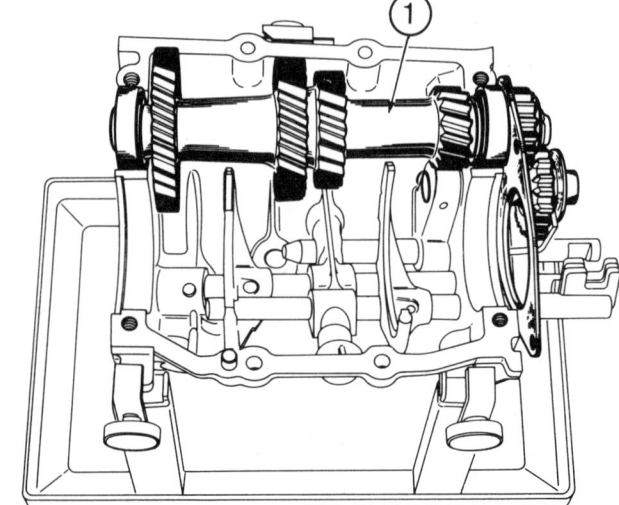

Fig. 6.16 Layshaft shim selection (Sec 14)

1   Layshaft

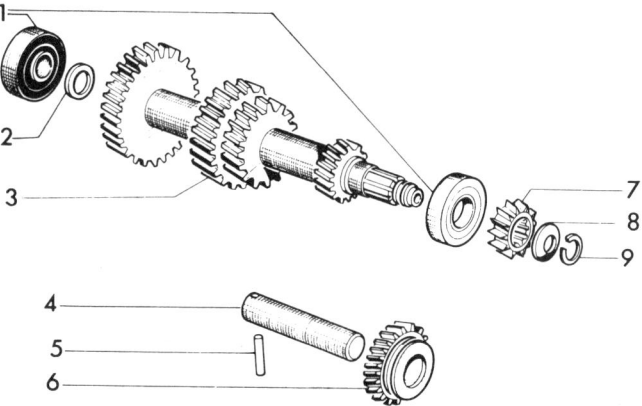

Fig. 6.17 Layshaft assembly (Sec 14)

1	*Bearing*	6	*Reverse idler gear*
2	*Selective shim*	7	*Reverse gear*
3	*Layshaft*	8	*Washer*
4	*Spindle*	9	*Snap-ring*
5	*Lock pin*		

7   Draw the front bearing off the layshaft and thread the shim over the shaft with its chamfered side towards the pinion. Refit the bearing ensuring it beds down firmly onto the shim.

15 Mainshaft and input shaft (manual gearbox) – reassembly

1   With the mainshaft, start by assembling the components shown in Fig. 6.5. Make sure when assembling the synchronizer hub and its sliding gear that they are in their original positions. Be careful when pressing on the bearing that pressure is exerted only on the part of the bearing that is in contact with the shaft (ie the inner track).

2   Leave the backing plate, reverse pinion and retaining nut and speedometer drive until later.

3   Working on the other end of the mainshaft, fit the third gear pinion and the third/fourth gear synchronizer, taking note of any previously make marks. Complete this assembly by fitting a new spring washer and snap ring. It will be necessary to push the snap ring down the shaft against the action of the spring washer before it will engage in its groove.

4   Fit the third/fourth gear sliding gear, positioning it in accordance with the previously made marks. Push it right home so that third gear is engaged.

5   Fig. 6.6 shows the order in which the components are assembled on the input shaft. There is no particular problem here except making quite sure that the snap ring is properly engaged in its groove. It will have to be pushed down against the pressure exerted by the spring washer. The spring washer and snap ring, as well as the snap ring on the bearing, should be renewed.

6   Install the needle cage in the end of the input shaft and slip the input shaft over the mainshaft.

16 Gearbox (manual) – final reassembly

1   Assemble the shaft to the mainshaft, not forgetting the needle cage in the end. Put the third/fourth sliding gear in the neutral position.

2   Carefully lower the assembly into the left-hand housing, engaging the selector forks with the synchromesh assemblies.

3   Next mesh and lower the layshaft assembly into the housing.

4   Slide the backing plate (rear bearing retainer) over the mainshaft and layshaft end and up to the housing (photo).

5   The gearbox should now appear as in the photograph. Check that all mating faces are clean (photo).

6   Lightly smear the mating surfaces of the half housings with a

16.4 Refitting the rear bearing retainer

16.5 The gear trains in position

16.6 Refitting the right-hand housing

16.9 Reverse pinion in position or mainshaft

16.11 Locking the reverse pinion retaining nut

16.12 Refitting the oil filler and chain plugs

16.13 Refitting the bellhousing

16.16 The speedometer drive gear on the mainshaft ready to be drifted into position

16.17 Lowering the rear housing into position

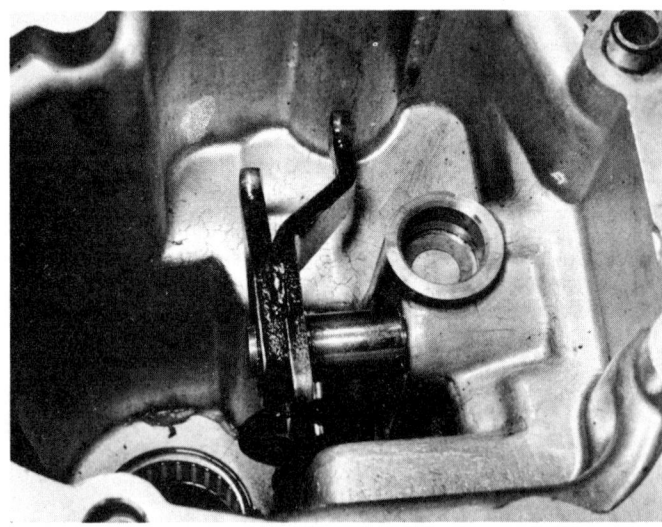

16.18 The internal selectors which engage with the selector fork rods

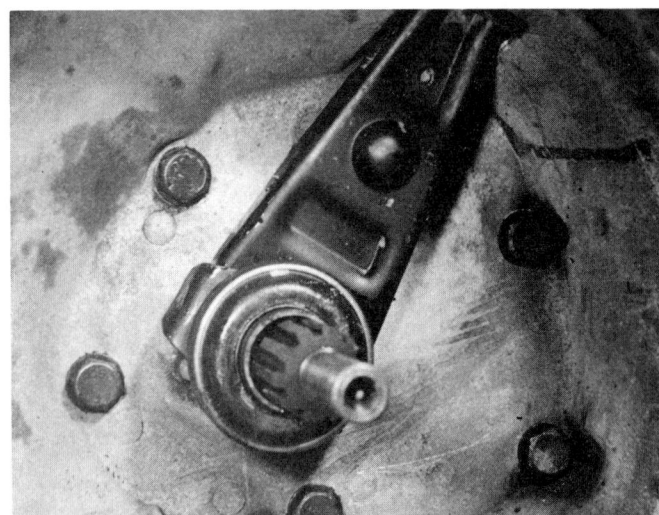

16.22 Clutch release fork and bearing in position

suitable sealing compound and carefully lower the right-hand housing into position (photo).

7   Secure the two halves together with the four corner bolts. Tighten to the specified torque wrench setting.

8   Secure the rear backing plate with its four socket-headed screws and tighten to the specified torque wrench setting.

9   Slide the reverse pinion onto the mainshaft ensuring that it is the correct way round (photo).

10 Refit the reverse pinion securing nut and tighten to the specified torque wrench setting.

11 Lock the nut to the mainshaft using a suitable diameter punch to depress part of the nut lip into the mainshaft indentation (photo).

12 Refit the gearbox oil level and drain plugs (photo).

13 Smear sealing compound on the rear face of the bellhousing and fasten it to the gearbox housing with six bolts. Tighten these in a progressive and diagonal manner (photo).

14 Now loosen the fout housing bolts and tap the half-housings with a soft-faced hammer whilst rotating the mainshaft. Retighten the four bolts to the specified torque wrench setting. When this is done the half-housings should not be out of flush at their rear mating surface by more than 0.02 mm. Check this with a dial indicator gauge or feeler gauges and a straight edge. If more than the permitted amount slacken the four bolts and repeat the operation.

15 Refit the remaining nuts and bolts securing the housing halves.

16 Refit the speedometer drive gear onto the end of the mainshaft and tap up to its original position using a suitable diameter tube (photo).

17 Make sure that the mating surfaces of the rear housing and the main housing are clean and dry. Smear the mating surfaces with a sealing compound and assemble it to the gearbox (photo).

18 There will be no problem in engaging the selectors if the external selector lever is pulled fully rearwards (photo).

19 Refit the rear housing securing nuts and bolts and tighten to the specified torque wrench setting.

20 On models equipped with a universal joint at the end of the mainshaft, this should now be refitted by engaging the yoke splines with those on the mainshaft and sliding the joint fully home. Secure the universal joint with the socket-headed retaining bolt.

21 Turning to the clutch housing, insert the rubber cup in the groove behind the ball head and fill with grease. The guide sleeve should be smeared with a little molybdenum disulphide grease.

22 Attach the clutch release fork to the ball head (photo).

23 It now only remains to refit the reverse light switch, and the speedometer drive socket assembly. Always use a new O-ring smeared with grease before refitting the speedometer drive socket assembly.

17 Fault diagnosis – manual gearbox

Symptom	Reason(s)
Weak or ineffective synchromesh	Synchronising cones worn, split or damaged
Jumps out of gear	Broken gearbox fork rod spring Gearbox coupling dogs badly worn Selector fork rod groove badly worn
Excessive noise	Incorrect grade of oil in gearbox or oil level too low Bush or needle roller bearings worn or damaged Gear teeth excessively worn or damaged
Excessive difficulty in engaging gear	Clutch problem – see Chapter 5

18 General description (automatic transmission)

An automatic transmission unit is fitted as an alternative to the manual gearbox on models covered by this manual. It is manufactured by Zahnradfabrik Friedrichshafen AG and is of the ZF type. The unit comprises three main parts, namely, hydraulic torque converter, gearbox and automatic control unit.

The torque converter is driven by the engine crankshaft, and automatic operation is obtained to the torque converter transmitting its hydrokinetic energy to the propeller shaft, via a hydraulically controlled epicyclic gear train.

The fluid or hydraulic drive is directly employed in all transmission stages, which results in the automatic selection of forward low and high gear ranges. This takes place with a smooth and continuously variable torque output governed by road speed and position of the accelerator pedal.

The gearbox position, as opposed to the torque converter, provides three forward ratios and one reverse, which are obtained by manipulating two concentric planetary pinions connected by three pairs of planet gears.

The automatic control unit is housed inside the oil pan located below the main gearbox casing, and controls the operation of the multi-plate clutches through a number of hydraulic valves.

The selector lever has six positions and are as follows:

Park (P)   The gearbox is in the neutral position and the rear wheels are locked by a mechanical device located inside the transmission unit. The starter motor may be operated to start the engine

Reverse (R)   This enables the car to be driven backwards. There us a safety notch to prevent accidental enagement when the car is being driven forwards

Neutral (N)   The gearbox is in the neutral position and the rear wheels are not locked. The starter motor may be operated to start the engine

3 (D)   Drive; Full automatic range for normal road use. Car starts in first and as speed increases automatically changes to second and third speeds. Change point depends on position of accelerator pedal

2   Locked in 2nd ratio. The first two gear ratios are used without passing from second to third. Useful for engine braking, for descending steep hills or fast overtaking

1   Locked in 1st ratio. The first gear ratio is used without passing to second. Useful for descending steep hills

Note: In '1' position the car may be started from standstill using the gear selector as with a conventional gearbox. For example: Start and accelerate in '1', change to position '2' for normal increase in speed and then to 3 for normal driving.

Due to the complexity of the automatic transmission unit, if performance is not up to standard or overhaul is necessary, it is imperative that this be left to the local Peugeot garage or a specialist who will have the special equipment and knowledge required for diagnosis and rectification of faults.

19 Automatic transmission – fluid level and maintenance

1 It is important that transmission fluid manufactured to the correct specification is used. The system should be drained and refilled at the recommended intervals (see 'Routine Maintenance' at the beginning of this manual).

2 Regularly check the hydraulic fluid level; the manufacturers recommend every 600 miles (1000 km). The car should be on level ground, the handbrake well applied and the unit at normal operating temperature after at least a 5 mile (8 km) run.

3 Select 'N', start the engine and allow to idle for two to three minutes. Withdraw the dipstick, wipe it clean and refit it. Quickly withdraw it again, and if the level is below the 'MINI' mark top up to the recommended 'MAXI' mark. The difference between the two marks is approximately 1 Imp pint (1.2 US pints, 0.56 litre). Do not overfill the unit as damage can result.

4 When draining the unit remember that if the unit has run recently the hydraulic fluid will be extremely hot so take care.

5 Refit the drain plug and refill with new fluid. It is recommended than 3.5 Imp pints (4.2 US pints, 2 litres) is poured at first. The engine is then started and allowed to idle. Topping up is then continued until the level of the hydraulic fluid is up to the 'MAXI' mark (paragraph 3).

20 Automatic transmission – removal and refitting

Note: Any suspected fault must be referred to the local Peugeot garage or specialist before unit removal, as with this type of transmission the fault must be confirmed, using specialist equipment, *before the unit has been removed from the car. As the car will probably be in the hands of the specialist already, they will prefer to remove the old unit and fit the new one, making any adjustments as necessary. To act as a guide, however, a summary of the necessary operations are given in the following paragraphs.*

1   For safety reasons, disconnect the battery.

2   Jack up the car and support on firmly based stands if a lift or pit are not available.

3   Detach the exhaust downpipe from the manifold and release the front support. Tie the system back out of the way.

4   Undo and remove the speedometer drive securing screw located at the rear end of the transmission casing and detach the speedometer drive. Also detach the cables from the starter lock/reverse light switch noting their exact locations.

5   Refer to Chapter 7 and remove the torque tube and propeller shaft assembly.

6   Disconnect the starter motor cables and remove starter motor.

7   Disconnect the manual selector lever from the lever on the side of the transmission casing.

8   Using a jack or overhead hoist take the weight of the engine.

9   Slacken the bolts securing the engine to the torque converter housing.

10 Withdraw the oil filler pipe and plug the hole to prevent loss of hydraulic fluid.

11 Undo and remove the lower torque converter housing cover plate bolts.

12 Undo and remove the four diaphragm securing bolts. Access to these is through the hole in the bellhousing. Rotate the crankshaft a quarter of a turn at a time.

13 Very carefully ease the engine upwards and towards the front as far as movement of the rubber mountings will allow.

14 Now remove the previously slackened engine to torque converter housing securing bolts.

15 Using a garage hydraulic jack take the weight of the transmission unit.

16 Make quite sure that the torque converter remains on the transmission unit and does not slip forwards. Remember it will be full of hydraulic fluid.

17 Push back the converter with a screwdriver inserted through the hole in the bellhousing as the transmission unit is withdrawn.

18 When the unit is free, lower and remove from under the car.

19 Refitting the automatic transmission unit is the reverse sequence to removal, but the following additional information should be of use.

20 Note the two dowel sleeves located in the front face of the converter housing. This is important when a factory or specialist exchange assembly is being fitted. A defective sleeve can cause serious damage to the converter and driving disc.

21 Tighten the four diaphragm securing bolts, that are located through the hole in the bellhousing to the specified torque wrench setting.

22 When refitting the cables to the starter lock/reverse light switch, the two opposed pins furtherst apart should be connected to the cables coloured green/black and green/white. The other two pins which are closer together should be connected to the cables coloured brown/black and brown.

23 Do not forget to refill the unit with the correct amount of hydraulic fluid before starting the engine

---

21 Fault diagnosis – automatic transmission

As has been mentioned previously, no service repair work or adjustment should be carried out by anyone without the specialist knowledge and equipment to undertake the work. This is also relevant to fault diagnosis. If a fault is evident, consult the local Peugeot garage or specialist.

Chapter 7 Propeller shaft

Contents

Specifications

Type .... Solid steel shaft enclosed in longitudinal torque tube

Maximum run-out of torque tube .... 2 mm (0.07 in)

Maximum warping of torque tube bearing surfaces .... 0.05 mm (0.0019 in)

Maximum run-out of propeller shaft .... 0.2 mm (0.0078 in)

Torque wrench settings	Nm	lbf ft
Torque tube to gearbox	60	44
Torque tube to differential	60	44

1 General description

The propeller shaft arrangement on the Peugeot 504 is of a rather unusual layout. The gearbox and differential unit are connected to each other by a torque tube, and it is inside this tube that the propeller shaft rotates.

On models equipped with independent rear suspension, the torque tube is bolted to the rear face of the gearbox at one end and to the front face of the differential at the other. The propeller shaft has splined ends which mate with female splines in the gearbox and differential unit. There are no universal joints.

On models fitted with a solid 'banjo' type rear axle, the gearbox attachment is slightly different as the propeller shaft and torque tube

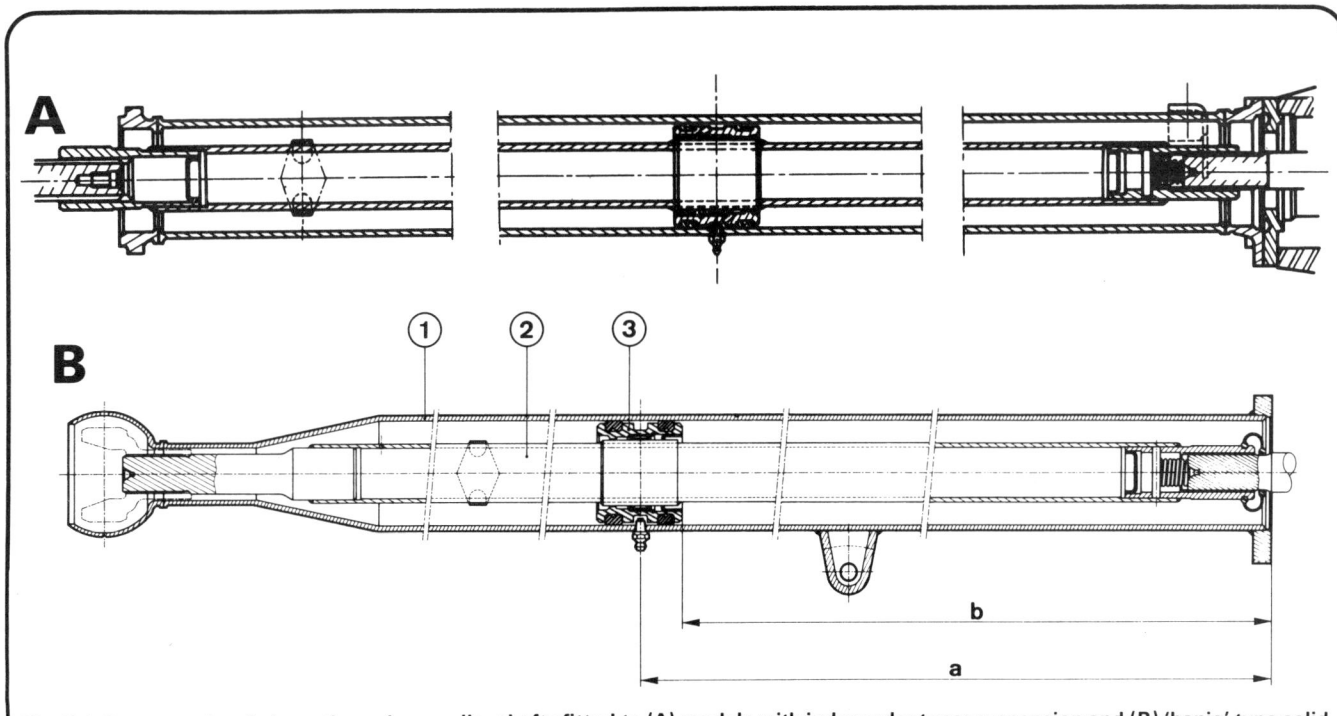

Fig. 7.1 Cross-sectional views through propeller shafts fitted to (A) models with independent rear suspension and (B) 'banjo' type solid rear axle (Sec 1)

1   Torque tube   2   Propeller shaft   3   Centre bearing

a = 956 mm (37.63 in)   b = 925 mm (36.41 in)

must move up and down to cater for suspension movement. The torque tube is therefore allowed to pivot on a spherical bearing bolted to the rear face of the gearbox. A universal joint is also fitted to the rear of the gearbox mainshaft.

On all models the propeller shaft is supported at its centre point by a needle bearing assembly located inside the torque tube. This bearing is lubricated by a grease nipple positioned half way along the tube.

At the end of the shaft which engages with the differential unit, a spring is inserted inside the shaft which prevents any fore-and-aft movement which might otherwise produce wear as well as transmission noise and vibration.

2   Propeller shaft and torque tube – removal

Models with independent rear suspension
1   There are two Peugeot special tools which considerably simplify the removal of the propeller shaft (Fig. 7.2). These are the rear crossmember guide rods, used to support the rear crossmember after detaching it from the car, and the propeller shaft holding plate, used to support the shaft in the torque tube after it has been removed from the gearbox.
2   It is considered worthwhile either borrowing these tools or making them up from scrap material. For example, long bolts and washers can be substituted for the guide rods, and the holding plate can be made from metal or plywood approximately 20 mm (0.78 in) thick.
3   Begin the removal operation by jacking up the rear of the car and supporting it on axle stands. Position the stands under a strong area of the body, not under the rear suspension forward crossmember, as this will be lowered in a subsequent operation. Most of the work will be carried out from beneath the car so make sure that you have adequate working clearance and that the car is quite secure on the stands.
4   Disconnect the exhaust system from its mountings and from the joint at the exhaust manifold. Allow the system to rest on the forward crossmember at the rear and tie it up out of the way at the front.
5   Undo and remove the two socket-headed bolts securing the differential assembly to the rear suspension upper crossmember. Allow the torque tube to rest on the forward crossmember.
6   From inside the car remove the rear seat cushion.
7   With the seat cushion removed, the three forward crossmember mounting nuts on each side of the car will now be visible.
8   Bend back the locktabs on all three nuts and then undo and remove the forwardmost nut. Lift up the locking plate and remove the plastic plug from the access hole.
9   Screw the Peugeot special guide rod, or alternative bolt and flat washer, into the threaded hole in the crossmember which can be seen through the access hole. If the guide rod and tommy bar are being used, leave the tommy bar in the guide rod.
10   Support the underside of the crossmember on a suitable jack, and then undo and remove the remaining two mounting nuts and locking plate.
11   Lower the jack until the weight of the crossmember is taken by the tommy bar in the guide rod, or bolt head if this is being used instead.
12   Now repeat paragraphs 8 to 11 inclusive for the other side of the car.
13   From under the car support the differential on a suitable jack and raise it slightly.
14   Undo and remove the four nuts securing the rear of the torque tube to the differential. Move the differential rearwards, while at the same time disengaging the torque tube and propeller shaft. Make sure the propeller shaft stays in the torque tube as you do this.
15   When sufficient clearance exists, remove the spring located in the rear of the propeller shaft and put it in a safe place, as it is easily lost.
16   Support the rear of the gearbox on a suitable jack and then undo and remove the four socket-headed bolts securing the torque tube to the rear of the gearbox. Withdraw the tube slightly and locate the holding plate in the groove in the propeller shaft. Fasten this plate to the torque tube flange.
17   The torque tube containing the propeller shaft can now be removed by drawing it forwards over the rear crossmember and out from under the car.

Models with solid 'banjo' type rear axle
18   The procedure for removing the propeller shaft on models fitted with a solid rear axle is rather more difficult. It is first necessary to

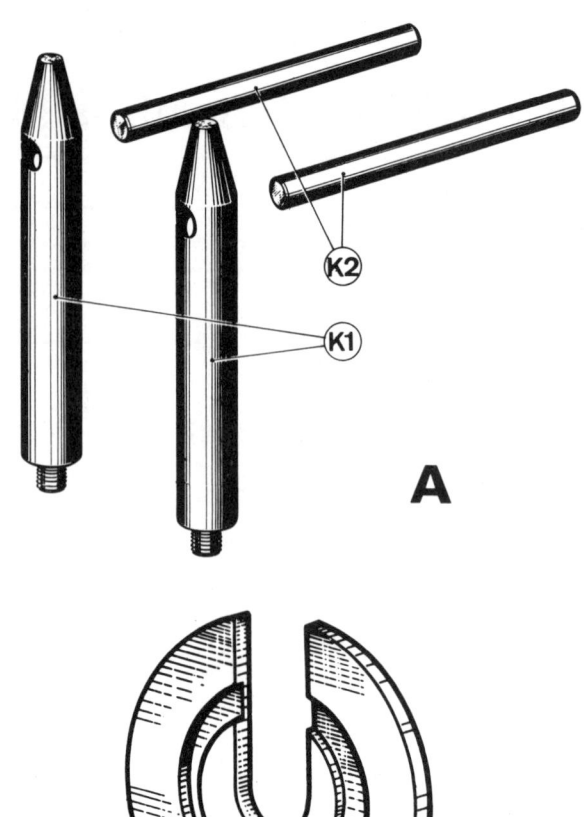

Fig. 7.2 Two special tools desirable for propeller shaft removal (Sec 2)

A   *Rear crossmember guide rods (K1) and tommy bars (K2)*
B   *Propeller shaft holding plate*

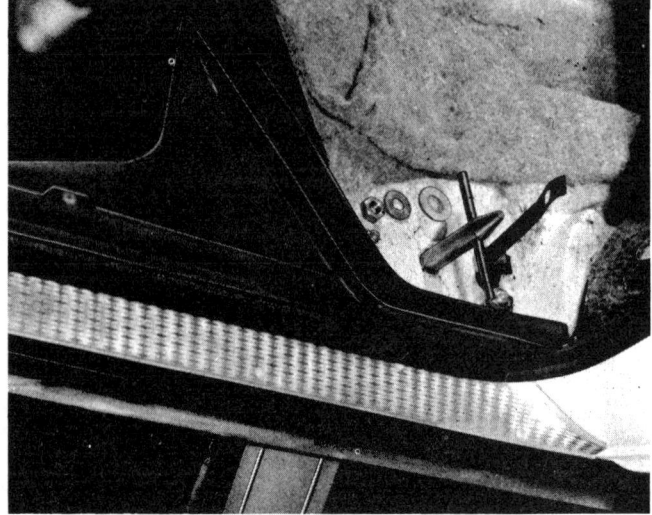

Fig. 7.3 Guide rod in position (Sec 2)

2.20 Vibration damper blocks fitted to rear of gearbox

2.21 Torque tube spherical bearing-to-gearbox mounting bolts

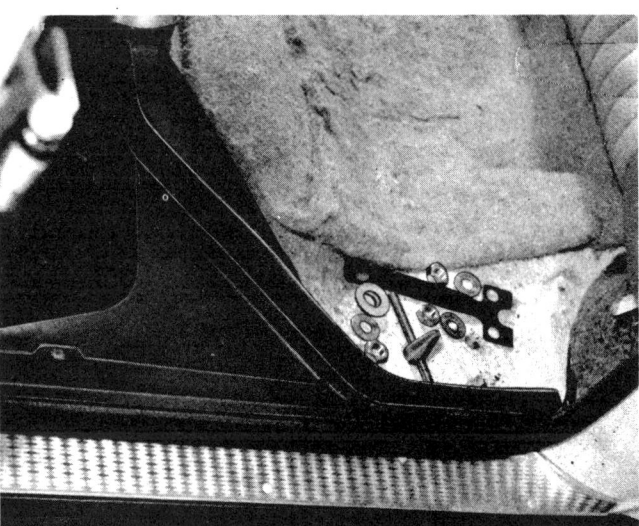

Fig. 7.4 Guide rod taking weight of rear crossmember (Sec 2)

remove the complete rear axle assembly from the car as described in Chapter 8. This is necessary to provide sufficient clearance to enable the propeller shaft and torque tube to be moved rearwards and thus disengaged from the gearbox.

19 With the rear axle removed, disconnect the exhaust system from its mountings and from the joint at the exhaust manifold, and lower the system to the ground.

20 At the rear of the gearbox remove the two rubber vibration damper blocks (if fitted), and also the exhaust bracket is still in position (photo).

21 Undo and remove the four socket-headed bolts securing the torque tube spherical bearing to the rear of the gearbox (photo).

22 Carefully slide the torque tube and propeller shaft rearwards and out of engagement with the gearbox universal joint splines. Lower the assembly to the ground and out from under the car.

3   Propeller shaft and torque tube – refitting

1   Refitting the propeller shaft is basically the reverse sequence to removal. There are, however, several importaant points to be noted and these are given in the following paragraphs.

2   Ensure that all mating surfaces are perfectly clean and that new gaskets are used where applicable.

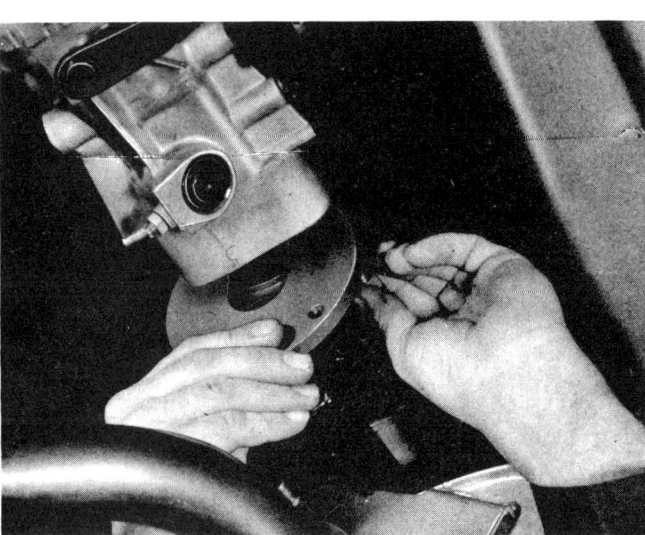

Fig. 7.5 Fitting propeller shaft holding plate (Sec 2)

Fig. 7.6 Removing the propeller shaft and torque tube (Sec 2)

3   Smear the propeller shaft splines with general purpose grease before fitting, and don't forget to fit the spring before connecting the rear of the shaft to the differential (photo).

4   Ensure that all nuts and bolts are tightened to the specified torque wrench settings, and where applicable locked with tab washers.

5   When refitting the exhaust system use a new manifold flange gasket and make sure that the system is clear of the body and suspension when installed.

6   On completion of the installation, grease the propeller shaft centre bearing and, on models equipped with a solid rear axle, the front spherical bearing. Check and, if necessary, top up the gearbox and rear axle oil levels.

4   Propeller shaft and torque tube – inspection

1   Before separating the shaft from the torque tube, give the outside a good clean using paraffin or soluble degreaser. Be careful that your cleaning operations do not allow dirt to enter the tube – a piece of rag wrapped round the propeller shaft where it emerges from the tube should prevent this.

2   When the tube and ends of the shaft are thoroughly clean, withdraw the shaft from the tube, being careful that no strain is placed on the needle bearing by too much lateral movement of the shaft (photo).

3   Clean the shaft as necessary, and inspect for signs of damage and wear – especially at the splines and at the centre where it is supported in the needle bearing.

4   Where a spherical bearing is fitted at the front end of the torque tube, this can be inspected and the oil seal renewed if necessary by undoing the two socket-headed bolts and separating the two bearing halves (photo).

5   Inspect the torque tube carefully for signs of damage. If it shows signs of having been damaged by driving over rough ground it must be checked for run-out as described in the next paragraph.

6   To carry out this check, the tube must be placed between centres and the run-out checked at the centre, close to the grease nipple. At the same time the warping of the bearing surfaces should also be checked. The maximum acceptable distortion of the tube is given in the Specifications.

7   The propeller shaft should be treated in the same way, referring to the Specifications for the maximum acceptable run-out.

8   It is unlikely that the average owner will be able to carry out these checks for himself, but there is nothing difficult about them, and any reasonably equipped engineering works or garage should be able to do them. Whatever course of action is decided upon, it is really only worthwhile if trouble is being experienced in the transmission system. Very often the propeller shaft is removed as part of some other job, such as removing the gearbox or differential, and in this case, though it seems a pity not to have a quick look at the propeller shaft and tube, more elaborate checking is unnecessary.

5   Centre bearing – removal, inspection and refitting

1   The remarks made about checking the shaft and tube in the previous Section apply equally to the removal and checking of the centre bearing. Unless vibration in the transmission has been experienced or inspection of the propeller shaft has indicated that all is not well, it is simplest to leave this bearing alone. However, it is not possible to inspect it properly unless it is removed, and removal is not very difficult.

2   A drift will be required and this can be of brass about 20 mm (0.8 in) thick. Something to drive it will also be required. This must be somewhat longer than the torque tube and should preferably have some means of holding the drift. A piece of pipe would do, or perhaps the wooden handle of a garden tool.

3   Before actually driving the bearing out, insert the drift at the differential end and push it up against the bearing with the rod to be used for drifting it out. Make a mark on this rod just where it enters the tube, so that when the new bearing is being fitted, its correct location in the middle of the torque tube lines up with the grease nipple. Remove the grease nipple.

4   Drive out the bearing until it leaves the tube at the gearbox end.

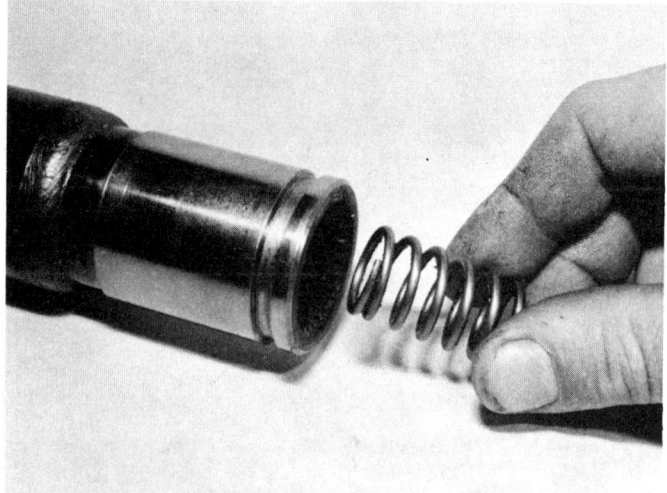

3.3 The preload spring is fitted to the differential end of the propeller shaft

4.2 Withdrawing the propeller shaft from the torque tube

4.4 Torque tube spherical bearing components

5   When the bearing is out of the tube, wash it thoroughly in cleaning fluid, giving it a final rinse with white spirit. Examine it carefully for signs of wear, blueing of the rollers or damage to the cage. If it passes this test, smear it very lightly with oil and put it on the propeller shaft in its correct position. Check for play, and if there is an appreciable amount the bearing should be renewed.

6   To fit the bearing, carry out the removal procedure in reverse. Lubricate the inside of the transmission tube with engine oil, then insert the bearing at the differential end being very careful that it is fitted squarely. Start it off by tapping it very gently with a soft-faced hammer. Once inserted into the tube, drift it along until the mark on the rod has been reached. At this stage go very carefully, checking through the grease nipple hole that the groove in the bearing is correctly placed. Finally refit the grease nipple. It is best not to grease the bearing until the propeller shaft is back into the tube. Do not forget to lubricate it otherwise the bearing will fail within a short period of time.

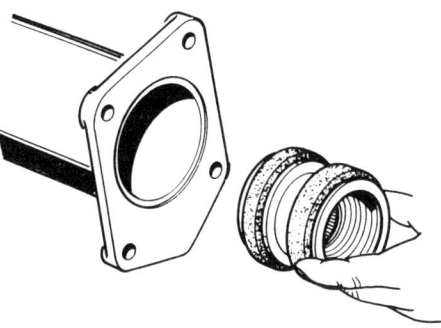

Fig. 7.7 Propeller shaft centre bearing (Sec 5)

6 Fault diagnosis – propeller shaft

Symptom	Reason(s)
Vibration	Wear in propeller shaft splines Torque tube distorted Excessive propeller shaft run-out Centre bearing worn Front universal joint worn (where applicable)
Knock or clunk when taking up drive	Wear in propeller shaft splines Front universal joint worn *See also Chapter 8 'Fault diagnosis – rear axle'*

Chapter 8 Rear axle

Contents

Specifications

Type .... Hypoid bevel; mounted on crossmember with driveshafts to rear wheels, or in conventional 'banjo' casing with halfshafts driving rear wheels

Axle ratios
Saloon .... 3.7 : 1
Estate .... 4.2 : 1
Family estate .... 4.1 : 1

Lubricant capacity .... 1.6 litres (2.8 Imp pints, 3.3 US pints)

Torque wrench settings

	Nm	lbf ft
Differential to crossmember	37	27
Rear hub to suspension arm	40	29
Driveshaft retaining nut	250	189
Roadwheels	60	44
Differential side covers	8	5.8
Torque tube to differential	60	44

1 General description

The Peugeot 504 Diesel models covered by this manual may be fitted with either a conventional 'banjo' type solid rear axle or, on models equipped with independent rear suspension, a fixed differential assembly and two equal length driveshafts.

Where a conventional axle is employed, the assembly comprises a hypoid gear differential housed in a 'banjo' type solid axle casing. Drive to the rear wheels is by solid steel halfshafts, splined at their inner ends into the differential gears and supported at their outer ends by ball bearings.

Fore-and-aft movement of the axle is controlled by the torque tube which is bolted to the front of the differential. Lateral movement is prevented by means of a Panhard rod and two tie-rods connected between the axle and torque tube. Coil spring suspension is used in conjunction with an anti-roll bar and double-acting shock absorbers.

On models equipped with independent rear suspension, the hypoid gear differential is attached to a crossmember which is secured to the underside of the body. Drive to the rear wheels is by two

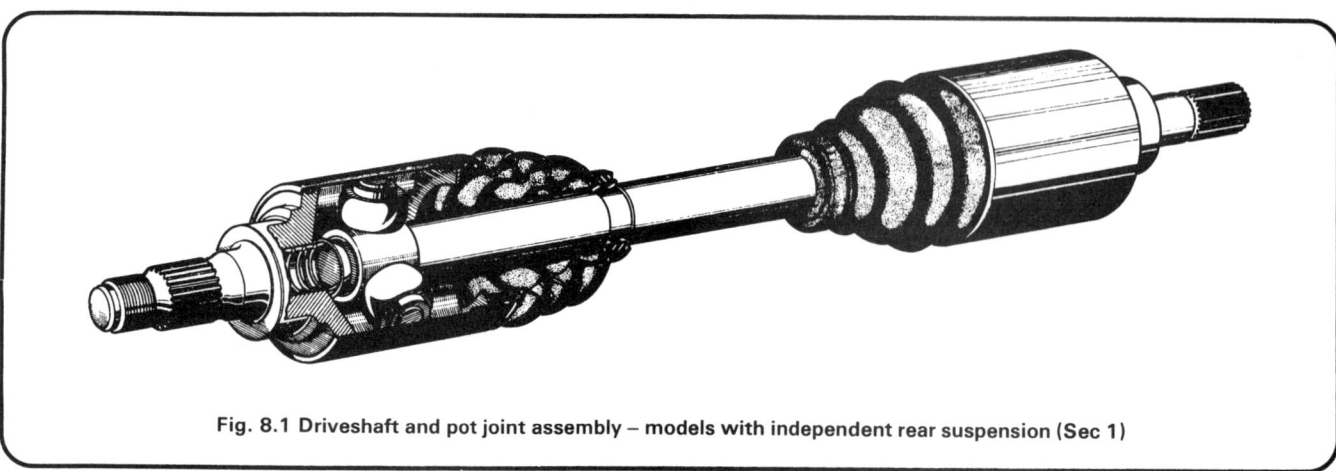

Fig. 8.1 Driveshaft and pot joint assembly – models with independent rear suspension (Sec 1)

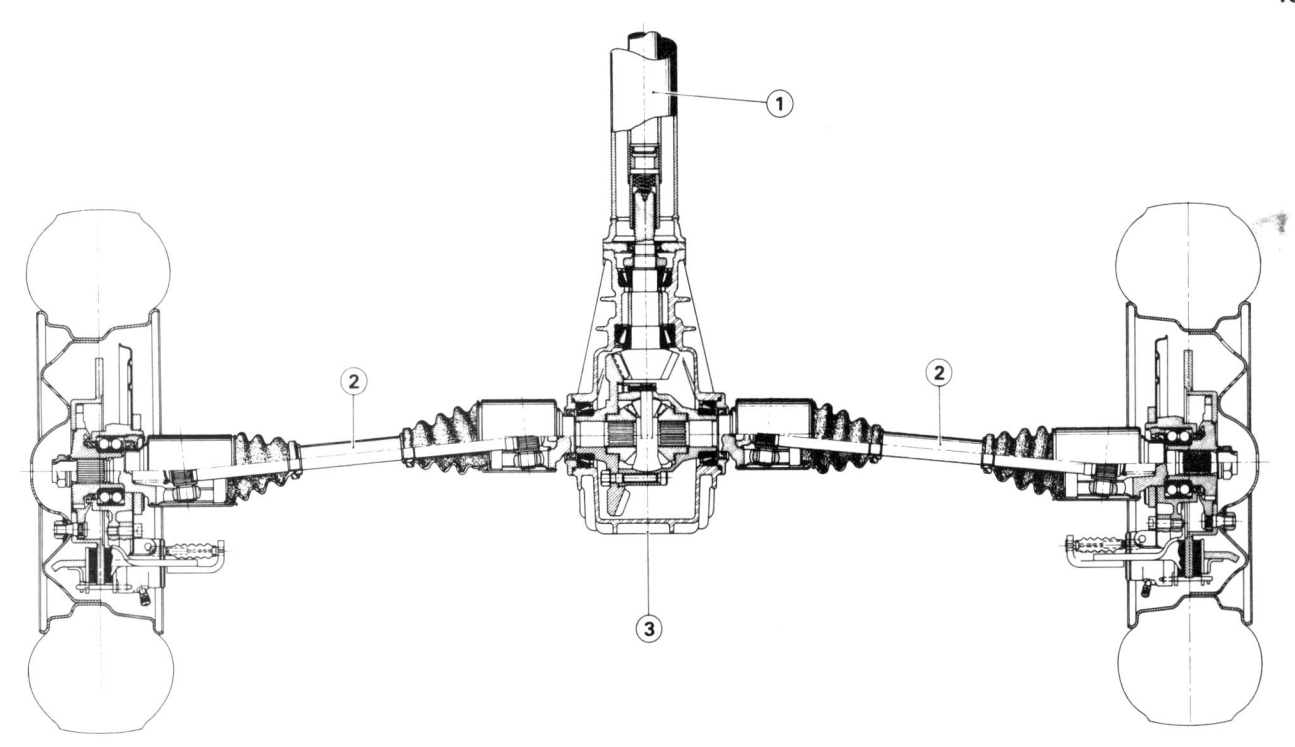

Fig. 8.2 Cross-sectional view of rear axle assembly – models with independent rear suspension (Sec 1)

1   Torque tube   2   Driveshafts   3   Differential

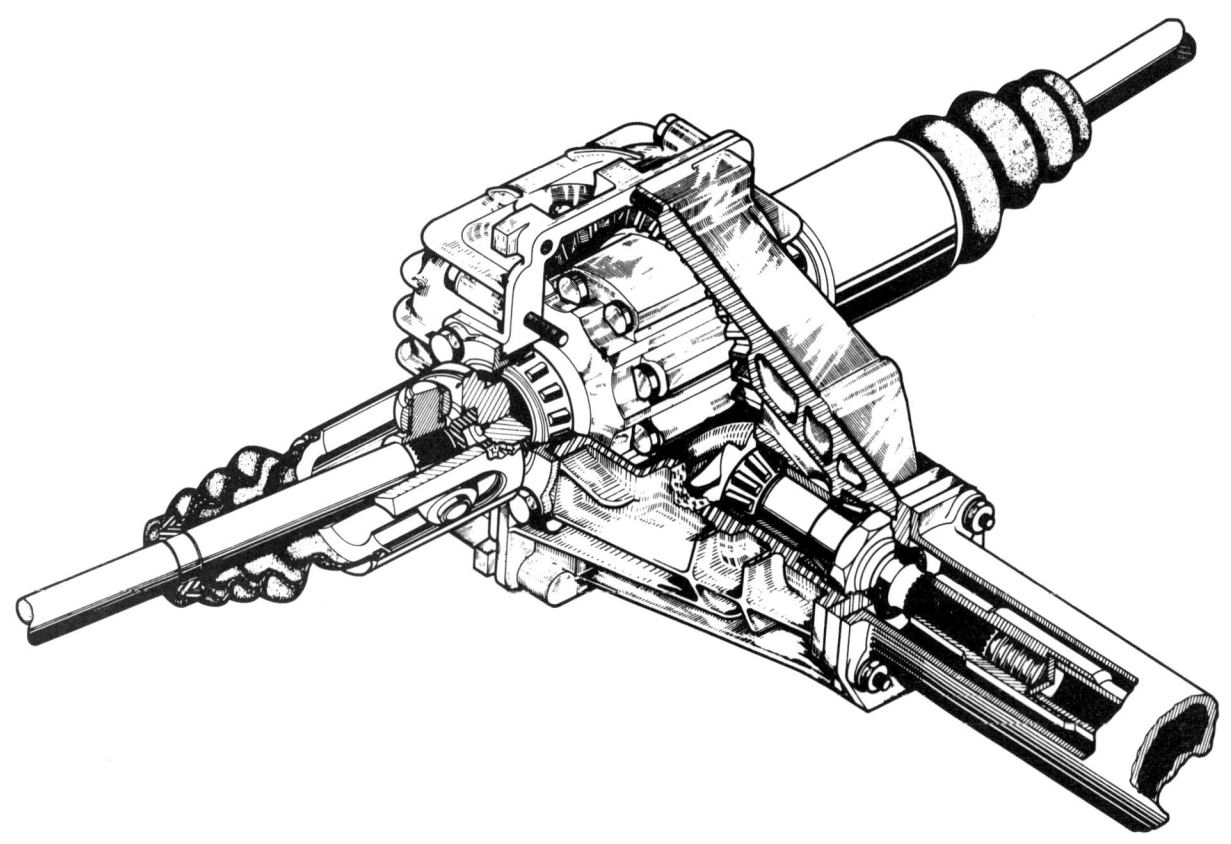

Fig. 8.3 Sectional view of differential assembly – models with independent rear suspension (Sec 1)

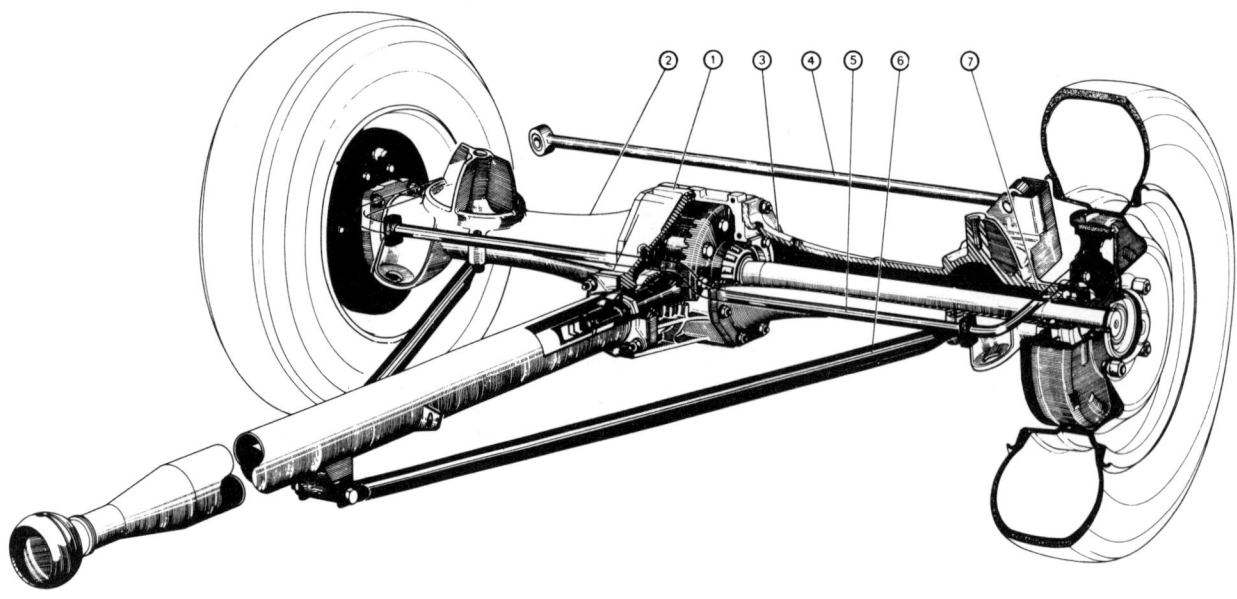

Fig. 8.4 Sectional view of 'banjo' type solid axle fitted to saloon models (Sec 1)

1 Differential housing	3 Axle casing (left)	5 Anti-roll bar	7 Oil seal
2 Axle casing (right)	4 Panhard rod	6 Tie-rod	

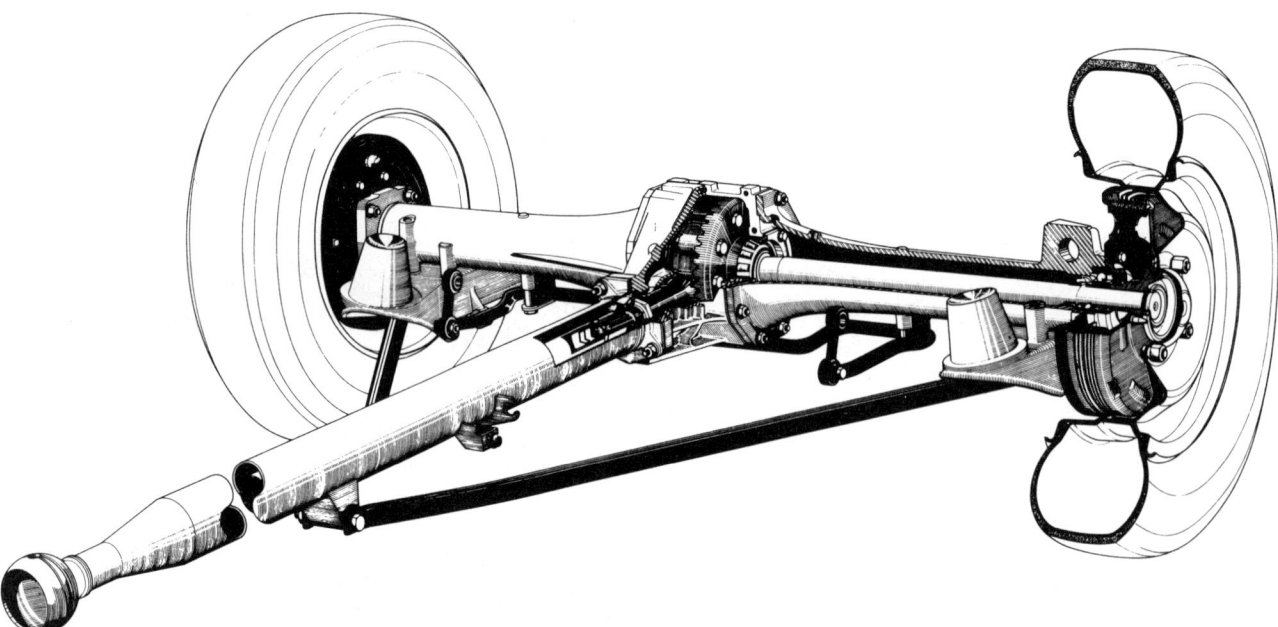

Fig. 8.5 Sectional view of 'banjo' type solid axle fitted to estate and family estate models (Sec 1)

driveshafts, each one fitted with two internal sliding, constant velocity, three-pronged pot joints. The outer (wheel end) pot joint ensures the sliding action of the shaft and includes a spring which exerts constant pressure on the shaft. This, combined with the high sliding qualities of the three pronged pot joint, allows the driveshaft to increase or decrease in length consistent with rear suspension movement.

The driveshafts are splined at both ends. The inner ends engage with the differential gears and the outer ends with the rear wheel hubs, which are supported by ball bearings. Suspension is by coil springs and trailing arms in conjunction with double-acting shock absorbers and an anti-roll bar.

Due to the complex nature of the differential assembly and the need for specialist knowledge and equipment, the repair and overhaul of this unit is considered outside the scope of this manual. Should a

problem occur on the differential, it is advisable to entrust the repair work to a Peugeot main dealer who will have the necessary special tools and equipment.

2   Rear axle (solid type) – removal and refitting

1   Jack up the rear of the car and support the body on axle stands.
2   Undo the rear axle drain plug and allow the oil to drain into a suitable container. When all the oil has drained, refit and tighten the drain plug.
3   Refer to Chapter 9 and disconnect the handbrake cables from the rear brake shoes and brake backplates. Remove the wire clips securing the cables to the axle tie-rods and lower the cables to the ground.

4 Disconnect the tension spring from the brake compensator and the bracket on the torque tube.

5 Using a brake hose clamp or self-gripping wrench with suitably protected jaws, firmly clamp the flexible rear brake hose. This will prevent loss of hydraulic fluid when the hose is disconnected.

6 Now undo and remove the rigid metal brake pipe union from the end of the hose, and then detach the hose from the bracket on the torque tube. Plug or tape over the disconnected ends to prevent dirt ingress.

7 Undo and remove the nuts securing the anti-roll bar links to each side of the axle casing and then detach the links from the axle (photo).

8 Extract the split pin and undo and remove the nut and bolt securing the Panhard rod to the axle casing.

9 Place a sturdy jack under the centre of the axle and jack it up slightly. Ensure that the axle is well supported and not likely to slip off.

10 Undo and remove the shock absorber lower mounting nuts and thrust pads (photo).

11 Carefully lower the axle until all tension is released from the coil road springs. When they are completely free, lift them out of their locations in the body crossmember and axle.

12 Undo and remove the nut and bolt securing the two axle tie-rods to the torque tube (photo).

13 Undo and remove the four nuts and washers securing the torque tube to the front of the differential housing (photo).

2.7 Removing the anti-roll bar links from the rear axle

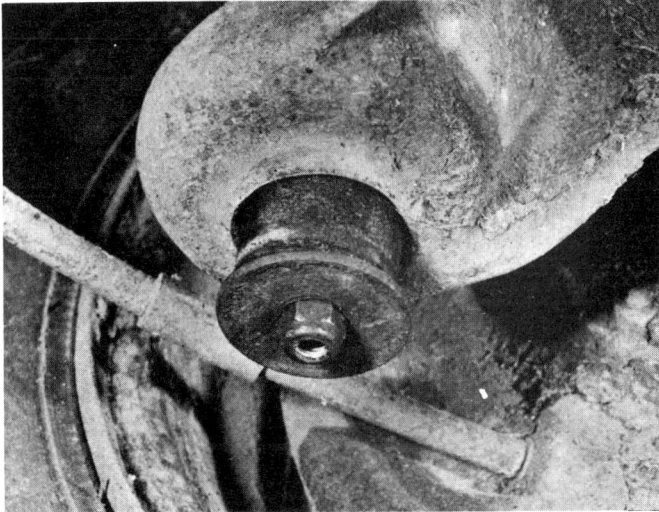

2.10 Removing the shock absorber lower nut, washer and thrust block

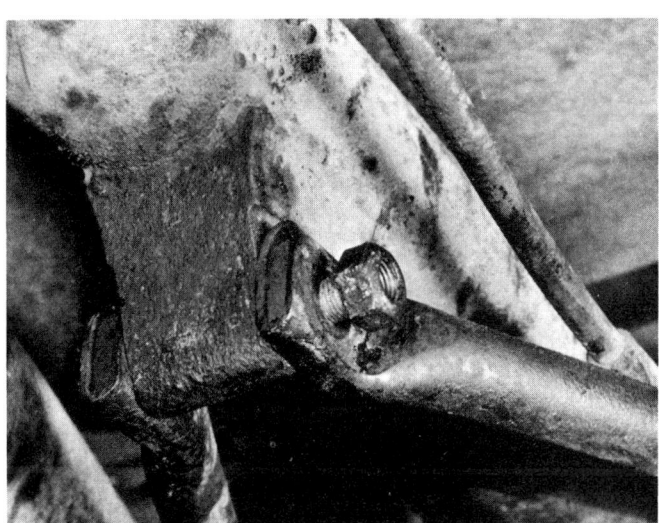

2.12 Axle tie-rod to torque tube retaining bolt removal

2.13 Torque tube to differential housing retaining nuts

2.14 Disengaging the rear axle from the torque tube

14 Make a final check that everything is disconnected and then lower the axle until there is just sufficient clearance to move it rearward and out of engagement with the torque tube (photo). As the axle comes free, ensure that the propeller shaft slides off the differential pinion splines and stays behind in the torque tube. Take care also that the preload spring in the end of the propeller shaft does not fall out unnoticed.

15 Once the axle is clear of the propeller shaft, it can be fully lowered and withdrawn from under the car.

16 Refitting the rear axle is the reverse sequence to removal bearing is mind the following points:

    (a) *Ensure that the preload spring is in place in the propeller shaft before reconnecting it to the differential housing.*
    (b) *Bleed the rear brakes on completion of the installation (Chapter 9)*
    (c) *Refill the rear axle with the specified grade of oil*
    (d) *Observe the correct torque wrench settings during refitting*

3.4a Withdraw the halfshaft ...

---

3   Rear axle halfshafts (solid type axle) – removal and refitting

1 Jack up the rear of the car and support it on axle stands. Remove the appropriate rear roadwheel.

2 Undo and remove the retaining screws, release fully the handbrake and then withdraw the brake drum. If it is tight, tap its circumference with a soft-faced mallet.

3 Undo and remove the seven nuts, at the rear of the brake backplate, that secure the halfshaft outer bearing and brake backplate to the axle flange.

4 The halfshaft can now be removed from the axle by tapping the wheel hub flange with a soft-faced mallet. **Note:** *After withdrawing the halfshaft, the brake backplate will remain in position on the axle supported only by the brake hydraulic pipe. To avoid straining the pipe temporarily attach the backplate to the axle flange using a scrap nut and bolt (photos).*

5 Should the outer halfshaft bearing or oil seal require renewal, this work should be entrusted to your Peugeot dealer, as a press and other special tools are needed to remove the bearing (photo).

6 Refit the halfshaft in the reverse sequence to removal, ensuring that the mating surfaces are perfectly clean and new gaskets are used where applicable. Remember to check and if necessary top up the rear axle oil level on completion of the installation.

3.4b ... and then secure the backplate with an old nut and bolt

---

4   Driveshafts (independent suspension) – removal and refitting

1 Jack up the rear of the car and support it securely on stands placed under the rear suspension arms. Remove the appropriate rear roadwheel.

2 Refer to Chapter 9 and remove the brake pads.

3 Using a small screwdriver, prise open the clip securing the hydraulic brake pipe to the rear suspension arm.

4 Undo and remove the two socket-headed bolts securing the brake caliper to the hub. Carefully lift the caliper off the disc and suspend it from a convenient place on the bodywork, using string or wire. Take care not to distort the brake pipe excessively.

5 Mark the relationship of the brake disc to the hub flange, undo and remove the two retaining screws and lift off the disc.

6 Using a socket and short extension bar inserted through the hole in the hub flange, undo and remove the four bolts securing the hub to the suspension arm.

7 The driveshaft assembly can now be withdrawn by tapping the edge of the hub flange with a soft-faced mallet. If it is a tight fit refit the roadwheel and strike the tyre firmly until the shaft is removed. Alternatively two long bolts screwed into the rear of the suspension arm will bear against the hub flange as they are tightened and force the hub out of the suspension arm.

8 With the driveshaft removed from the car, mount the hub flange in a strong vice and then undo and remove the driveshaft retaining nut. This nut will be *very* tight so ensure that the flange is securely gripped in the vice.

9 Now tap the driveshaft out of the hub flange using a soft-faced mallet. However, if it is tight it will be necessary to resort to using a press.

3.5 The halfshaft and bearing assembly

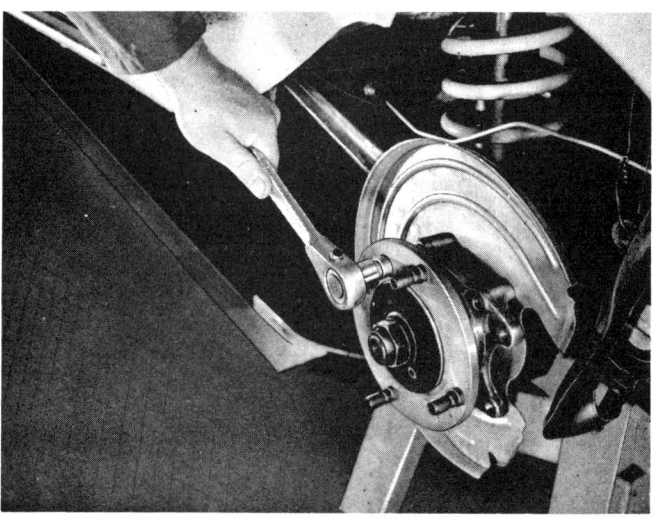

Fig. 8.6 Removing the hub carrier retaining bolts (Sec 4)

10 To refit the driveshaft first make sure that all parts are thoroughly clean.

11 Smear some general purpose grease onto the driveshaft splines and then engage the driveshaft into the hub. Refit the washer and new retaining nut, and with the hub flange securely supported, tighten the nut to the specified torque wrench setting and lock it with a punch.

12 Check that the oil seal in the differential is in good order, and then fill the space between the seal lips with general purpose grease. Also apply some grease to the driveshaft splines.

13 Introduce the driveshaft through the suspension arm and engage the inner end of the shaft into the differential.

14 Using a soft-faced mallet, tap the driveshaft until the hub is fully home in the suspension arm.

15 Refit the retaining bolts and tighten them to the specified torque wrench setting.

16 Refit the brake disc, making sure that the previously made marks are aligned, and then refit the retaining screws.

17 Position the brake caliper over the disc and refit the retaining bolts, tightened to the specified torque (Chapter 9). Affix the brake pipe to the suspension arm using the small clip.

18 Refer to Chapter 9 and refit the brake pads.

19 Check and, if necessary, top up the differential oil level, refit the roadwheel and lower the car to the ground.

Fig. 8.7 Removing the driveshaft retaining nut (Sec 4)

1   Hub   3   Hub nut
2   Thrust washer

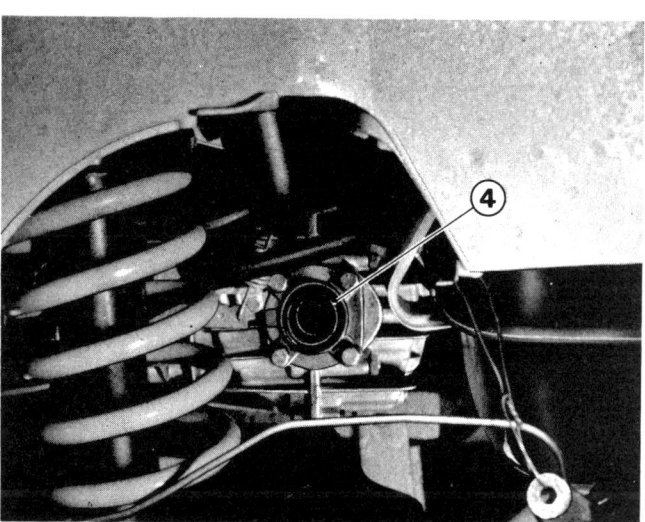

Fig. 8.8 Differential side cover oil seal (4) (Sec 4)

Fig. 8.9 Bending back the end of the driveshaft pot joint cover
(Sec 5)

a   Adhesive tape

Fig. 8.10 Removal of cover (Sec 5)

Fig. 8.11 Using adhesive tape to retain bearing pack (Sec 5)

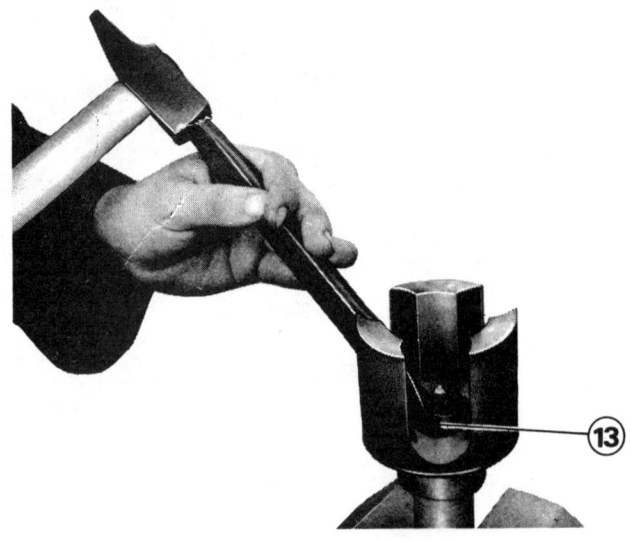

Fig. 8.12 Chiseling out the nylon stop (13) (Sec 5)

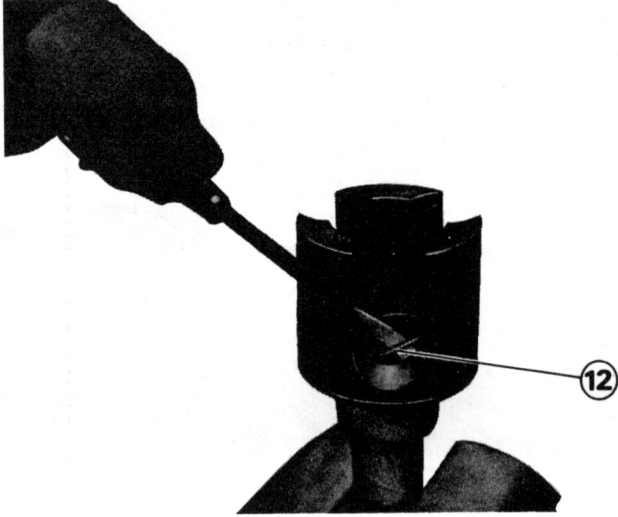

Fig. 8.13 Removing the retaining washer (12) (sec 5)

5 Driveshafts (independent suspension) – dismantling, overhaul and reassembly

1   Mount the driveshaft vertically in a vice.
2   Wrap some adhesive tape around the oil seal bearing face of the tulip to protect it from damage.
3   Using a pair of end cutters carefully bend back the end of the cover. Now tap the end of the cover downwards to disengage it from the tulip.
4   The tulip can now be removed by lifting it up vertically off the end of the driveshaft. If working on the outer (wheel side) joint, recover the spring and thrust cap.
5   Wrap some adhesive tape around the bearing pack. This is a matched assembly and the components must not be separated or interchanged.
6   Using old rags carefully remove as much grease as possible from the bearing pack. *Do not use any solvents on this assembly.*
7   Place the bearing pack over suitably protected vice jaws. Using a brass drift of suitable diameter, drift the driveshaft downwards and out of the bearing pack. Don't forget to hold the driveshaft or it will drop on the floor. If the shaft is very tight it may be necessary to resort to using a press. **Note:** *There is no need to remove the three punch marks on the shaft as they will disappear during removal.*

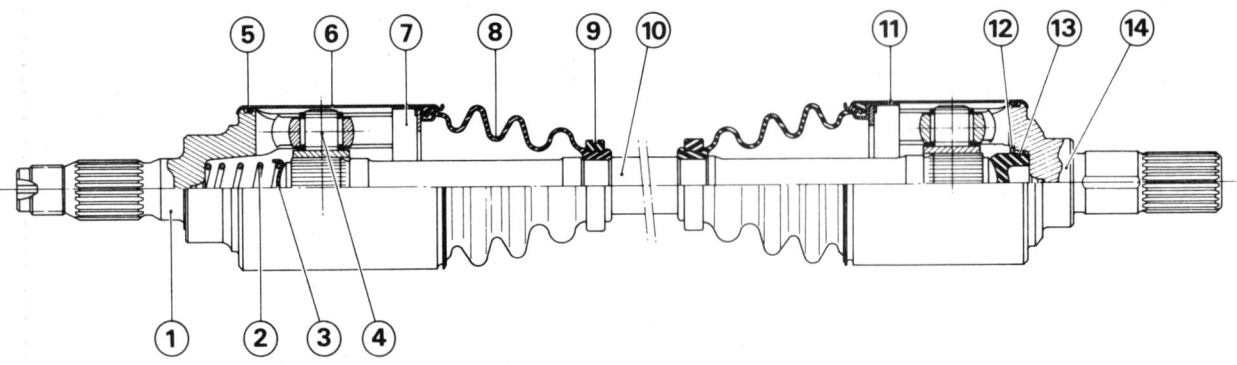

Fig. 8.14 Sectional view of the assembled driveshaft (Sec 5)

1 Tulip	5 O-ring	9 Retaining ring	12 Thrust washer
2 Spring	6 Cover (length 113 mm)	10 Shaft	13 Stop
3 Cup	7 Spacer	11 Cover (length 99 mm)	14 Tulip
4 Journal and bearing pack	8 Gaiter		

8 Once the bearing pack is removed, the cover and rubber gaiter can be withdrawn from the end of the driveshaft.

9 The pot joint at the other end of the driveshaft can now be removed, if necessary, using the above procedure.

10 Should it be necessary to renew both covers and rubber gaiters it is only necessary to remove one bearing pack. Both covers and rubber gaiters can be withdrawn from one end of the shaft.

11 Remove the O-ring seal from the groove in the end of the tulip and then clean away all traces of old grease.

12 In the event of wear or damage to the differential side tulip nylon stop, cut this away using a sharp chisel. Now, using a screwdriver, hook out the nylon stop retaining thrust washer.

13 Remove the punch marks from inside the tulip using a small rotary file or stone.

14 Finally clean out the tulip thoroughly so that all traces of abrasive metal are removed.

15 Inspect the dismantled components for wear, distortion or damage, paying close attention to the bearing pack and its track in the tulip, and also the splines on the driveshaft and tulip. A new protector kit consisting of rubber gaiter, cover, spacer, O-ring and retainer should be obtained for each dismantled joint as a matter of course. It will also be necessary to obtain the special grease for lubrication of the bearing pack. This is obtainable from Peugeot dealers pre-packed in exact quantities for each joint.

16 Before proceeding with reassembly, refer to Fig. 8.15 and note the direction of fitment of the driveshaft and joint covers. The outer (wheel side) pot joint (the one with the spring and thrust cup) must be fitted to the end of the driveshaft having the widest rubber gaiter stop collar. The longer of the two joint covers is also fitted to this end of the shaft.

17 Begin reassembly by fitting the rubber gaiter over the spacer and then inserting this assembly into the cover. When correctly assembled, the spacer should abut the inside flange of the cover.

18 Clamp the driveshaft vertically in a vice and slide on the retaining ring and previously assembled gaiter and cover.

19 Refit the bearing pack to the driveshaft, tapping it fully home using a tube of suitable diameter as a drift. Check that the lower part of the bearing pack is flush with the bottom of the groove in the driveshaft when installed.

20 Using a centre punch make three equidistant punch marks so as to spread the splines on the shaft toward the hub of the bearing pack.

21 If the nylon stop has been removed from the pot joint fitted to the inner (differential end) of the shaft, refit a new stop to the interior of the tulip.

22 Refit the locking thrust washer over the stop and then, using a centre punch, make three equidistant punch marks on the inner flange of the tulip to retain the washer.

23 Pack the inside of the tulip and rubber gaiter with the correct quantity of the specified grease.

24 Remove the adhesive tape from the bearing pack.

25 Place a new O-ring oil seal into the groove in the tulip and then refit the tulip to the shaft. If working on the outer (wheel end) pot joint ensure that the cup and spring are in position on the end of the shaft before fitting the tulip.

26 Slide the tulip into the cover as far as it will go and hold it in this position, while at the same time crimping over the top edge of the cover with a small hammer.

27 Slide the retaining ring over the small end of the rubber gaiter.

28 It is now necessary to expel all the trapped air from inside the rubber gaiter. To do this, insert a small screwdriver between the small end of the gaiter and the shaft. Take care not to puncture the gaiter as you do this.

29 Now with the screwdriver in position push the outer (wheel end) pot joint toward the centre of the driveshaft until the gaiter is compressed to a dimension of 88 mm (3.46 in). Hold the joint in this position and pull out the screwdriver.

30 If working on the inner (differential end) pot joint, push the joint towards the centre of the driveshaft as far as it will go and then pull out the screwdriver.

31 Finally check the operation of the joints, they must slide and swivel freely with no deformation of the rubber gaiter.

---

6 Differential (independent suspension) – removal and refitting

1 Jack up the rear of the car and support it securely on axle stands positioned under the rear suspension arms.

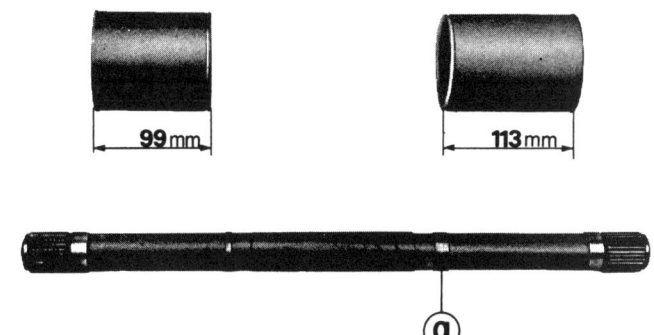

Fig. 8.15 The wide stop collar (a) of the driveshaft must be fitted to the wheel side pot joint (Sec 5)

Fig. 8.16 Brake compensator lever detached from pivot (Sec 6)

Fig. 8.17 Removing the differential retaining bolts (Sec 6)

2   Refer to Section 4, and remove the left-hand driveshaft assembly.
3   Remove the drain plug from the differential housing and allow the oil to drain into a suitable container. When the oil has drained, refit and tighten the drain plug.
4   Detach the brake compensator lever pivot from the underside of the bodywork and allow it to hang from its spring.
5   Undo and remove the four bolts securing the torque tube to the differential housing (photo).
6   Undo and remove the two socket-headed bolts securing the differential housing to the upper crossmember.
7   Disengage the differential housing from the propeller shaft and torque tube by moving it rearwards. Now move the housing to the left to disengage the right-hand driveshaft. The differential can now be withdrawn from under the car. Take care during this operation not to lose the preload spring from the end of the propeller shaft which may fly out as the differential is moved rearwards.
8   Refitting the differential is the reverse sequence to removal, bearing in mind the following points:

    (a) *Check the condition of the oil seals in the differential housing before refitting, and if necessary renew them as described in Section 7. If satisfactory, pack the space between the lips with general purpose grease*
    (b) *Apply grease to the driveshaft splines before inserting them into the differential*
    (c) *Ensure that the preload spring is in place in the end of the propeller shaft*
    (d) *Ensure that all nuts and bolts are tightened to the specified torque wrench settings*
    (e) *Don't forget to refill the differential with the correct grade of oil on completion of the installation*

7   Differential oil seal (independent suspension) – removal and refitting

1   Refer to Section 4, and remove the appropriate driveshaft.
2   Undo and remove the drain plug and allow the oil to drain into a suitable container placed beneath the differential. When the oil has drained refit the drain plug.
3   Undo and remove the four bolts securing the differential side cover to the casing. Now lift off the side cover complete with oil seal, and recover the O-ring.
4   Suitably support the side cover on blocks of wood or over open protected vice jaws, and drift out the old oil seal using a tube of suitable diameter or a lever.
5   To refit a new oil seal first ensure that the side cover is thoroughly cleaned with all traces of old gasket removed (where applicable).
6   Dip the new oil seal in engine oil and then place it in position squarely over the side cover. The open side of the seal must face toward the differential when fitted.
7   Using a block of wood to keep the seal square and spread the load, tap the seal into place until the outer face of the seal is flush with the edge of the side cover.
8   Position a new O-ring into the recess in the differential housing.
9   Refit the side cover and retaining bolts to the differential (using a new gasket where applicable), and tighten the bolts to the specified torque wrench settings. Tighten the bolts diagonally to avoid distorting the side cover.
10   Refer to Section 4, and refit the driveshaft assembly.
11   When reassembly is complete, refill the differential with the correct grade of lubricant.

8   Rear hubs, bearings and oil seals (independent suspension) – dismantling and reassembly

1   The dismantling and reassembly of the rear hub assembly is considered to be beyond the scope of the home mechanic.
2   The bearing is retained in the hub by a threaded collar and can only be satisfactorily removed using Peugeot special tools. Once the collar is removed further special tools are needed to extract the bearing and oil seals.
3   Should the bearing or oil seals require renewal, the best course of action is to remove the hub assembly from the driveshaft as described in Section 5, and then entrust the overhaul work to your nearest Peugeot dealer.

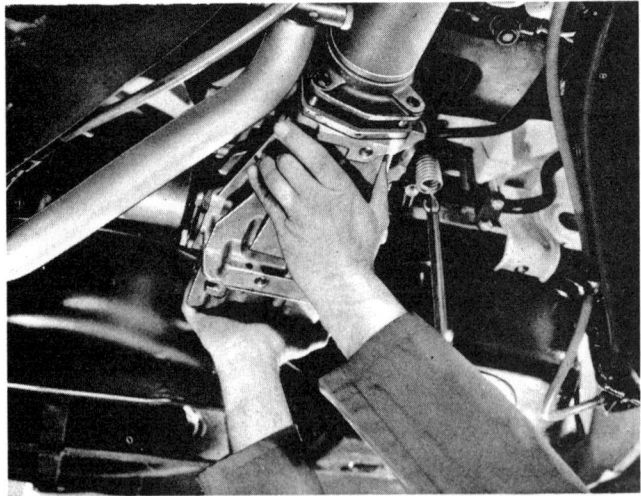
Fig. 8.18 Removing the differential (Sec 6)

6.5 Removing the torque tube retaining bolts

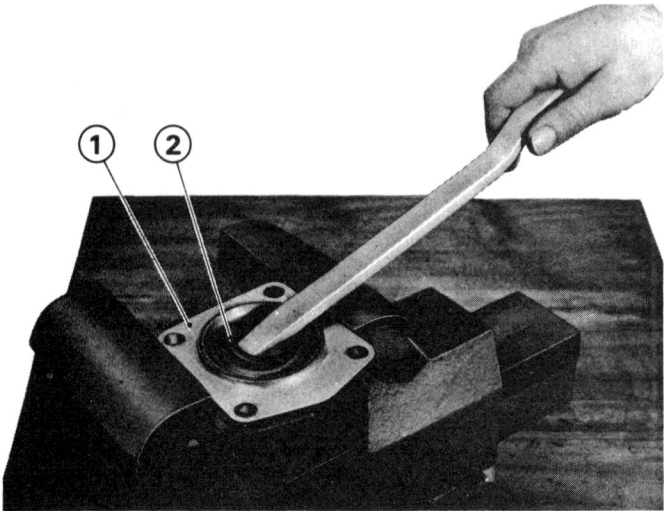
Fig. 8.19 Removing the oil seal (2) from the differential side cover (1) (Sec 7)

9 Fault diagnosis – rear axle

Symptom	Reason(s)
Vibration	Worn driveshaft pot joints Worn halfshaft or driveshaft bearings Excessive run-out or distortion of driveshafts Wheels out of balance Defective tyre
Noise	Insufficient lubricant Excessive wear of gears or bearings
Clunk on acceleration or deceleration	Incorrect mesh of crownwheel and pinion Worn driveshaft pot joints Worn halfshaft or driveshaft splines Worn drive pinion splines *See also Chapter 7 'Fault diagnosis – propeller shaft'*
Oil leakage	Defective or worn pinion, side cover or halfshaft oil seal Blocked differential housing breather

Chapter 9 Braking system

Contents

Specifications

General

System type	Single or dual circuit hydraulic, servo assisted, on all four wheels
Front brakes	Disc with twin piston, floating armature caliper
Rear brakes:	
Models with independent rear suspension	Disc with twin piston, floating armature caliper
Models with 'banjo' solid axle	Drum with single leading and trailing shoe
Handbrake	Mechanical on rear wheels only

Front brakes

Disc diameter	273 mm (10.75 in)
Disc thickness:	
New	12.75 mm (0.5 in)
Machined (minimum)	10.00 mm (0.4 in)
Disc run-out (maximum)	0.07 mm (0.003 in)
Minimum brake pad thickness	2.5 mm (0.1 in) and before warning light operates (where fitted)

Rear disc brakes

Disc diameter	273 mm (10.75 in)
Disc thickness:	
New	11.25 mm (0.44 in)
Machined (minimum)	9 mm (0.35 in)
Disc run-out (maximum)	0.07 mm (0.003 in)
Minimum brake pad thickness	2.5 mm (0.1 in), and before warning light operates (where fitted)

Rear drum brakes

Drum diameter	280 mm (11.03 in)
Wheel cylinder piston diameter	22 mm (0.86 in)
Minimum lining thickness	1.52 mm (0.06 in)

Torque wrench settings

	Nm	lbf ft
Bleed screws	7	5
Caliper securing bolts:		
Front	70	51
Rear	43	31
Disc-to-hub bolts	47	34
Handbrake lever casing nuts	6	4.5
Outer cable retaining collar	10	7
Disc brake pad retaining fork	17	12

1 General description

Disc brakes are fitted to the front wheels on all models, and either disc or drum brakes are employed at the rear. This is dependent on whether the car is equipped with a 'banjo' type solid rear axle or independent rear suspension.

The disc is of cast iron and is secured to the hub by four bolts. The caliper, which is mounted over the disc and contains the pads, incorporates two pistons mounted on one side of the disc. The pad on the other side of the disc is brought into contact with the disc by using an armature which slides in the caliper body.

Basically the rear disc brakes are similar to those fitted to the front with the exception that the brake pads are slightly smaller.

The rear drum brakes (when fitted) are of the leading/trailing shoe type and operated by a hydraulic wheel cylinder.

All four brakes are hydraulically operated via a pendant pedal positioned under the instrument panel. When the pedal is depressed, a master cylinder, which is connected to the brake pedal, is brought into operation. To assist the driver and reduce brake pedal pressures a vacuum servo unit is located between the brake pedal and master cylinder. Vacuum for the system is created by a pump, mounted on the front of the engine, and a tank located on the left-hand inner wing panel. The pump is driven from the water pump pulley by a V-belt.

The master cylinder incorporates a brake fluid reservoir which supplies both the clutch and brake hydraulic circuits. On some models is a special float contact in the reservoir cap. This is in circuit with a warning light on the instrument panel which comes on when the level of fluid is too low for safety. This warning light also indicates when the brake pads have reached their minimum thickness, and when the handbrake has been applied. On some models the warning light also indicates a drop in hydraulic pressure.

A brake hydraulic pressure compensating device is fitted into the system and this varies the front-to-rear brake line pressure. It is also attached to the rear suspension to accommodate differences in vehicle load. Basically it comprises a hollow piston having two different parts, each fitted with a sealing ring. A hollow plug with a slot on its front face is screwed to the piston to act as a guide for a regulator valve which is held on its seat by a spring. A metal link connects the device to the rear suspension by a spring, and it is this which enables the hydraulic pressure to the rear brakes to be varied.

The mechanical handbrake system is cable operated and provides an independent means of rear brake application.

On models equipped with drum brakes at the rear, these will be either self-adjusting or manually adjustable by two eccentric cam adjusters accessible from the rear of the brake backplate.

Disc brake systems are self-adjusting in that as the lining material of the brake pads becomes worn, so hydraulic fluid will be drawn from the reservoir to supplement that already in the brake system. No means of manual adjustment therefore is provided.

2 Hydraulic system – bleeding

1   If any of the hydraulic components in the braking system have been removed or disconnected, or if the fluid level in the master cylinder has been allowed to fall appreciably, it is inevitable that air will have been introduced into the system. The removal of all this air from the hydraulic system is essential if the brakes are to function correctly, and the process of removing it is known as bleeding.

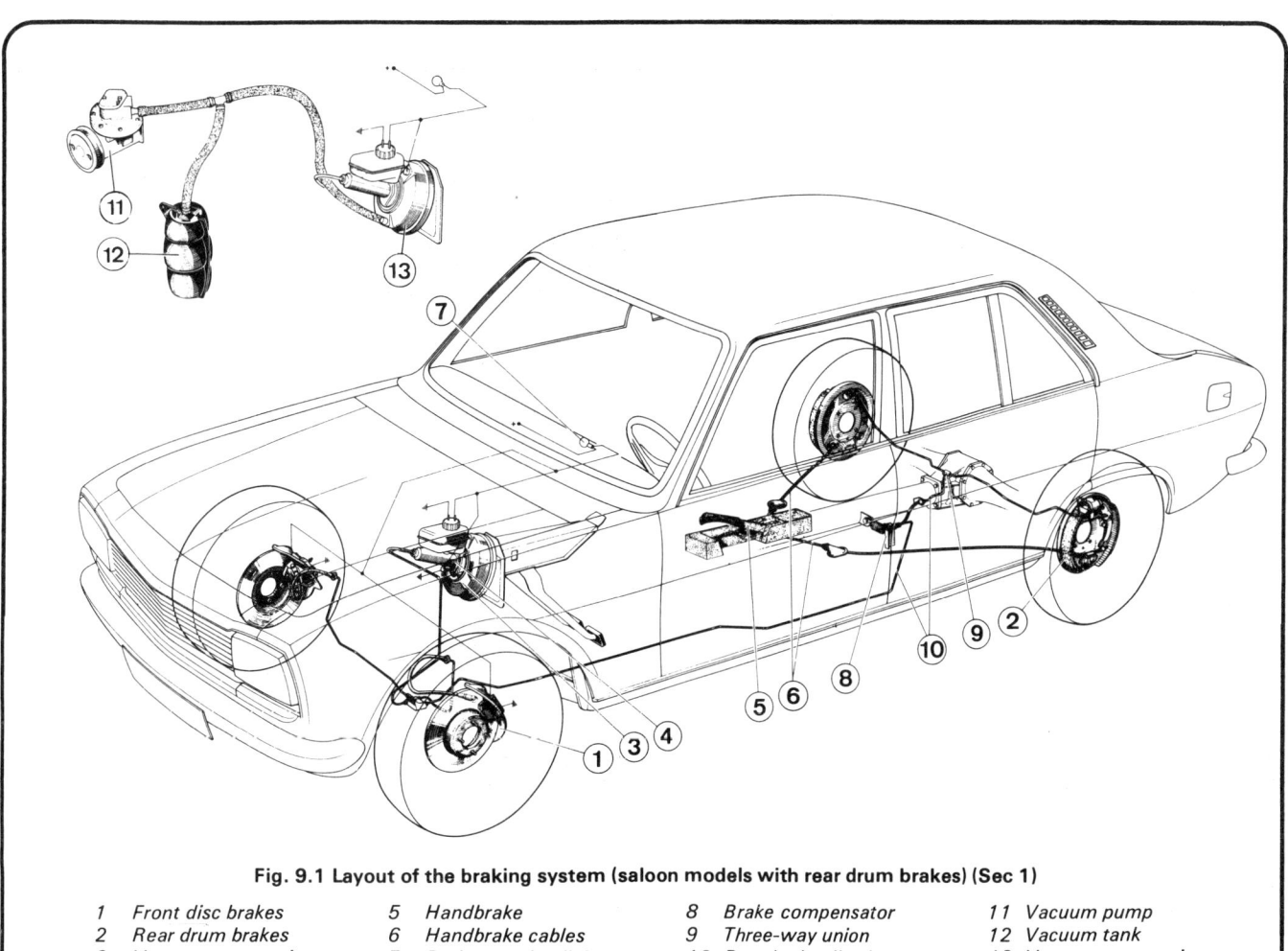

Fig. 9.1 Layout of the braking system (saloon models with rear drum brakes) (Sec 1)

1	Front disc brakes	5	Handbrake	8	Brake compensator
2	Rear drum brakes	6	Handbrake cables	9	Three-way union
3	Vacuum servo unit	7	Brake warning light	10	Rear hydraulic pipes
4	Master cylinder				

11 Vacuum pump
12 Vacuum tank
13 Vacuum servo unit

2.8 One-man brake bleeding kit in position on front caliper

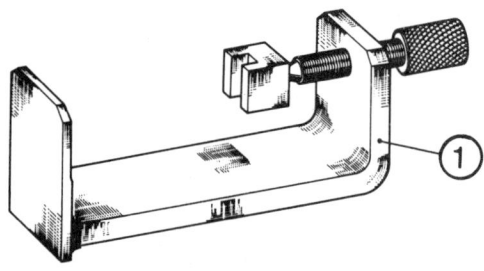

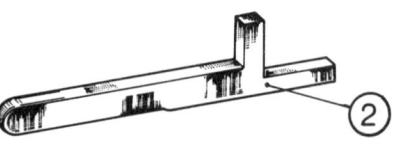

Fig. 9.2 Two special tools that are desirable to use when working on disc brakes (Sec 2)

1 Clamp (use a G-clamp and wooden block if tool not available)
2 Key (can be made from scrap metal)

2   There are a number of one-man, do-it-yourself, brake bleeding kits currently available from motor accessory shops. It is recommended that one of these kits should be used wherever possible, as they greatly simplify the bleeding operation and also reduce the risk of expelled air and fluid being drawn back into the system.

3   If one of these kits is not available then it will be necessary to gather together a clean jar and a suitable length of clear plastic tubing which is a tight fit over the bleed screw, and also to engage the help of an assistant.

4   Before commencing the bleeding operation, check that all rigid pipes and flexible hoses are in good condition and that all hydraulic unions are tight. Take great care not to allow hydraulic fluid to come into contact with the vehicle paintwork, otherwise the finish will be seriously damaged. Wash off any spilled fluid immediately with cold water.

5   If hydraulic fluid has been lost from the master cylinder, due to a leak in the system, ensure that the cause is traced and rectified before proceeding further, or a serious malfunction of the braking system may occur.

6   To bleed the system, clean the area around the bleed screw at the wheel cylinder to be bled. If the hydraulic system has only been partially disconnected and suitable precautions were taken to prevent further loss of fluid, it should only be necessary to bleed that part of the system. However, if the entire system is to be bled, start at the wheel furthest away from the master cylinder.

7   Remove the master cylinder filler cap and top up the reservoir. Periodically check the fluid level during the bleeding operation and top up as necessary.

8   If a one-man brake bleeding kit is being used, connect the outlet tube to the bleed screw (photo) and then open the screw half a turn. If possible position the unit so that it can be viewed from the car, then depress the brake pedal to the floor and slowly release it. The one-way valve in the kit will prevent dispelled air from returning to the system at the end of each stroke. Repeat this operation until clean hydraulic fluid, free from air bubbles, can be seen coming through the tube. Now tighten the bleed screw and remove the outlet tube.

9   If a one-man brake bleeding kit is not available, connect one end of the plastic tubing to the bleed screw and immerse the other end in the jam jar containing sufficient clean hydraulic fluid to keep the end of the tube submerged. Open the bleed screw half a turn and have your assistant depress the brake pedal to the floor and then slowly release it. Tighten the bleed screw at the end of each downstroke to prevent expelled air and fluid from being drawn back into the system. Repeat this operation until clean hydraulic fluid, free from air bubbles, can be seen coming through the tube. Now tighten the bleed screw and remove the plastic tube.

10   If the entire system is being bled, the procedures described above should now be repeated at each wheel, finishing at the wheel nearest to the master cylinder. Do not forget to recheck the fluid level in the master cylinder at regular intervals and top up as necessary.

Fig. 9.3 Key (G) fitted in groove in piston (Sec 2)

Fig. 9.4 Key (G) pivoted through $\frac{1}{8}$ turn (Sec 2)

11 When completed, recheck the fluid level in the master cylinder, top up if necessary and refit the cap. Check the 'feel' of the brake pedal, which should be firm and free from any 'sponginess' which would indicate air still present in the system.

12 Discard any expelled hydraulic fluid as it is likely to be contaminated with moisture, air and dirt which makes it unsuitable for further use.

13 It should be noted that if the rear disc brakes have been removed or overhauled, a condition can arise whereby the caliper cylinders must be refilled using a different procedure to that already described. Only use this second method 'as a last resort' because a special clamp and key are required (Fig. 9.2). Then proceed as described in the following paragraphs.

14 Remove the brake pads (Section 8).

15 Engage the end of the special key in the groove on the piston (Fig. 9.3).

16 Pump the brake pedal until the armature of the caliper comes into contact with the outer face of the disc, and the key is pinched between the piston and the other face of the disc.

17 Now bleed the system as previously described.

18 Pivot the piston about $\frac{1}{8}$th of a turn until the arm of the key abuts against the angle of the brake pad guide. This will free the automatic play take-up device of the handbrake (Fig. 9.4).

19 Remove the key.

20 Refer to Fig. 9.5 and mount the clamp as shown. Open the bleed screw one turn to facilitate the return of the pistons.

21 Tighten the clamp knurled screw until it abuts and then, tighten the bleed screw.

22 Remove the clamp.

23 Return the piston to its initial position using the key, and then remove the key.

24 Refit the brake pads.

25 Check the hydraulic fluid level in the reservoir and top up if necessary.

26 Refit the roadwheels and road test.

---

3 Hydraulic hoses (flexible) – inspection, removal and refitting

---

1 Inspect the condition of the flexible hydraulic hoses leading to the front and rear brakes, referring to Section 26 for further information.

2 If they are swollen, damaged or chafed, they must be renewed.

3 Wipe the top of the brake master cylinder reservoir and unscrew the cap. Place a piece of polythene sheet over the top and secure to make an airtight joint. This is to stop hydraulic fluid syphoning out during subsequent operations. If the cap is refitted the float contact could be damaged.

4 To remove a flexible hose wipe the union and any supports free of dust and undo the union nuts from the metal pipe ends (photo).

5 Undo and remove the locknut and washer securing the flexible hose end to the bracket.

6 Unscrew the hose from the caliper or connector as applicable.

7 Refitting the flexible hose is the reverse sequence to removal. It will be necessary to bleed the brake hydraulic system as described in Section 2.

---

4 Disc brake pads (front) – removal, inspection and refitting

---

Note: *It is important that the pads for both front brakes are renewed as a complete set*

1 Chock the rear wheels, jack up the front of the car and support on firmly based axle stands. Remove the roadwheel.

2 Disconnect the brake wear warning lead (where fitted) at the terminal connector (photo).

3 Remove the brake pads thrust spring (photo).

4 Undo and remove the nut and washer securing the pads retaining fork (photo).

5 Withdraw the pads retaining fork (photo).

6 The pads may now be removed (photos). Should the pads be difficult to remove, it is permissible to release them using a screwdriver or lever placed squarely between the metal lips of the brake pads.

7 Clean down the caliper and disc assembly and generally inspect for fluid leakage, wear or damage.

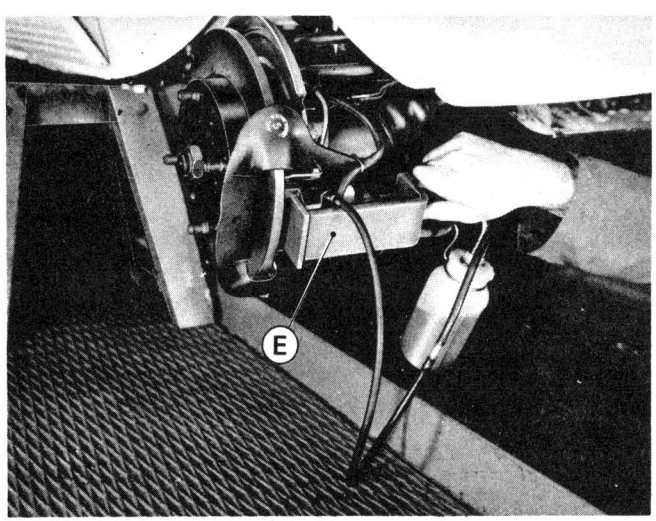

Fig. 9.5 Returning piston using clamp (E) (Sec 2)

3.4 Rear brake hose-to-metal pipe union

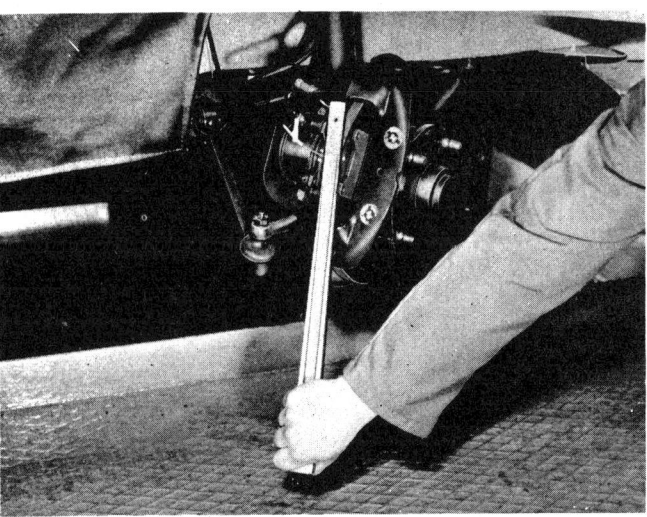

Fig. 9.6 Using a lever to release the brake pads (Sec 4)

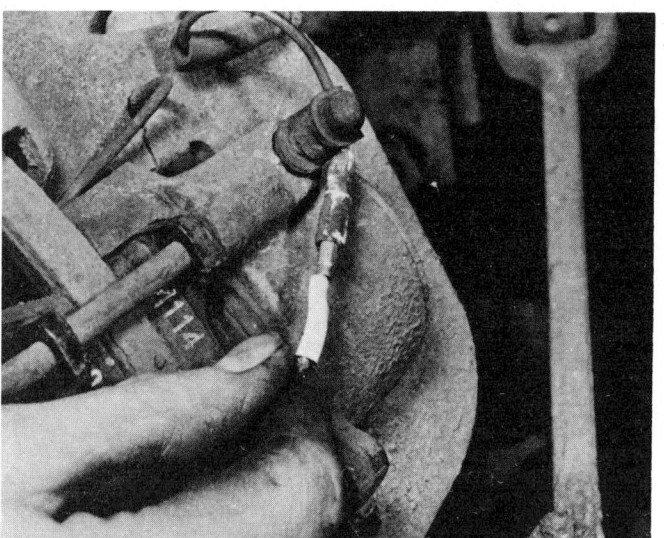

4.2 Disconnect the brake wear warning light lead

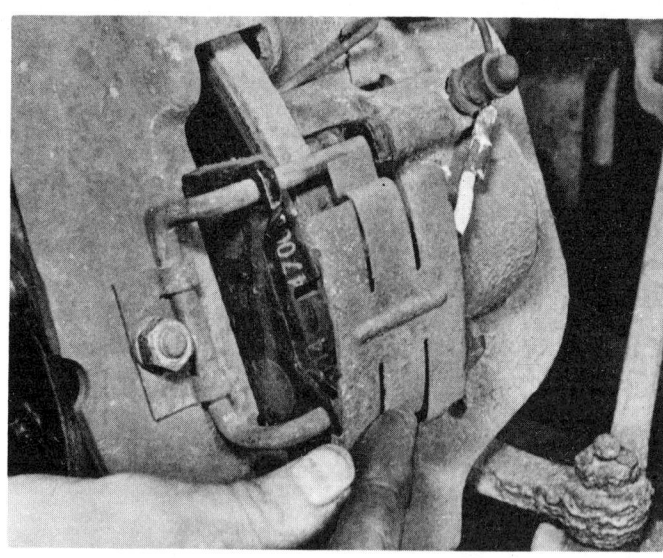

4.3 Remove the thrust spring

4.4 Remove the retaining fork securing nut ...

4.5 ... then slide out the fork ...

4.6a ... followed by the outer pad ...

4.6b ... and inner pad

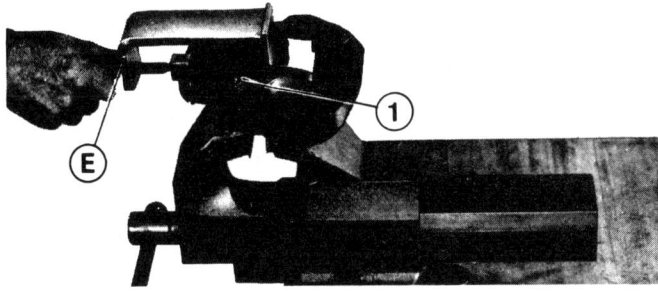

Fig. 9.7 Using a clamp to retract the caliper pistons (Sec 6)

E   Clamp   1   Caliper

8   Measure the thickness of the pad lining, if it is badly worn the pads must be renewed – see Specifications.
9   If new pads are to be fitted push the piston into the bore using a block of wood and a G-clamp. To stop hydraulic fluid overflowing from the reservoir, slacken the caliper bleed screw while moving the pistons back, then retighten.
10 Refitting the pads is the reverse sequence to removal but the following additional points should be noted:

(a) Fit the brake pads thrust spring with the arrow pointing upwards
(b) Tighten the pads retaining fork securing nuts to the specified torque wrench setting
(c) Check the brake fluid level and top up if necessary
(d) Operate the brake pedal several times until a strong resistance is felt. This will ensure that the pads have settled correctly then road test the car

Fig. 9.8 Removing the caliper pistons (Sec 6)

3   Nylon spacer

---

5   Disc brake caliper (front) – removal and refitting

1   Chock the rear wheels, apply the handbrake, jack up the front of the car and support on firmly based axle stands. Remove the roadwheel.
2   Disconnect the brake wear warning lead (where fitted) at the terminal connector.
3   Disconnect the union of the flexible hose from the caliper body. Tape the end to stop loss of hydraulic fluid.
4   Undo and remove the two bolts securing the caliper assembly to the front suspension member.
5   It should now be possible to lift the caliper assembly from over the disc. If the pads are binding it is permissible to release them using a screwdriver placed squarely between the metal lips of the brake pads.
6   Refitting the caliper assembly is the reverse sequence to removal, but the following additional points should be noted:

(a) Use new 'Blocfor' washers for the caliper securing bolts
(b) Tighten the caliper securing bolts to the specified torque wrench setting
(c) Reconnect the flexible hosing using new sealing washers
(d) Refer to Section 2, and bleed the brake hydraulic system

Fig. 9.9 Hooking out the caliper piston sealing rings (Sec 6)

---

6   Disc brake caliper (front) – overhaul

Note: If hydraulic fluid is leaking from the caliper, it will be necessary to fit new seals or renew the caliper. Should brake fluid be found running down the side of the wheel, or if it is noticed that a pool of fluid forms alongside one wheel, or the level in the master cylinder reservoir drops excessively, it is also indicative of seal failure.

1   Refer to Section 4, and remove the caliper pads.
2   Refer to Section 5, and remove the caliper.
3   Using a G-clamp and wooden block, retract the pistons as shown in Fig. 9.7.
4   Remove the thrust spring from the armature.
5   Disengage the armature from the guide grooves in the caliper body.

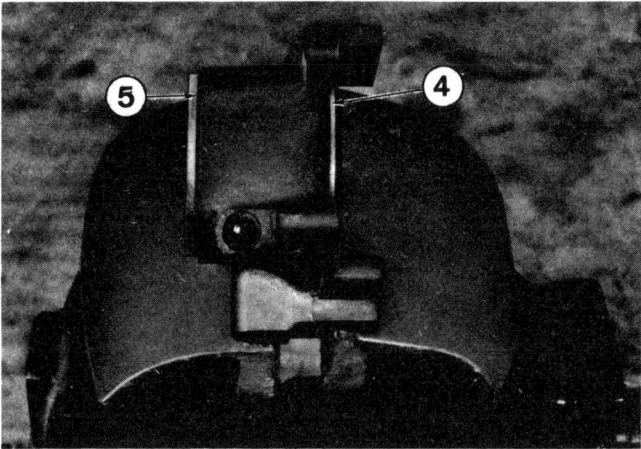

Fig. 9.10 Refitting the protector rubber spring clips with the narrow clip (4) on the disc side and thicker clip (5) on the armature side (Sec 6)

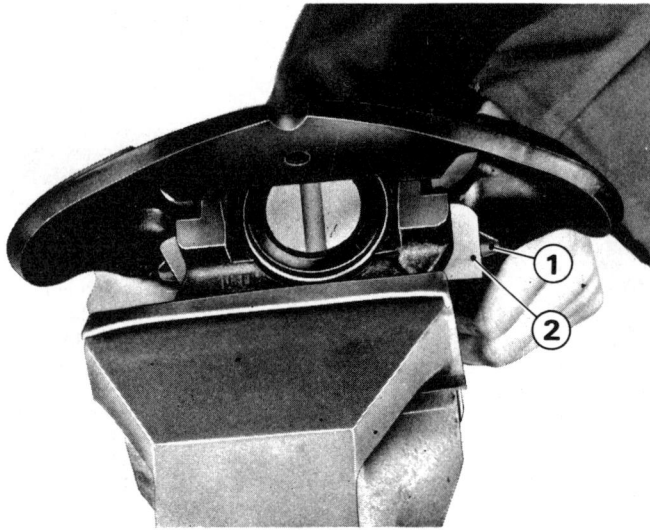

Fig. 9.11 Using shim steel (2) to aid refitment of the thrust plates (1) (Sec 6)

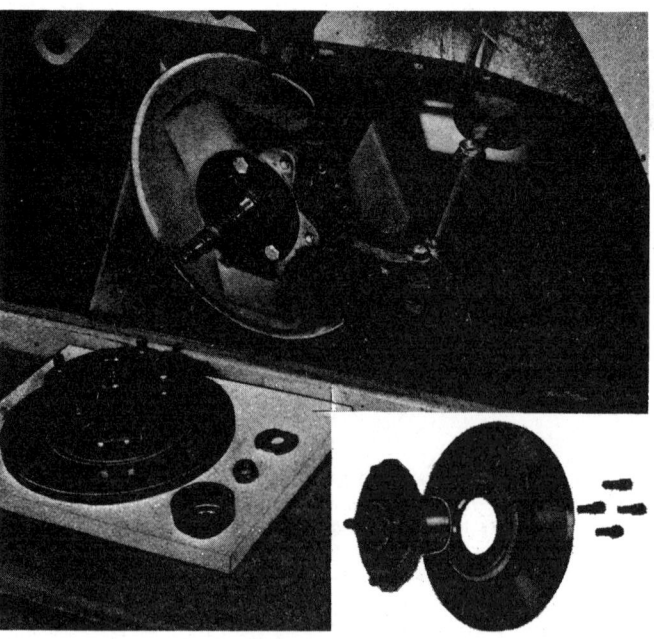

Fig. 9.12 Removal of a front hub and disc assembly (Sec 7)

Fig. 9.13 Key (G)fitted in groove in piston (Sec 7)

Fig. 9.14 Key (G) pivoted through $\frac{1}{8}$ turn (Sec 7)

6   Carefully remove the spring clips that secure the piston protectors.
7   Remove the two protectors.
8   Carefully push the two pistons out of the cylinder.
9   Remove the nylon spacer from the piston on the armature side.
10 Using a non-metallic rod, remove the sealing rings from the caliper cylinder body.
11 Thoroughly wash all parts in methylated spirit or clean hydraulic fluid. During reassembly new rubber seals must be fitted and these should be well lubricated with clean hydraulic fluid before fitment.
12 Inspect the pistons and bore for signs of wear, score marks or other damage. If evident a new caliper assembly will be necessary.
13 To reassemble, first clamp the cylinder body in a soft-faced vise.
14 Lubricate the rubber seals and position in the grooves inside the cylinder body.
15 Place the nylon spacer in the piston which will be fitted to the armature side.
16 Lubricate the pistons and insert them one at a time into the cylinder body.
17 Fit the two protector rubbers and their spring clips. Note that the narrow clip must be on the disc side and the thicker clip to the armature side.

18 If the thrust plates have been removed, refit them to the armature.
19 Place a piece of shim steel 0.008 in (0.20 mm) thick against each of the plates to facilitate their engagement in the grooves on the cylinder body.
20 Engage the armature in the cylinder body grooves whilst compressing the thrust plates. When in position, remove the two strips of shim steel.
21 Refit the thrust spring to the upper part of the armature.
22 Finally retract the pistons fully using the G-clamp and wooden block.
23 Reassembly is now complete and the unit is ready to refit to the car. The pads are then refitted as described in Section 4.

7   Brake disc and hub assembly (front) – removal and refitting

1   Refer to Section 5, and remove the caliper assembly. It is not necessary to disconnect the flexible hose if the caliper does not require attention. Suspend the caliper on wire or string to prevent straining the flexible hose.
2   Carefully remove the grease cap from the wheel spindle.

3   Unscrew and remove the hub nut and washer.
4   Grip the hub and disc assembly and pull it from the wheel spindle.
5   Thoroughly clean the disc and inspect for signs of deep scoring or excessive corrosion. If evident the surfaces may be refaced, but leave this to the experts. It is desirable however to fit a new disc if at all possible.
6   To remove the disc from the hub, first mark the hub to disc assembly relationship if the original parts are to be used.
7   Undo and remove the four securing socket-headed screws and part the disc from the hub.
8   On reassembly, first make sure that the mating faces are really clean and then refit the four socket-headed screws using new 'Blocfor' washers. Tighten to the specified torque wrench setting.
9   Grease the hub bearings and refit the assembly to the steering swivel.
10   Refit the washer with the inner shoulder against the inner race of the bearing.
11   Refer to Chapter 11 and adjust the front hub bearings, but do not lock the hub nut yet.
12   It is now necessary to check for disc run-out. For this a dial indicator gauge or feeler gauge pack is required.
13   Rotate the disc and check for run-out at a point approximately 1 in (25 mm) from the outer circumference. With a dial indicator this is easy, but when using a feeler gauge pack this should be positioned between the backplate and disc at the caliper location.
14   The maximum run-out should not exceed that specified. If it does however, first remove the disc and hub assembly, part the two and check for dirt. Reposition the disc through a quarter of a turn relative to the hub.
15   Recheck for run-out and when satisfactory lock the hub nut using a suitable punch. Refit the grease cap.
16   Refit the caliper assembly as described in Section 5.

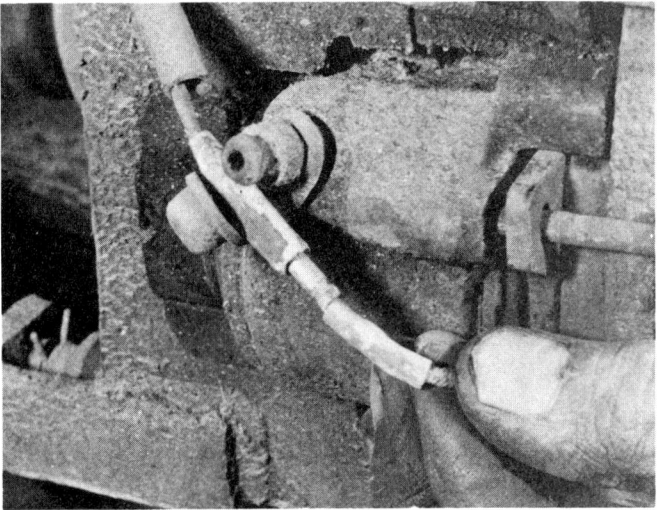

8.2 Disconnect the brake pad wear warning light lead

8   Disc brake pads (rear) – removal, inspection and refitting

Note: *It is important that the pads for both rear brakes are renewed as a complete set.*
1   Chock the front wheels, jack up the rear of the car and support on firmly based axle stands. Remove the roadwheel.
2   Disconnect the brake wear warning lead at the terminal connector (photo), where fitted.
3   Undo and remove the bolt and nut securing the pads retaining fork and pad support (photo). Lift away the pad support.
4   Withdraw the pads retaining fork (photo).
5   The pads may now be removed (photos). Should the pads be difficult to remove, it is permissible to release them using a screwdriver placed squarely between the metal lips of the brake pads.
6   Clean down the caliper and disc assembly and generally inspect for fluid leakage, wear or damage.
7   Measure the thickness of the pad lining, and if it is badly worn the pads must be renewed – see Specifications.
8   To return the brake pistons for the rear brakes, a special piston positioning key is required (Fig. 9.2). It should not be too difficult to manufacture an alternative.
9   Place the key in the inner brake pad position in such a manner that it is lodged in the groove on the piston.

8.3 Remove the retaining fork securing nut and bolt ...

10   Rotate the piston one eighth of a turn so as to bring the arm of the key against the angle of the brake pad guide, in order to release the automatic handbrake play take-up device.
11   Remove the key and ensure that the handbrake lever on the piston is well down onto its nylon stop.
12   Push the piston into the bore using a block of wood and a G-clamp. To stop hydraulic fluid overflowing from the reservoir, slacken the caliper bleed screw while moving the piston back, then retighten.
13   Now return the piston to its initial position using the key.
14   Refitting the pads is now the reverse sequence to removal, but the following additional points should be noted:

   (a)   When fitted, the brake pads thrust spring should be refitted with the arrow pointing upwards
   (b)   Tighten the pads retaining fork securing bolt and new washer to the specified torque wrench setting
   (c)   Check the brake fluid level and top up if necessary
   (d)   Operate the brake pedal several times until a strong resistance is felt. This will ensure that the pads have settled correctly. Road test the car

8.4 ... then withdraw the fork ...

8.5a ... followed by the outer pad ...

8.5b ... and inner pad

9 Disc brake caliper (rear) − removal and refitting

1 Chock the front wheels, jack up the rear of the car and support on firmly based axle stands. Remove the roadwheel.
2 Disconnect the brake wear warning lead at the terminal connector, where fitted.
3 Disconnect the brake hydraulic fluid line and plug the ends to stop dirt ingress or loss of hydraulic fluid.
4 Disconnect the handbrake cable and outer casing.
5 Undo and remove the two bolts that secure the caliper and lift away from over the disc. If the pads are binding it is permissible to release them using a screwdriver between the metal lips of the brake pads. As a last resort remove the pads, as described in Section 8.
6 Refitting the caliper assembly is the reverse sequence to removal but the following additional points should be noted:

   (a) Use new 'Blocfor' washers for the caliper securing bolts
   (b) Tighten the caliper securing bolts to the specified torque wrench setting
   (c) Reconnect the handbrake and adjust as described in Section 22
   (d) Refer to Section 2 and bleed the brake hydraulic system

10 Disc brake caliper (rear) − overhaul

Note: If hydraulic fluid is leaking, it will be necessary to fit new seals or renew the caliper. Should brake fluid be found running down the side of the wheel, or if it is noticed that a pool of fluid forms alongside one wheel, or the level in the master cylinder reservoir drops excessively, it is also indicative of seal failure.

1 Refer to Section 8, and remove the caliper pads.
2 Refer to Section 9, and remove the caliper.
3 To return the brake pistons a special piston positioning key is required (Fig. 9.2). It should not, however, be too difficult to manufacture an alternative.
4 Using the key rotate the piston until it abuts on the brake pad guide.
5 Using a G-clamp and wooden blocks, return the pistons into the cylinder.
6 Detach and remove the thrust spring from the armature.
7 Slide the armature to disengage it from the grooves in the cylinder body.
8 Carefully remove the 'Truarc' ring (Fig. 9.15) and then the handbrake lever return spring.
9 Raise the handbrake lever and recover the nylon spacer.
10 Carefully remove the spring clips that secure the piston protectors.
11 Remove the two protectors.

12 To remove the pistons, push on the 'grooved' one and eject from the end of the bore.
13 Using a non-metallic rod, remove the sealing rings from the caliper cylinder body.
14 Thoroughly wash all parts in methylated spirit or clean hydraulic fluid. During reassembly new rubber seals must be fitted, and these should be well lubricated with clean hydraulic fluid before fitment.
15 Inspect the pistons and bore for signs of wear, score marks or other damage. if evident a new caliper assembly will be necessary.
16 To reassemble, first clamp the cylinder body in a soft-faced vice.
17 Lubricate the rubber seals and position in the grooves inside the cylinder body.
18 Lubricate the pistons, and then referring to Fig. 9.17 insert piston (5) positioning the handbrake lever as shown.
19 Refit piston (6) with its groove inclined at one eighth of a turn from the vertical.
20 Fit the two protector rubbers and their spring clips. Note that the narrow clip must be on the disc side and the thicker clip to the armature side.
21 Raise the handbrake lever and position the nylon spacer on the piston.

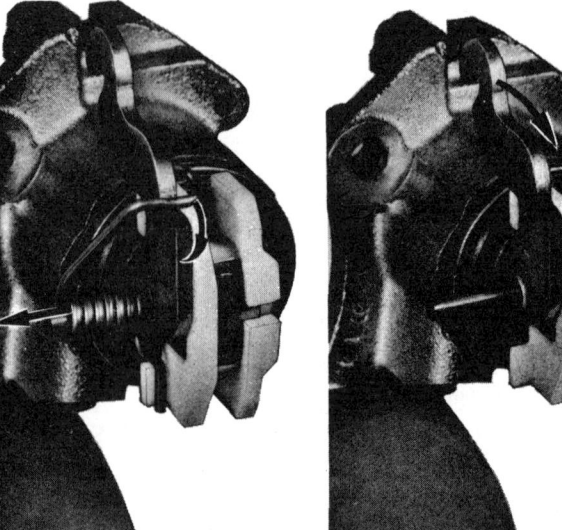

Fig. 9.15 Removing the 'Truarc' ring, the handbrake lever return spring and the nylon spacer from the rear brake caliper (Sec 10)

Fig. 9.16 Removing the rear brake caliper pistons (Sec 10)

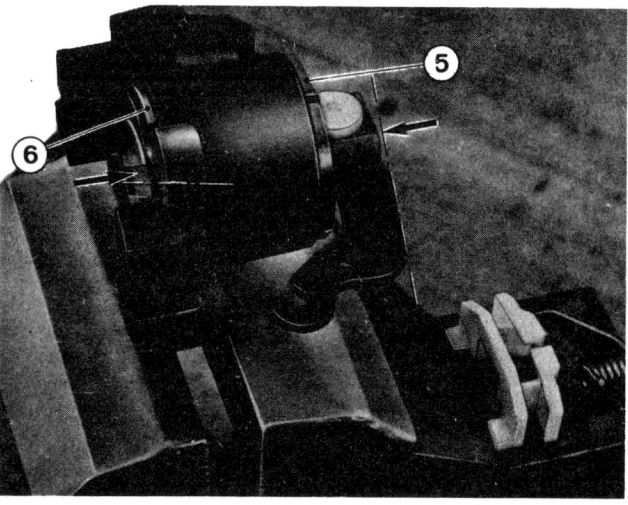

Fig. 9.17 Initial reassembly of rear brake caliper pistons (Sec 10)

5   Correct position of piston and handbrake lever
6   Piston groove inclined at $\frac{1}{8}$ turn from vertical

Fig. 9.18 Refitting the handbrake lever nylon spacer to the piston (Sec 10)

Fig. 9.19 Final assembly of rear caliper (Sec 10)

3   Handbrake return spring   4   Thrust spring

22 If the thrust plates have been removed, refit them to the armature.
23 Place a piece of shim steel 0.008 in (0.20 mm) thick against each of the plates to facilitate their engagement in the grooves on the cylinder body.
24 Engage the armature in the cylinder body grooves whilst compressing the thrust plates. When in position remove the two strips of shim steel.
25 Slide the handbrake return spring onto its pivot and hook over the two ends.
26 Lock the spring on its pivot using a new 'Truarc' ring.
27 Refit the thrust spring onto the upper part of the armature.
28 Reassembly is now complete and the unit is ready for refitting to the car. The pads are then refitted as described in Section 8.

11 Brake disc (rear) – removal and refitting

1 Refer to Section 9, and remove the caliper assembly. Note, however, that it is not necessary to disconnect the flexible hose if the caliper does not require attention.

2 In the latter case, proceed as follows:

(a) Slacken the hose nut on the rear arm support and disengage the hose from it
(b) Open the clamp that holds the brake line onto the rear arm
(c) Detach the handbrake cable from the rear arm
(d) Refer to Section 8 and remove the brake pads
(e) Now remove the two caliper securing bolts and lift from over the disc
(f) Suspend the caliper on wire or string to prevent straining the flexible hose

3 Mark the position of the disc relative to the hub.
4 Undo and remove the one cross-head screw securing the disc to the hub.
5 Lift away the disc and carefully clean the hub without removing it.
6 Thoroughly clean the disc and inspect for signs of deep scoring or excessive corrosion. If evident the surfaces may be refaced, but leave this to the experts. It is desirable, however, to fit a new disc if at all possible.
7 To reassemble, first make sure the mating faces are really clean.

Fig. 9.20 Using a dial indicator to check rear disc run-out (Sec 11)

8   Offer up the disc and secure with the cross-head screw. Also temporarily fit two nuts on the wheel studs and tighten these to secure the disc.
9   It is now necessary to check for disc run-out. For this a dial indicator gauge or feeler gauge pack is required.
10 Rotate the disc and check for run-out at a point approximately 1 in (25 mm) from the outer circumference. With a dial indicator this is easy, but when using a feeler gauge pack, this should be positioned between the backplate and disc at the caliper location.
11 The maximum run-out should not exceed that specified. If it does, however, remove the disc and check for dirt. Reposition the disc through half a turn relative to the hub.
12 Recheck for run-out. When satisfactory, remove the nuts from the wheel studs and refit the caliper, referring to Section 9.

---

12 Drum brake shoes (rear) – inspection, removal and refitting

Note: *After high mileages, it will be necessary to fit replacement shoes with new linings. Refitting new brake linings to old shoes is not considered economic, or possible, without the use of special equipment. However, if the services of a local garage or workshop having brake relining equipment are available, then there is no reason why the original shoes should not be successfully relined. Ensure that the correct specification linings are fitted to the shoes.*

1   Chock the front wheels, jack up the rear of the car and place on firmly based axle stands. Remove the roadwheel.
2   Release the handbrake, remove the brake drum retaining screws (photo) and, using a soft-faced hammer on the outer circumference of the brake drum, remove the brake drum.
3   Should the brake drum be difficult to remove due to the shoes fouling the drum, back off the brake adjusters (where applicable) accessible from the rear of the brake backplate. If the brakes are of the self-adjusting type, remove the inspection plug from the rear of the backplate and push the brake lever with a screwdriver to retract the shoes.
4   The brake linings should be renewed if they are so worn that they are down to the specified minimum thickness. Never let the linings get so thin that the rivet heads are flush with the lining surface – scoring of the brake drum is then inevitable.
5   Depress each shoe holding-down spring and detach the anchor plate located at the rear of the brake backplate.
6   Ease each shoe from its location slot in the fixed pivot, and then detach the other end of each shoe from the wheel cylinder.
7   Note which way round, and into which holes in the shoes, the retracting springs fit and detach the retracting springs.
8   Lift away the front shoe followed by the operating link.

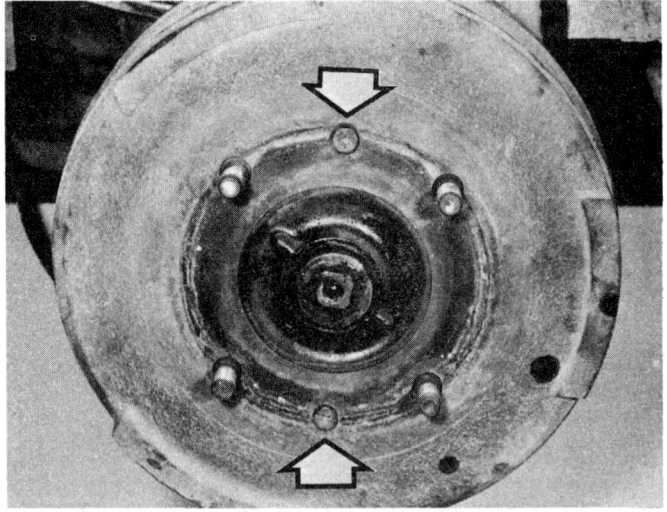

12.2 Brake drum retaining screws (arrowed)

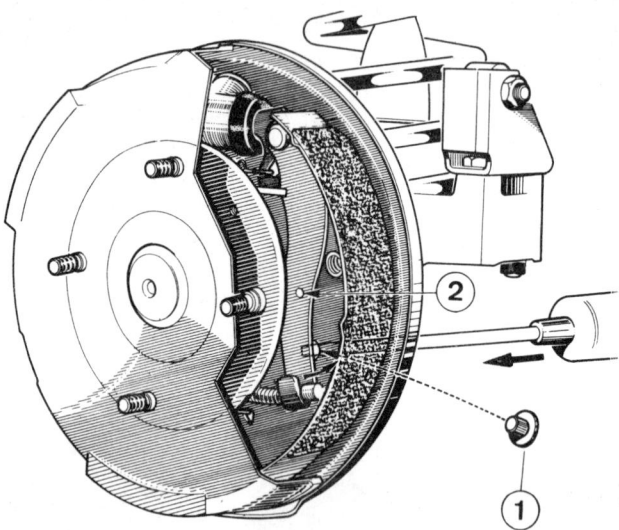

Fig. 9.21 Using a screwdriver to retract the self-adjusting rear brake shoes (Sec 12)

1   Inspection plug   2   Brake lever

Fig. 9.22 Removing the brake shoe hold-down springs, using tool L as shown in inset (Sec 12)

9   Detach the handbrake inner cable from the rear shoe lever and lift away the rear shoe together with lever.

10   If the shoes are to be left off for a while, place a warning on the steering wheel as accidental depression of the brake pedal will eject the pistons from the wheel cylinder.

11   If new shoes are being fitted the levers will have to be transferred.

12   Thoroughly clean all traces of dust from the shoes, backplates and brake drums using a stiff brush. It is recommended that compressed air is not used, as brake lining dist should not be inhaled. Brake dust can cause judder or squeal and therefore, it is important to clean out as described.

13   Check that the pistons are free in the cylinder, that the rubber dust covers are undamaged and in position, and that there are no hydraulic fluid leaks.

14   Prior to reassembly smear a trace of brake grease on the shoe support pads, brake shoe pivots and on the ratchet pawl teeth.

15   Reassembly is the reverse sequence to removal, and provided that care was taken to note the location of each part as it was removed, no problems should arise.

16   On completion of reassembly, adjust the rear brakes as described in Section 15, where manually adjustable brakes are fitted. On self-adjusting systems operate the hand and foot brake several times to take up the brake shoe-to-drum clearance.

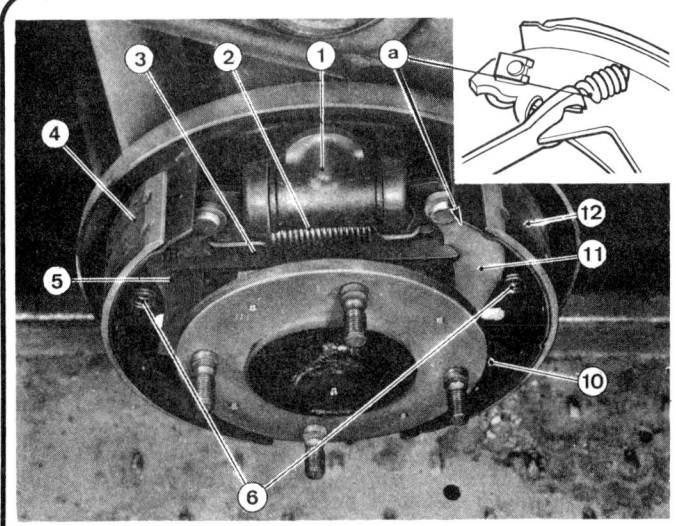

Fig. 9.23 Layout of the self-adjusting rear drum brakes fitted to saloon models (Sec 12)

1	Wheel cylinder	5	Adjusting lever	9	Retaining springs	a	Location of upper retaining spring
2	Return spring	6	Hold-down springs	10	Handbrake cable	b	Location of lower retaining spring
3	Brake lever	7	Pawl	11	Handbrake lever		
4	Leading shoe	8	Pawl spring	12	Trailing shoe	c	Handbrake cable spring

Fig. 9.24 Layout of the manually adjusted rear drum brakes fitted to estate and family estate models (Sec 12)

1	Wheel cylinder	4	Leading shoe	7	Handbrake cable	a	Correct spring fitting
2	Upper return spring	5	Hold-down spring	8	Handbrake lever	b	Correct cable fitting
3	Link	6	Lower return spring	9	Trailing shoe		

13 Wheel cylinder (rear drum brakes) – removal and refitting

Note: *If hydraulic fluid is leaking from the brake wheel cylinder, it will be necessary to dismantle it and renew the seals or renew the complete cylinder. Should brake fluid be found running down the side of the wheel, or if it is noticed that a pool of liquid forms alongside one wheel, or the level in the master cylinder reservoir drops significantly it is also indicative of failed seals.*

1   Refer to Section 12 and remove the brake drums and shoes. Clean down the rear of the backplate using a stiff brush. Place a quantity of rag under the backplate to catch any hydraulic fluid that may issue from the open pipe or wheel cylinder.
2   Using an open-ended spanner, carefully unscrew the hydraulic pipe connection union to the rear of the wheel cylinder. To prevent dirt ingress tape the end of the pipe.
3   Undo and remove the two bolts and spring washers that secure the wheel cylinder to the backplate.
4   Withdraw the wheel cylinder from the front of the brake backplate.
5   Refitting the wheel cylinder, shoes and drums is the reverse sequence to removal. On completion it will be necessary to bleed the brake hydraulic system as described in Section 2.

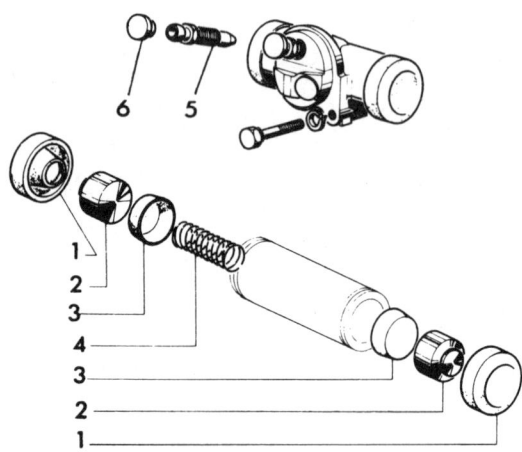

Fig. 9.25 Rear drum brake wheel cylinder (Sec 14)

1	*Rubber boot*	4	*Spring*
2	*Piston*	5	*Bleed screw*
3	*Cup seal*	6	*Cap*

14 Wheel cylinder (rear drum brakes) – inspection and overhaul

1   With the wheel cylinder removed, thoroughly clean down and wipe dry with a non-fluffy rag.
2   Ease off each rubber dust cover and draw out the pistons, cup seals and spring. Note which way round the seals are fitted.
3   Inspect the inside of the cylinder for score marks caused by impurities in the hydraulic fluid. If any are found, the complete cylinder assembly will require renewal.
4   If the cylinder is sound, thoroughly clean it out with fresh hydraulic fluid.
5   The old rubber seals will probably be swollen and visibly worn. Smear the new rubber seals with hydraulic fluid and fit the spring, cup seals, pistons and rubber dust cover to the wheel cylinder.
6   The wheel cylinder is now ready for refitting to the brake backplate.

15 Drum brakes (rear) – adjustment

1   On models having manually adjustable rear brakes, the two adjusters per wheel are accessible from the rear of the backplate, and adjustment is carried out as follows.
2   Chock the front wheels, release the handbrake, jack up the rear of the car and support it on axle stands.

3   Remove all dirt from around the area of the brake adjusters and lightly lubricate each adjuster with penetrating oil.
4   Turn one of the adjusters until the brake shoe is in firm contact with the drum and the wheel is locked.
5   Now back off the adjuster until the wheel again turns freely. A slight rubbing noise may be heard as the wheel is rotated, due to dust or high spots in the drum. This is acceptable providing the drum does not bind.
6   Now carry out this procedure again for the second adjuster.
7   Repeat paragraphs 3 to 6 inclusive for the other rear brake.

16 Master cylinder (single circuit) – removal and refitting

1   For safety reasons, disconnect the battery.
2   Wipe down the outside of the master cylinder and reservoir. Unscrew the reservoir cap.
3   With a clean glass jar ready, detach the clutch master cylinder hydraulic fluid supply pipe from the underside of the reservoir. Catch the hydraulic fluid as it drains out from the reservoir.
4   Plug the end of the clutch master cylinder hydraulic fluid supply pipe with a pencil or suitable dowel to stop loss of fluid or dirt ingress.
5   Undo and remove the union nut from the end of the brake master cylinder.
6   Undo and remove the two nuts and washers securing the master cylinder to the vacuum servo unit.
7   The master cylinder and reservoir may now be lifted away. *Do not allow brake fluid to contact any paintwork as it acts as a solvent.*
8   Refitting the brake master cylinder is the reverse sequence to removal, but the following additional points should be noted:

   (a)   *If the rubber pipe is squeezed as it is connected to the reservoir, and at the same time the reservoir is refilled, it should not be necessary to bleed the clutch hydraulic system. However, should air be in the clutch pipe it will be necessary to bleed the system, as described in Chapter 5*

   (b)   *Bleed the brake hydraulic system, as described in Section 2, upon completion of refitting*

17 Master cylinder (dual circuit) – removal and refitting

Later models and certain export versions of early models are fitted with a dual circuit braking system. Models so fitted use a 'tandem' master cylinder of either Lockheed or Teves manufacture. Removal and refitting of this master cylinder is basically the same as that for the single circuit type, with the exception that one additional hydraulic pipe must be detached (photo). Refer to Section 16 for full information.

17.1 Dual circuit master cylinder, showing retaining nuts (A), clutch master cylinder supply pipe (B), and hydraulic pipe unions (C)

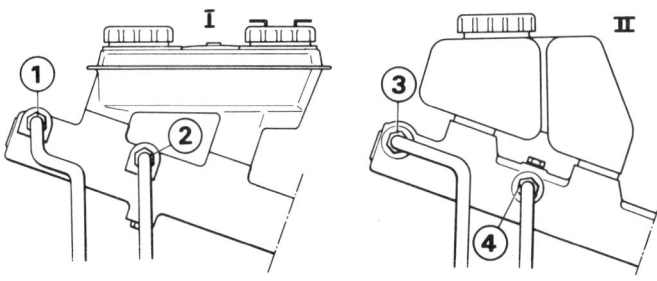

Fig. 9.26 Hydraulic pipe connections on Lockheed (I) and Teves (II) dual circuit master cylinders (Sec 17)

1 Feed to rear brakes	3 Feed to front brakes
2 Feed to front brakes	4 Feed to rear brakes

18 Master cylinder (single circuit) – dismantling, examination and reassembly

Note: *If a replacement master cylinder is to be fitted, it will be necessary to lubricate the seals before fitting to the car, as they have a protective coating when originally assembled. Remove the blanking plug from the hydraulic pipe union seat. Inject some clean hydraulic fluid into the master cylinder and operate the piston with a screwdriver several times so that the fluid spreads over all the internal working surfaces. If the master cylinder is to be dismantled after removal proceed as follows.*

1   Thoroughly clean the exterior of the master cylinder and reservoir and wipe dry with a non-fluffy rag.
2   Using a pair of circlip pliers remove the circlip from the end of the bore.
3   The internal parts may now be removed in the following order: plain washer, secondary cup, piston, disc (some models), main cup and spring.
4   Examine the bore of the cylinder carefully for any signs of scores or ridges. If this is found to be smooth all over, new seals can be fitted. If, howver, there is any doubt of the condition of the bore then a new master cylinder must be fitted.
5   Always fit new seals when reassembling the master cylinder never re-use the old ones. Swelling and distortion will have taken place on the old seals even though this may not be obvious during a visual inspection. Also, once their position in the master cylinder has been disturbed, they can never be relied upon to maintain hydraulic fluid pressure without leakage. New seals are available as a repair kit from your Peugeot dealer or brake and clutch factor.
6   Thoroughly clean all parts in clean hydraulic fluid or methylated spirit. Ensure that the ports are clear.
7   All components should be assembled wet after dipping in fresh brake fluid.
8   Carefully fit the internal parts in the following order: spring, main cup, disc (when fitted), piston and secondary cup, and plain washer.
9   Retain the fitted parts with the circlip located in the end of the bore.
10 Check that the piston is free to move by pushing with a screwdriver, and then refit to the car.

19 Master cylinder (dual circuit – Lockheed) – dismantling, examination and reassembly

1   Refer to the introduction to Section 18.
2   Thoroughly clean the exterior of the master cylinder and reservoir and wipe dry with a non-fluffy rag.
3   Using a pair of circlip pliers, remove the circlip from the end of the bore. Also unscrew the stop screw located on the underside of the master cylinder.
4   The internal parts may now be removed in the following order; plain washer, primary piston and seals, spring, shaped washer, secondary piston and seals and finally a spring.
5   Inspect the master cylinder bore and seals, as described in Section 18, paragraphs 4 to 7 inclusive.
6   Carefully fit the internal parts in the reverse order to removal.

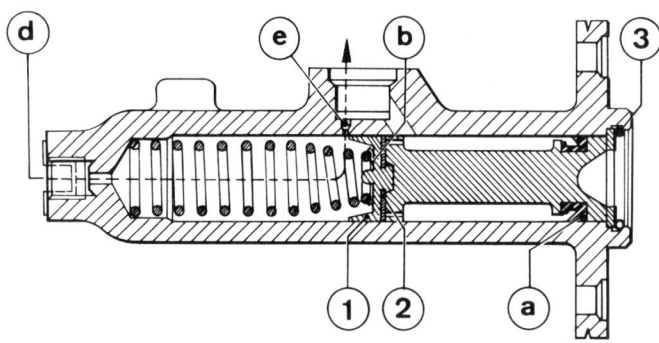

Fig. 9.27 Sectional view of single circuit master cylinder (Sec 18)

1 Main cup	a Secondary cup
2 Security disc	b Spring
3 Circlip	d Outlet
	e Return orifice

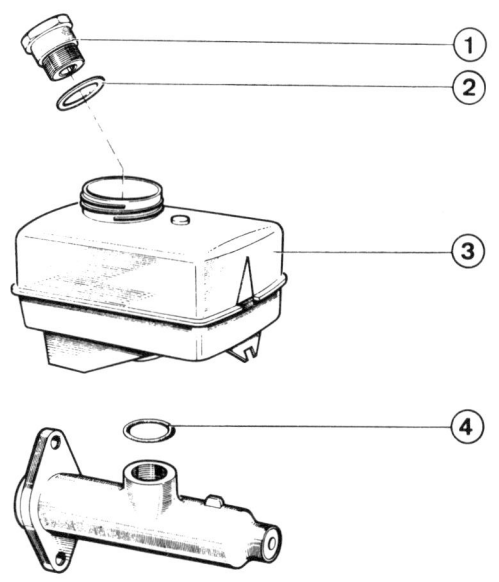

Fig. 9.28 Single circuit master cylinder reservoir (Sec 18)

1 Union nut	3 Reservoir
2 Washer	4 Rubber seal

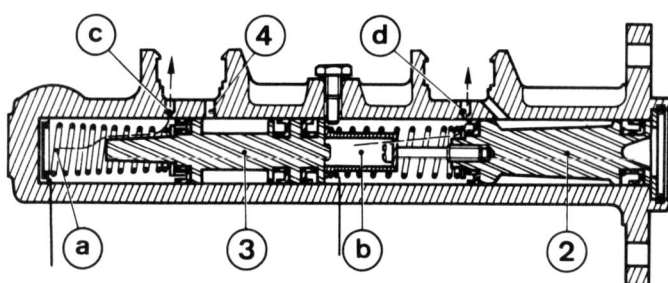

Fig. 9.29 Sectional view of Lockheed dual circuit master cylinder (Sec 19)

a Secondary return spring	2 Primary piston
b Primary outlet	3 Secondary piston
c Secondary return orifice	4 Secondary outlet
d Primary return orifice	

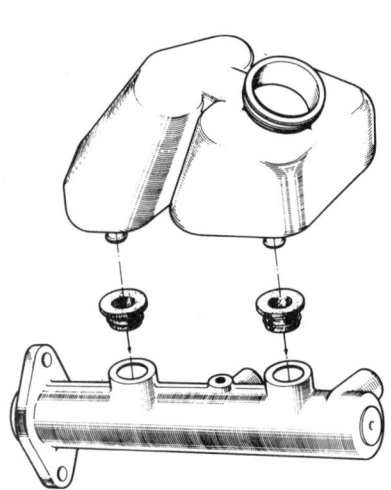

Fig. 9.30 Teves dual circuit master cylinder, standard reservoir
fitting (Sec 20)

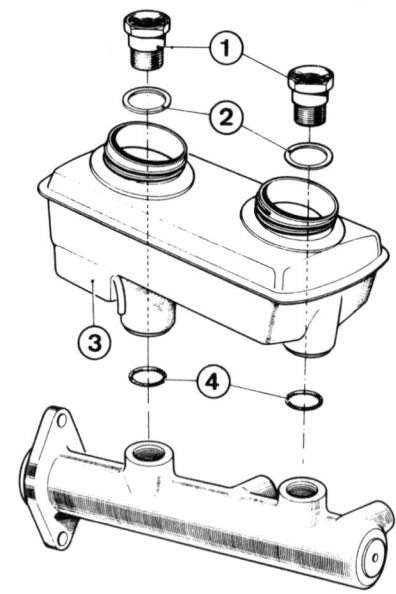

Fig. 9.31 Teves dual circuit master cylinder, alternative reservoir
fitting (Sec 20)

| 1 | Union nuts | 3 | Reservoir |
| 2 | Washer | 4 | Rubber seals |

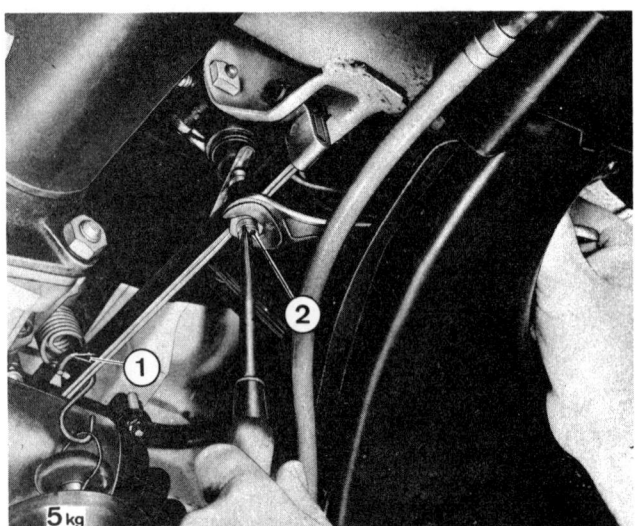

Fig. 9.32 Compensator adjustment – models with independent
rear suspension (Sec 21)

| 1 | Weight | 2 | Adjusting screw |

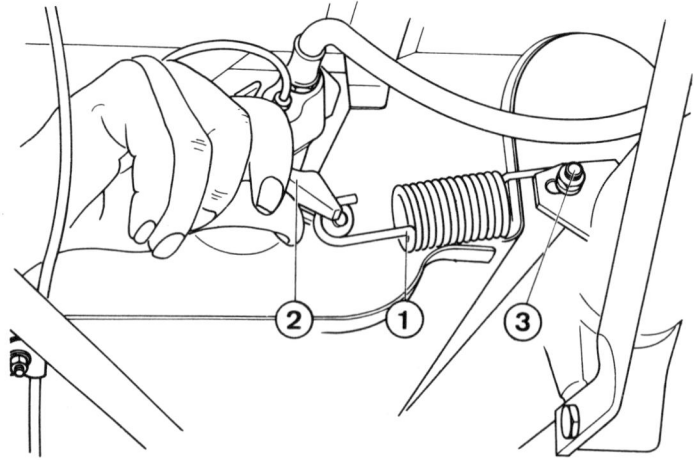

Fig. 9.33 Compensator adjustment – saloon models with 'banjo'
type axle (Sec 21)

| 1 | Spring | 3 | Retaining bolt |
| 2 | Operating lever | | |

7   Retain the fitted parts with the circlip located in the end of the
bore.
8   Refit the stop screw and new sealing O-ring.
9   Check that the pistons are free to move by pushing with a
screwdriver and then refit to the car.

20 Master cylinder (dual circuit – Teves) – dismantling, examination and reassembly

The overhaul sequence is basically the same as that described in
Section 19, but there are minor differences in the internal parts which
are apparent upon comparison. Provided that care is taken, no
problems will arise. One point worth noting, however, is that a range
of reservoirs can be fitted depending on local market requirements. For
models originally fitted with a Lockheed tandem master cylinder, the

front and rear circuits connections must be reversed when fitting a
Teves tandem master cylinder.

21 Compensator – adjustment

Models with independent rear suspension
1   With the car normally laden and on its wheels over a pit or on a
horizontal ramp, suspend a 5 kg (11 lb) weight from the slot in the
compensator lever adjacent to the spring.
2   Push the compensator piston in as far as it will go.
3   Slacken the locknut and turn the adjusting screw in the required
direction until a feeler blade of the correct thickness will just slide
between the piston and adjusting screw. The thickness of feeler
required varies according to whether the fuel tank is full or empty, and
according to the type of regulator fitted. Later GL Saloon models with

drum brakes are fitted with a regulator of ratio 0.47 : 1 (in place of the standard 0.31 : 1); this type may be identified by the fact that it is marked with a dab of white paint. Feeler gauge thicknesses are:

Regulator ratio	Fuel tank full	Fuel tank empty
0.31 : 1	1.4 mm (0.055 in)	1.6 mm (0.063 in)
0.47 : 1	0.7 mm (0.028 in)	0.8 mm (0.032 in)

Saloon models with 'banjo' type solid rear axle

4   Jack up the rear of the car and support it on chassis stands with the wheels and suspension free of any load.
5   Push the operating lever toward the torque tube (photo).
6   Now adjust the spring retaining bolt in its elongated slot so that the spring is without tension or free play. Lower the car to the ground.

Estate and Family Estate models

7   Adjustment of the rear brake compensator on these models requires the use of special Peugeot distance gauges. It is recommended that if the rear brakes seem ineffective or over-effective, adjustment be entrusted to your Peugeot garage.

22 Handbrake – adjustment

1   Jack up the rear of the car and support it on axle stands. Release fully the handbrake.

Models with rear disc brakes

2   If the handbrake is dashboard mounted, slacken the two locknuts on the compensating arm located just in front of the rear suspension crossmember. Now tighten the first adjusting nut until the dished washer behind the nut just starts to compress. Hold the nut in this position and tighten the other locknut.
3   If the handbrake is mounted between the seats, slacken the locknuts at the ends of the handbrake outer cables. Now turn the threaded collars on the ends of the outer cables until the lever on the disc brake caliper just moves off its nylon stop. Now tighten the outer cable locknut.

Models with rear drum brakes

4   First make sure the brake shoes are correctly adjusted as described in Section 15.
5   If the handbrake is dashboard mounted, slacken the two locknuts at the compensating lever under the car. Turn the rod to give four to seven notches of handbrake lever travel and then tighten the locknut.
6   If the handbrake is mounted between the seats, undo the retaining screws and lift up the centre console to expose the cables and compensating lever. Slacken the locknut and turn the rod to give four to seven notches of handbrake lever travel, and then tighten the locknut.

23 Handbrake primary cable – removal and refitting

1   Working under the car, disconnect the control cable yoke from its lever.
2   Remove the clamp and rubber union fixing the rear extremity of the primary outer cable to the car floor.
3   Now working inside the car, raise the mat and underfelt from the gearbox tunnel.
4   Unclip the primary cable from under the front seat support.
5   Remove the clip that secures the plastic counter pulley.
6   Undo and remove the upper and lower handbrake lever case securing nuts and primary outer cable retaining collar nut.
7   Detach the handbrake lever and case assembly from the top and then move towards the counter pulley.
8   Remove the pulley and retaining collar from the lower support.
9   Push the handbrake lever fully into its case.
10   Unhook the cable from the lever.
11   Working under the car again pull the primary cable towards the rear through the opening in the rear floor of the car.
12   Recover the securing collar from the cable outer casing.
13   Refitting the handbrake primary cable is the reverse sequence to removal, but tighten the upper and lower lever case securing nuts and

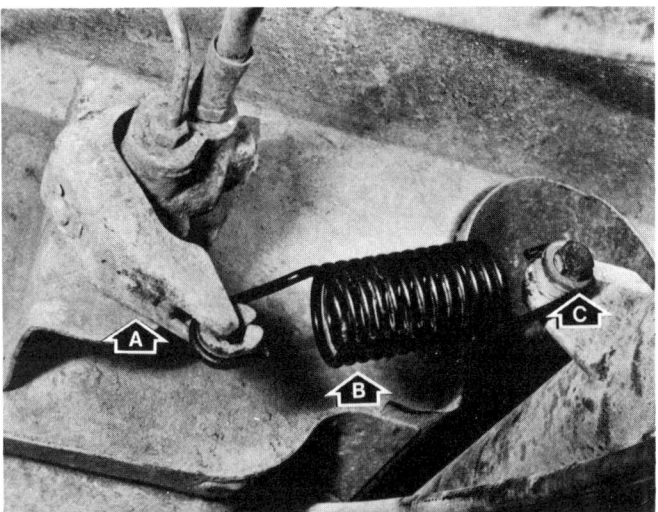

21.5 Rear brake compensator assembly (Teves), showing operating lever (A), spring (B), and adjustment bolt (C)

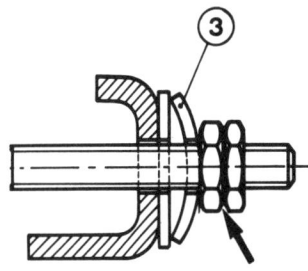

Fig. 9.34 Handbrake lever compensating arm dished washer (3) and locknuts (arrowed) (Sec 22)

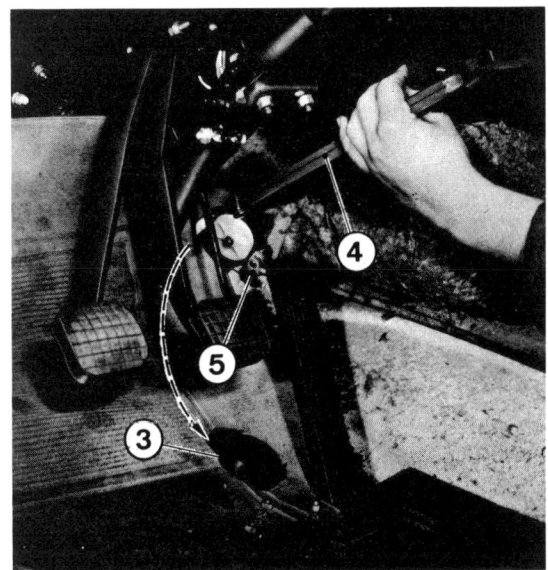

Fig. 9.35 Handbrake lever removal – dashboard mounted type (Sec 23)

3	Pulley shield	5	Stop collar
4	Lever casing		

the outer cable retaining collar to the specified torque wrench settings, as given in the Specifications. Adjust the handbrake as described in Section 22.

24 Vacuum servo unit – removal and refitting

1 Slacken the clip securing the vacuum hose to the servo unit and carefully withdraw the hose from its union.
2 Disconnect the electrical leads to the warning light switch (where fitted).
3 Remove the brake master cylinder as described in the relevant Section.
4 Using a pair of pliers remove the spring clips in the end of the brake pedal-to-pushrod clevis pin. Lift out the clevis pin.
5 Undo and remove the nuts and spring washers that secure the servo unit to the bulkhead. Now carefully lift off the servo unit.
6 Refitting the servo unit is the reverse sequence to removal. On completion of the installation, it will be necessary to bleed the hydraulic system as described in Section 2.

25 Vacuum servo unit – overhaul

It is very rare for a servo unit to develop an internal fault and therefore it should not need any maintenance or servicing. However, should it develop a fault which has been confirmed after checking the vacuum hose, vacuum pump and clips, it is strongly recommended that a replacement unit be obtained and fitted. Normally these units are available on an exchange basis. No overhaul procedures are given because special tools are required, and it is considered far more economical to fit a replacement unit rather than try to obtain a service kit and do the job oneself. The following two points should be noted:

(a) The unit is supplied with the master cylinder pushrod preset to a determined protrusion and this must not be altered under any circumstances
(b) The rod from the reaction disc must never be withdrawn, because if the disc falls into the cylinder it cannot be refitted in its correct position without dismantling

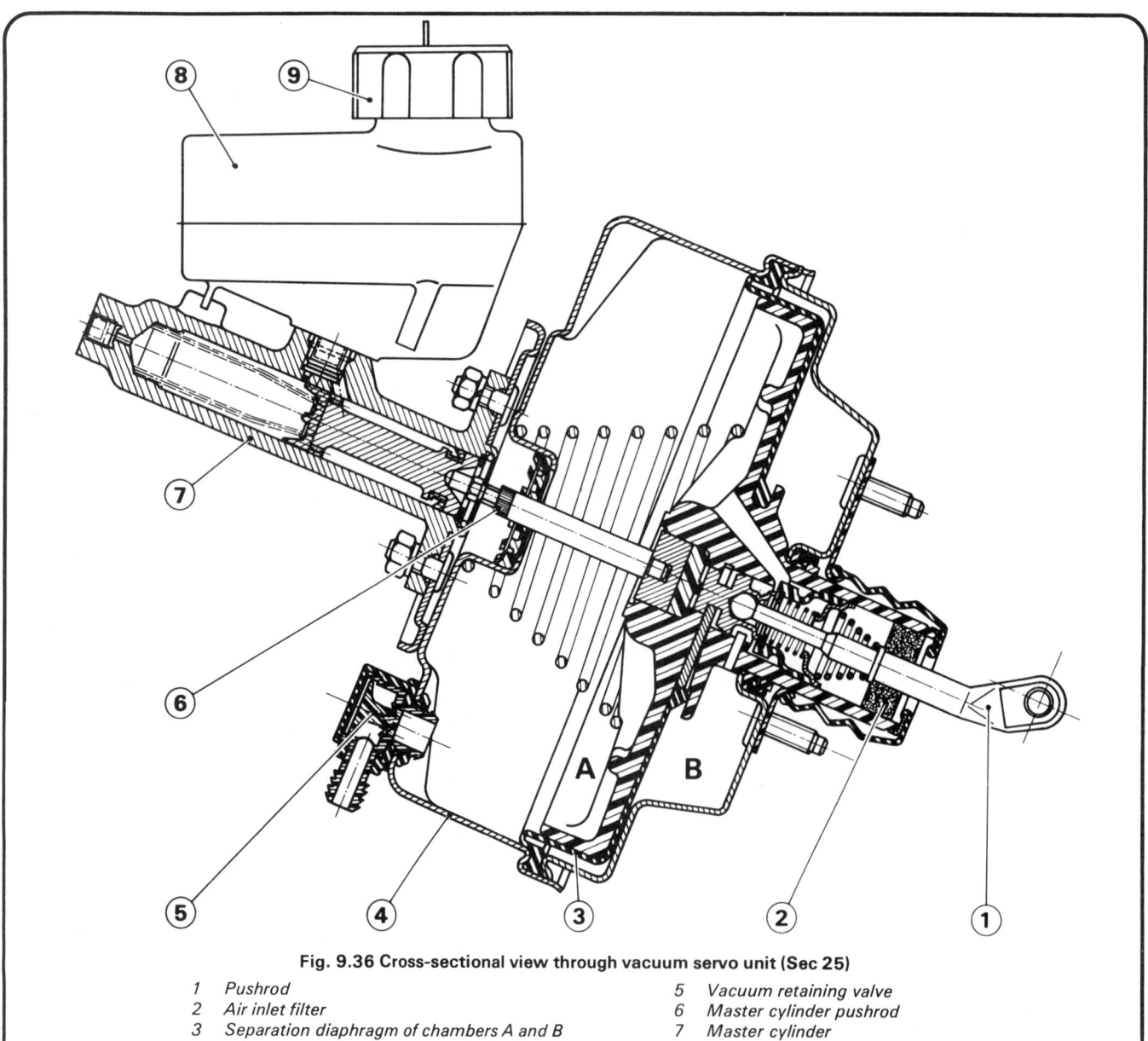

Fig. 9.36 Cross-sectional view through vacuum servo unit (Sec 25)

1 Pushrod
2 Air inlet filter
3 Separation diaphragm of chambers A and B
   A – Chamber subject to engine vacuum
   B – Chamber at atmospheric pressure
4 Vacuum servo unit body

5 Vacuum retaining valve
6 Master cylinder pushrod
7 Master cylinder
8 Brake and clutch fluid reservoir
9 Reservoir cap with level indicator

26 Hydraulic pipes and hoses – general inspection and renewal

1   Periodically all brake pipes, pipe connections and unions should be carefully examined.

2   First examine for signs of leakage where the pipe unions occur. Then examine the flexible hoses for signs of chafing and fraying and, of course, leakage. This is only a preliminary part of the flexible hose inspection, as exterior condition does not necessarily indicate the interior condition, which will be considered later.

3   The steel pipes must be examined carefully and methodically. They must be cleaned off and examined for any signs of dents or other percussive damage, rust or corrosion. Rust and corrosion should be scraped off, and if the depth of pitting in the pipes is significant the pipes should be renewed. This is particularly likely in those areas underneath the car body and along the rear axle where the pipes are exposed to full force of road and weather conditions.

4   Rigid pipe removal is usually quite straightforward. The unions at each end are undone, the pipe and union pulled out, and the centre sections of the pipe removed from the body clips. The joints may sometimes be very tight. As one can only use an open-ended spanner and the unions are not large, burring of the flats is not uncommon when attempting to undo them. For this reason, a self-locking grip wrench is often the only way to unscrew a stubborn union.

5   Removal of flexible hoses is described in Section 3.

6   With the flexible hose removed, examine the internal bore. If it is blown through first, it should be possible to see through it. Any specks of rubber which comes out, or signs of restriction in the bore mean that the rubber lining is breaking up and the hose must be renewed.

7   Rigid pipes which need renewal can usually be purchased from any Peugeot garage where they have the pipes, unions and special tools to make them up. All they need to know is the total length of pipe, the type of flange used at each end with the unions, and the length and thread of the union. It is a good idea to take the old pipe along as a pattern.

8   Refitting of the pipe is a straightforward reversal of the removal procedure. If the rigid pipes have been made up it is best to get all the bends in them before trying to install them. Also, if there are any acute bends ask your supplier to put these in for you on a special tube bender – otherwise you may kink the pipe and thereby decrease the bore area and fluid flow.

9   With the pipes refitted it will be necessary to bleed the brake hydraulic system, as described in Section 2.

27 Brake pedal – removal and refitting

1   Working underneath the dashboard, remove the spring clips in the end of the brake pedal-to-vacuum servo unit pushrod clevis pin using a pair of pliers. Lift out the clevis pin.

2   At the top of the brake pedal, remove the sring clip from the brake pedal pivot pin and slide out the pin. Space is extremely limited in this area, and the removal of the spring clip and pivot pin is a fiddly operation requiring a good deal of patience.

3   Having removed the pivot pin, carefully lower the brake pedal out from under the dash and recover the bushes, washers and spacer (if fitted).

4   Examine the bushes for wear, and check that the pivot pin is a slide fit in them with very little side play. Renew the bushes or pivot pin if worn.

5   Refitting the brake pedal is the reverse sequence to removal.

28 Stop-light switch – removal and refitting

1   The stop-light switch is located on a bracket beneath the dashboard and is activated by movement of the brake pedal (photo).

2   To remove the switch, disconnect the electrical connections and then slacken the two switch retaining locknuts.

3   Remove the locknut nearest the brake pedal and then lift out the switch.

4   To refit the switch, place it in position on the mounting bracket and loosely refit the locknuts. Reconnect the electrical leads to the switch.

5   Depress the brake pedal just sufficiently to take up the free play of the servo unit and master cylinder. With the pedal in this position, adjust the switch by repositioning the locknuts so that the stop lights are just illuminated.

29 Vacuum pump – removal and refitting

1   Make a note of the positions of the two hoses and then detach them from the pump.

2   Slacken the pump tensioning bolt and the pump mounting nut and bolt, push the pump inwards and lift off the drivebelt (photo).

3   Now remove the pump adjusting bolt and mounting nut and bolt and lift the pump off the engine.

4   Refitting the vacuum pump is the reverse sequence to removal. Position the pump to give a deflection of approximately 7 mm (0.25 in) of the drivebelt using hand pressure, midway between the two pulleys.

30 Vacuum pump – testing, dismantling and reassembly

1   Should a fault develop on the vacuum pump it can only be accurately tested using specialist gauges. However, a reasonable guide to the performance of the pump can be obtained by placing your fingers over the two ports and turning the pulley by hand. A reasonable

28.1 Brake pedal assembly and stop-light switch (arrowed)

29.2 Vacuum pump assembly

A   Drivebelt tensioning bolt   B   Pump mounting bolt and nut

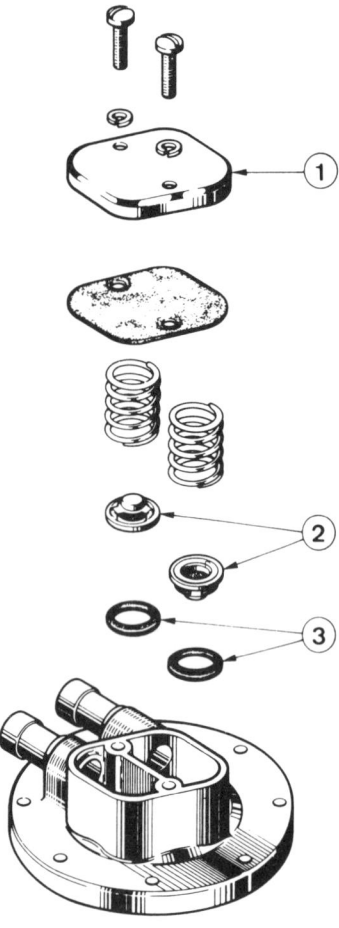

Fig. 9.37 Vacuum pump upper body assembly (Sec 30)

1   Top cover   3   Seals
2   One-way valves

suction should be felt at the ports accompanied by a slight increase in effort needed to turn the pulley. If this is not the case the pump may be dismantled and new valves and a diaphragm obtained as necessary.

2   With the pump on the bench, undo and remove the two screws securing the top cover and lift off the cover.

3   Recover the gasket and then lift out the two springs.

4   Note the position of the two one-way valves (one will be facing upwards and one downwards) and then lift them out together with their seals.

5   Now mark the relationship of the upper and lower pump body and then undo and remove the retaining screws. Lift off the upper pump body.

6   Undo and remove the socket-headed bolt securing the diaphragm to the piston, and then lift off the small washer, the diaphragm and then the large washer.

7   Examine the diaphragm, the valves and valve seals for puncturing, splitting or general deterioration, and renew as necessary.

8   Reassembly of the vacuum pump is the reverse of the dismantling sequence, bearing in mind the following points:

(a)   When reassembling the diaphragm, the large washer is fitted below the diaphragm and the small washer above. Ensure that the chamfered sides face the diaphragm

(b)   Line up the marks made during dismantling when reassembling the upper and lower bodies

(c)   Ensure that the one-way valves are fitted in the same positions as noted during dismantling

(d)   Refill the pump with the correct grade of oil to the level of the filler plug after reassembling the pump. Ensure that the mark on the pulley hub is uppermost when checking or refilling with oil.

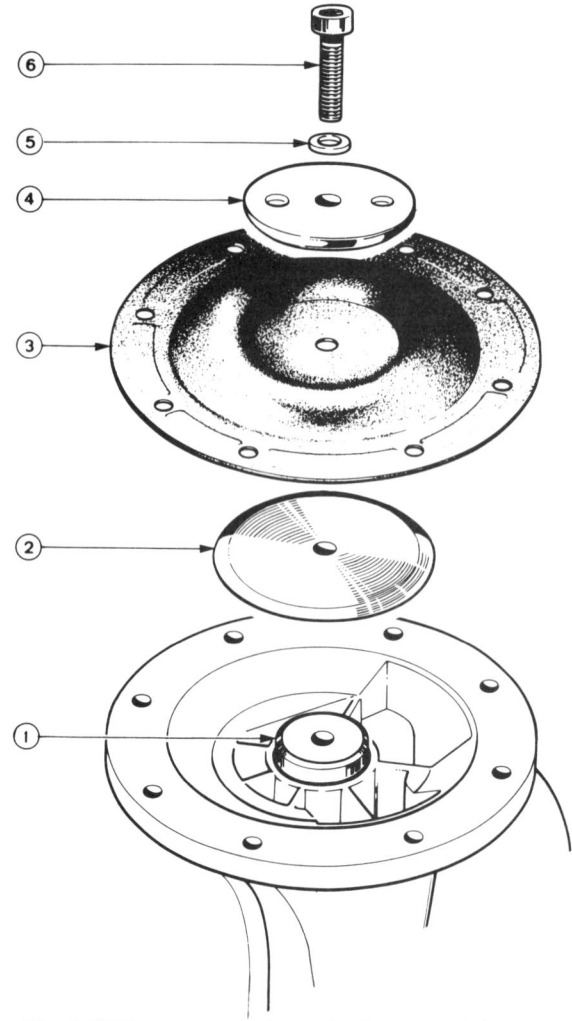

Fig. 9.38 Vacuum pump lower body assembly (Sec 30)

1   Piston   4   Small washer
2   Large washer   5   Washer
3   Diaphragm   6   Bolt

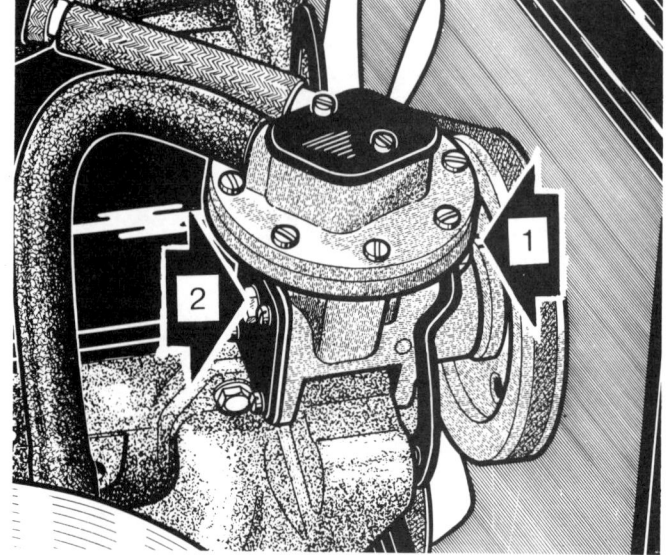

Fig. 9.39 Checking vacuum pump oil level (Sec 30)

1   Pump TDC mark on pulley   2   Oil level/filler plug

31 Fault diagnosis – braking system

Symptom	Reason(s)
Excessive brake pedal travel	Rear brakes out of adjustment Self-adjusting mechanism inoperative (where fitted) Excessive front (or rear) wheel bearing endfloat Excessive front (or rear) disc run-out
Vehicle pulls to one side under braking	Front disc pads contaminated with oil, grease or hydraulic fluid on one side Disc brake caliper pistons seized or partially seized on one side Excessive wear of brake pad friction material A mixture of brake pad materials fitted between sides Wear, incorrect or out-of-adjustment steering or suspension components, tyres or tyre pressures
Judder felt through brake pedal and/or steering wheel under braking	Excessive run-out of front discs Front discs worn, scored or grooved Excessively worn brake pads Rear drums (or discs) worn, scored or out-of-round Brake component mountings loose or insecure
Brake pedal appears spongy	Air in hydraulic system Bulging in hydraulic flexible hose(s) Master cylinder or servo unit mountings insecure Master cylinder faulty
Excessive effort required to stop vehicle	Lack of servo assistance Worn brake pads or linings One or more brake caliper or wheel cylinder pistons seized Incorrect brake pads or linings fitted Brake pads or linings contaminated with oil, grease or hydraulic fluid Failure of one braking circuit (dual circuit system)
Lack of servo assistance	Vacuum hose connections loose or disconnected Vacuum pump drivebelt slipping or broken Vacuum pump faulty Servo unit faulty
Pedal travels to floor with little resistance	Hydraulic pipe, hose, or union leaking Leaking brake caliper piston or wheel cylinder seals Leaking or faulty master cylinder
Binding, juddering, overheating	One of a combination or reasons given in the foregoing Sections Handbrake overadjusted

Chapter 10 Electrical system

Contents

Specifications

System type .... 12 volt, negative earth

Battery .... 12 volt, 65 amp hour

Alternator
Type .... Paris-Rhone A13 series or SEV-Marchal 71229302
Output at 14 volts .... 32 to 48 amps, depending on model and specification
Maximum speed .... 12 000 rpm

Starter motor
Type .... Ducellier 6207 or 6109; Bosch JF 12V 2KW; Paris-Rhone D11E series
Actuator .... Pre-engaged, solenoid operated

Windscreen wipers
Type .... Bosch or SEV-Marchal
Number of speeds 2

Heater plugs
Type .... Bosch or Beru
Voltage .... 9.5 volts
Current .... 10 amps

Fuses
Quantity .... 4 or 5, depending on model (see text)

Bulbs
	Wattage
Headlights	45/40W
Sidelights	5W
Direction indicators	21W

Stop lights	21W
Reversing lights	21W
Panel lights	4W
Warning lights	2W
Interior lights	4W
Number plate light	5W

Torque wrench settings

	Nm	lbf ft
Alternator pulley nut	40	29
Starter motor retaining bolts	20	14
Heater plugs	45	33

1 General description

The electrical system is of the 12 volt negative earth type, and the major components comprise a 12 volt battery, an alternator which is driven from the crankshaft pulley, and a starter motor.

The battery supplies a steady amount of current for the starting, lighting and other electrical circuits, and provides a reserve of electricity when the current comsumed by the electrical equipment exceeds that being produced by the alternator.

The alternator has its own integral regulator which ensures a high output if the battery is in a low state of charge, or the demand from the electrical equipment is high, and a low output if the battery is fully charged and there is little demand for the electrical equipment.

When fitting electrical accessories to cars with a negative earth system it is important, if they contain silicon diodes or transistors, that they are connected correctly, otherwise serious damage may result to the components concerned. Items such as radios, tape recorders, etc, should all be checked for correct polarity.

It is important that the battery is disconnected before removing the alternator output lead, as this is live at all times. Also, if body repairs are to be carried out using electric arc welding equipment, the alternator must be disconnected otherwise serious damage can be caused to the more delicate components. Whenever the battery has to be disconnected, the negative terminal should always be removed first and refitted last. Do *not* disconnect the battery with the engine running. If 'jumper cables' are used to start the car, they must be connected correctly – positive to positive and negative to negative.

2 Battery – removal and refitting

1   The battery is on a carrier fitted to the left-hand wing valance of the engine compartment. It should be removed once every three months for cleaning and testing. Disconnect the negative and then the positive leads from the battery terminals by undoing and removing the terminal post clamps. Note that two cables are attached to the positive terminal (photos).

2   Release the battery clamp and carefully lift the battery from its carrier, holding it vertically to ensure that none of the electrolyte is spilled.

3   Refitting is a direct reversal of this procedure. Refit the positive lead before the negative lead and smear the terminals with petroleum jelly to prevent corrosion. *Never* use an ordinary grease.

3 Battery – maintenance and inspection

1   Normal weekly battery maintenance consists of checking the electrolyte level of each cell to ensure that the separators are covered by $\frac{1}{4}$ inch (6 mm) of electrolyte. If the level has fallen, top up the battery using distilled water only, but do not overfill. If a battery is overfilled or any electrolyte spilled, immediately wipe away the excess, as electrolyte attacks and corrodes any metal it comes into contact with very rapidly.

2   If the battery has the Autofil device as fitted on original production of the car, a special topping up sequence is required. The white balls in the Autofil battery are part of the automatic topping up device which ensures correct electrolyte level. The vent chamber should remain in position at all times except when topping up or taking specific gravity readings. If the electrolyte level in any of the cells is below the bottom of the filling tube top up as follows:

   (a) Lift off the vent chamber cover
   (b) With the battery level, poor distilled water into the trough until all the filling tubes and trough are full
   (c) Immediately refit the cover to allow the water in the trough and tubes to flow into the cells. Each cell will automatically receive the correct amount of water

3   As well as keeping the terminals clean and covered with petroleum jelly, the top of the battery, and especially the top of the cells, should be kept clean and dry. This helps prevent corrosion and ensures that the battery does not become partially discharged by leakage through dampness and dirt.

4   Once every three months remove the battery, and inspect the battery securing bolts, the battery clamp plate, tray and battery leads

2.1a Remove the battery negative terminal first ...

2.1b ... followed by the positive terminal

for corrosion (white fluffy deposits on the metal which are brittle to touch). If any corrosion is found clean off the deposit with ammonia and paint over the clean metal with an anti-rust anti-acid paint.

5   At the same time inspect the battery case for cracks. Cracks are frequently caused to the top of the battery case by pouring in distilled water in the middle of winter *after* instead of *before* a run. This gives the water no chance to mix with the electrolyte and so the former freezes and splits the battery case.

6   If topping up the battery becomes excessive, and the case has been inspected for cracks that could cause leakage but none are found, the battery is being overcharged and the voltage regulator will have to be checked and reset.

7   With the battery on the bench at the three monthly interval check, measure the specific gravity with a hydrometer to determine the state of charge and condition of the electrolyte. There should be very little variation between the different cells and, if a variation in excess of 0.025 is present it will be due to:

(a) Loss of electrolyte from the battery at some time caused by spillage or a leak. This results in a drop in the specific gravity of the electrolyte when the deficiency is replaced with distilled water instead of fresh electrolyte

(b) An internal short circuit caused by buckling of the plate or similar malady pointing to the likelihood of total battery failure in the near future

8   The specific gravity of the electrolyte for fully charged conditions, at the electrolyte temperature indicated, is listed in Table A. The specific gravity of a fully discharged battery at different temperatures of the electrolyte is given in Table B.

Table A – Specific gravity – battery fully charged
  1.268 *at 100°F or 38°C electrolyte temperature*
  1.272 *at 90°F or 32°C electrolyte temperature*
  1.276 *at 80°F or 27°C electrolyte temperature*
  1.280 *at 70°F or 21°C electrolyte temperature*
  1.284 *at 60°F or 16°C electrolyte temperature*
  1.288 *at 50°F or 10°C electrolyte temperature*
  1.292 *at 40°F or 4°C electrolyte temperature*
  1.296 *at 30°F or -1.5°C electrolyte temperature*

Table B – Specific gravity – battery fully discharged
  1.098 *at 100°F or 38°C electrolyte temperature*
  1.102 *at 90°F or 32°C electrolyte temperature*
  1.106 *at 80°F or 27°C electrolyte temperature*
  1.110 *at 70°F or 21°C electrolyte temperature*
  1.114 *at 60°F or 16°C electrolyte temperature*
  1.118 *at 50°F or 10°C electrolyte temperature*
  1.122 *at 40°F or 4°C electrolyte temperature*
  1.126 *at 30°F or -1.5°C electrolyte temperature*

4   Battery – electrolyte replenishment

1   If the battery is in a fully charged state and one of the cells maintains a specific gravity reading which is 0.025 or more lower than the others, it is likely that electrolyte has been lost from the cell at some time.

2   Top up the cell with a solution of 1 part sulphuric acid to 2.5 parts of water obtainable ready mixed from your garage. If the cell is already fully topped up syphon some electrolyte out.

5   Battery – charging

1   In winter time when heavy demand is placed upon the battery, such as when starting from cold, and much electrical equipment is continually in use, it is a good idea to occasionally have the battery

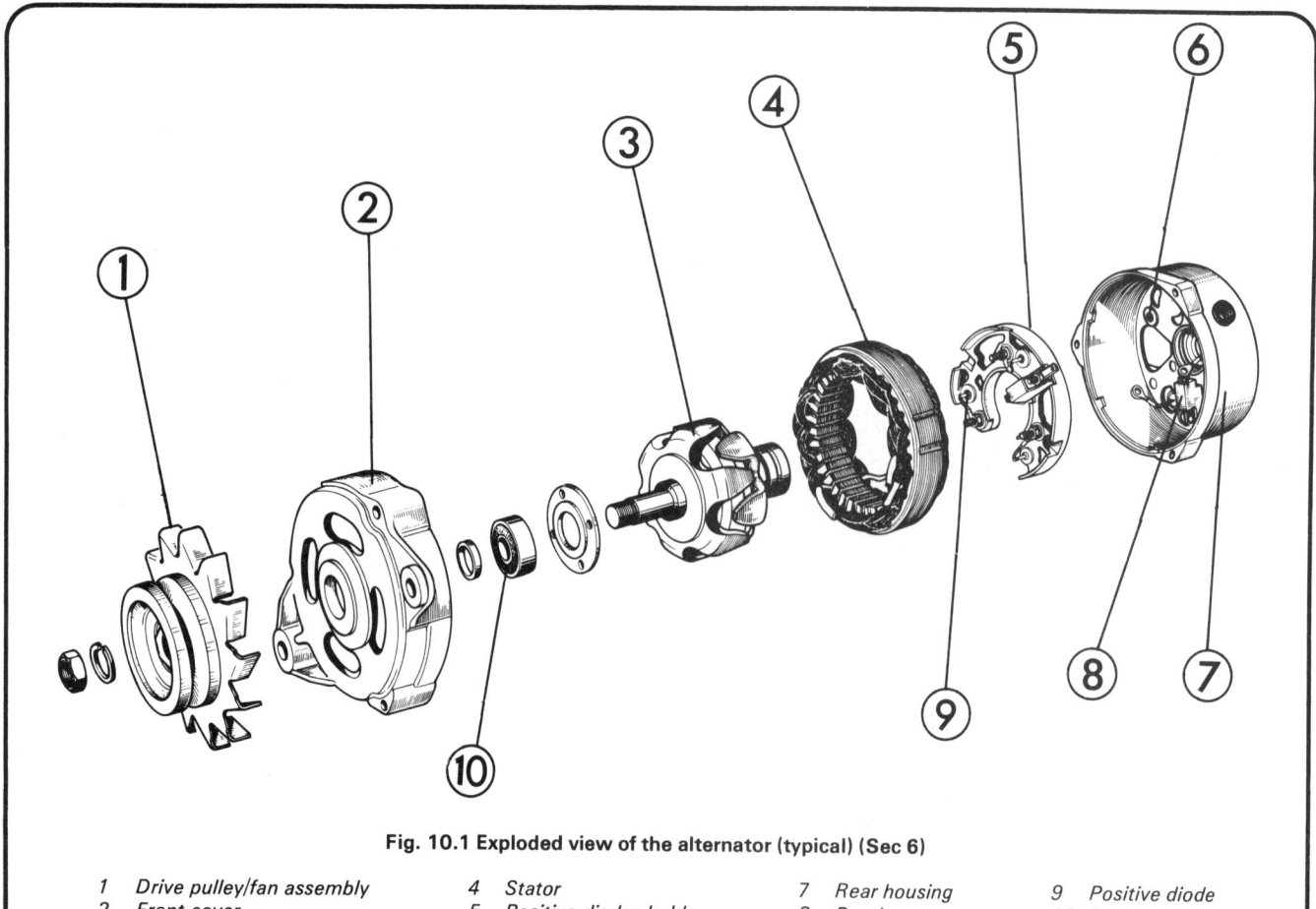

Fig. 10.1 Exploded view of the alternator (typical) (Sec 6)

1	Drive pulley/fan assembly	4	Stator	7	Rear housing	9	Positive diode
2	Front cover	5	Positive diodes holder	8	Brush	10	Ball bearing
3	Rotor	6	Negative diode				

fully charged from an external source at the rate of 3.5 to 4 amps.
2   Continue to charge the battery at this rate, until no further rise in specific gravity is noted over a four hour period.
3   Alternatively, a trickle charger charging at the rate of 1.5 amps can be safely used overnight.
4   Specially rapid 'boost' charges, which are claimed to restore the power of the battery in 1 to 2 hours, are not recommended as they can cause serious damage to the battery plates through overheating.
5   While charging the battery note that the temperature of the electrolyte should not exceed 100°F (37.8°C).

6   Alternator – general description

All models covered by this manual are fitted with alternators. The alternator generates alternating current (ac) which is rectified by diodes into direct current (dc) and is the current needed for charging the battery.

The main advantage of the alternator lies in its ability to provide a high charge at low speed. Driving slowly in heavy traffic with a dynamo invariably means no charge is reaching the battery. In similar conditions even with the heater, wiper, lights and perhaps radio switched on, the alternator will ensure a charge reaches the battery.

The alternator is of the rotating field ventilated design, and comprises principally; a laminated stator on which is wound the output winding; a rotor carrying the field windings – each end of the rotor shaft runs in ball race bearings which are lubricated for life; natural finish die-cast end brackets; and an output control regulator.

The rotor is belt-driven from the engine through a pulley keyed to the rotor shaft. A fan adjacent to the pulley draws air through the unit. This fan forms an integral part of the alternator specification. It has been designed to provide adequate airflow with minimum noise, and to withstand the high stresses associated with the maximum speed. Rotation is clockwise when viewed from the drive end.

The regulator is set during manufacture and requires no further attention. However, should its operation be faulty, it must be renewed as a complete unit.

7   Alternator – special procedures

Whenever the electrical system of the car is being attended to, or external means of starting the engine is used, there are certain precautions that must be taken, otherwise serious and expensive damage can result.
1   Always make sure that the negative terminal of the battery is earthed. If the terminal connections are accidentally reversed, or if the battery has been reverse charged, the alternator diodes will burn out.
2   Whenever the alternator is to be removed, or when disconnecting the terminals of the alternator circuit, always disconnect the battery earth terminal first.
3   The alternator must never be operated without the battery-to-alternator cable connected.
4   If the battery is to be charged by external means, always disconnect both battery cables before the external charge is connected.
5   Should it be necessary to use a booster charger or booster battery to start the engine, always double check that the negative cable is connected to negative terminal and the positive cable to positive terminal.

8   Alternator – maintenance

1   The equipment has been designed for the minimum amount of maintenance in service, the only items subject to wear being the brushes and bearings.
2   Brushes should be examined after about 75 000 miles (120 000 km) and renewed if necessary. The bearings are pre-packed with grease for life, and should not require further attention.
3   Regularly check the drivebelt tension, and if slack, adjust as described in Section 9.

9   Alternator – removal and refitting

1   Disconnect the battery earth terminal.

9.2 Electrical connections at rear of alternator

9.3 Alternator adjustment arm bolt (A) and mounting bolt (B)

2   Note the terminal connections at the rear of the alternator and disconnect the plug, multi-pin connector or terminals (photo).
3   Undo and remove the alternator adjustment arm bolt, slacken the alternator mounting bolts and push the alternator inwards towards the engine. Lift away the drivebelt from the pulley (photo).
4   Remove the retaining two mounting bolts and carefully lift the alternator away from the car.
5   Take care not to knock or drop the alternator, as this can cause irreparable damage.
6   Refitting the alternator is the reverse sequence to removal. Before fully tightening the adjustment arm bolt, move the alternator away from the engine until it is just possible to deflect the drivebelt by hand approximately 13 mm (0.5 in) at a point midway between the pulleys. Hold the alternator in this position and tighten the mountings and adjustment arm bolt.

10   Alternator – fault diagnosis and repair

Due to the specialist knowledge and equipment required to test or service an alternator, it is recommended that if the performance is suspect, the car be taken to an automobile electrician who will have the facilities for such work. Because of this recommendation, information given in this Chapter is limited to the inspection and renewal

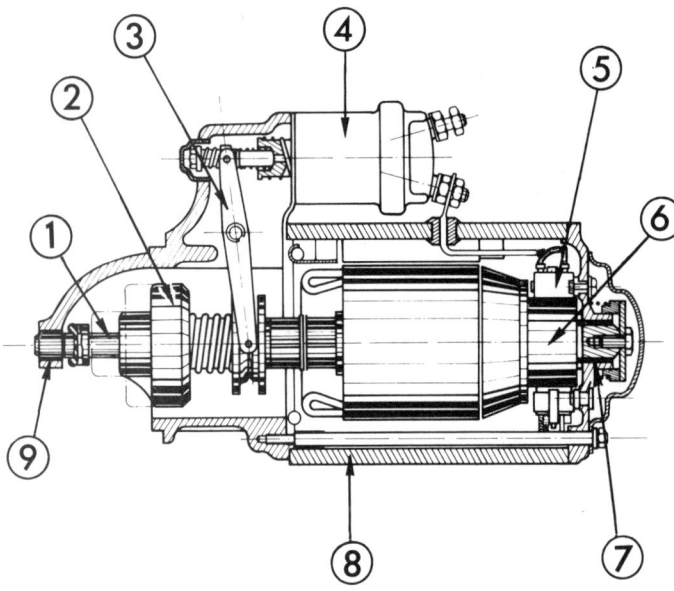

Fig. 10.2 Sectional view of the starter motor (typical) (Sec 11)

1	Driveshaft	6	Commutator/armature
2	Freewheel		assembly
3	Fork	7	Rear end bearing
4	Solenoid	8	Motor body
5	Brushes	9	Front end bearing

of the brushes. Should the alternator not charge or the system be suspect, the following points may be checked before seeking further assistance:

(a) Check the drivebelt tension, as described in Section 9
(b) Check the battery, as described in Section 3
(c) Check all electrical cable connections for cleanliness and security

11 Starter motor – general description

The starter motor is of the pre-engaged type with a series parallel wound four-pole, four-brush motor fitted with a pre-engagement solenoid. Incorporated in the pinion assembly is a roller clutch which is able to transmit torque from the starter motor to the engine but not in the reverse direction, thereby ensuring that the armature is not driven by the engine at any time.

The solenoid comprises a soft iron plunger, starter switch contacts, main closing winding (series winding) and a hold-on winding

(short winding). When the starter/ignition switch is operated, both the coils are engaged in parallel, but the closing winding is shorted out by the starter switch contacts when they are closed.

12 Starter motor – testing on engine

1   If the starter motor fails to turn the engine when the switch is operated there are four possible reasons why:

(a) The battery is discharged or faulty
(b) The electrical connections between switch, solenoid, battery and starter motor are somewhere failing to pass the necessary current from the battery, through the starter to earth
(c) The solenoid has an internal fault
(d) The starter motor is either jammed or electrically defective

2   To check the battery, switch on the headlights. If they go dim after a few seconds the battery is discharged. If the lamps glow brightly, next operate the starter switch and see what happens to the lights. If they do dim it is indicative that power is reaching the starter motor but failing to turn it. Therefore check that it is not jammed by placing the car in gear and rocking it to-and-fro (except automatic). If it is not jammed the starter will have to be removed for examination. If the starter should turn very slowly go on to the next check.

3   If, when the starter switch is operated, the lights stay bright, then the power is not reaching the starter motor. Check all connections from the battery to solenoid for cleanliness and tightness. With a good battery fitted this is the most usual cause of starter motor problems. Check that the earth cable between the engine and chassis is also intact and cleanly connected. This can sometimes be overlooked when the engine is taken out.

4   If no results have yet been achieved, turn off the headlights, otherwise the battery will soon be discharged. It may be possible that a clicking noise was heard each time the ignition/starter switch was operated. This is the solenoid switch operating but it does not necessarily follow that the main contact is closing properly. (If no clicking has been heard from the solenoid it is certainly defective). The solenoid contact can be checked by putting a voltmeter or bulb across the main cable connection on the starter side of the solenoid and earth. When the switch is operated there should be a reading or a lighted bulb. If not the switch has a fault.

13 Starter motor – removal and refitting

1   Disconnect the battery positive and negative leads from the terminals.
2   Make a note of the cable connections to the rear of the solenoid and detach the cable terminals from the solenoid (photo).
3   Undo and remove the starter motor securing nuts, bolts and spring washers and lift away the starter motor (photos).
4   Refitting the starter motor is the reverse sequence to removal.

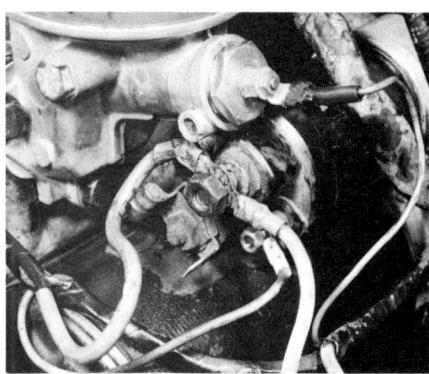

13.2 Electrical connections at starter motor solenoid

13.3a Starter motor lower support bolt

13.3b Removing the starter motor

14 Starter motor – dismantling, overhaul and reassembly

Such is the inherent reliability of the starter motor, it is unlikely that a motor will ever need dismantling until it is totally worn out and in need of renewal. It is not a task for the home mechanic because, although reasonably easy to undertake, the reassembly and adjustment before refitting is beyond his scope because of the need for specialist equipment. It would under all circumstances be realistic for the work to be undertaken by the specialist auto-electrician.

15 Headlight bulb – removal and refitting

1   Working in the engine compartment, withdraw the wiring pulley from the rear of the headlight bulb (photo).
2   Now spring back the two spring clips that retain the bulb in the lens unit and lift out the bulb (photo).
3   Refitting the bulb is the reverse sequence to removal.

16 Headlight – alignment

1   It is always advisable to have the headlights aligned on proper optical beam setting equipment, but if this is not available the following procedure may be used.
2   Position the car on level ground 10ft (3 metres) in front of a dark wall or board. The wall or board must be at right-angles to the centreline of the car.
3   Draw a vertical line on the board or wall in line with the centreline of the car.
4   Bounce the car on its suspension to ensure correct settlement and then measure the height between the ground and the centre of the headlights.
5   Draw a horizontal line across the board or wall at this measured height. On this horizontal line mark a cross on either side of the vertical centreline the distance between the centre of the light unit and the centre of the car.
6   On models equipped with a twin headlight system, remove the external headlight surround to gain access to the adjusting screws. It will be seen that there are two adjusters for each light unit, one at the top for vertical movement and one at the side for horizontal movement.
7   With the remaining light units, two adjusters are located at the rear of each unit. One at the top for vertical movement (photo), and the other halfway down the rim on the radiator side. This is for horizontal adjustment (photo).
8   On some models there is an extra adjustment device which is used purely to compensate for the different load conditions of the vehicle. This is used to prevent dazzling oncoming drivers when using dipped beams with a heavy load in the rear. This device is a plastic spacer placed on the vertical adjuster rod of each headlight (see photo 16.7a). The spacer has a small lug moulded onto it. With the lug uppermost, the lights are set up for the normal or light load condition. For heavy loads, the lug is turned 90° clockwise. It should be noted that this is merely a compensation device – the headlamps must still be initially adjusted using the appropriate adjusters as below.
9   Switch the headlights onto full beam.
10 By careful adjustment of the horizontal and vertical adjusting screws on each light, align the centres of each beam onto the crosses which were previously marked on the horizontal line.
11 Bounce the car on its suspension again and check that the beams return to the correct positions. At the same time check the operation of the dip switch. Refit the headlight rims if removed.

17 Front side and direction indicator lights – removal and refitting

Bulb renewal
1   The front sidelight bulbs may be fitted either to the headlight unit (photo) (in which case sidelight bulb renewal follows the same procedure as for the headlight bulb described in Section 15), or to a separate unit with the direction indicator as described below.
2   To renew a light bulb it is not necessary to remove the light body.

3   Undo and remove the two screws securing the lens to the light body. Lift away the lens and gasket (photo).
4   Depress the bulb and turn anti-clockwise to release the bayonet fitting. Withdraw the bulb.
5   Refitting the bulb and lens is the reverse sequence to removal.

Light body – removal and refitting
6   Undo and remove the two screws securing the lens to the light body. Lift away the lens and gasket.
7   Detach the two electric cables from the terminal connectors.
8   Carefully ease the light body forwards from its aperture. Recover the gasket (photo).
9   Refitting the light body is the reverse sequence to removal.

18 Rear light cluster and bulbs – removal and refitting

Bulb renewal
1   Undo and remove the screws that secure the lens assembly to the light body. Lift away the lens and gasket (photo).
2   Depress the relevant bulb and turn anti-clockwise to release the bayonet fitting. Withdraw the bulb (photo).
3   Refitting the bulb and lens is the reverse sequence to removal.

Light body – removal and refitting
4   Detach the electric cables from the terminal connectors located inside the luggage compartment.
5   *Saloon models:* Undo and remove the nut and washer securing the light body and draw away from its aperture.
6   *Other models:* Undo and remove the screws securing the light body and draw away from its aperture.
7   Refitting the light body is the reverse sequence to removal.

19 Rear number plate light – removal and refitting

Bulb renewal
1   *All models except Utility:* Working inside the rear of the car, detach the transparent covers, depress the bulb and turn anti-clockwise to release the bayonet fitting. Withdraw the bulb (photo). Refitting the bulb is the reverse sequence to removal.
2   *Utility models:* Undo and remove the two screws securing the lens to the light body. Lift away the lens and gasket. Depress the bulb and turn anti-clockwise to release the bayonet fitting. Withdraw the bulb. Refitting the bulb is the reverse sequence to removal.

Light body – removal and refitting
3   *All models except Utility:* Working inside the car, detach the electric cables from the wiring harness. Undo and remove the two securing nuts and washers. Lift away the light body. Refitting the light body is the reverse sequence to removal.
3   *Utility models:* Undo and remove the nuts, washers and bolts securing the light body to the rear panel. Detach the electric cables from the wiring harness and lift away the light body. Refitting the light body is the reverse sequence to removal.

20 Windscreen wiper blades – removal and refitting

1   To remove a windscreen wiper blade, depress the tab and pull the blade from the arm (photo).
2   Refitting the windscreen wiper blade is the reverse sequence to removal.

21 Windscreen wiper arms – removal and refitting

1   Before removing a wiper arm, turn the windscreen wiper switch on and off to ensure that the arms are in their normal parked position, with the blades parallel with the bottom of the windscreen.
2   To remove the arm, lift up the end cap and undo the retaining nut. Now lift the arm off the spindle (photo).
3   Refitting is the the reverse sequence to removal.

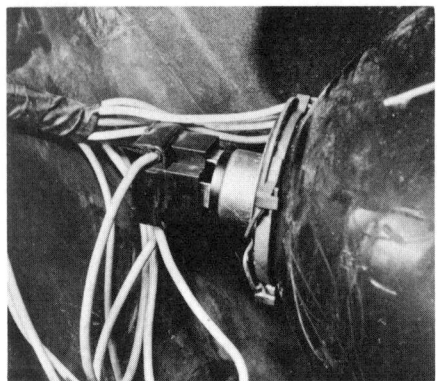

15.1 Headlight bulb wiring connector

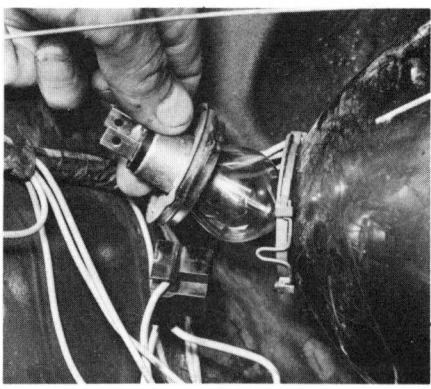

15.2 Removing the headlight bulb

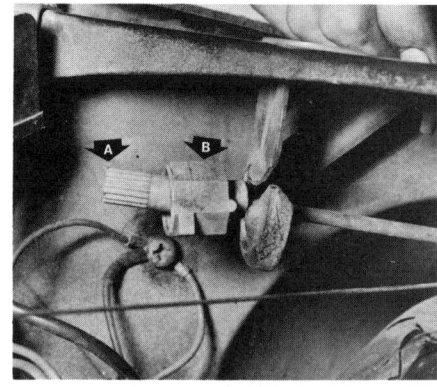

16.7a Headlight vertical movement adjuster (A) and compensator (B)

16.7b Headlight horizontal movement adjuster

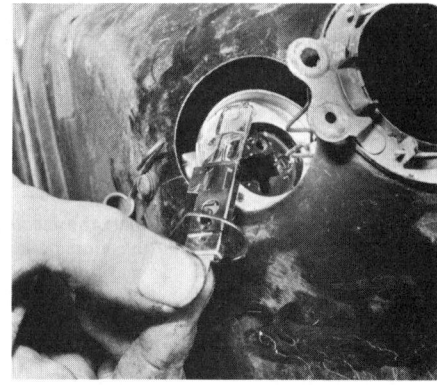

17.1 Removing a headlight mounted sidelight bulb

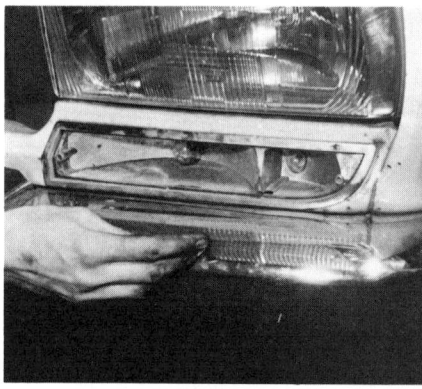

17.3 Removing the front light cluster lens

17.8 Light body removal

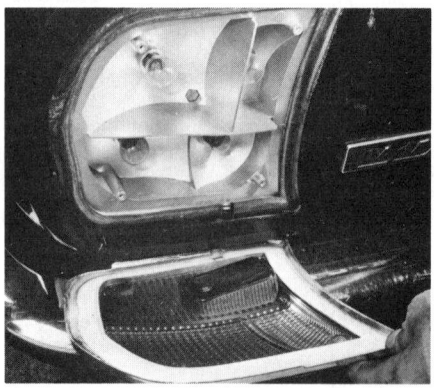

18.1 Remove the rear light cluster lens ...

18.2 ... to provide access to the bulbs

19.1 Rear number plate light bulb location

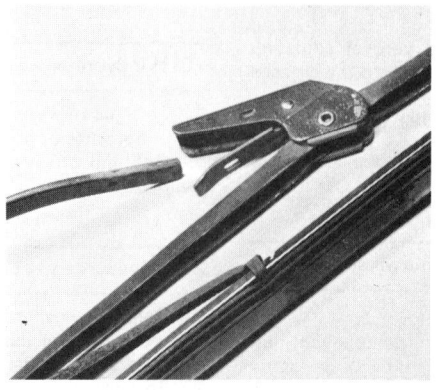

20.1 Remove the wiper blade from the cam by depressing the tab

21.2 Remove the wiper arm by lifting the cap and unscrewing the nut

22 Windscreen wiper mechanism – fault diagnosis and rectification

1   Should the windscreen wipers fail, or work very slowly, then check the terminal connectors for security and make sure the insulation of all the wiring is not damaged, so causing a short circuit. If this is in order then check the current the motor is taking by connecting an ammeter in the circuit and turning on the wiper switch. Consumption should be between 2 and 3 amps.

2   If no current is passing through the motor, check that the switch is operating correctly.

3   If the wiper motor takes a very high current, check the wiper blades for freedom of movement. If this is satisfactory check the gearbox cover or linkage for damage.

4   If the wiper motor takes a very low current, ensure that the battery is fully charged. Check the brushgear and ensure the brushes are bearing on the commutator. If not, check the brushes for freedom of movement and, if necessary, renew the tension springs. If the brushes are very worn they should be replaced with new ones. Check the armature by substitution if this part is suspect.

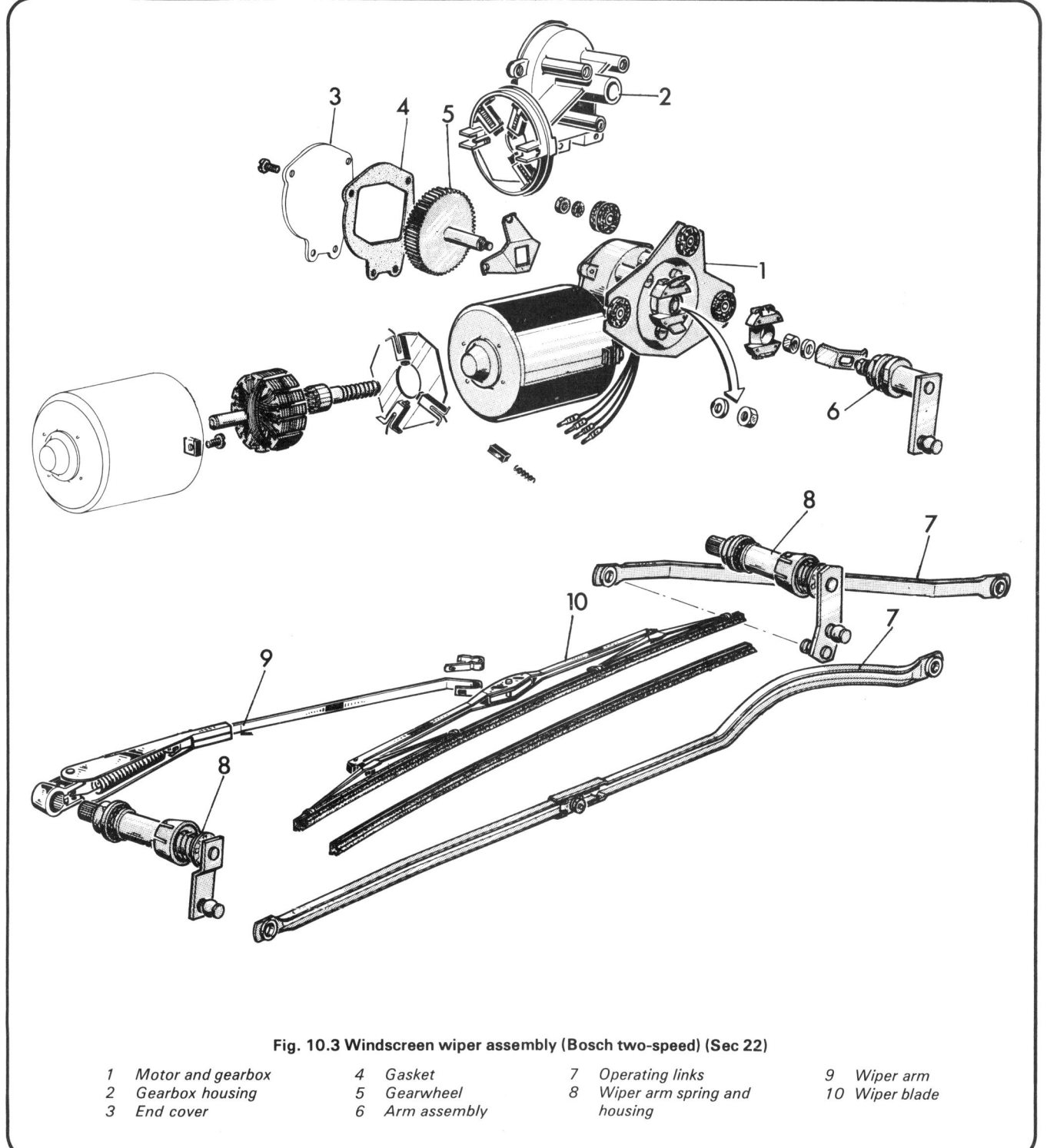

Fig. 10.3 Windscreen wiper assembly (Bosch two-speed) (Sec 22)

1 Motor and gearbox	4 Gasket	7 Operating links	9 Wiper arm
2 Gearbox housing	5 Gearwheel	8 Wiper arm spring and	10 Wiper blade
3 End cover	6 Arm assembly	housing	

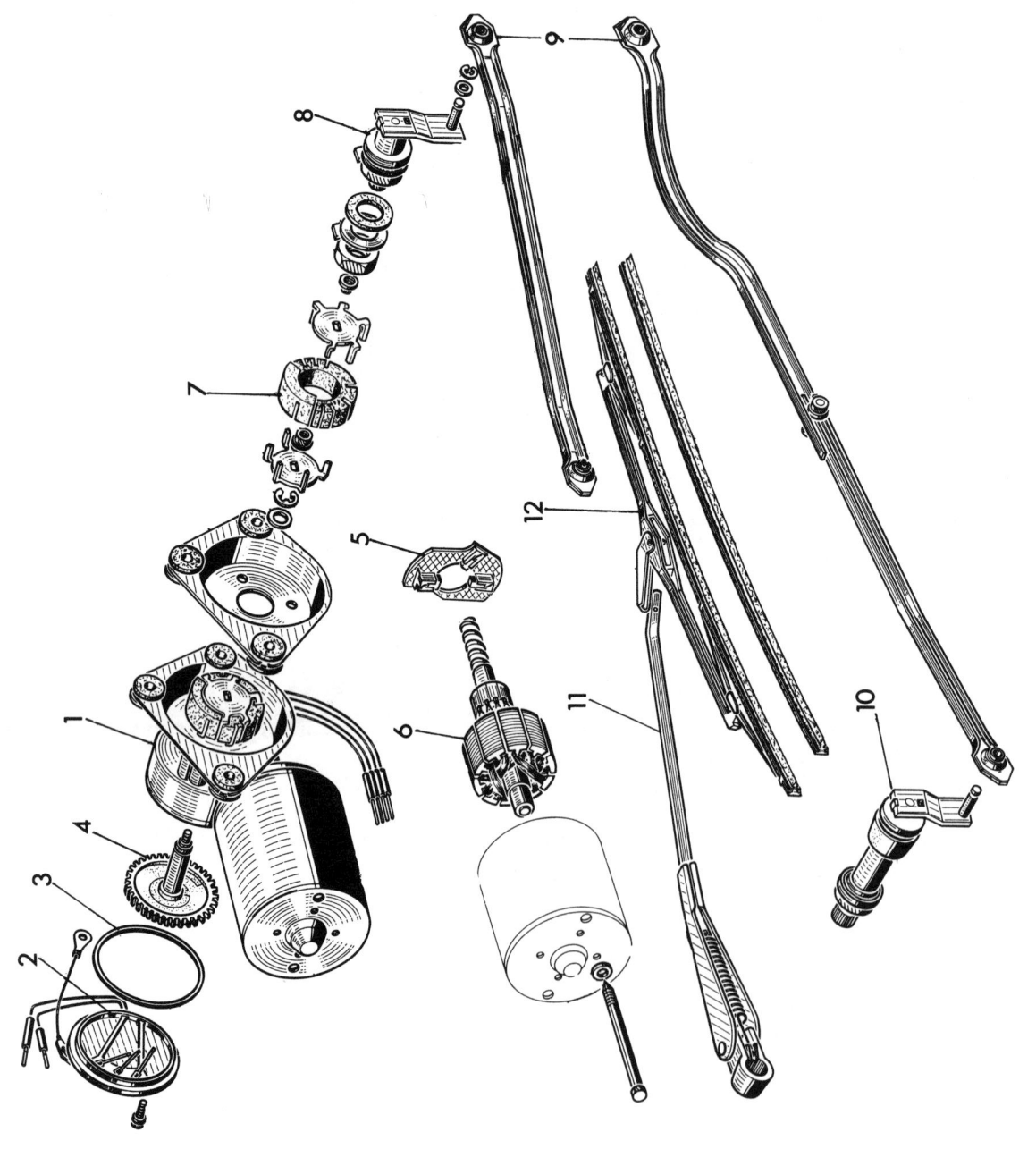

Fig. 10.4 Windscreen wiper assembly (Ducellier two-speed) (Sec 22)

1	Motor and gearbox	4	Gearwheel	7	Limit switch cam	10	Wiper arm spring and
2	End cover	5	Brush holder	8	Arm assembly		housing
3	Gasket	6	Armature	9	Operating links	11	Wiper arm
						12	Wiper blade

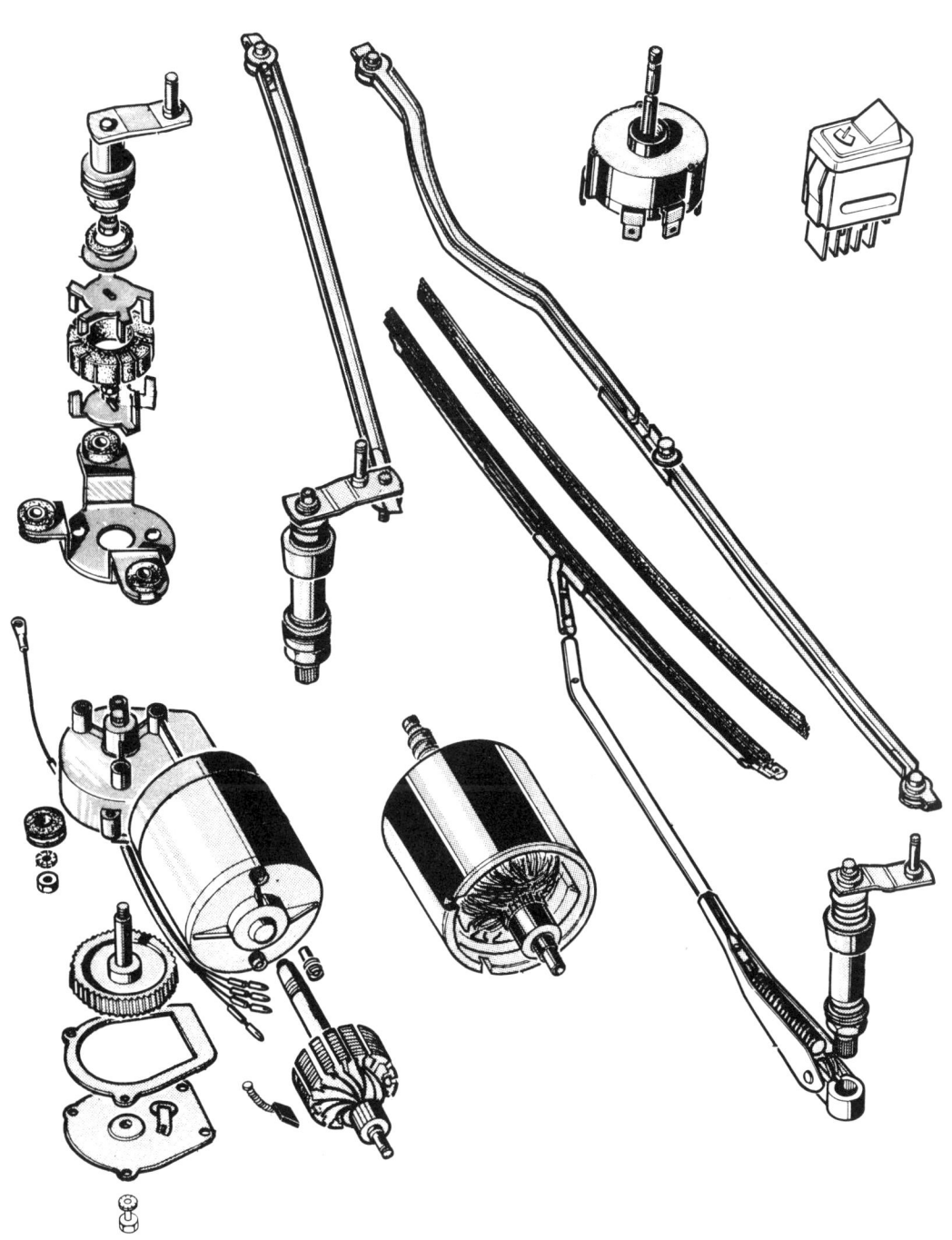

Fig. 10.5 Windscreen wiper assembly (SEV) (Sec 22)

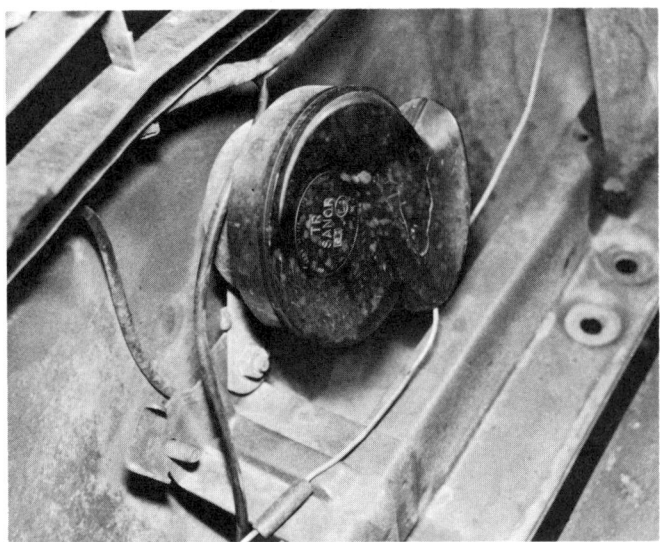

23.1 Horn location behind front grille panel

25.3 Lifting off the dashboard crash pad

25.4 Instrument panel front retaining screw

25.6 Electrical connections at rear of instrument panel

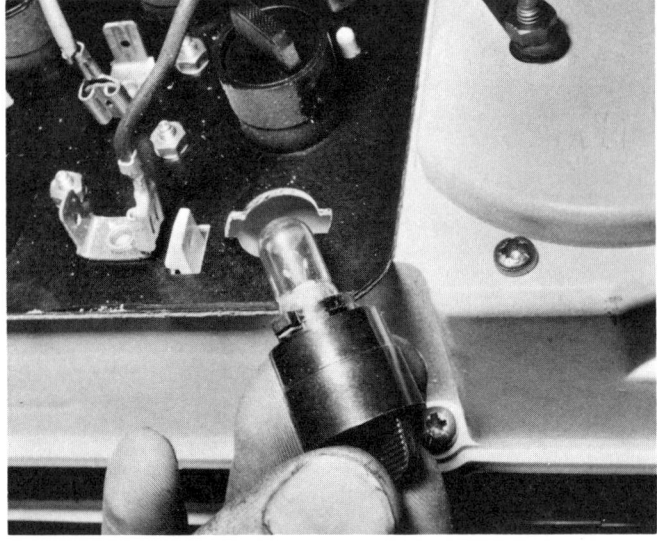

26.2 Instrument panel bulb holders are removed by turning anti-clockwise

27.2 The speedometer cable is retained in the gearbox by a grub screw

23 Horn – fault diagnosis and rectification

1 If the horn works badly or fails completely, check the wiring leading to the horn. Make sure that all connections are clean and secure (photo).
2 Using a test light check that current is reaching the horn and then ensure that the horn switch is operating correctly.
3 Check that the horn is secure on its mounting and that there is nothing lying on the horn body.
4 If all appears to be well test the horn and circuit by substitution.

24 Direction indicator light circuit – fault diagnosis and rectification

1 Should the flasher unit fail to operate, or work very slowly or rapidly, check out the circuit as detailed before assuming that there is a fault in the unit.
2 Examine the direction indicator light bulbs, both front and rear, for broken filaments.
3 If the external flashers are working, but either of the internal flasher warning lights have ceased to function, check the filaments in the warning light bulb and replace with a new bulb if necessary.
4 If a flasher bulb is sound but does not work, check all the flasher circuit connections with the aid of the relevant wiring diagram at the end of this Chapter.
5 With the ignition switched on, check that the correct voltage is reaching the flasher unit.
6 Should all appear to be well then check the flasher unit by substitution.

25 Instrument panel – removal and refitting

1 The procedure for removing and refitting the instrument panel varies according to model and accessories fitted. The main differences from model to model are the location and number of the retaining screws. Make a note during removal of any differences found between the model being worked on and the text as a guide to refitting.
2 Before removing the instrument panel, it is first necessary to remove the dashboard crash pad to provide clearance and access to the instrument panel retaining screws. Begin this procedure by disconnecting the battery earth terminal, and then locating the screws or clips that secure the crash pad to the dashboard.
3 Undo and remove the crash pad retaining screws or clips and then lift the crash pad up and off the top of the dashboard (photo).
4 Now undo and remove the screws on the front face of the instrument panel and the bolts on the mounting bracket at the rear of the panel (photo).
5 When the retaining screws are undone, lift up the instrument panel and pull it forward sufficiently to allow the speedometer cable to be unscrewed from the rear of the panel.
6 Now withdraw the panel further, make a note of the location of the electrical leads at the rear of the panel and disconnect them (photo).
7 The instrument panel can now be removed from the car.
8 Refitting is the reverse sequence to removal.

26 Instrument panel – dismantling and reassembly

1 With the instrument panel removed from the car as described in the previous Section, the panel warning lights, illumination lights, printed circuit, voltage stabilizer and instruments can all be removed. Once these components have been removed, further dismantling is not possible as the remaining components are all sealed units. If trouble arises on any of the instrument panel components they must be renewed as complete assemblies.
2 Begin dismantling by removing the bulb holders by turning them anti-clockwise and lifting out. The bulbs are a simple push fit in their holders (photo).
3 To remove the printed circuit, undo the nuts and washers, ease back the retaining lugs and lift the circuit off the rear of the instrument panel.
4 The instruments can be removed next. First pull off the knobs for

the trip reset and clock reset from the front of the panel (where applicable).
5 Undo and remove the screws securing the two halves of the instrument panel together and lift off the front half.
6 The instruments can now be removed by undoing the appropriate retaining screws and lifting out the instrument.
7 Reassembly of the instrument panel is the reverse sequence to removal.

27 Speedometer cable – removal and refitting

1 Jack up the front of the car and support it on axle stands. Disconnect the battery earth terminal.
2 From under the car, slacken the locknut and then unscrew the grub screw securing the speedometer cable to the rear of the gearbox (photo). Slide the cable out of its location and allow it to hang down.
3 From inside the car remove the dashboard crash pad as described in Section 25.
4 It will now be possible to reach over the top of the instrument panel and unscrew the speedometer cable from the rear of the panel (photo).
5 Once the cable is disconnected from the instrument panel it can be pulled through the bulkhead grommet and into the engine compart-

27.4 ... and to the rear of the instrument panel by a threaded collar

28.1 Electrical connections on rear heater plug

ment. Disconnect any clips securing the cable to the vehicle under-body and remove it from the car.

6   Refitting the speedometer cable is the reverse sequence to removal.

28 Heater plugs – removal, testing and refitting

1   Unscrew the knurled nut from the plug nearest to the engine compartment bulkhead and lift off the electrical lead (photo).

2   Now unscrew the nuts from the top of the remaining heater plugs and lift off the connecting electrical strip.

3   Unscrew and remove the heater plug from the cylinder head.

4   Scrape off any carbon from the base of the plug and element. Do *not* use ordinary spark plug sandblasting equipment.

5   Examine the element for signs of fracture and the seating for scoring. If these conditions are evident, renew the plug.

6   To test the heater plug internal circuit for continuity, connect the plug and a 12 volt sidelamp bulb in circuit to a 12 volt battery as shown in Fig. 10.6.

7   If the bulb fails to light, there is an open circuit in the heater plug and it must be renewed.

8   Refitting the heater plug is the reverse sequence to removal, observing the correct torque wrench setting.

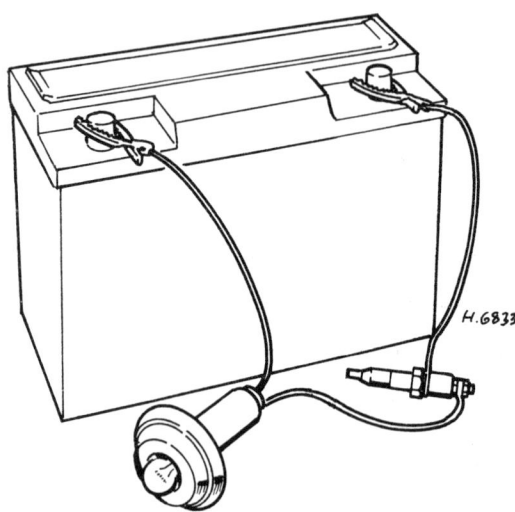

Fig. 10.6 Testing heater plugs (Sec 28)

A	12 volt battery	D	Seating
B	12 volt bulb	E	Insulation
C	Element	F	Terminal nuts

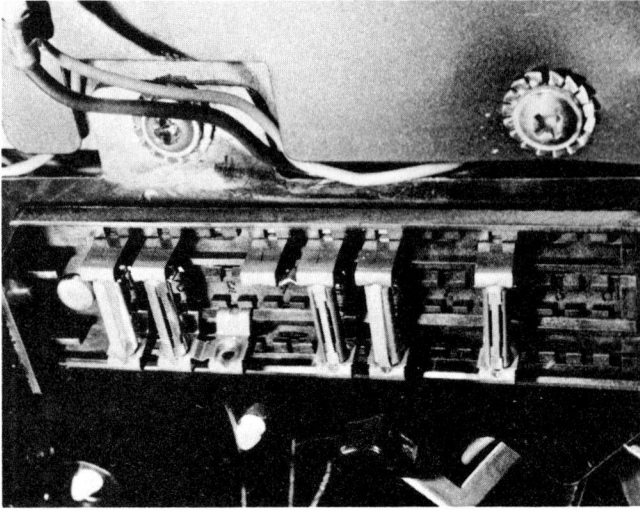

29.1 Fuse box location under the left-hand side of the dashboard

29 Fuses

1   The fuse box is located on the left-hand side of the dashboard, and the fuses are accessible after lifting off the plastic cover (photo). Do not renew a blown fuse until the cause is found and rectified. The circuits protected are as follows:

Saloon models

Fuse	Rating	Circuit protected
1	5 amp	Front and rear sidelights
		Rear number plate light
		Instrument panel lights
2	10 amp	Horns
		Interior lights
		Cigarette lighter
		Hazard warning light
		Clock
3	10 amp	Stop lights
		Reversing lights
		Electro-magnetic fan
		Heater plug warning light
4	15 amp	Windscreen wipers/washers
		Heated rear screen
5	10 amp	Heater fan
		Direction indicators
		Instruments
		Oil pressure warning light
		Brake warning light
		Alternator warning light
		Any additional accessories

Family Estate

Fuse	Rating	Circuit protected
1	5 amp	Front and rear sidelights
		Instrument panel lights
		Rear number plate light
		Heater control lights
2	15 amp	Horns
		Cigarette lighter
		Clock
		Interior lights
		Glovebox light
		Rear roof light
3	10 amp	Reversing lights
		Stop lights
		Electro-magnetic fan
4	10 amp	Direction indicators
		Oil pressure warning light
		Instruments
		Brake warning light
		Heater plug warning light
5	10 amp	Windscreen wiper and washer

Estate

Fuse	Rating	Circuit
1	5 amp	Front and rear sidelights
		Instrument panel lights
		Rear number plate light
2	15 amp	Horn
		Roof light
3	10 amp	Direction indicators
		Stop lights
		Oil pressure warning light
		Brake warning light
		Instruments
		Heater plug warning light
4	10 amp	Windscreen wiper and washer
		Heater fan

2   In addition to the fuses listed above, an in-line fuse is incorporated in the heater plug circuit, and other in-line fuses are used to protect optional equipment and accessories as and when fitted.

30 Radios and tape players – fitting (general)

A radio or tape player is an expensive item to buy and will only give its best performance if fitted properly. If you do not wish to do the fitting yourself there are many in-vehicle entertainment specialists who can do the fitting for you.

Make sure the unit purchased is of the same polarity as your vehicle and ensure that units with adjustable polarity are correctly set before commencing the fitting operation.

It is difficult to give specific information with regard to fitting, as final positioning of the radio/tape player, speakers and aerial is entirely a matter of personal preference. However, the following paragraphs give guidelines, which are relevant to all installations.

Radios

Most radios are a standardised 7 in wide by 2 inches deep; this ensures that they will fit into the radio aperture provided in most vehicles. If your car does not have such an aperture, the radio must be fitted in a suitable position either in, or beneath, the dashpanel. The following points should be borne in mind before deciding where to fit the unit.

(a) *The unit must be within easy reach of the driver wearing a seat belt*

(b) *The unit must not be mounted close proximity to the flasher unit and associated wiring*

(c) *The unit must be mounted within reach of the aerial lead and in such a place that the aerial lead will not have to be routed near the component detailed in preceeding paragraph (b)*

(d) *The unit should not be positioned where it might cause injury to the vehicle's occupants in an accident; for instance, under the dashpanel above the driver's or passenger's legs*

(e) *The unit must be fitted really securely*

Some radios will have mounting brackets provided together with instructions: others will need to be fitted using drilled and slotted metal strips, bent to form mounting brackets. These strips are available from most accessory shops. The unit must be properly earthed by fitting a separate earthing lead between the casing of the radio and the vehicle frame.

Use the radio manufacturer's instructions when wiring into the vehicle's electrical system. A 1 to 2 amp 'in-line' fuse must be fitted in the radio's 'feed' wire; a choke may also be necessary (see next Section).

The type of aerial used, and its fitted position, is a matter of personal preference. In general, the taller the aerial, the better the reception. It is best to fit a fully retractable aerial, especially, if a mechanical car-wash is used or if you live where cars tend to be vandalised. In this respect, electric aerials which are raised and lowered automatically when switching the radio on or off are convenient, but are more likely to give trouble than the manual type.

When choosing a site for the aerial, the following points should be considered:

(a) *The aerial lead should be as short as possible; this means that the aerial should be mounted at the front of the vehicle*

(b) *The part of the aerial which protrudes beneath the mounting point must not foul the roadwheels, or anything else*

(c) *If possible the aerial should be positioned so that the coaxial lead does not have to be routed through the engine compartment*

(d) *The plane of the panel on which the aerial is mounted should not be so steeply angled that the aerial cannot be mounted vertically (in relation to the 'end-on' aspect of the car). Most aerials have a small amount of adjustment available*

Having decided on a mounting position, a relatively large hole will have to be made in the panel. The exact size of the hole will depend upon the aerial being fitted, although, generally, the hole required is of $\frac{3}{4}$ inch (19 mm) diameter. On metal bodies cars, a 'tank-cutter' of the relevant diameter is the best tool to use for making the hole. This tool needs a small diameter pilot hole drilled through the panel, through which the tool clamping bolt is inserted. On GRP bodies cars a 'hole-saw' is the best tool to use. Again, this tool will require the drilling of a small pilot hole. When the hole has been made the raw edges should be de-burred with a file and then painted, to prevent corrosion.

Fit the aerial according to the manufacturer's instructions. If the aerial is very tall, or if it protrudes beneath the mounting panel for a considerable distance, it is a good idea to fit a stay between the aerial and the vehicle frame. This can be manufactured from the slotted and drilled metal strips previously mentioned. The stay should be securely screwed or bolted in place. For best reception it is advisable to fit an earth lead between the aerial body and the vehicle frame – this is essential for GRP bodies cars.

It will probably be necessary to drill one or two holes through bodywork panels in order to feed the aerial lead into the interior of the car. Where this is the case ensure that the holes are fitted with rubber grommets to protect the cable, and to stop possible entry of water.

Positioning and fitting of the speaker depends mainly on the type. Generally, the speaker is designed to fit directly into the aperture already provided in the car (usually in the shelf behind the rear seats, or in the top of the dashpanel). Where this is the case, fitting the speaker is just a matter of removing the protective grille from the aperture and screwing or bolting the speaker in place. Take care not to damage the speaker diaphragm whilst doing this. It is a good idea to fit a 'gasket' between the speaker frame and the mounting panel, in order to prevent vibration – some speakers will already have such a gasket fitted.

If a 'pod' type speaker was supplied with the radio, the best acoustic results will normally be obtained by mounting it on the shelf behind the rear seat. The pod can be secured to the panel with self-tapping screws.

When connecting a rear mounted speaker to the radio, the wires should be routed through the vehicle beneath the carpets, or floor mats – preferably the middle, or along the side of the floorpan, where they will not be trodden on by passengers. Make the relevant connections as directed by the radio manufacturer.

By now you will have several yards of additional wiring in the car; use PVC tape to secure this out of harm's way. Do not leave electrical leads dangling. Ensure that all new connections are properly made (wires twisted together will not do), and completely secure.

The radio should now be working, but before you pack away your tools it will be necessary to 'trim' the radio to the aerial. If specific instructions are not provided by the radio manufacturer, proceed as follows. Find a station with a low signal strength on the medium-wave band. Slowly turn the trim screw of the radio in, or out, until the loudest reception of the selected station is obtained – the set is then trimmed to the aerial.

Tape players

Fitting instructions for both cartridge and cassette stereo tape players are the same and in general the same rules apply as when fitting a radio. Tape players are not prone to electrical interference like radio – although it can occur – so positioning is not so critical. If possible the player should be mounted on an 'even keel'. Also, it must be possible for a driver wearing a seat belt to reach the unit to change or turn over tapes.

For the best results from speakers designed to be recessed into a panel, mount them so that the back of the speaker protrudes into an enclosed chamber within the car (eg door interiors or the boot cavity).

To fit recessed type speakers in the front doors, first check that there is sufficient room to mount the speakers in each door without fouling the latch or window winding mechanism. Hold the speaker against the skin of the door, and draw a line around the periphery of the speaker. With the speaker removed draw a second 'cutting' line, within the first, to allow enough room for entry of the speaker back, but at the same time, providing a broad seat for the speaker flange. When you are sure that the 'cutting-line' is correct, drill a series of holes around its periphery. Pass a hacksaw blade through one of the holes and cut through the metal between the holes until the centre section of the panel falls out.

De-burr the edges of the hole and paint the raw metal to prevent corrosion. Cut a corresponding hole in the door trim panel – ensuring that it will be completely covered by the speaker grille. Now drill a hole in the door edge and a corresponding hole in the door surround. These holes are to feed the speaker leads through – so fit grommets. Pass the speaker leads through the door trim, door skin and out through the holes in the side of the door and door surround. Refit the trim panel and then secure the speaker to the door using self-tapping screws. Note: If the speaker is fitted with a shield to prevent water dripping on it, ensure that this shield is at the top.

Pod type speakers can be fastened to the shelf behind the rear seat, or anywhere else offering a corresponding mounting point on each side of the car. If the pod speakers are mounted on each side of the shelf behind the rear seat, it is a good idea to drill several large diameter holes through to the boot cavity beneath each speaker – this will improve the sound reproduction. Pod speakers sometimes offer a better reproduction quality if they face the rear window – which then acts as a reflector – so it is worthwhile to do a little experimenting before finally fixing the speaker.

31 Radios and tape players – suppression of interference (general)

To eliminate unwanted noises costs very little and is not as difficult as sometimes thought. With common sense and patience, and following the instructions in the following paragraphs, interference can be virtually eliminated.

The first cause for concern is the generator. The noise this makes over the radio is like an electric mixer and speeds up when you rev up (if you wish to prove the point, remove the drivebelt and try it). The remedy for this is to connect a 1.0 μf to 3.0 μf capacitor between earth, probably the bolt that holds down the generator base, and the output (B+) terminal on the alternator or dynamo. This is most important, for if you connect it to the small terminal, you will probably damage the generator permanently (see Fig. 10.7).

Check that the case of the radio and the fixings for the aerial make good electrical contact with the metalwork of the vehicle. Ensure that the aerial plug is pushed fully into the socket in the radio and that the radio has been trimmed (see preceding Section). Make sure that the radio has an in-line fuse and that the rating of the fuse cartridge is not higher than 2 amps.

Unwanted noises on the radio can also be produced by the electric motors of the windscreen wiper, windscreen washer, heater fan and electric aerial (if fitted). Other sources of interference are electric fuel pumps, flashing turn signals and instrument voltage stabilizers: Fig. 10.8 shows the way to suppress interference from an electric motor and Fig. 10.9 shows instrument voltage stabilizer suppression. Turn signals are not normally suppressed.

Modern radios usually have a choke as well as a fuse in the live line, as shown in Fig. 10.10. If your installation lacks one of these, put one in as shown. For a transistor radio, a choke having a current carrying capacity of 2 amps is adequate. For any other equipment, use a choke of the same current rating as the protective fuse. Components for radio interference suppression are available from radio and car accessory shops.

An electric clock should be suppressed by connecting a 0.5 μf capacitor across it as shown for a motor in Fig. 10.8.

If after all this, you are still experiencing radio interference, first assess how bad it is, for the human ear can filter out unobtrusive unwanted noises quite easily. But if you are still adamant about eradicating the noise, then continue.

As a first step, a few experts seem to favour a screen between the radio and the engine. This is OK as far as it goes, for the whole set is screened anyway and if interference can get past that then a small piece of aluminium is not going to stop it.

A more sensible way of screening is to discover if interference is coming down the wires. First, take the live lead; interference can get between the set and the choke (hence the reason for keeping the wires short). One remedy here is to screen the wire and this is done by buying screened wire and fitting that. The loudspeaker lead could be screened also to prevent 'pick-up' getting back to the radio, although this is unlikely.

Now for the really impossible cases, here are a few tips to try out. Where metal comes into contact with metal, an electrical disturbance is caused which is why good clean connections are essential. To remove interference due to overlapping or butting panels you must bridge the join with a wide braided earth strap (like that from the frame to the engine/transmission). The most common moving parts that could create noise and should be strapped are, in order of importance:

(a)   Silencer to frame
(b)   Exhaust pipe to engine block and frame
(c)   Air cleaner to frame
(d)   Front and rear bumpers to frame
(e)   Steering column to frame
(f)   Bonnet to frame

These faults are most pronounced when the engine is idling or labouring under load. Although the moving parts are already connected with nuts, bolts etc, these do tend to rust and corrode, thus creating a high resistance interference source.

If you have a ragged sounding pulse when mobile, this could be wheel or tyre static. This can be cured by buying some anti-static powder and sprinkling it liberally inside the tyre.

If the interference takes the shape of a high pitched screeching noise that changes its note when the vehicle is in motion and only comes now and then, this could be related to the aerial, especially if it is of the telescopic or whip type. This source can be cured quite simply by pushing a small rubber ball on top of the aerial as this breaks the electric field before it can form; but it would be much better to buy yourself a new aerial of a reputable brand. If, on the other hand, you are getting a loud rushing sound every time you brake, this is brake static. This effect is most prominent on hot dry days and is cured only by fitting a special kit, which is quite expensive.

In conclusion, it is pointed out that it is relatively easy, therefore cheap, to eliminate 95 per cent of all noise, but to eliminate the final 5 per cent is time and money consuming. It is up to the individual to decide if it is worth it. Please remember also, that you cannot get a concert hall performance out of a cheap radio.

Finally, cassette and eight track players are not usually affected by vehicle noise, but in a very bad case, the best remedy is the first suggestion, plus using a 3 to 5 amp choke in the live line, and in incurable cases, screening the live and speaker wires.

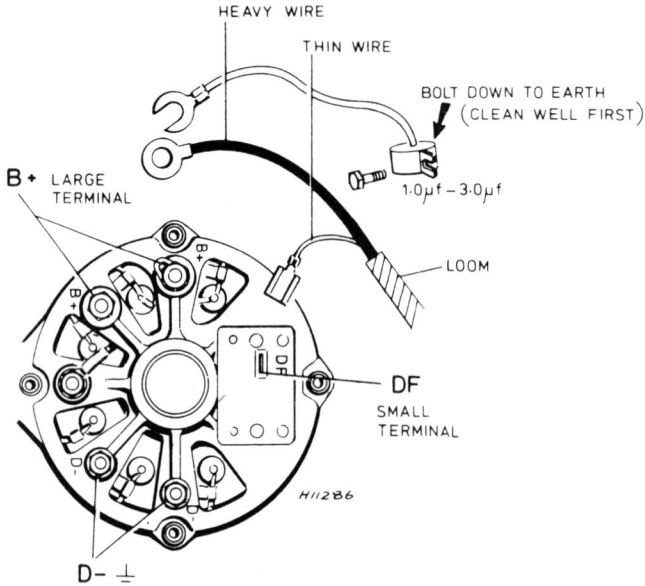

Fig. 10.7 The correct way to connect a capacitor to the alternator (Sec 31)

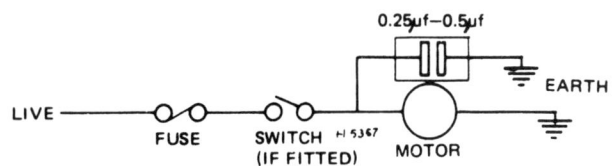

Fig. 10.8 Correct method of suppressing electric motors (Sec 31)

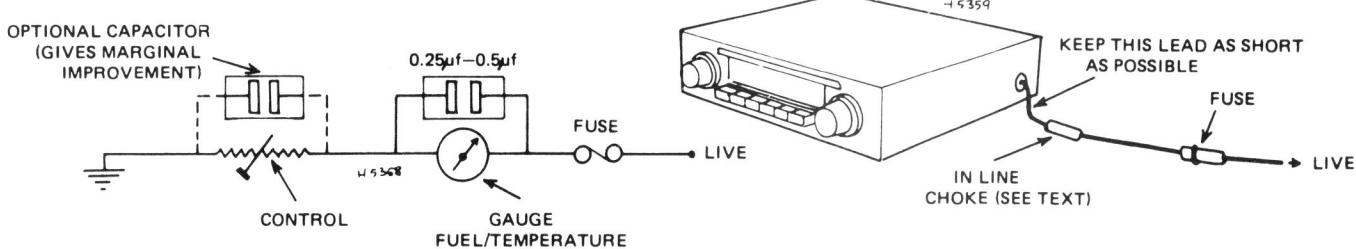

Fig. 10.9 Method of suppressing gauges and their control units (Sec 31)

Fig. 10.10 An in-line choke should be fitted into the live supply lead as close to the unit as possible (Sec 31)

32 Fault diagnosis – electrical system

Symptom	Reason(s)
Starter motor fails to turn engine	Battery discharged
	Battery defective internally
	Battery terminal leads loose or earth lead not securely attached to body
	Loose or broken connection in starter motor circuit
	Starter motor switch or solenoid faulty
	Starter brushes badly worn, sticking, or brush wires loose
	Commutator dirty, worn or burnt
	Starter motor armature faulty
	Field coils earthed
Starter motor turns engine very slowly	Battery in discharged condition
	Starter brushes badly worn, sticking or brush wires loose
	Loose wires in starter motor circuit
Starter motor operates without turning engine	Pinion or flywheel gear teeth broken or worn
Starter motor noisy or excessively rough engagement	Pinion or flywheel gear teeth broken or worn
	Starter motor retaining bolts loose
Battery will not hold charge for more than a few days	Battery defective internally
	Electrolyte level too low or electrolyte too weak due to leakage
	Plate separators no longer fully effective
	Battery plates severely sulphated
	Fan/alternator belt slipping
	Battery terminal connections loose or corroded
	Alternator not charging properly
	Short in lighting circuit causing continual battery drain
Warning lights fail to go out, battery runs flat in a few days	Drivebelt loose and slipping or broken
	Alternator faulty
Fuel gauge gives no reading	Fuel tank empty!
	Electric cable between tank unit and gauge broken
	Fuel gauge case not earthed
	Fuel gauge supply cable interrupted
	Fuel gauge unit broken
Fuel gauge registers 'full' all the time	Electric cable between tank and gauge earthed or shorting
Horn operates all the time	Horn push earthed or stuck down
	Horn cable to horn push earthed
Horn fails to operate	Blown fuse
	Cable or cable connection loose, broken or disconnected
	Horn has an internal fault
Horns emits intermittent or unsatisfactory noise	Cable connections loose
Lights do not come on	Blown fuse
	If engine not running, battery discharged
	Light bulb filament burnt or bulbs broken

Symptom	Reason(s)
	Wire connections loose, disconnected or broken
	Light switch shorting or otherwise faulty
Lights come on but fade out	If engine not running, battery discharged
Lights give very poor illumination	Poor earth connection
	Reflector tarnished or dirty
	Lamp badly out of adjustment
	Incorrect bulb with too low wattage fitted
	Existing bulbs old and badly discoloured
Wiper motor fails to work	Blown fuse
	Wire connections loose, disconnected or broken
	Brushes badly worn
	Armature worn or faulty
Wiper motor works very slowly and takes excessive current	Commutator dirty, greasy or burnt
	Drive to wheelboxes bent or unlubricated
	Wheelbox spindle binding or damaged
	Armature bearings dry or unaligned
	Armature badly worn or faulty
Wiper motor work slowly and takes little current	Brushes badly worn
	Commutator dirty, greasy or burnt
	Armature badly worn or faulty
Wiper motor works but wiper blades remain static	Wiper linkage damaged or worn
	Wiper motor gearbox parts badly worn

Key to Figs. 10.11, 10.12 and 10.13. Due to the numerous model variants it is only possible to include a typical selection

Note: This key contains certain references applicable to petrol engined models – these should be disregarded

1 Headlight
2 Front direction indicators
3 Front sidelights
4 Direction indicators relay
5 Starter relay
6 Alternator
7 Oil pressure switch
8 Electro-magnetic or motor driven fan
8A Motor driven fan relay
9 Thermal switch for electro-magnetic fan or motor driven fan
9A Thermal switch in water circuit for electro-magnetic fan
9B Thermal switch in oil circuit for electro-magnetic fan
10 Horn
10A Seat belt audible warning signal (USA)
10B Seat belt warning tell-tale (USA)
10C Seat belts warning system switch (USA)
11 Headlights relay
12 Battery
12A Battery cut-out terminal
13 Starter
14 Brake pad electrode
15 Water temperature transmitter
15A Water temperature thermostat
15B Water temperature tell-tale switch or water temperature tell-tale
16 Brake fluid reservoir
17 Stoplights switch
18 Reversing lights switch
19 Starter inhibitor switch
20 Carburettor idling circuit cut-out resistor
21 Regulator
22 Ignition coil
22A Coil relay
22B Coil resistor
22C Coil resistor relay (USA and Sweden)
23 Distributor
24 Front screen wiper
24A Screen wiper relay
24B Screen wiper timer
24C Rear window wiper
25 Front screen washer pump
25A Rear window washer pump
26 Car heater blower
26A Car heater blower to rear
26B Car heater blower switch
27 Heater blow switch or rheostat
27A Rheostat resistors or heater blower resistor
27B Switch for car heater blower to rear
28 Switch to choke tell-tale
28A Choke actuating motor (USA)
28B Choke thermostat (USA)
29 Heated rear window switch
29A Heated rear window
30 Screen wash/wipe switch
30A Rear window wash/wipe switch
31 Direction indicators unit
32 Lights-screen wash/wipe dual purpose switch

33 Headlights flasher relay
34 Sidelights
35 Cigarette lighter
36 Clock
37 Direction indicators tell-tale
38 Fuel gauge
38A Reserve fuel tell-tale
39 Headlights tell-tale
40 Hazard warning tell-tale
41 Tachometer
42 Sidelights tell-tale
43 Brakes system warning light
43A Brakes system warning light control diode
44 Water temperature tell-tale or water temperature gauge
45 Oil pressure tell-tale
46 Choke tell-tale
47 Oil and water tell-tale
48 Preheating tell-tale
49 Charge indicator
50 Facia lighting
50A Gearplate lighting
50B Facia lighting rheostat
50C Switch lighting
51 Heater controls lighting
51A Console lighting
51B Console lighting rheostat (USA)
52 Glove compartment lighting
52A Glove compartment lighting switch
53 Front door light switch
53A Rear door light switch
54 Vehicle interior lights
54A Below facia lighting
54B Map reading light
55 Handbrake tell-tale switch
56 Hazard warning switch
57 Sliding roof panel switch
57A Sliding roof panel motor
57B Sliding roof panel max travel cut-out
57C Sliding roof panel safety cut-out
58 Ignition/anti-theft lock
58A Ignition switch warning buzzer (USA)
59 Preheating/starter switch
59A Preheating plugs
60 Pump electric motor or solenoid valve cut-out
61 Preheating tell-tale operating switch
62 Preheating relay
63 Direction indicators/horns dual purpose switch
64 Boot or tailgate light
64A Boot or tailgate light switch
65 Fuel tank unit, with or without reserve fuel tell-tale switch
65A Fuel tank unit external resistor
66 Rear number plate light
67 Reversing lights
68 Stop lights
68B Stop and sidelights (twin filament)
69 Rear direction indicators

70 Rear lights
71 Tailgate light switch
72 Open door warning light
73 Rear LH window winder switch
74 Front LH window winder switch
75 Cut-out switch for rear windows and cigarette lighter
76 Front RH window winder switch
77 Rear RH window winder switch
78 Rear LH window winder switch
79 Front LH window winder switch
80 Window winder motor
80A Window winder motor relay
86 Fuel pump
87 Solenoid valve
87A Switch to solenoid valve
88 Sensor
89 Electronic control unit
90 Rear foglights
90A Rear foglights switch
90B Rear foglights tell-tale
91 Relay
91A Seat belts timer relay (USA)
92 Terminal
93 Multiple junction box
94 Conductive tailgate stay
95 Brakes system pressure switch
96 Brake pedal travel switch
97 Headlights wash/wipe switch
98 Headlights washer pump
99 Headlights wiper motor
100 Oil pressure drop warning light
101 Tachometer
102 Flasher (roof mounted)
102A Flasher switch
103 Centre rooflight
103A Centre rooflight switch
104 Main feed tell-tale
104A Main feed tell-tale switch
105 Ventilation fan
105A Ventilation fan switch
106 Call bell
106A Call bell switch
107 Socket
108 Compressor clutch
108A Compressor clutch cut-in/out
109 Thermostat
110 Pressure switch
111 Idling compensation solenoid
118 Control pressure regulator
119 Supplementary air control
120 Air sensor switch
121 Thermal time switch
122 Cold start injector
+P Continous feed
+aa Feed to accessories
+ac Feed after switch-on

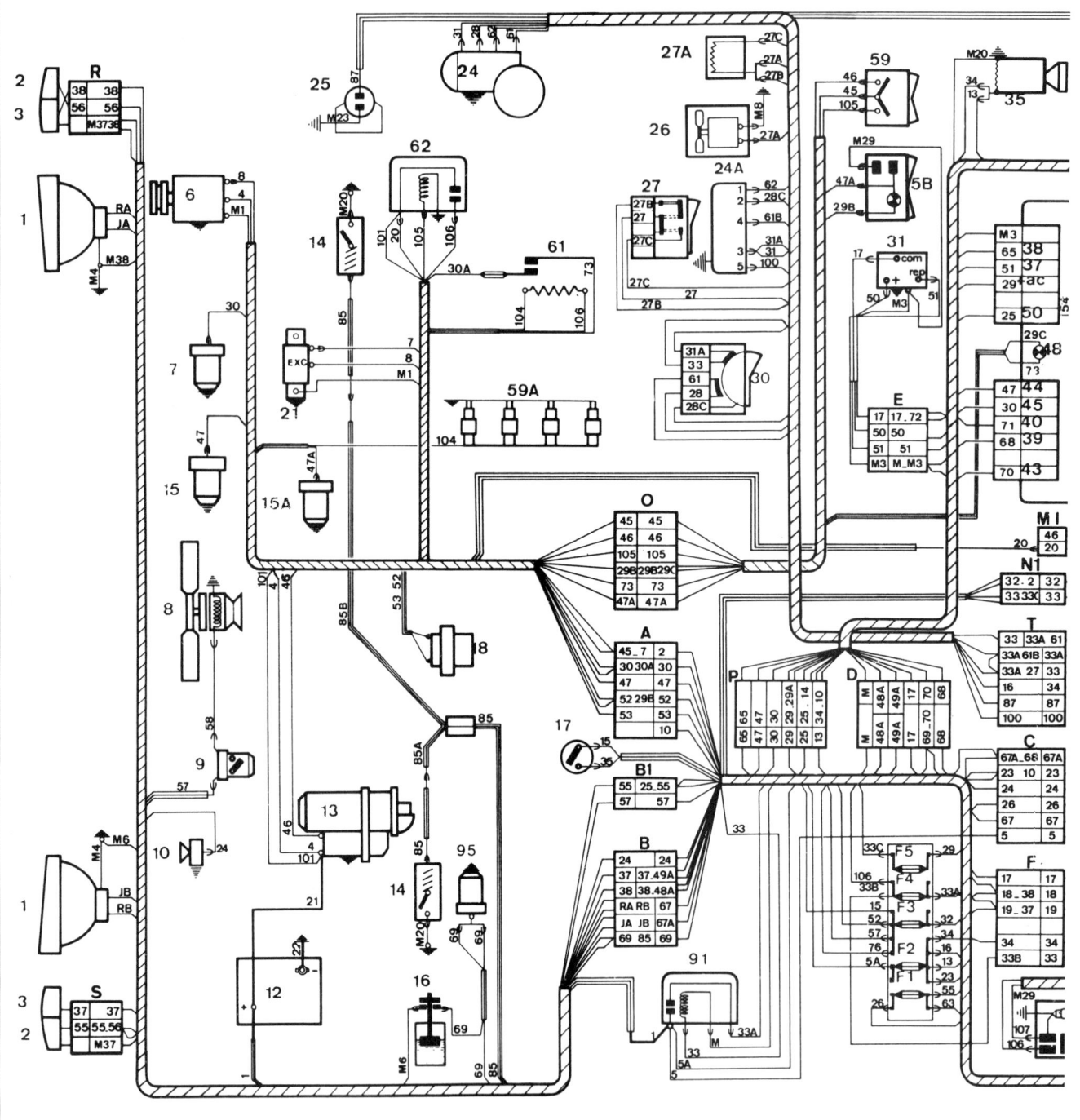

Fig. 10.11 Typical wiring diagram for 504 Diesel Saloon – 1975 models

153

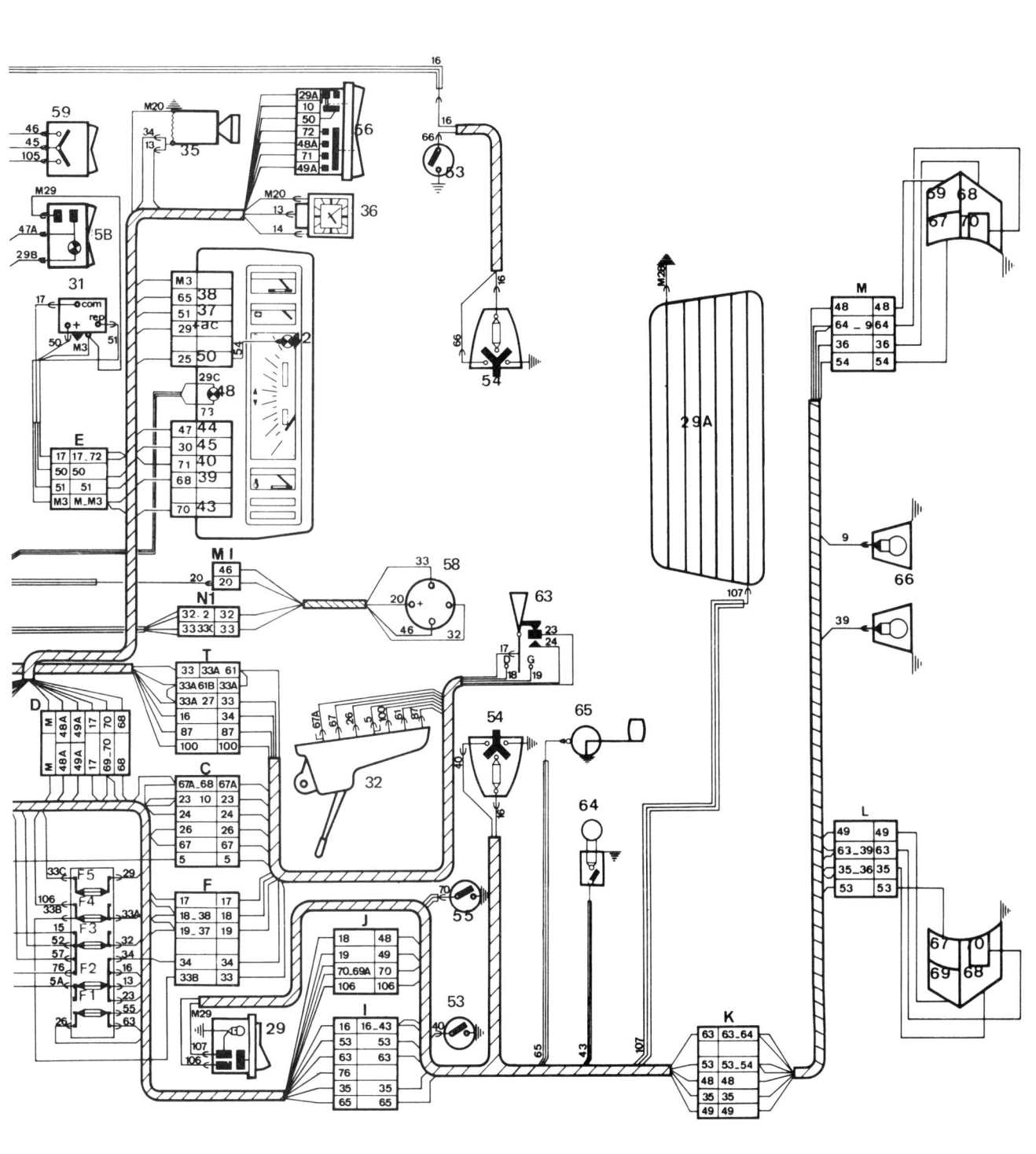

Fig. 10.11 Typical wiring diagram for **504 Diesel Saloon** – **1975 models** – continued

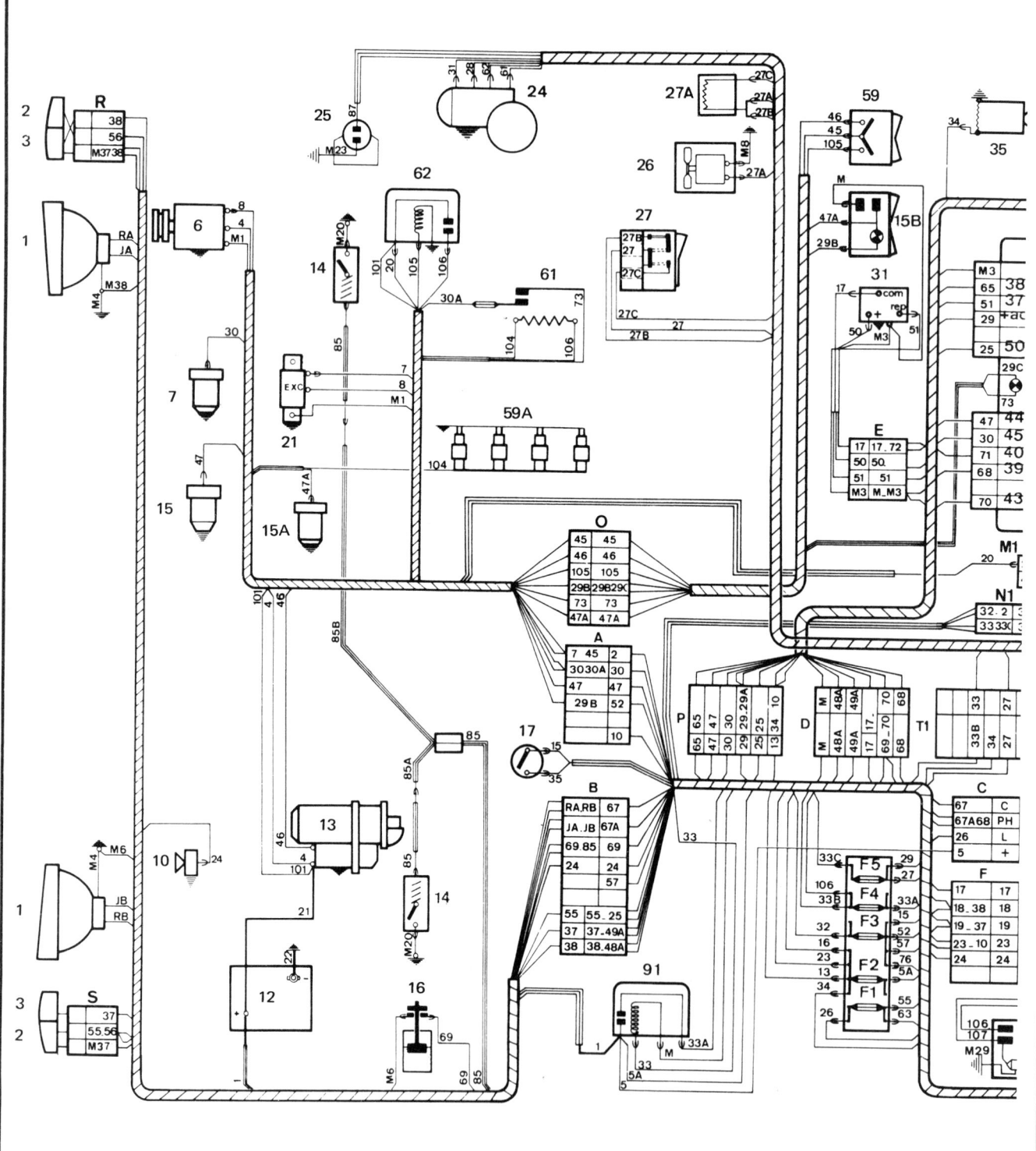

Fig. 10.12 Typical wiring diagram for 504 Diesel Estate – 1976 models

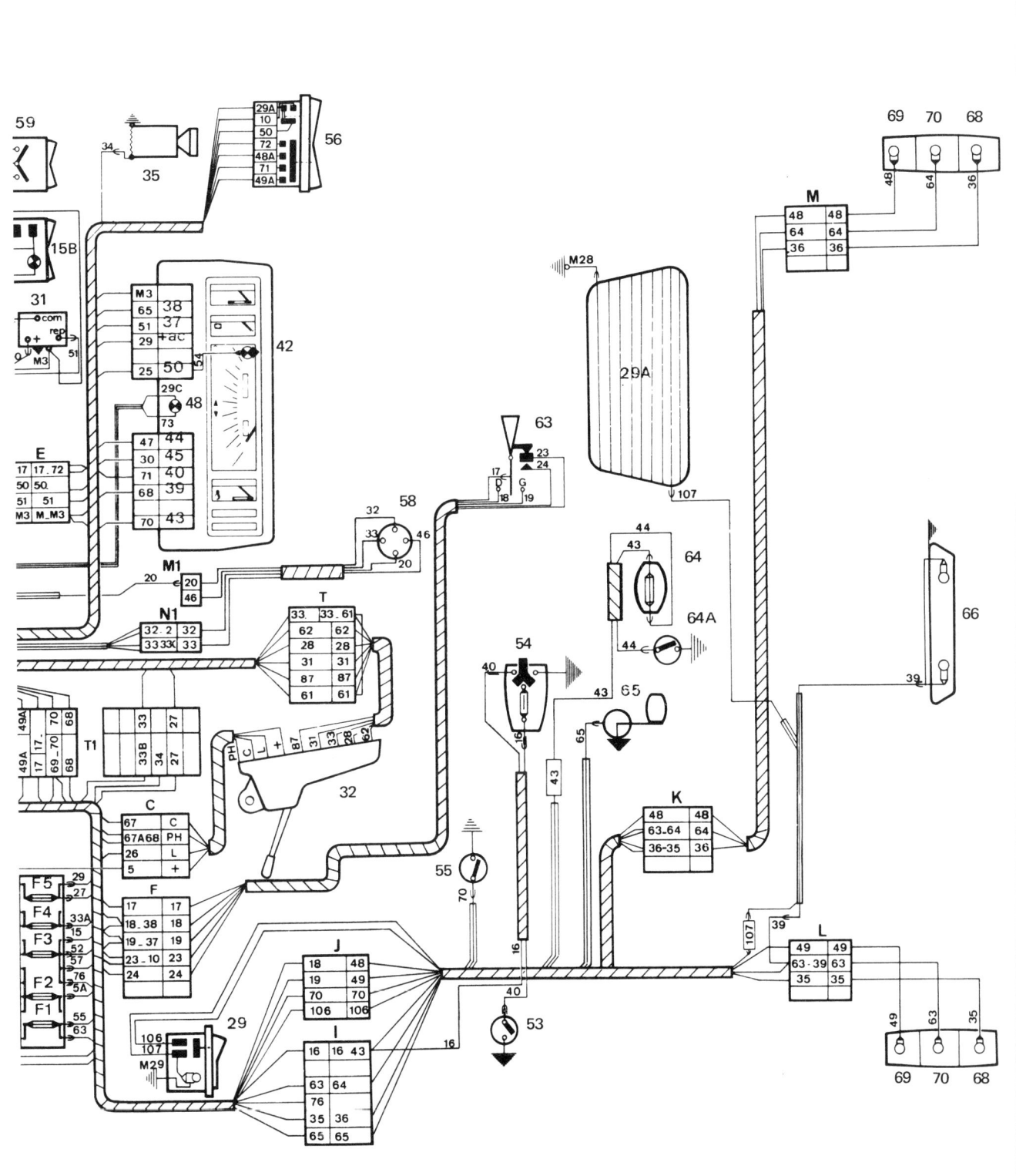

Fig. 10.12 Typical wiring diagram for 504 Diesel Estate – 1976 models – continued

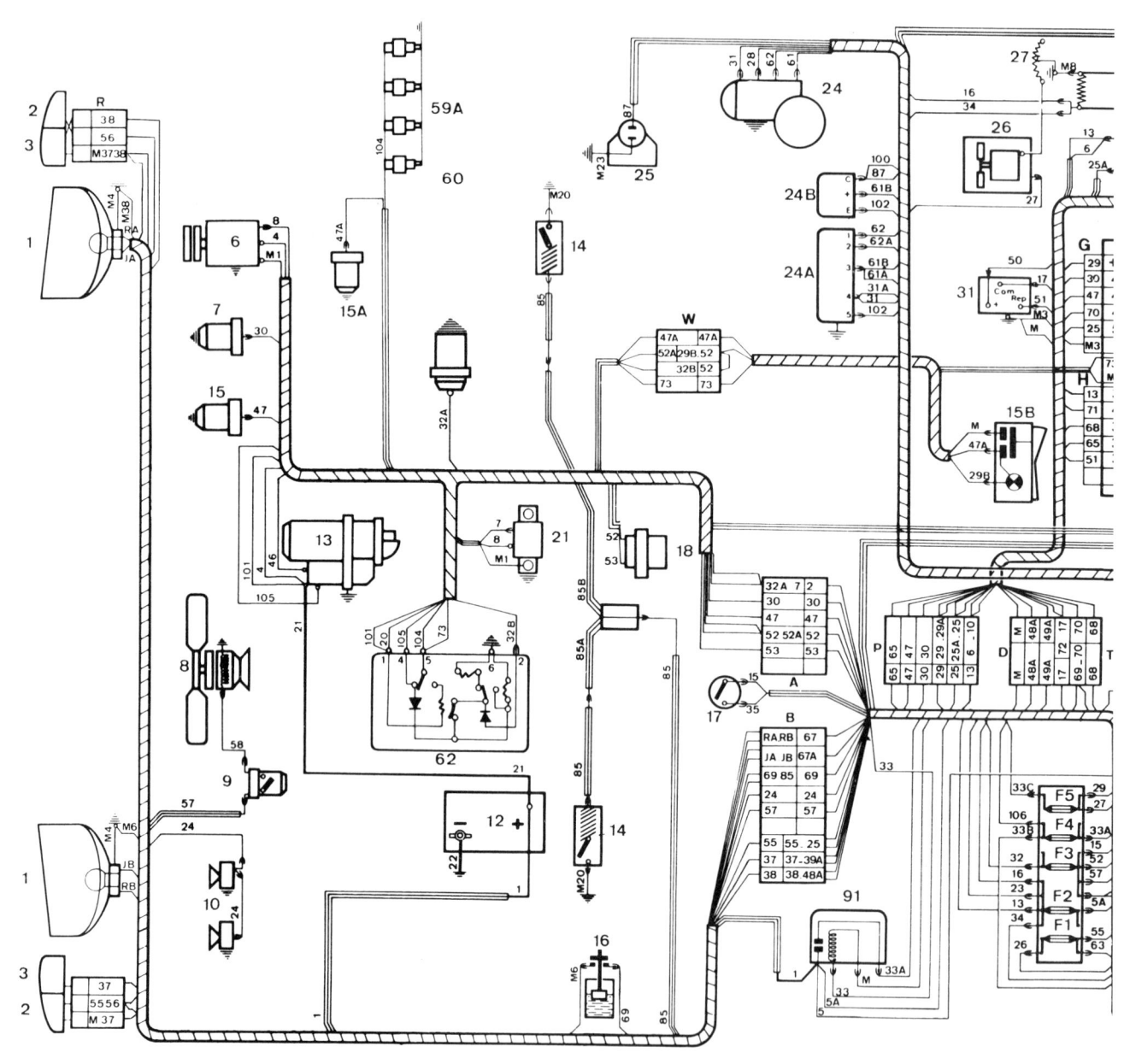

Fig. 10.13 Typical wiring diagram for 504 Diesel Family Estate – 1977 onwards models

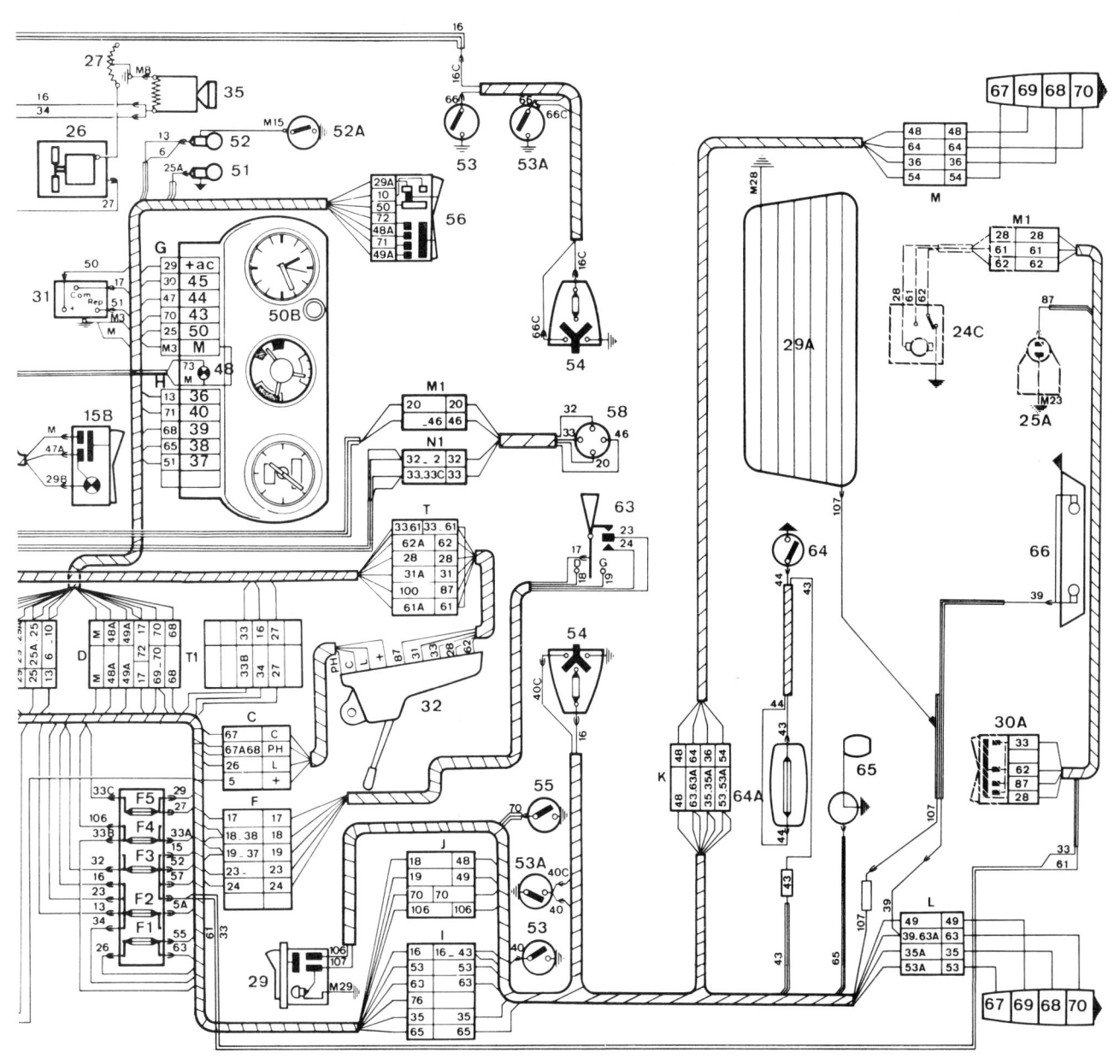

Fig. 10.13 Typical wiring diagram for 504 Diesel Family Estate – 1977 onwards models – continued

158

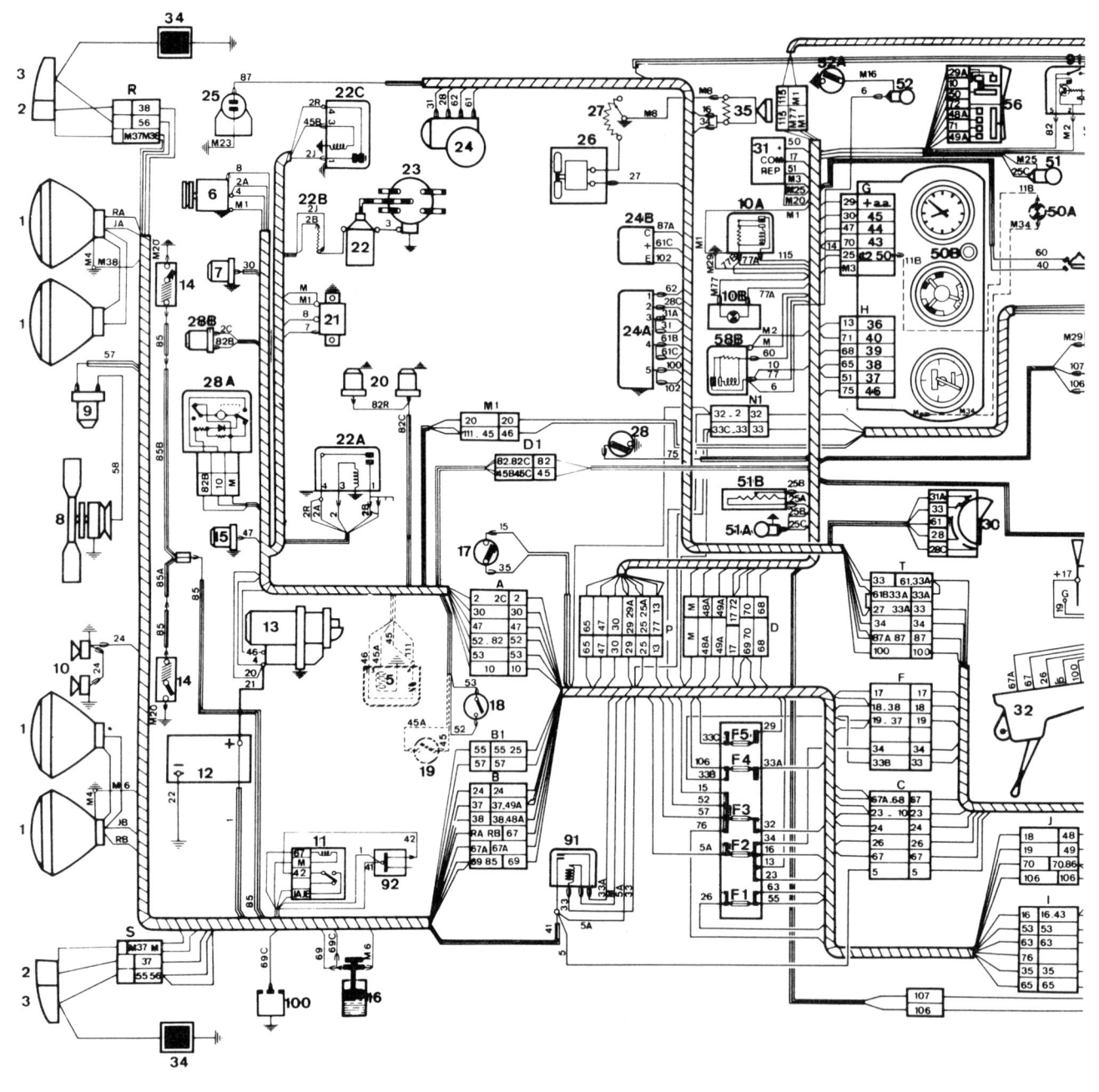

Fig. 10.14a Typical wiring diagram for 504; use in conjunction with Fig. 10.14b – 1976 USA models

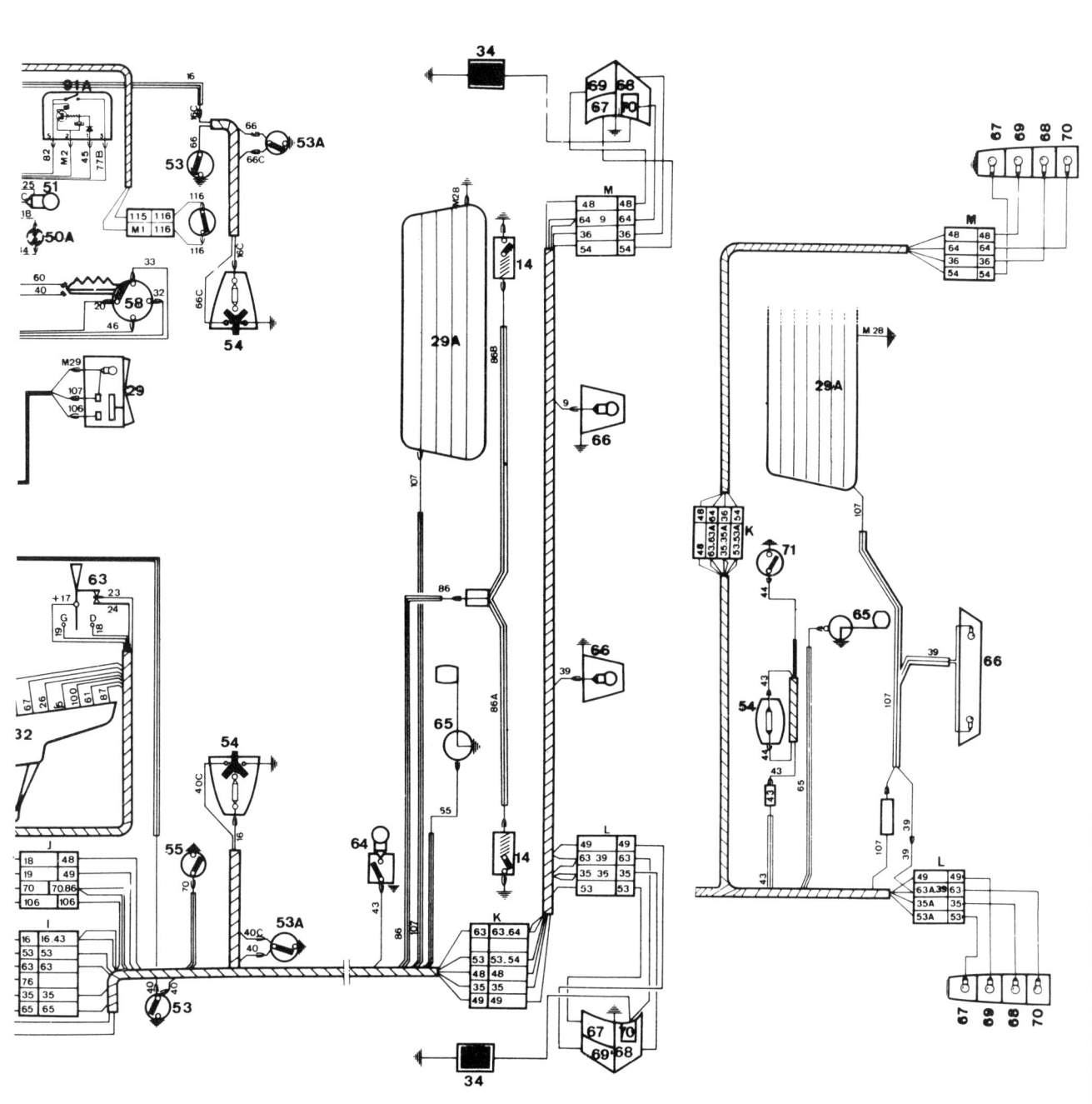

Fig. 10.14a Typical wiring diagram for 504; use in conjunction with Fig. 10.14b – 1976 USA models – continued

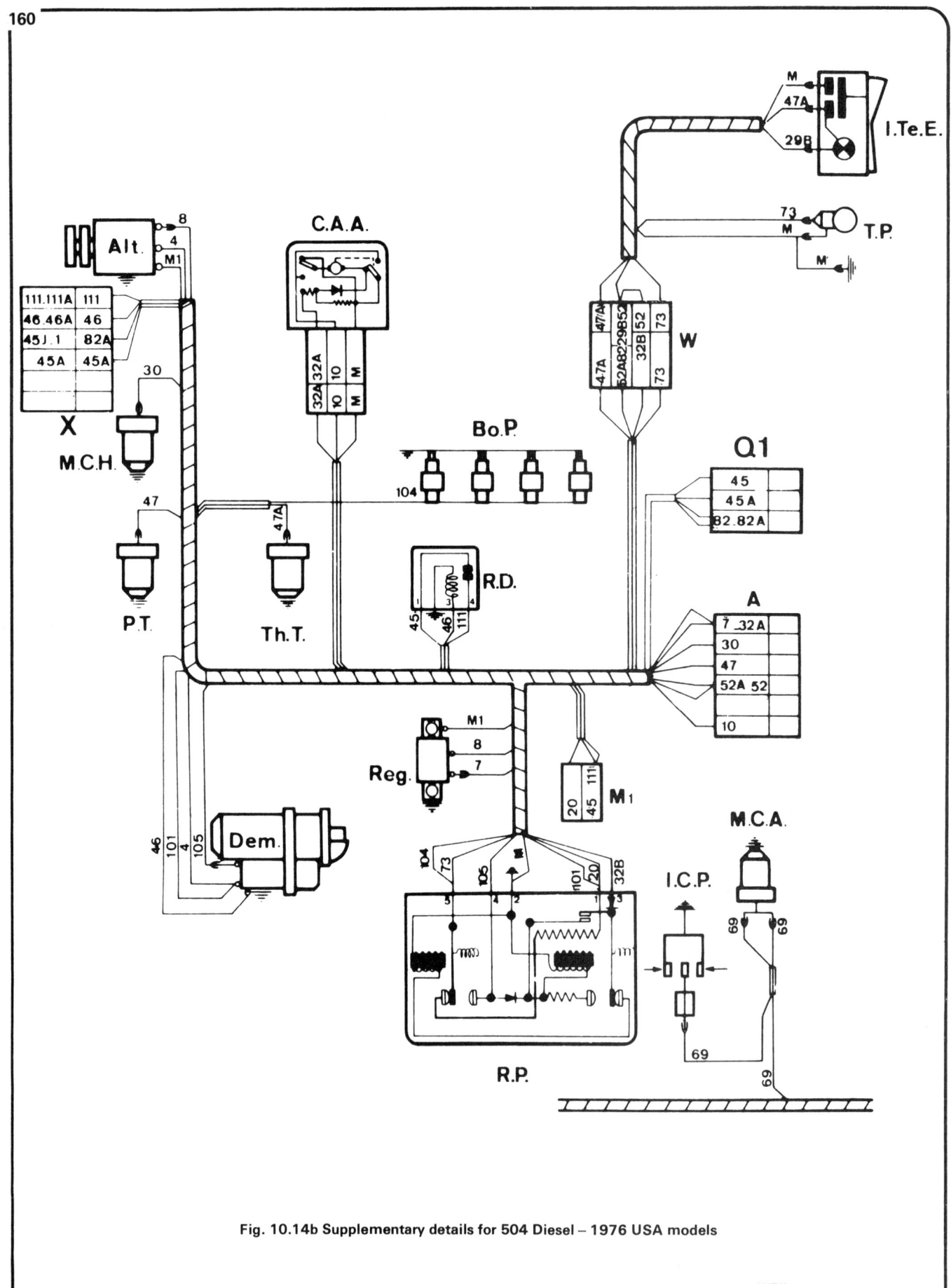

Fig. 10.14b Supplementary details for 504 Diesel – 1976 USA models

Key to Figs. 10.14a and 10.14b. Due to the numerous model variants it is only possible to include a typical diagram

Note: *504 petrol (gasoline) model shown in Fig. 10.14a – use in conjunction with Fig. 10.14b*

1	Headlights
2	Front direction indicators
3	Front parking light
5	Starter motor relay
6	Alternator
7	Oil pressure switch
8	Electro-magnetic or motor driven fan
9	Electro-magnetic fan thermostat
10	Horns
10A	Seat belts warning buzzer
10B	Seat belts tell-tale light
10C	Seat belts warning system cut-out
11	Headlights relay
12	Battery
13	Starter
14	Brake pad electrodes
15	Water temperature transmitter
16	Brake fluid reservoir
17	Stoplights switch
18	Back-up lights switch
19	Starter protection cut-out
20	Idling circuit cut-out
21	Regulator
22	Coil
22A	Coil relay
22B	Coil resistor
22C	Coil resistor relay
23	Distributor
24	Windshield wiper
24A	Windshield wiper relay
24B	Windshield wiper delayed action timer
25	Windshield washer pump
26	Heater blower
27	Heater blower rheostat
28	Choke tell-tale switch
28A	Choke control motor
28B	Choke control thermostat
29	Heated rear screen switch
29A	Heated rear screen
30	Windshield wiper switch
31	Direction indicators switch
32	Combined switch; lights/windshield wash-wipe
34	Parking lights
35	Cigar lighter
36	Clock
37	Direction indicators tell-tale
38	Fuel gauge
39	Headlights tell-tale
40	Hazard warning tell-tale
41	Tachometer (Sedan SL)
42	Parking lights tell-tale
43	Brakes system warning light
44	Water temperature indicator
45	Oil pressure warning light
46	Choke tell-tale
50	Instrument panel light
50A	Gear indicator plate light
50B	Gear indicator plate light rheostat
51	Heater controls lighting
51A	Console lighting
51B	Console light rheostat
52	Glove compartment lighting
52A	Glove compartment light switch
53	Front door light switch
53A	Rear door light switch
54	Interior lighting
55	Handbrake tell-tale switch
56	Hazard warning lights switch
58	Combined ignition switch and anti-theft lock
58A	Ignition in ON position warning buzzer
63	Combination switch: direction indicators/horns
64	Trunk light
65	Fuel tank unit
66	Rear license plate lighting
67	Back-up lights
68	Stop lights
69	Rear direction indicators
70	Rear parking lights
71	Tailgate light switch (Station wagon)
74	Front LH window winder switch
76	Front RH window winder switch
80	Window winder electric motor
91	Relay
91A	Safety belts system timer relay
92	Connection terminal
100	Pressure drop tell-tale
+aa	Feed to accessories

A,M1,Q1,W,X	Connectors
Alt.	Alternator
Bo.P	Preheating plug
C.A.A.	Automatic stop control
Dem.	Starter control: solenoid
I.C.P.	Pressure drop indicator
I.Te.E.	Water temperature switch
M.C.A.	Brake warning switch
M.C.H.	Oil pressure switch
P.T.	Temperature gauge transmitter
Reg.	Regulator
R.D.	Starter relay
R.P.	Preheating relay
T.P.	Preheating warning light
Th.T.	Water temperature switch

162

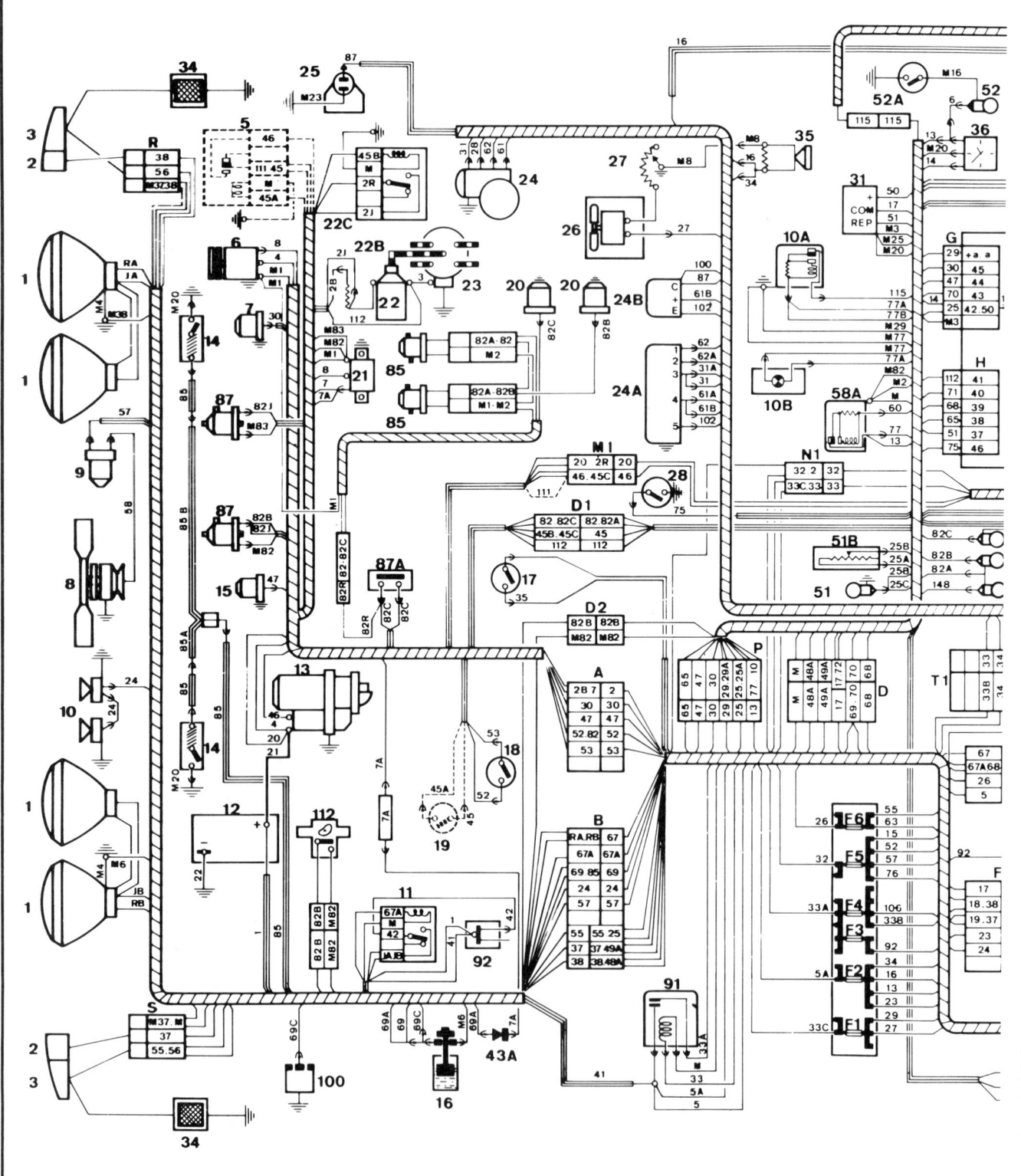

Fig. 10.15a Typical wiring diagram for 504; use in conjunction with Fig. 10.15b – 1978 USA models

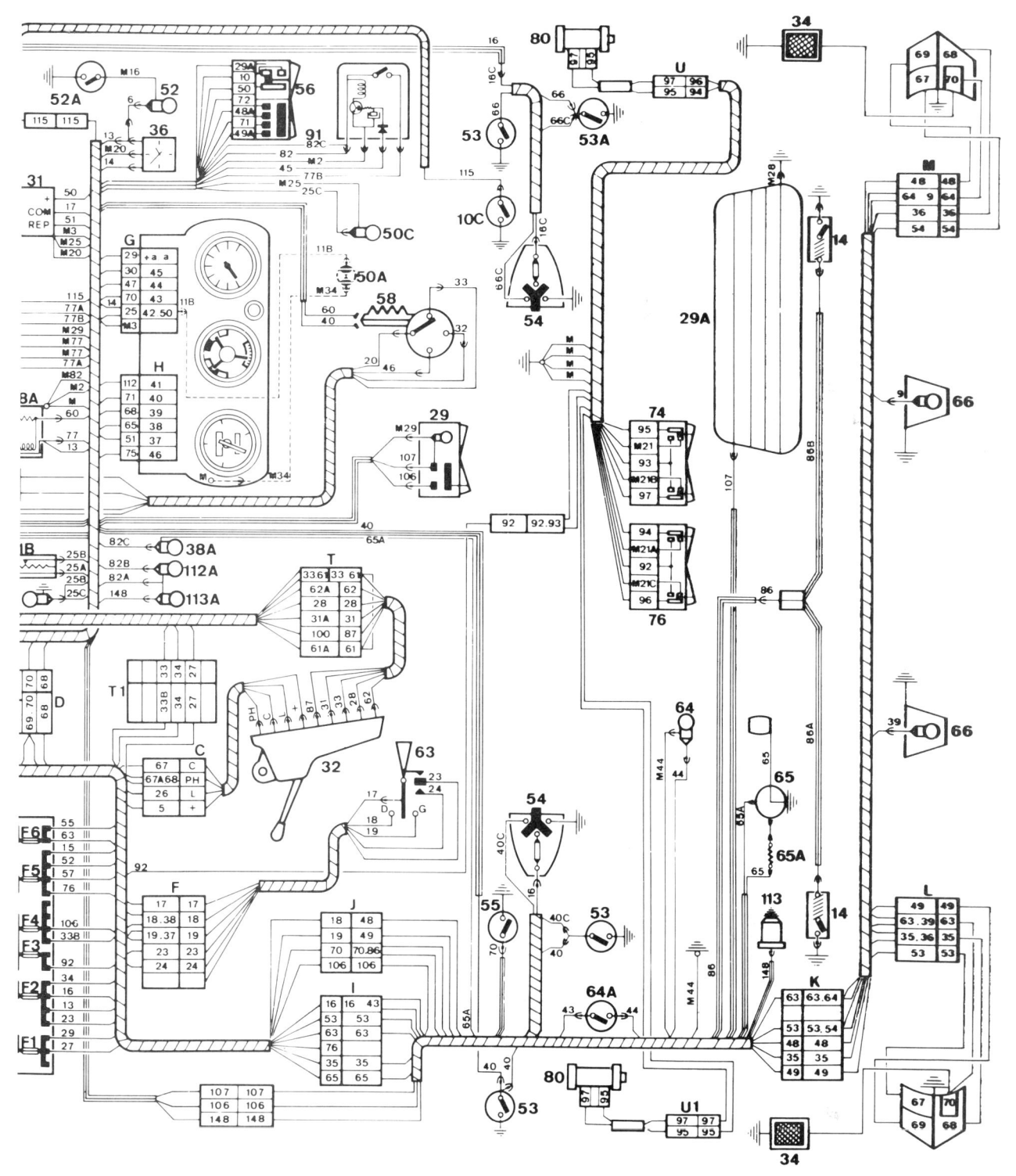

Fig. 10.15a Typical wiring diagram for 504; use in conjunction with Fig. 10.15b – 1978 (USA) models – continued

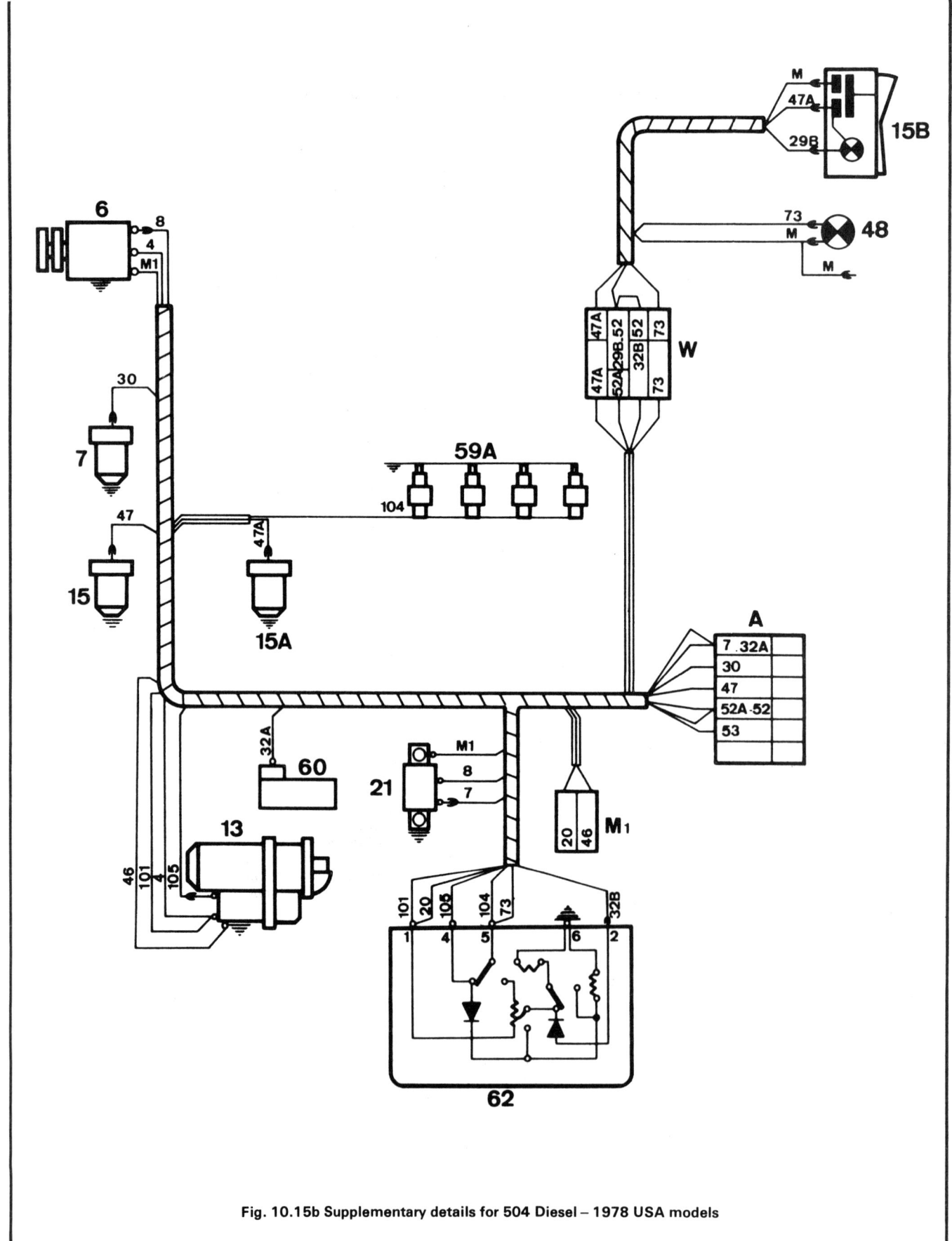

Fig. 10.15b Supplementary details for 504 Diesel – 1978 USA models

Key to Figs. 10.15a and 10.15b. Due to the numerous model variants it is only possible to include a typical diagram

Note: *504* petrol (gasoline) model shown in Fig. 10.15a – use in conjunction with Fig. 10.15b

1	Headlight		40	Hazard warning indicator
2	Front direction signal		41	Tachometer (Sedan SL)
3	Front parking light		42	Parking light indicator
5	Starter motor relay		43	Brake function indicator
6	Alternator		43A	Brake warning light diode
7	Oil pressure switch		44	Water temperature gauge
8	Self-disengaging fan		45	Oil pressure indicator
9	Self-disengaging fan thermostat		46	Choke indicator
10	Horns		50	Dashboard lighting
10A	Seat belts warning buzzer		51	Heater controls lighting
10B	Seat belts warning light		51B	Heater control and hazard switch lights rheostat
10C	Seat belt switch		52	Glove compartment lighting
11	Headlights relay		52A	Glove compartment light switch
12	Battery		53	Front door switch
13	Starter		53A	Rear door switch
14	Brake pad wear warning indicator		54	Interior lighting
15	Water temperature transmitter		55	Handbrake switch
16	Brake fluid reservoir		56	Hazard warning switch
17	Brake light switch		58	Ignition switch
18	Back-up lights switch		58A	Ignition warning buzzer
19	Starter safety switch		63	Direction signal/horns switch
20	Idling solenoid		64	Trunk light
21	Regulator		64A	Trunk light switch
22	Coil		65	Gauge transmitter (fuel)
22B	Coil resistor		66	License plate light
22C	Coil resistor relay		67	Back-up light
23	Distributor		68	Brake light
24	Windshield wiper		69	Rear directional signal
24A	Windshield wiper relay		70	Rear parking light
24B	Windshield wiper time delay relay		71	Tailgate light switch (estate)
25	Windshield wiper pump		74	Front LH power window regulator
26	Heater blower		76	Front RH power window regulator
27	Heater blower rheostat		80	Power window regulator motor
28	Choke tell-tale switch		85	Emission control electro-valve
29	Rear window heater switch		87	Anti-pollution electrovalve
29A	Rear window heater		87A	Electrovalve contact control
31	Directional signal unit		91	Relay
32	Lighting/windshield wiper/washer switch		91A	Seat belt time delay relay
34	Side marker light		92	Connector terminal
35	Cigar lighter		100	Brake pressure indicator
36	Clock		112	Periodic maintenance switch
37	Directional signal indicator		112A	EGR periodic maintenance warning light
38	Fuel gauge		113	Underbody overheating thermoswitch
38A	Fuel gauge warning light		113A	Underbody overheating warning light
39	High beam indicator			

6	Alternator
7	Oil pressure switch
13	Starter control: solenoid
15	Temperature gauge transmitter
15A	Water temperature switch
15B	Water temperature switch
21	Regulator
48	Preheating warning light
59A	Preheating plug
60	Electric solenoid fuel cut-off valve
62	Preheating relay

Chapter 11 Suspension and steering

Contents

Specifications

Front suspension

Type .... Independent, with MacPherson struts, coil springs, telescopic shock absorbers and anti-roll bar

Toe-in setting .... 3 mm $\pm$ 1 mm (0.1 in $\pm$ 0.03 in)
Castor .... 2° 40' $\pm$ 30'
Camber .... 0° 38' $\pm$ 30'
King pin inclination .... 8° 54' $\pm$ 30'

Rear suspension

Type .... Independent, with coil springs, trailing arms, telescopic shock absorbers and anti-roll bar; or 'banjo' type solid axle with coil springs, telescopic shock absorbers and anti-roll bar

Toe-in setting* .... 4.5 $\pm$ 0.5 mm (0.16 in $\pm$ 0.01 in)
Camber* .... 1° 0' $\pm$ 0° 40'
*models with independent rear suspension only

Standard steering

Type .... Rack-and-pinion
Turns lock-to-lock 4.5
Rack plunger free play .... 0.1 mm $\pm$ 0.05 mm (0.003 in $\pm$ 0.001 in)

Power assisted steering

Type .... Rack-and-pinion, hydraulically assisted
Power steering fluid capacity .... 0.65 litre (1.2 pints)
Power steering drivebelt tension .... 12 mm (0.5 in) deflection at centre of run

Roadwheels

Wheel size .... 5J x 14
Tyre pressures .... For correct pressures according to vehicle load and speed condition, consult manufacturer's handbook or Peugeot dealer

Torque wrench settings

	Nm	lbf ft
Front Suspension		
Suspension strut upper mounting	10	7
Main crossmember to body	42	31
Front crossmember to body	37	27
Rear triangle arm inner pivot	45	33
Front triangle arm mountings	45	33
Anti-roll bar connecting link	45	33
Hub to stub axle:		
Initial	30	22
Final	10	7
Wheel nuts	60	44
Rear suspension		
Shock absorber upper locknut	12	9
Shock absorber lower locknut	12	9
Shock absorber lower pivot bolt	45	33
Crossmember-to-body nuts (inner)	32	23
Crossmember-to-body nuts (outer)	65	47
Suspension arm pivot nuts	65	47
Anti-roll bar connecting link	12	9
Support block nuts:		
Front	32	23
Rear	12	9
Intermediate support to crossmember	32	23
Crossmember front nuts	17	13
Crossmember rear nuts	32	23
Panhard rod nuts	32	23
Wheel nuts	60	44
Standard setting		
Steering gear to crossmember	32	23
Track rod end balljoint	42	31
Flexible coupling bolts and nuts	17	13
Flexible coupling clamp bolts	10	7
Steering wheel	45	33
Steering column to dashboard	10	7
Universal joint clamp bolt	10	7
Steering gear pinion nut	15	11
Thrust plate bolts	10	7
Rack eye locknut	35	25
Track rod yoke to rack	45	33
Power assisted steering		
Steering gear to crossmember	32	23
Hydraulic ram to crossmember	55	40
Flexible coupling to steering gear flange	20	14

1 General description

The front suspension on all models is fully independant with integral shock absorbers and coil springs. A steel crossmember acts as a mounting for the engine as well as the rack-and-pinion steering gear. At the ends of the crossmember are transverse suspension links which pivot in bushes on the crossmember. The outer ends of the links are connected to the stub axles. Resilient 'Silentblock' mountings are used.

A second crossmember, located in front of the first crossmember, is connected to the transverse suspension links by front triangle arms, again mounted in 'Silentblock' bushes. When an anti-roll bar is fitted, it is mounted on the front crossmember and connected to the transverse arms by a short link.

Two coil springs are mounted vertically and rest on the telescopic double-acting shock absorber cylinders, which are integral with the stub axles. At the lower end, each suspension unit is accurately positioned by the transverse suspension links and triangle arms. When fitted, the anti-roll bar links the two suspension units together. The top ends of the suspension units are attached to the body at the top wheel arch panels.

On models with independant rear suspension the final drive and rear suspension assembly is supported by two pressed steel crossmembers which form a subframe. This is attached to the main body using resilient 'Silentblock' mountings. The front crossmember acts as a mounting for the trailing arm which carry the coil springs and dampers. These are located at their upper ends by the rear crossmember, which is mounted at a higher level.

On models equipped with a 'banjo' type solid rear axle, coil springs are fitted at each end in conjunction with telescopic double-acting shock absorbers. Fore-and-aft movement of the axle in controlled by the torque tube and two additional steady arms. A Panhard rod is used to restrict lateral movement and an anti-roll bar is also fitted.

The steering gear used on all models is of the rack-and-pinion type. When the steering wheel is turned, the steering shaft, onto which is attached a helically toothed gear, also turns. This gear is located in the steering gearbox which is mounted on the front crossmember. The helically toothed gear, called the pinion, meshes with the rack which is located in a tubular housing. Gaiters are fitted at either end to contain the lubricant and exclude road dirt. When the pinion rotates, the rack is caused to move transversely in the housing. Universal joints are fitted to each end of the rack and connect it to the track rods. Movement of the rack causes the track rods and steering arms on the front swivel hubs to move, thereby giving movement to the front wheels.

On early models the left-hand track rod only is adjustable in length to allow the alteration of the front wheel alignment. On later models and all models equipped with power assisted steering, both track rods are adjustable.

Where power assisted steering is fitted, steering effort is reduced by applying hydraulic pressure to a new ram incorporated in the steering rack housing. Hydraulic fluid pressure for this purpose is generated by a pump mounted on the engine and driven by a V-belt

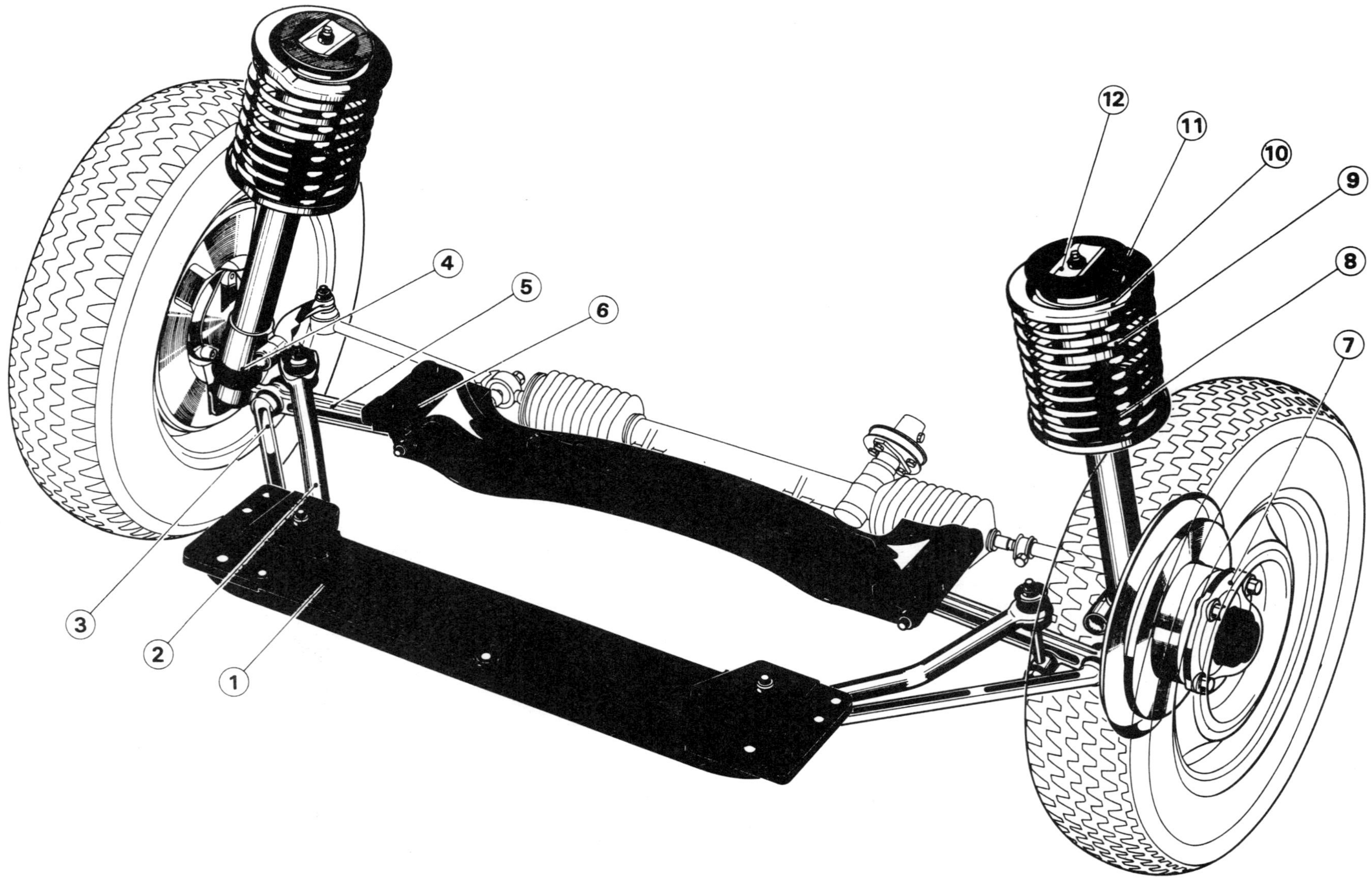

Fig. 11.1 Front suspension assembly (Sec 1)

1 Front crossmember	4 Balljoint assembly	7 Front hub assembly	9 Coil spring	11 Upper mounting
2 Anti-roll bar	5 Rear triangle arm	8 Rebound stop	10 Spring upper seat	12 Rebound seating cup
3 Front triangle arm	6 Main crossmember			

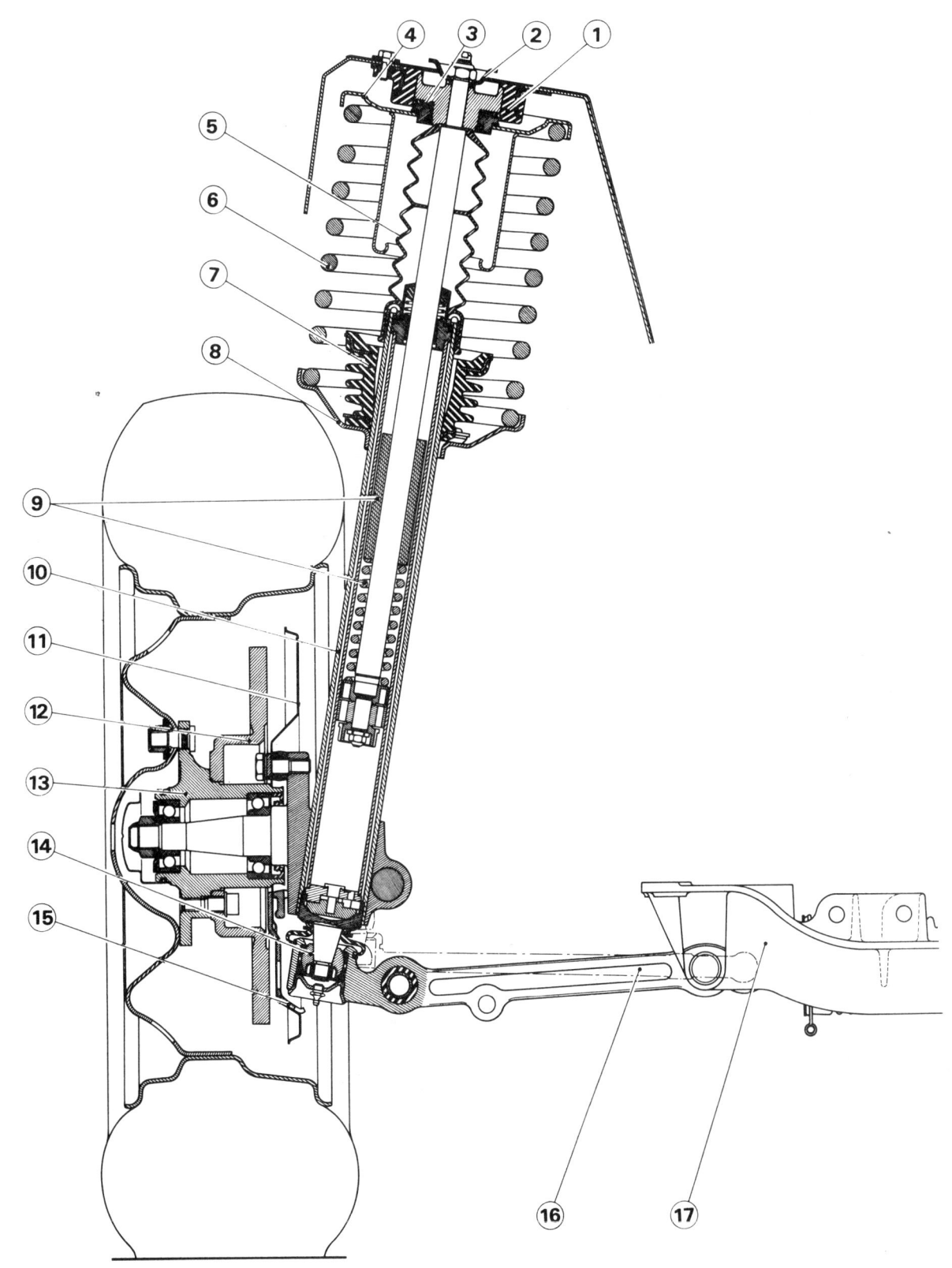

Fig. 11.2 Sectional view of front suspension (Sec 1)

1	Upper flexible mounting	7	Rebound stop or block	11	Brake disc shield
2	Safety cup	8	Lower spring seating cup	12	Brake disc
3	Needle thrust bearing	9	Nylon spacer and damper limiting spring	13	Hub
4	Upper spring seating cup	10	Shock absorber body	14	Lower steering knuckle balljoint
5	Damper shaft protector			15	Balljoint grease nipple protector
6	Suspension spring			16	Rear arm of triangle
				17	Main crossmember

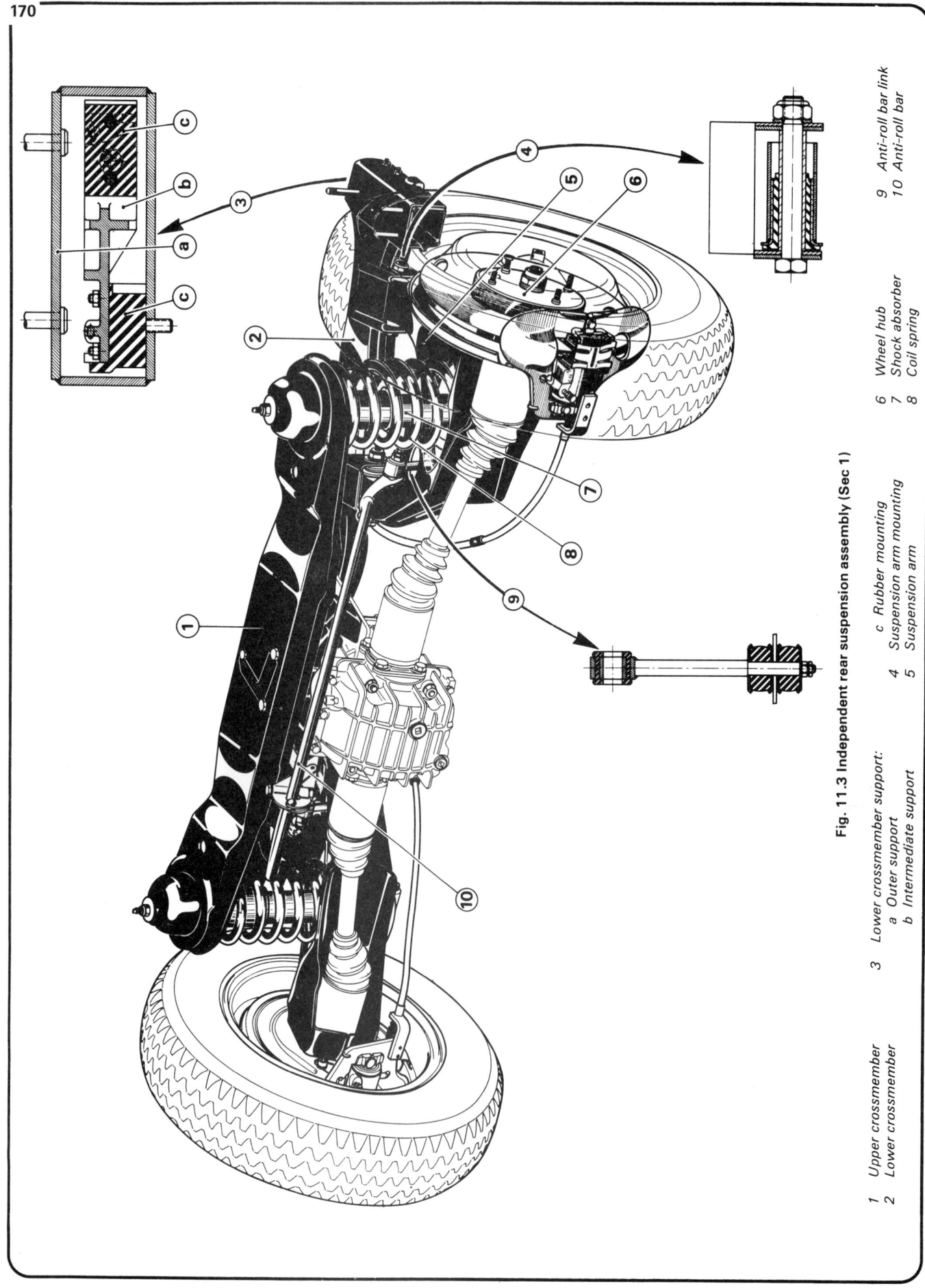

Fig. 11.3 Independent rear suspension assembly (Sec 1)

1 Upper crossmember
2 Lower crossmember

3 Lower crossmember support:
  a Outer support
  b Intermediate support
  c Rubber mounting
4 Suspension arm mounting
5 Suspension arm

6 Wheel hub
7 Shock absorber
8 Coil spring

9 Anti-roll bar link
10 Anti-roll bar

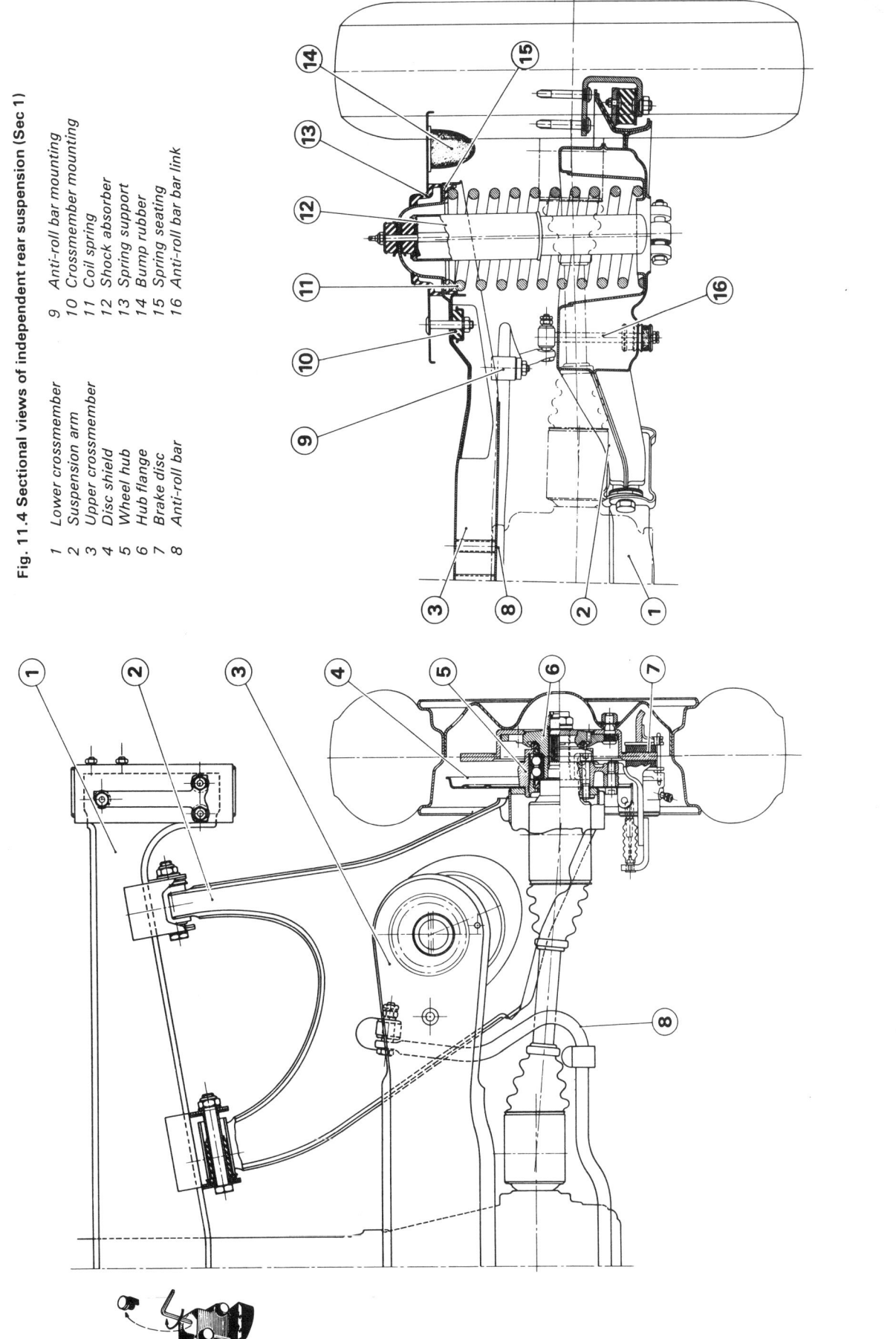

Fig. 11.4 Sectional views of independent rear suspension (Sec 1)

1 Lower crossmember
2 Suspension arm
3 Upper crossmember
4 Disc shield
5 Wheel hub
6 Hub flange
7 Brake disc
8 Anti-roll bar
9 Anti-roll bar mounting
10 Crossmember mounting
11 Coil spring
12 Shock absorber
13 Spring support
14 Bump rubber
15 Spring seating
16 Anti-roll bar bar link

from the crankshaft pulley. In the event of failure of the hydraulic system the steering can still be operated, but extra effort will be required.

2   Front hub bearings – adjustment

1   To check the condition of the hub bearings, jack up the front of the car and support it on axle stands. Grasp the roadwheel at the '12 o'clock' and '6 o'clock' positions and try to rock it. Watch carefully for any movement in the steering gear which can easily be mistaken for hub movement.

2   If the front wheel hub movement is excessive, proceed as follows.

3   Remove the roadwheel and, by judicious tapping and levering, withdraw the dust cap from the centre of the hub.

4   Using a small punch, tap up the staking that locks the hub nut to the stub axle. Now undo and remove the hub nut.

5   Refit a *new* hub nut to the stub axle and tighten it initally to the torque wrench setting given in the Specifications, while at the same time rotating the hub.

6   Now slacken the nut and then retighten to the final specified torque wrench setting. **Note**: *If the hub bearings are of the taper roller bearing type, now slacken the hub nut by $\frac{1}{8}$ of a turn.*

7   Spin the hub and check that it turns freely with just a trace of endfloat.

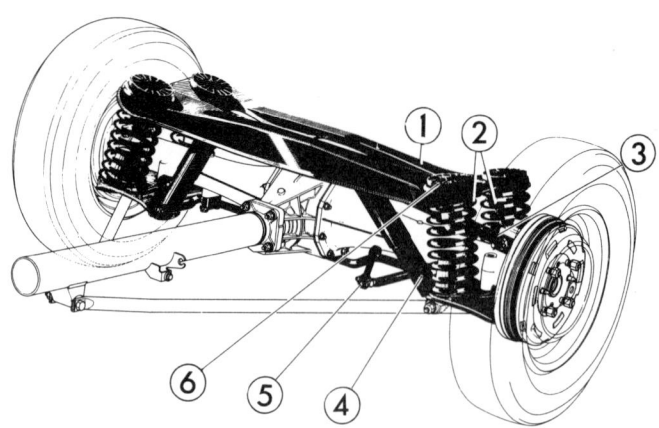

Fig. 11.5 Rear suspension assembly as fitted to estate and family Estate models (Sec 1)

1	Rear crossmember	4	Shock absorber
2	Rear springs	5	Anti-roll bar
3	Panhard rod	6	Crossmember pad

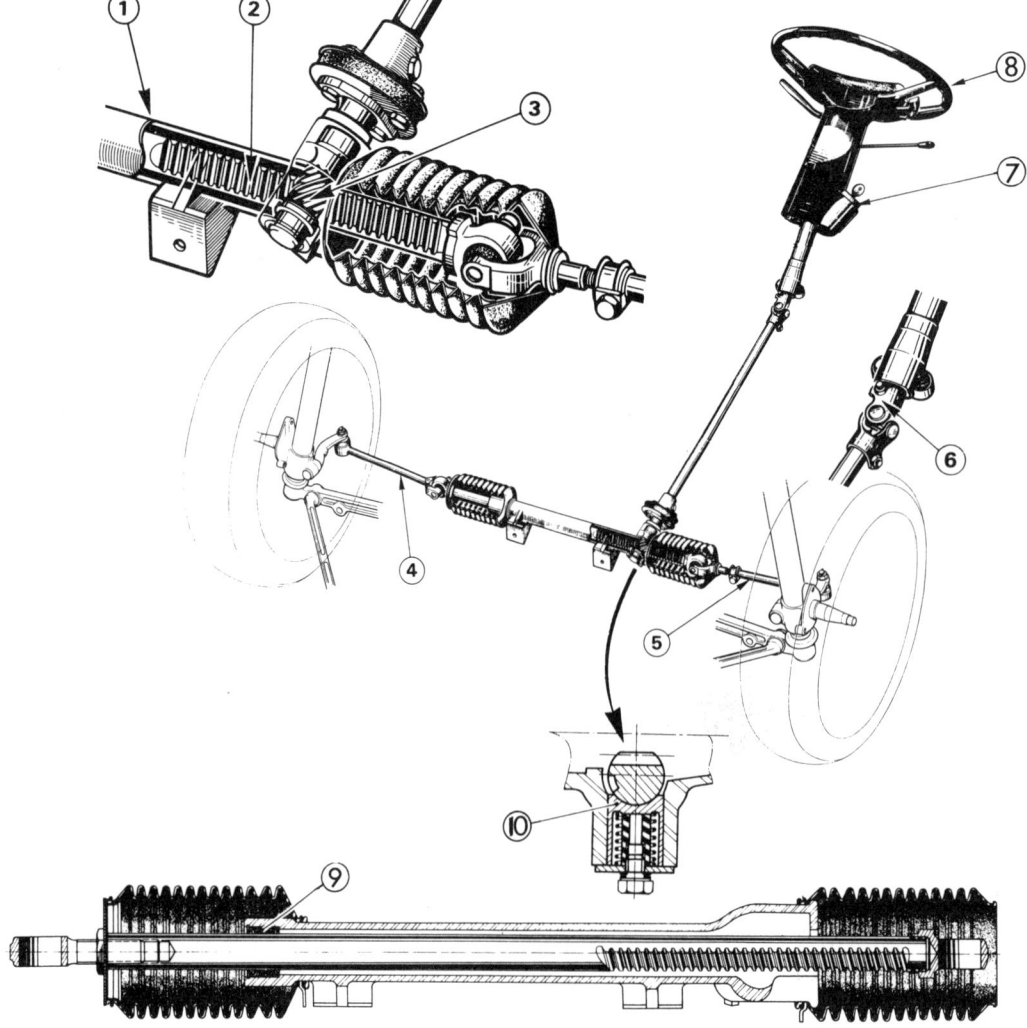

Fig. 11.6 Layout of the rack-and-pinion steering gear (Sec 1)

1	Rack housing	4	Right-hand track rod	7	Starter switch	9	Rack bushing
2	Steering rack	5	Left-hand track rod	8	Steering wheel	10	Rack plunger
3	Pinion	6	Universal joint				

8   Using a small punch, stake the nut into the grooves on the stub axle and then refit the dust cap and roadwheel.

3   Front hub and bearings – removal, overhaul and refitting

Note: *Depending on model, either ball bearings or taper roller bearings may be fitted to the front hubs. The procedure for removal, overhaul and refitting is similar for both types, any differences will be described where necessary.*
1   Jack up the front of the car and support it on axle stands. Remove the appropriate front roadwheel.
2   Refer to Chapter 9, and remove the front disc brake pads. Undo and remove the brake caliper retaining bolts, withdraw the caliper and tie it up out of the way using string or wire. Avoid placing undue strain on the flexible brake hose.
3   By judicious tapping and levering, withdraw the dust cap from the centre of the hub.
4   Using a small punch, knock up the staking securing the hub nut to the stub axle.
5   Carefully slide the complete hub and disc assembly off the stub axle. If it is initially tight, tap the circumference of the hub flange with a soft-faced mallet. **Note**: *On models equipped with taper roller bearings, it is likely that the inner bearing race and oil seal will remain on the stub axle as the hub assembly is withdrawn. If this happens remove the bearing from the stub axle using two screwdrivers or a universal puller.*
6   To remove the bearings, support the rear face of the disc on blocks of wood. Using a tapered drift inserted through the hole in the centre of the hub, tap out the inner bearing and oil seal. As the parts are released, note which way round they are fitted as a guide to installation.
7   Turn the hub over and remove the outer bearing in a similar fashion.
8   Thoroughly wash all parts in paraffin and wipe dry using a non-fluffy rag.
9   Inspect the bearings for signs of rusting, pitting or overheating. If evident a new set of bearings must be fitted.
10   Inspect the oil seal journal face of the stub axle for signs of damage. If evident polish with fine emery tape: if very bad a new stub axle will have to be fitted. This will of course be very expensive, as it is incorporated in the front suspension unit.
11   To reassemble, carefully drift the new bearings into position using a suitable diameter drift. Make sure they are fitted the correct way round.
12   Work some grease into the bearings and hub assembly.
13   Smear a new oil seal with a little engine oil and fit it with the lip

innermost using a tube of suitable diameter. The final fitted position should be flush with the hub flange.
14   Fit the hub assembly to the stub axle and check that the inner bearing track is flush against the shoulder of the stub axle.
15   Fit the washer with the inner shoulder against the inner track of the outer bearing.
16   Refit a *new* hub nut to the stub axle and tighten it initially to the torque wrench setting given in the Specifications, while at the same time rotating the hub.
17   Now slacken the nut and retighten to the final specified torque wrench setting. **Note**: *If the hub bearings are of the taper roller bearing type, now slacken the hub nut by $\frac{1}{8}$ of a turn.*
18   Spin the hub and check that it turns freely with just a trace of endfloat.
19   Using a small punch, stake the nut into the grooves on the stub axle and then refit the dust cap.
20   Refit the brake caliper, observing the correct torque wrench settings for the mounting bolts, and then refit the brake pads as described in Chapter 9.
21   Refit the roadwheel and lower the car to the ground.

4   Front suspension strut assembly – removal and refitting

1   Jack up the front of the car and support it on axle stands. Remove the appropriate front roadwheel.
2   Refer to Chapter 9 and remove the front disc brake pads. Now undo and remove the brake caliper retaining bolts and suspend the caliper from the bodywork using string on a wire. Take care not to stretch the flexible brake hose.
3   Undo and remove the nut securing the track rod end balljoint to the steering arm.
4   Release the track rod end from the steering arm using a universal balljoint separator. Alternatively, strike the end of the steering arm sharply using a medium hammer to release the taper.
5   Undo and remove the nut and pivot bolt securing the anti-roll bar connecting link to the rear triangle arm (photo).
6   Undo and remove the nut and then carefully tap out the splined pivot bolt securing the rear triangle arm to the front suspension crossmember. Now lever the triangle arm out of its location in the crossmember.
7   Undo and remove the nut securing the front triangle arm. Move the suspension strut assembly rearwards to disengage the two triangle arms. Recover the Silentblock bushes.
8   Position a jack beneath the wheel hub and *just* take the weight of the suspension strut assembly.
9   From inside the engine compartment detach the earth lead from the tag on the suspension strut upper mounting (photo).
10   Undo and remove the three bolts securing the suspension strut upper mounting to the inner wing panel.
11   Slowly lower the jack while at the same time supporting the assembly by one of the spring coils. Carefully withdraw the unit from under the wheel arch.
12   Refitting the front suspension strut assembly in the reverse sequence to removal, bearing in mind the following points:

   (a)   *Use new locknuts and washers whenever possible*
   (b)   *Tighten all suspension mountings finger tight only during initial assembly*
   (c)   *Finally tighten all suspension mountings to the specified torque wrench settings with the full weight of the vehicle on its roadwheels.*

5   Front suspension strut assembly – overhaul

This job is not considered to be suitable for the do-it-yourself motorist as six special tools are required. Without these the coil spring cannot be removed in safety, and also the unit cannot be dismantled or reassembled without damaging various parts. If the unit is in need of overhaul, then it is far better for the local Peugeot garage to transfer the spring to a reconditioned or new unit.

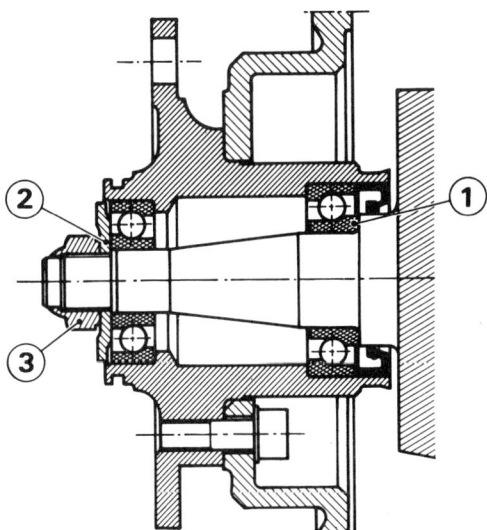

Fig. 11.7 Sectional view of front hub and ball bearings (Sec 3)

1 Inner race	*3 Nut*
2 Thrust washer	

6   Anti-roll bar – removal and refitting

1   Jack up the front of the car and support it on axle stands.

4.5 Anti-roll bar connecting link (A), rear triangle arm inner mounting (B), front-to-rear triangle arm retaining nut (C) and track rod end balljoint retaining nut (D)

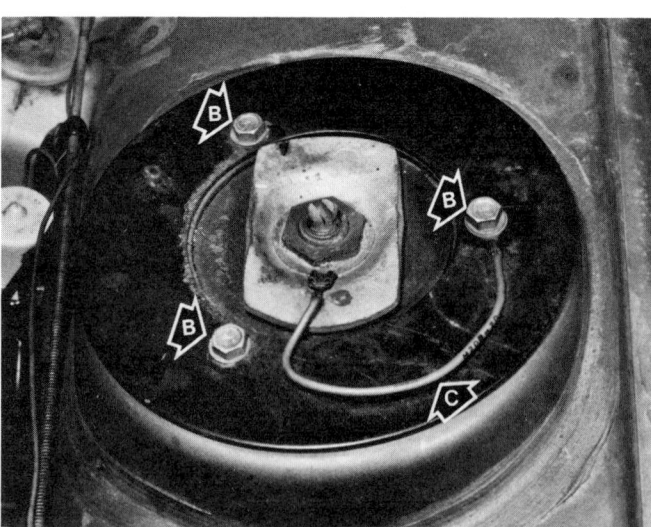

4.9 Front suspension strut earth lead (A) and upper mounting bolts (B)

6.2 Anti-roll bar mountings on front crossmember

7.3 Front triangle arm mounting on crossmember

2   From beneath the front of the car, undo and remove the bolts securing the anti-roll bar mountings to both sides of the front crossmember (photo).

3   Now undo and remove the nut and pivot bolt securing the anti-roll bar links to the rear triangle arms.

4   The anti-roll bar can now be withdrawn from under the car.

5   If necessary the connecting links can be removed after undoing the retaining nuts and lifting off the rubber bushes and thrust washers.

6   Examine the rubber bushes and Silentblock mountings for signs of swelling, splitting or general deterioration and renew as necessary.

7   Refitting the anti-roll bar in the reverse sequence to removal. Finally tighten the mountings to the specified torque wrench settings with the full weight of the vehicle on its roadwheels.

7   Front triangle arm – removal and refitting

1   Jack up the front of the car and support it on axle stands. Remove the appropriate front roadwheel.

2   Undo and remove the nut and splined pivot bolt securing the rear triangle arm to the front suspension crossmember. Using a large screwdriver, ease the arm out of its location in the crossmember.

3   Undo and remove the nuts, thrust washers and half bushes securing the front triangle arm to the crossmember and to the rear

triangle arm (photo).

4   Move the suspension assembly rearwards sufficiently to disengage the front triangle arm from the crossmember and rear triangle arm.

5   With the arm removed from the car, carefully examine the mounting half bushes for signs of deterioration and compression damage and renew as necessary.

6   Refitting the front triangle arm in the reverse sequence to removal. Ensure that all mountings are tightened to the specified torque wrench settings when the full weight of the car is on its roadwheels.

8   Rear triangle arm – removal and refitting

The outer end of the rear triangle arm is attached to the base of the front suspension strut by means of a steering knuckle balljoint. To remove the arm this balljoint must be dismantled and a number of special tools are required to do this. The improvisation of these tools is not really feasible as these are a number of small components in the balljoint which are easily damaged. Should it be necessary to remove the arm or overhaul the balljoint it is recommended that the front suspension strut complete with rear triangle arm be removed from the car as described in Section 4 and then taken to a Peugeot dealer to have the necessary repair work caried out.

9 'Silentblock' or 'Metalastic' bushes – removal and refitting

1 The procedure for the removal and refitting of metalastic bushes is the same no matter from where they came on the car.
2 Drift the old bush out of its bore. This may be extremely difficult if the bush has distorted or broken up. However, it does not matter if the bush is damaged during removal as it is to be renewed.
3 Smear the new bush with soap or washing up liquid *(on no account use oil or grease)* and also its bore. This will ease refitting a great deal.
4 Tap the new bush into its bore with a soft faced hammer. Alternatively, and more desirable, use a bench vice as a press to force the bush into its bore. If movement is continuous, the job is easier and there is little chance of the bush 'picking-up' half way in.

10 Rear shock absorbers – removal and refitting

1 Jack up the rear of the car and support its weight on axle stands placed under the rear axle or rear suspension arms, depending on model.

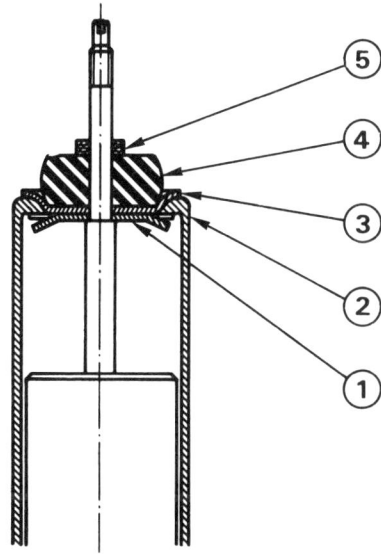

Fig. 11.8 Correct assembly order for upper mounting (Sec 10)

1	Thrust cap	4	Rubber washer
2	Rod protector	5	Nylon spacer
3	Centering cup		

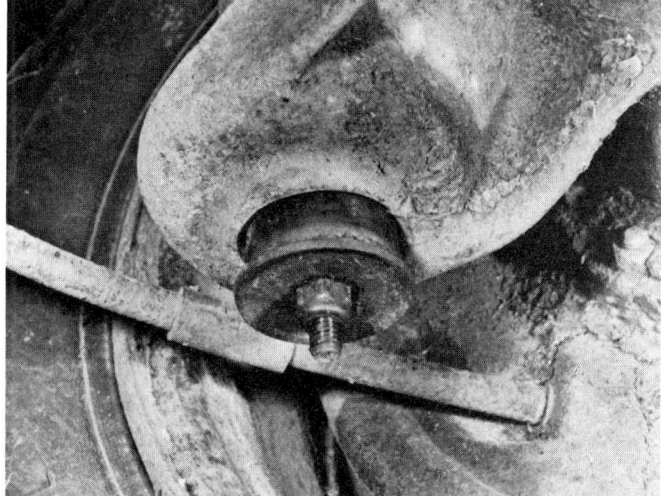

10.4 Shock absorber lower mounting

2 Working inside the car, undo and remove the locknut at the top end of the shock absorber. It will be necessary to hold the shock absorber rod with a spanner to prevent it from turning as the nut is undone.
3 Now lift off the upper sheet metal cup and rubber washer.
4 Working underneath the car, undo and remove the lower nut and pivot bolt on models fitted with independent rear suspension, or the lower locknut, sheet metal cup and rubber washer where a 'banjo' type solid rear axle is fitted (photo).
5 On models with independent rear suspension, remove the shock absorber by lowering it through the aperture in the rear suspension arm.
6 On models fitted with a 'banjo' type solid rear axle, lift the shock absorber to clear the lower mounting and then lower it downwards and out from under the car.
7 To test the shock absorber, alternatively compress and extend it throughout its full movement. If the action is jerky or weak, either it is worn or there is air in the hydraulic cylinder. Continue to compress and extend it, and if the action does not become more positive a new shock absorber should be obtained. If the shock absorber is showing signs of leaking it should be discarded as it is not possible to overhaul it.
8 Check the rubber washers and bushes; if they show signs of deterioration a new set of rubbers should be obtained and fitted. Ideally this should be done every time the shock absorber is removed.
9 Fully extend the shock absorber rod and fit on the following parts: thrust cap, rod protector, centering cup, rubber washer, and nylon spacer.
10 Engage the shock absorber in its recess with the rod positioned in the suspension crossmember hole.
11 From inside the car, fit the following parts to the shock absorber rod: rubber washer, upper sheet metal cup with the raised edge facing upwards, and a new locknut tightened to the specified torque wrench setting.
12 On models with independent rear suspension, engage the lower securing pivot bolt and refit the nut. Tighten the nut to the specified torque wrench setting.
13 On models with a 'banjo' type solid rear axle, fit the centering cup and rubber washer to the shock absorber, and then engage the lower mounting with the lug on the axle casing. Fit the rubber washer and lower sheet metal cup followed by the locknut. Tighten the locknut to the specified torque wrench setting.

11 Rear suspension arm (models with independent rear suspension) – removal and refitting

1 Refer to Chapter 8, and remove the driveshaft.
2 Raise the rear of the car and support it under each crossmember support.
3 Place a jack under the rear arm and raise the rear arm so that the shock absorber is not fully extended.
4 Remove the shock absorber, as described in Section 10.
5 Unclip the handbrake cable from the rear arm.
6 Undo and remove the nut that secures the anti-roll bar link under the rear arm.
7 Withdraw the metal cup and the rubber washer and immediately refit the nut to prevent the upper parts from falling inside the arm.
8 Unscrew the rear arm pivot nuts.
9 Carefully lower the jack until the suspension spring is fully extended.
10 Remove the spring and its upper rubber cup.
11 Finally withdraw the rear arm pivots and lift away the rear arm.
12 Check the rear suspension arm for damage or excessive corrosion and renew if evident. Inspect the bushes and if they have deteriorated, renew them as described in Section 9.
13 When refitting the rear suspension arm always use new 'Nylstop' nuts and 'Blocfor' or 'Orduflex' type washers.
14 To refit, first position the rear arm in the corresponding yokes on the crossmember.
15 Insert a rod through the inner joint and fit the outer pivot into its housing.
16 Withdraw the rod and fit the inner pivot into its housing.
17 Fit new 'Nylstop' nuts but do not fully tighten yet.
18 Place a jack under the rear part of the arm.
19 Smear the upper rubber spring cup with a little soap or washing up liquid. This will make its final positioning easier.

20 Place the spring in between its upper and lower mountings.
21 Carefully raise the arms, taking care that the spring centres correctly in its housing. At the same time guide the anti-roll bar connecting link into position in the rear arm.
22 Refit the shock absorber as described in Section 10.
23 Refit the rubber washer and metal cup onto the anti-roll bar connecting link. Tighten the nut to the specified torque wrench setting.
24 Refit the driveshaft as described in Chapter 8.
25 Reattach the handbrake cable to the rear arm.
26 Refit the roadwheel and lower the car to the ground.
27 With two people sitting in the rear seat, tighten the rear suspension pivot nuts to the specified torque wrench setting.
28 Finally check the oil level in the differential housing and top up if necessary.

12 Rear anti-roll bar (models with independant rear suspension) – removal and refitting

1 Jack up the rear of the car and support it on axle stands placed under the rear suspension crossmember.
2 Working under the rear of the car, undo and remove the nuts securing the anti-roll bar links to each rear suspension arm.
3 Withdraw the metal cup and rubber washers from each link and then immediately refit the nut to prevent the upper parts from falling inside the arm.

Fig. 11.9 Removing the anti-roll bar from the suspension arm (Sec 12)

Fig. 11.10 Removing the anti-roll bar-to-body mountings (Sec 12)

4 Undo and remove the bolts from the two anti-roll bar clamps and then disengage the anti-roll bar from the bodywork.
5 Disengage the anti-roll bar links from the suspension arms and then withdraw the bar rearwards and out from under the car.
6 With the anti-roll bar removed, the nut and bolt securing each connecting link may be removed and the links lifted off.
7 Inspect the anti-roll bar for damage and distortion and the bushes for wear. Renew any suspect components.
8 Refitting the anti-roll bar in the reverse sequence to removal. Ensure that all nuts and bolts are tightened to the specified torque wrench settings.

13 Rear suspension upper crossmember (models with independent rear suspension) – removal and refitting

1 Preferably place the car over a pit or on a ramp, but if these are not available jack up the rear of the car and place axle stands in front of the lower crossmember.
2 Remove the roadwheels.
3 Remove the rear nut that secures the exhaust pipe to the underside of the body.
4 Remove the two securing clamps of the anti-roll bar flexible bushes and disengage the anti-roll bar from the bodywork.
5 Undo and remove the two socket-headed bolts that secure the differential unit to the suspension crossmember.
6 Rest the rear section of the connecting tube on the rear crossmember.
7 Slacken the rear arm pivot nuts.
8 Remove the petrol pipe rear securing clamp.
9 Place a jack under the crossmember left-hand lateral bracket.
10 Carefully remove the rear seat cushion.
11 Unlock the three crossmember securing nuts.
12 Undo and remove the front securing nut.
13 Prise up the lockwasher and remove the plastic plug from the guide hole.
14 Two long bolts and washers are now required. One must be screwed into each side of the suspension at the point of the guide holes. There must be a protrusion of about 76 mm (3 in) into the car. Illustrations in Chapter 7 show the special tool in use, but bolts and large washers do just as well.
15 Remove the crossmember rear securing nuts and the thrust washers.
16 Carefully lower the crossmember until the bolt is supporting its weight.
17 Repeat the previously described sequence for the right-hand side of the crossmember.
18 Place chocks under the rear arms.
19 Refer to Section 10 and remove the two shock absorbers.
20 Carefully raise the rear of the car until the coil springs are completely detached.
21 Remove the springs and their upper rubber cups.
22 Undo and remove the suspension crossmember securing nuts from under the body.
23 Remove the sheet metal cups and the rubber washers.
24 Carefully disengage the crossmember from the bodywork and then pull it sideways to avoid contact with the final drive housing.
25 Finally remove the rubber thrust caps.
26 To refit the rear suspension upper crossmember, first place the rubber thrust caps on the suspension crossmember. To facilitate positioning them, smear with soap or washing-up liquid.
27 Place the crossmember between the final drive housing and underside of the body.
28 Secure the crossmember to the body using rubber washers, sheet metal cups, nuts and new Blocfor washers. Tighten the nuts to the specified torque wrench setting.
29 Locate the rear spring upper rubber cap in the recess in the crossmember. For this it is suggested that some adhesive is used.
30 Place the springs between the their upper and lower supports.
31 Carefully lower the rear of the car and position the springs in their upper cups.
32 Refer to Section 10 and refit the two rear shock absorbers.
33 Refit the roadwheels and lower the car to the ground.
34 Place a jack under the right-hand lateral holder and raise the crossmember until it comes into contact with the floor.

35 Remove the bolt and washer and close the guide hole using the plastic plug.
36 Fit the following onto the studs in this order: flat washers, a new tab lock and securing nuts.
37 Tighten the nuts to the specified torque wrench setting.
38 Lock the nuts by bending the tab tongue over the nuts.
39 Repeat the sequence previously described for the second side.
40 Refit the rear seat cushion.
41 Secure the final drive housing to the suspension crossmember using socket-headed bolts with new 'Blocfor' washers. Tighten to the specified torque wrench settings.
42 Smear a little rubber grease onto the anti-roll bar bushes.
43 Fit and secure the anti-roll bar to the underside of the body.
44 Refit the petrol pipe securing clamp.
45 Reconnect the rear portion of the exhaust pipe to the body.
46 Refit the roadwheels and lower the car to the ground.
47 With two people sitting in the rear seats, tighten the rear suspension arm pivot nuts to the specified torque wrench setting.

14 Rear suspension lower crossmember (models with independent rear suspension) – removal and refitting

1 Preferably place the car over a pit or on a ramp, but if these are not available jack up the rear of the car and support it on axle stands placed in front of the lower crossmember.
2 Remove the roadwheels.
3 Unscrew, but do not remove, the nuts that secure the rear brake flexible hoses to the supports on the underside of the rear floor panel. Carefully detach the hoses.
4 Release the brake pipes from their supports.
5 Place a jack under the left-hand lateral crossmember support in contact with it.
6 Remove the rear seat cushion.
7 Unlock the three nuts that secure the crossmember.
8 Undo and remove the front securing nut.
9 Prise up the lockwasher and remove the plastic plug from the guide hole.
10 Two long bolts and washers are now required. One must be screwed into each side of the suspension at the point of the guide holes. There must be a protrusion of about 76 mm (3 in) into the car. Illustrations in Chapter 7 show the special tool in use, but bolts and large washers will do just as well.
11 Remove the crossmember rear securing nuts and the thrust washers.
12 Carefully lower the crossmember until the bolt is supporting its weight.

13 Repeat the previously described sequence for the right-hand side of the crossmember.
14 Unhook the handbrake control lever return spring.
15 Straighten the handbrake cable stop tongues on the relay arm and slide the cable sideways out of the arm.
16 Remove the lever and arm assembly.
17 Remove the protector covers and withdraw the brake cables from their respective guides on the crossmember.
18 Remove the inner rear arm pivots and slide in two rods to support its weight.
19 Remove the outer rear arm joints and slide out the two rods.
20 Using a lever, disengage the left-hand rear arm joints followed by the right-hand rear arm joints.
21 Support the crossmember so as to release the tension on the two bolts suspending the crossmember from the floor. Remove the two bolts.
22 The crossmember may now be removed from under the car.
23 To refit the rear suspension lower crossmember, position under the car and support using the two bolts and washers.
24 Using a lever, reposition the rear arm pivots into the crossmember yokes.
25 Insert rods through the pivots to take the weight of the rear arm.
26 Remove the inner rods and insert the pivots. Follow this by removing the outer rods and inserting the pivots. Fit new locknuts on the pivots, but do not fully tighten yet.
27 Raise the car at the rear and support under the crossmember lateral mounting.
28 Lower the rear of the car until the crossmember is against the underside of the body.
29 Remove the bolts and washer and close the guide hole using the plastic plug.
30 Fit the following onto the studs in the order of: flat washers, a new tab lock and securing nuts.
31 Tighten the nuts to the specified torque wrench setting.
32 Lock the nuts by bending the tab tongues over the nuts.
33 Repeat the sequence previously described for the second side.
34 Refit the rear seat cushion.
35 Coat the rubber stop rings with a little washing-up liquid and introduce the outer cable ends in their respective guides.
36 Refit the protector covers.
37 Refit the handbrake control equipped with new relay arm.
38 Carefully bend over the cable retaining tongues on the relay arm.
39 Refer to Chapter 9, and adjust the handbrake.
40 Reconnect the flexible hoses to the supports on the underside of the rear floor panel.
41 Refit the rear wheels and lower the car to the ground.
42 With two people sitting in the rear seats, tighten the rear arm pivot nuts to the specified torque wrench setting.

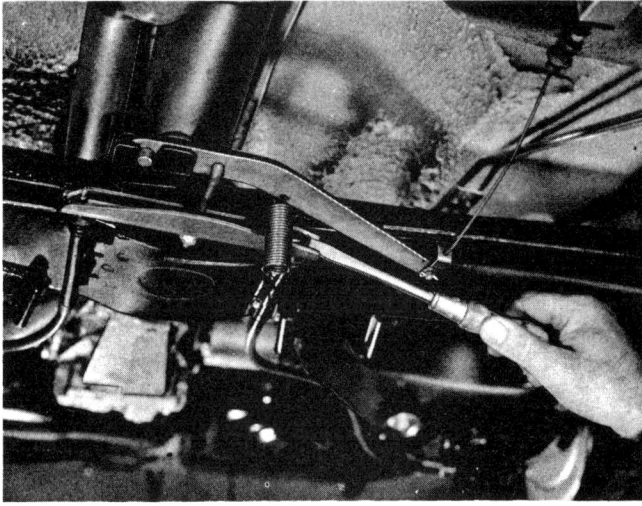

Fig. 11.11 Straightening the handbrake cable retaining tongues on the relay arm (Sec 14)

Fig. 11.12 Crossmember supported on blocks (Sec 14)

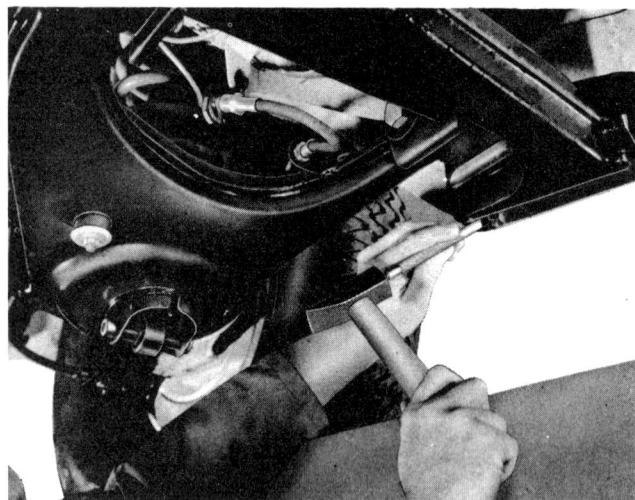

Fig. 11.13 Unlocking the shouldered nut on the rear support block
(Sec 15)

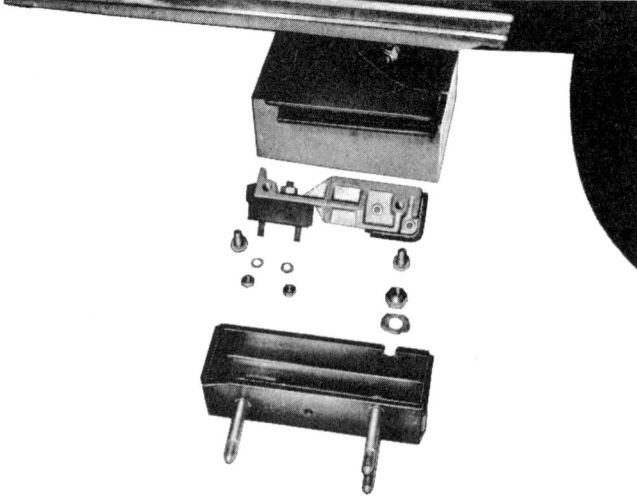

Fig. 11.14 Crossmember support components (Sec 15)

15 Rear suspension lower crossmember support (models with independent rear suspension) – removal and refitting

1   Preferably place the car over a pit or on a ramp, but if these are not available jack up the rear of the car and support it on axle stands placed in front of the lower crossmember.
2   Remove the roadwheel.
3   Unscrew, but do not remove, the nut that secures the rear brake flexible hose to the support on the underside of the rear floor panel. Carefully detach the hose.
4   Unlock the rear support shouldered nut on the rear support block.
5   Place a jack under the crossmember support and in contact with it.
6   Remove the rear seat cushion.
7   Bend back the tabs on the locking plate, and then undo and remove the three crossmember securing nuts.
8   Carefully lower the crossmember until the three studs are clear of the body.
9   Undo and remove the nuts and washers securing the crossmember support to the intermediate support bracket and withdraw the support.
10 If necessary the cast alloy intermediate support together with its rubber mounting blocks may now be removed.
11 Carefully inspect the components for wear or damage, paying particular attention to the rubber blocks on the intermediate support. Renew any suspect parts.
12 Begin reassembly by refitting the intermediate support bracket and crossmember support to the crossmember. Tighten the mountings to the specified torque wrench settings.
13 Slowly jack up the crossmember while at the same time guiding the three studs on the crossmember support through the holes in the body.
14 Refit the thrust washers, the locking plate and the three nuts tightened to the specified torque wrench setting. Lock the nuts by bending up the locking plate.
15 Refit the rear seat cushion.
16 Refit the rear brake flexible hose to the support bracket.
17 Refit the roadwheel and lower the car to the ground.

16 Panhard rod (models with 'banjo' type solid rear axle) – removal and refitting

1   Jack up the rear of the car and place axle stands under the rear axle.
2   Extract the split pins and then undo and remove the nuts, and where applicable the pivot bolts, securing the Panhard rod to the axle

casing and support bracket on the underbody.
3   Carefully ease the Panhard rod from its location and withdraw it from under the car.
4   Check the rod for damage or distortion and the bushes for wear. If the bushes require renewal refer to Section 9.
5   Refitting the Panhard rod is the reverse sequence to removal. Tighten the mountings to the specified torque wrench settings and always use new split pins.

17 Rear anti-roll bar (models with 'banjo' type solid rear axle) – removal and refitting

1   Jack up the rear of the car and place axle stands under the rear axle.
2   Undo and remove the nuts securing the anti-roll bar connecting links to the mounting studs at each end of the axle casing (photo).
3   Using a stout screwdriver, ease the connecting links off the mounting studs.
4   Now undo and remove the bolts securing the two anti-roll bar mounting blocks to the underbody (photo).

17.2 Rear anti-roll bar connecting link

17.4 Anti-roll bar-to-body mounting block

18.4 Steering gear flexible coupling and clamp bolt (arrowed) (viewed from above)

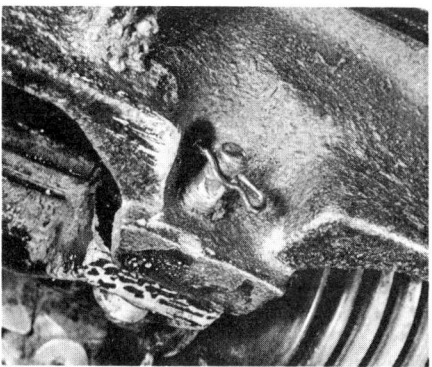

18.5 Steering gear retaining bolt circlips

5   The anti-roll bar can now be withdrawn from under the car.
6   If necessary, undo and remove the nuts and bolts and lift the connecting links off the anti-roll bar.
7   Examine the parts for damage or distortion and for wear of the rubber bushes. Renew any suspect components.
8   Refitting the anti-roll bar is the reverse sequence to removal. Ensure that the mountings are tightened to the specified torque wrench settings.

18 Rack-and-pinion steering gear – removal and refitting

1   Jack up the front of the car and support it on axle stands placed under the front crossmember.
2   Extract the split pins (where fitted) and then undo and remove the nuts securing the track rod end balljoints to the steering arm.
3   Extract the tapered balljoint shank from the steering arm using a universal balljoint separator. Alternatively strike the end of the steering arm with a few sharp blows from a medium hammer to free the taper.
4   Next undo and remove the clamp bolt securing the steering column shaft to the flexible coupling (photo).
5   Withdraw the circlips from the threaded ends of the two bolts securing the rack assembly to the crossmember (photo). Now undo and remove the two bolts.
6   Lower the rack assembly while at the same time rocking the flexible coupling to disengage the steering column shaft.
7   The steering gear can now be withdrawn from under the car.
8   To refit the steering gear, first position the steering wheel so that the spokes are horizontal in the normal driving position.
9   Centralize the steering gear by turning the flexible coupling from full left lock to full right lock while counting the number of turns of the coupling. Now turn the coupling back half the number of counted turns.
10 Engage the steering column shaft with the flexible coupling, turning the coupling slightly if necessary to align the flat on the shaft with the clamp bolt hole.
11 Refit the steering gear mounting bolts and tighten them to the specified torque wrench setting. Refit the circlips to the ends of the bolts (where applicable).
12 Refit the clamp bolt to the flexible coupling, tightened to the specified torque wrench setting.
13 Engage the track rod end balljoint shanks with the steering arms, refit and fully tighten the retaining nuts and secure with new split pins (where applicable).
14 Remove the stands and lower the car to the ground.
15 If during removal the steering gear was dismantled in any way or the settings of the track rod altered, it will now be necessary to reset the front wheel alignment. Refer to Section 22 for full information.

19 Rack-and-pinion steering gear – dismantling, overhaul and reassembly

Note: *Certain export models are fitted with steering gear incorporating two adjustable track rods and a balljoint instead of a yoke pivot at the point where the track rod is connected to the steering rack. The dismantling, overhaul and reassembly sequence is similar for both*

types of steering gear, and any differences will be stated where necessary
1   Wash the outside of the rack-and-pinion assembly using paraffin or a proprietary cleaner and wipe dry with a non-fluffy rag.
2   Mount the assembly horizontally between soft faces in a bench vice.
3   Mark the position of the flexible coupling collar with the rack in the straight-ahead position.
4   Remove the four rubber rack gaiter securing clips and push the two gaiters away from the centre of the steering assembly.
5   Unlock and remove the two track rod yoke pivots, or undo and remove the two inner track rod balljoints.
6   Remove the two track rods and if fitted the rack eye on the opposite side to the pinion. For this, clamp the rack directly between soft faces in a vice and slacken the locknut.
7   Remove the rack plunger thrust plate securing bolts and washers. Lift away the plunger retaining plate complete with grease nipple and nylon stop, the plunger spring, rack plunger, bearing sealing cup, pinion nut and finally the pinion together with its thrust washer and O-ring.
8   The rack may now be withdrawn from the pinion side.
9   Remove the flexible bush retaining circlips. Withdraw the bush and the two steel thrust washers.
10 Remove the pinion bearing retaining circlips. Dip the steering box in boiling water to loosen the bearing. Lift out the bearing.
11 The steering rack is now fully dismantled. Clean all the parts in paraffin and wipe dry with a non-fluffy rag.
12 Thoroughly inspect the rack and pinion teeth for signs of wear, cracks or damage. Check the ends of the rack for wear, especially where it moves in the bushes.
13 Examine the rubber gaiters for signs of cracking, perishing or other damage – if evident new gaiters must be obtained.
14 Inspect the rack eyes and yoke pivots for wear – if evident, new

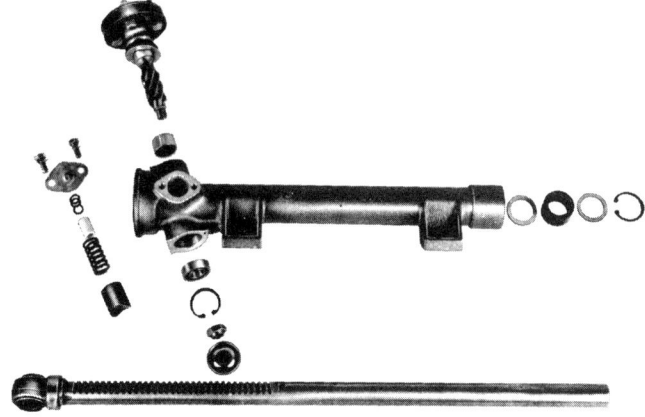

Fig. 11.15 Steering rack-and-pinion dismantled (Sec 19)

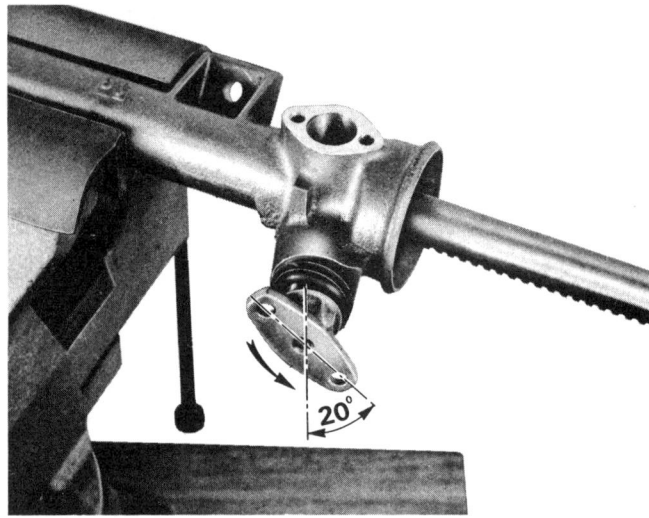

Fig. 11.16 Rotating pinion flange through 20° (Sec 19)

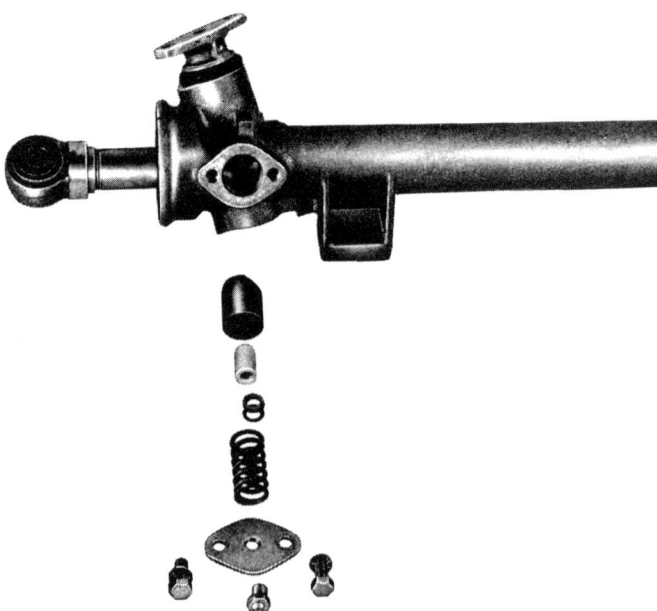

Fig. 11.17 Thrust plate and plunger components (Sec 19)

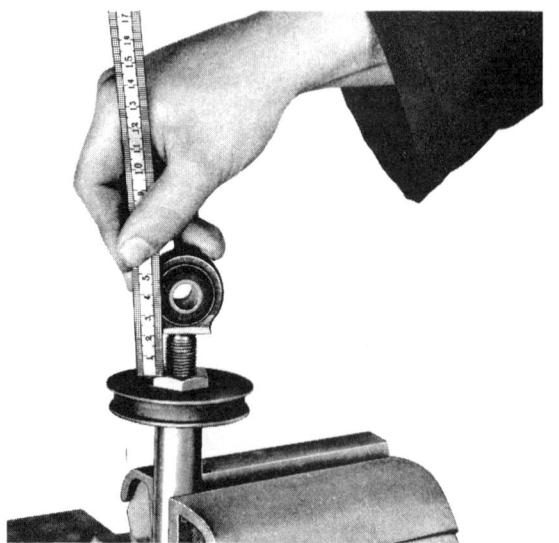

Fig. 11.18 Correct positioning of rack eye (Sec 19)

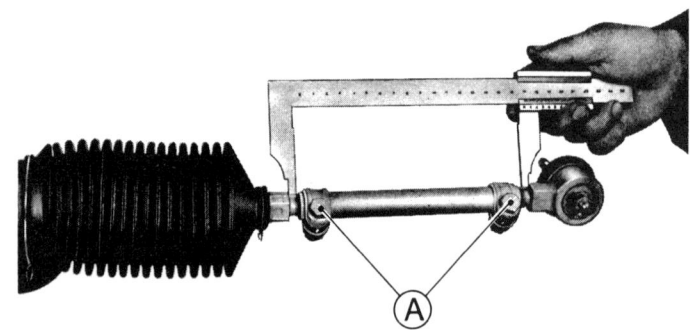

Fig. 11.19 Pinion side track rod initial adjustment, showing clamp bolts (A) (Sec 19)

parts will be necessary. Any other parts that show wear or damage must be renewed.

15 Should it be necessary to renew the pinion bush, it should be drifted out into the steering box with a suitable diameter drift.

16 To fit the new bush, heat the steering box in boiling water and then carefully but quickly insert the new bush tapping, if necessary, with a soft-faced hammer.

17 Grease the end bearing and immerse the end of the steering box in boiling water for a few minutes. Carefully but quickly insert the bearing into its housing, pressing on the outer race.

18 Fit the retaining circlip.

19 Fit into the housing on the opposite end to the pinion, the inner thrust washer, the flexible bush complete with two rubber rings, the outer thrust washer and the circlip.

20 Grease the rack and flexible bush well. Insert the rack into the box from the pinion side.

21 Temporarily thread the second eye (where applicable) onto the rack together with its locknut. Lightly tighten the locknut.

22 Push the rack until the locknut comes into contact with the steering box.

23 Grease the pinion well. Fit the O-ring and thin metal thrust washer

to the pinion housing.

24 Place the pinion into its bore. The nut locking groove must be away from the plunger housing.

25 Starting from the vertical position of the pinion flange, rotate it to the left through about 20°.

26 Push in the pinion until it abuts its bearing. The pinion flange should now be vertical with the locknut still in contact with the extremity of the steering box.

27 Clamp the pinion flange between soft faces in a bench vice.

28 Screw on a new nut and tighten to the specified torque wrench setting.

29 Lock the nut by tapping the nut collar into the groove on the pinion.

30 Grease the bearing housing well and then fit a new sealing cup, tapping it into place with a soft-faced hammer.

31 Assemble the thrust plate by first refitting the grease nipple. Tighten to the specified torque wrench setting. Then refit the shim pack and the nylon stop.

32 Well grease and then place the plunger and spring in its housing in the steering box.

33 Secure the thrust plate assembly with the two bolts and new

'Blocfor' washers. Tighten the bolts to the specified torque wrench setting.

34 Remove the eye from the rack on the opposite end to the pinion, (where applicable).

35 Fit the rack rubber gaiter.

36 Refit and adjust the rack eye to a distance of 20 to 21 mm between the locknut and shoulder of the eye (where applicable).

37 Align the moveable eye with the fixed eye using two 12 mm diameter rods, inserted in the inner rings of the 'Silentblocs', (where applicable).

38 Tighten the locknut firmly but not excessively.

39 Turn the pinion to release the rack from the housing and clamp the rack horizontally in the vice again.

40 Tighten the eye locknut to the specified torque wrench setting.

41 Position the yoke of the track rod on the pinion side of the rack.

42 Place the track rod in line with the track. The head of the bolt should be on the same side as the pinion flange. On racks having two adjustable track rods, refit the pinion side track rod and balljoint.

43 Fit the rack gaiter on the pinion side so that the larger axis is perpendicular to the bearing faces of the mounting flanges on the steering box on the main crossmember. The prongs of the clips must face the lower part of the steering box when fitted to the car.

44 Check and, if necessary, adjust the distance between the shoulders of the yoke and balljoint housing on the pinion side track rod to 180 mm. Equalise the distance between the shoulders and the adjuster rod. Retighten the two clamp bolts.

45 Fit the rack gaiter on the opposite end to the pinion. Refit the one-piece track rod onto the rack and position the track rod as described in paragraph 37. On racks having two adjustable track rods, refit the second track rod and balljoint.

46 Fit four new 'Blockfor' washers and bolts to the flexible coupling. The heads of the bolts should be towards the steering box.

47 Position the plates on both sides of the coupling with the holes forming a cross.

48 Secure the coupling to the pinion flange.

49 Centre the rack relative to the steering box so that it is in the straight-ahead position.

50 Fit the clamp to the coupling using the reference marks made during dismantling. In the straight-ahead position the bore of the collar bolt hole must be parallel to the rack.

51 The thrust faces of the pinion flange and the collar should be in contact with the coupling through the holes in the plates. Tighten the four nuts to the specified torque wrench setting.

52 Lock the bolts by spreading the threads with a cold chisel.

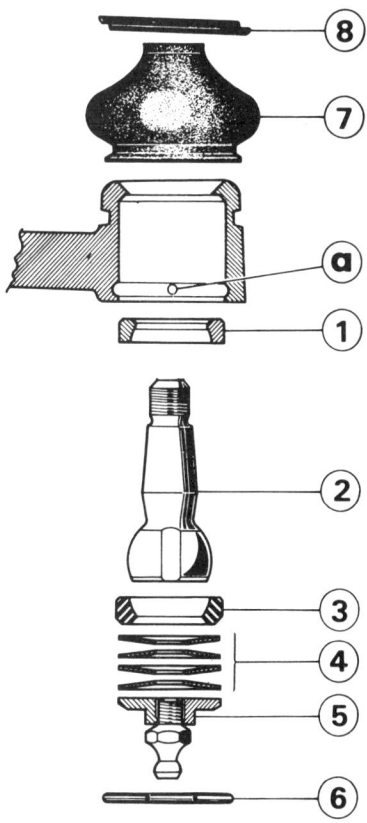

Fig. 11.20 Exploded view of track rod end balljoint (Sec 20)

1 Half cup	6 Spring clip
2 Ball head	7 Rubber boot
3 Nylon half cup	8 Retaining clip
4 Belleville washers	a Hole
5 Balljoint cover	

20 Track rod end balljoints – removal, overhaul and refitting

1 Jack up the front of the car and support it on axle stands placed under the main crossmember. Remove the appropriate front roadwheel.

2 Extract the split pin (where applicable) and then undo and remove the nut securing the balljoint shank to the steering arm.

3 Release the balljoint shank from the steering arm using a universal balljoint separator. Alternatively, strike the end of the steering arm with a few sharp blows from a medium hammer to release the taper.

4 Slacken the securing clamp bolt on the outer end of the track rod.

5 Make a note of the number of exposed threads between the end of the track rod and the shoulder of the balljoint. This will act as a guide to refitting.

6 Grip the track rod using a self-gripping wrench or similar tool and unscrew the track rod end balljoint.

7 With the joint removed from the car, clamp it in a vice and remove the clip and rubber gaiter.

8 Carefully disengage the spring clip securing the balljoint cover using a pin punch inserted in the hole provided.

9 The following parts can now be lifted out: the balljoint cover, Belleville washers, lower nylon half cup, steel ball head and upper steel half cup.

10 Examine all the parts carefully for wear, damage or signs of lack of lubrication. Renew all the internal parts if any of the components are suspect.

11 Begin reassembly by first inserting the steel half cup. Liberally lubricate the steel ball head with general purpose grease and refit to the joint. Now insert the lower nylon half cup, the Belleville washers, balljoint cover and the retaining spring clip.

12 Slide the rubber gaiter over the balljoint shank and secure it in place with the retaining clip.

13 To refit the assembly to the car, screw the balljoint onto the track rod until approximately the same number of threads are exposed as were previously noted.

14 Refit the balljoint shank to the steering arm and secure with the retaining nut. Tighten the nut to the specified torque wrench setting and lock with a new split pin (where applicable).

15 Tighten the track rod outer clamp retaining bolt and then have the front wheel alignment checked and if necessary reset. Refer to Section 22 for full information.

21 Steering column – removal and refitting

1 Open the bonnet and disconnect the battery earth terminal.

2 Jack up the front of the car and support it on axle stands placed under the main crossmember.

3 From under the car undo and remove the clamp bolt securing the steering column shaft to the flexible coupling.

4 Working inside the car undo and remove the securing screws and lift off the lower half of the steering column shroud (photo).

5 Undo and remove the clamp bolt securing the steering column shaft to the lower universal joint (photo). Now move the shaft downward as far as it will go.

6 Disconnect the starter switch and steering column wiring harness block connectors.

7 Undo and remove the four nuts securing the steering column to the dashboard.

8 Withdraw the upper steering column assembly and lift it out of the car.

21.4 Steering column with lower half of shroud removed

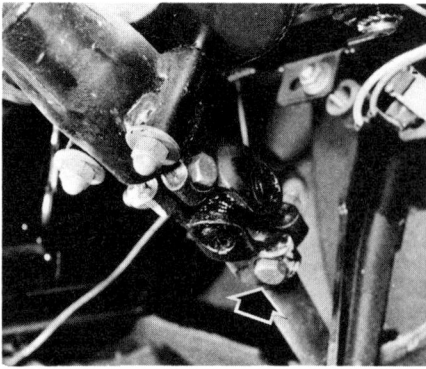

21.5 Steering column universal joint lower clamp bolt

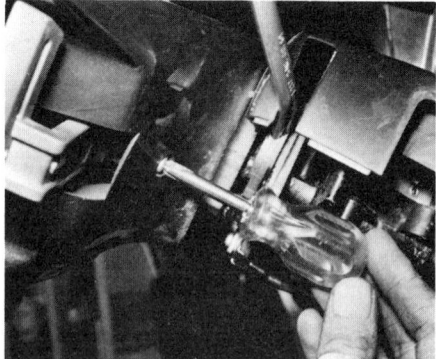

23.1a Remove the retaining screws ...

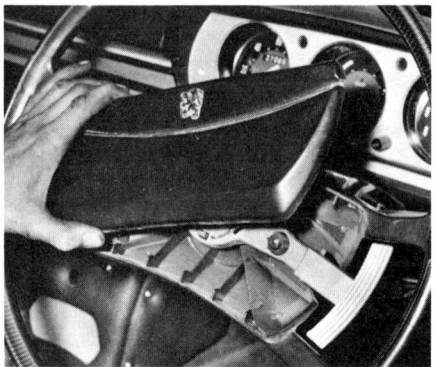

23.1b ... and lift off the steering wheel trim

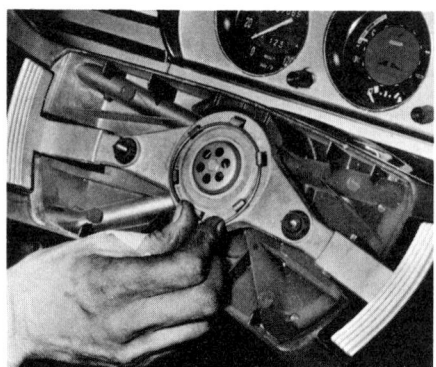

23.2a Remove the horn control ...

23.2b ... and switch snap-rings

9   Lift out the steering column shaft.

10   Refitting the steering column is the reverse sequence to removal. Ensure that the roadwheels are in the straight-ahead position and that the spokes of the steering wheel are horizontal when refitting the steering column shaft. Ensure also that all mountings are tightened to the specified torque wrench settings.

22   Front wheel alignment

The front wheels are correctly aligned when they are turning in at

Fig. 11.21 Adjusting the front wheel alignment (Sec 22)

1   *Adjustable track rod*   2   *Track rod end balljoint*

the front by the specified amount. This toe-in setting is the amount by which the distance between the front inside edges of the front roadwheels (measured at hub height) differs from the diametrically opposite distance measured between the rear inside edges of the front roadwheels.

Adjustment is best left to the local Peugeot garage as accurate alignment requires the use of special equipment. If the wheels are not in alignment, tyre wear will be heavy and uneven, and the steering will be stiff and unresponsive.

23   Steering wheel – removal and refitting

1   The procedure for removal and refitting of the steering wheel varies slightly according to model type and location of the horn button. In all cases the steering wheel trim must be removed either by carefully prising off or releasing the retaining screws (photos).

2   If the horn button or switch is incorporated in the steering wheel, first disconnect the battery earth terminal and then lift off the snap-rings securing the horn switch assembly to the steering wheel (photos).

3   Bend back the locktab (where fitted) and then, using a socket and extension bar, undo and remove the steering wheel retaining nut.

4   Tap the steering wheel upward with the palm of your hand to release it from the splines and then lift off. Be careful it doesn't come off suddenly and cause injury.

5   Refitting the steering wheel is the reverse sequence to removal. Ensure that the roadwheels are in the straight-ahead position and the steering wheel spokes are horizontal when fitting.

24   Power assisted steering system – checking the fluid level

1   Remove the power assisted steering pump filler cap/dipstick. Wipe the dipstick with a non-fluffy cloth and refit the cap. Remove the cap again and check the level of fluid on the dipstick. **Note:** *The fluid level in the system will vary according to the temperature in the system.*

2   On one side of the dipstick the markings 'Full Cold' will appear. On the other side of the dipstick are the markings 'Full Hot'. Top up if necessary, with the specified power steering fluid to the appropriate mark on the dipstick.

3   Where topping up is necessary, check all hoses and pipes in the system for leaks and rectify as required.

25 Power assisted steering gear – removal and refitting

1   Jack up the front of the car and support it on axle stands placed under the front crossmember.

2   Disconnect the battery earth terminal.

3   Remove the power assisted steering pump filler cap.

4   Working under the car, undo and remove the union nut securing the high pressure hose to the rear of the steering pump. Allow the fluid to drain into a suitable container. To assist the draining of the fluid, slowly move the steering wheel back and forth from lock to lock a few times.

5   When the fluid has drained completely, tape over or plug the high pressure union in the pump and the end of the hose to prevent dirt ingress.

6   Slacken the hose clip and withdraw the low pressure hose from the steering pump.

7   Undo and remove the two bolts securing the flexible coupling to the flange on the steering gear.

8   Undo and remove the nuts securing the track rod end balljoints to the steering arms. Release the taper of the balljoint shanks using a universal balljoint separator. Alternatively, strike the ends of the steering arms with a few sharp blows from a medium hammer to release the taper.

9   Extract the circlips from the protruding end of the two steering gear mounting bolts and then undo and remove the bolts.

10 Undo and remove the nut securing the end of the hydraulic ram to the main crossmember.

11 Move the steering gear rearwards and then lower it to the ground. Take care not to foul any of the components in the engine compartment with the hydraulic hoses as the steering gear is removed.

12 Refitting the power assisted steering gear is the reverse sequence to removal bearing in mind the following points:

(a) Set the roadwheels in the straight-ahead position and the steering wheel with the spokes horizontal before refitting

(b) Observe the correct torque wrench settings when tightening all mounting nuts and bolts

(c) On completion of the installation, bleed the hydraulic system as described in Section 27

26 Power assisted steering gear – overhaul

Due to the complex nature of this unit and the need for specialist knowledge and equipment, the overhaul of the power assisted steering gear is considered beyond the scope of the average home mechanic.

Fig. 11.22 Fluid pipes disconnected from rear of power steering pump (Sec 25)

1   High pressure hose   2   Low pressure hose

Fig. 11.23 The power assisted steering gear (Sec 25)

1 Rack housing	4 High pressure hose	7 Left-hand lock feed	10 Ram-to-rack attachment
2 Control valve	5 Low pressure hose	8 Ram pivot pin	11 Track rod
3 Ram	6 Right-hand lock feed	9 Spacer	

Should a fault develop on the steering gear, it is recommended that the unit be removed from the car as described in Section 25 and then taken to your Peugeot dealer for attention.

27 Power assisted steering system – bleeding

1   Remove the power assisted steering pump filler cap and fill the reservoir with approximately 0.3 litre (0.6 pint) of the specified power steering fluid.
2   Slowly turn the steering wheel to full lock in both directions.
3   Top up the reservoir to the 'Full Cold' mark on the dipstick.
4   Start the engine and turn the steering wheel to full lock in both directions again.
5   Switch off the engine and recheck the fluid level in the reservoir.

28 Power assisted steering pump drivebelt – removal and refitting

1   Slacken the belt tensioning nut and the pump mounting bolts on the front face of the pump.
2   Move the pump inwards toward the engine and lift the belt off the pump pulley.
3   Now remove the belt from the crankshaft pulley and withdraw it from the engine compartment.
4   To refit a new belt ease it over the crankshaft pulley and then the pump pulley.
5   Move the pump away from the engine to tension the belt. The tension is correct when it is just possible to deflect the belt using light finger pressure by approximately 12 mm (0.5 in) at a point midway between the two pulleys.
6   Hold the pump in this position and tighten the tensioning nut and pump mounting bolts.
7   If a new belt has been fitted, it is advisable to recheck the belt tension after a short run to eliminate any extra slack caused by stretching that may occur.

29 Power assisted steering pump – removal and refitting

1   Jack up the front of the car and support it on axle stands placed under the main crossmember.
2   Undo and remove the high pressure union at the rear of the pump and allow the hydraulic fluid to drain into a suitable container.
3   When the fluid has drained, tape over or plug the union in the pump and the end of the hose to prevent dirt ingress.
4   Slacken the drivebelt tensioning nut and the mounting bolts on the front face of the pump. Move the pump inwards toward the engine and lift the drivebelt off the pump pulley.
5   Slacken the hose clip and withdraw the low pressure hose from the pump. Plug the hose to prevent dirt ingress.
6   Now remove the pump mounting bolts and lift the pump off the engine.
7   Refitting the steering pump is the reverse of the removal sequence bearing in mind the following points:
   (a) Adjust the drivebelt tension as described in Section 28
   (b) On completion of the installation bleed the hydraulic system as described in Section 27

30 Power assisted steering pump – overhaul

The power assisted steering pump is a sealed unit and cannot be

Fig. 11.24 Removing the power steering pump (Sec 29)

3   Drivebelt tensioning nut   5   Pump mounting bolt
4   Pump mounting bolt

dismantled. Should a fault occur on the pump, it should be removed from the car as described in the previous Section and a factory exchange unit obtained from your Peugeot dealer.

31 Wheels and tyres – general maintenance

1   The roadwheels are of the pressed steel type, and the tyres are of the radial ply type.
2   Check the tyre pressures weekly, including the spare.
3   The wheel nuts should be tightened to the appropriate torque as shown in the Specifications, and it is an advantage if a smear of grease is applied to the wheel stud threads.
4   Every 6000 miles (10 000 km) the roadwheels should be moved round the vehicle (this does not apply where the wheels have been balanced on the vehicle) in order to even out the tyre tread wear. With radial types it is recommended that the wheels are moved front-to-rear and rear-to-front, not from side-to-side. To do this, remove each wheel in turn, clean it thoroughly (both sides) and remove any flints which may be embedded in the tyre tread. Check the tyre wear pattern which will indicate any mechanical or adjustment faults in the suspension or steering components. Examine the wheel bolt holes for elongation or wear. If such conditions are found, renew the wheel.
5   Renewal of the tyres should be carried out when the thickness of the tread pattern is worn to the legal minimum of 1 mm (0.03 in) or the wear indicators (if incorporated) are visible.
6   Always adjust the front and rear tyre pressures after moving the wheels round as previously described.
7   All wheels are balanced initially, but have them done again halfway through the useful life of the tyres.

32 Fault diagnosis – suspension and steering

Symptom	Reason(s)
Vehicle pulls to side	Tyre pressures uneven Defective tyre Excessive wear in suspension or steering components Wheel alignment incorrect Brakes binding
Excessive pitching and rolling on corners and during braking	Defective, broken or badly worn shock absorbers Broken, disconnected or worn anti-roll bar or connecting link bushes Broken or weak roadspring
Excessively stiff steering	Lack of lubricant in steering gear Lack of power assistance (where applicable) Incorrect tyre pressures Seized or partially seized suspension or steering balljoints Bent or damaged steering rack or steering column Wheel alignment incorrect
Excessive play in steering	Worn or out-of-adjustment steering gear Excessive wear in suspension or steering balljoints and components Worn steering column universal joint or flexible coupling
Lack of steering power assistance (where applicable)	Power assisted steering pump drivebelt broken or slipping Hoses or pipes restricted Fluid level low Worn or faulty steering pump Faulty steering gear hydraulic ram or control valve
Wheel wobble and vibration	Tyres out of balance Roadwheels buckled or damaged Worn suspension or steering balljoints and components Wheel bearings out of adjustment Out-of-balance propeller shaft (see Chapter 7). Excessive run-out of brake disc or drum (see Chapter 9) Worn rear axle or driveshaft components (see Chapter 8)
Excessive tyre wear	Incorrect tyre pressures Worn steering or suspension components Incorrect front wheel alignment Incorrect suspension geometry due to accident damage Tyres out of balance Wheels buckled or damaged

Chapter 12 Bodywork and fittings

Contents

1 General description

The combined body and underframe is of all-steel welded construction. This makes a very strong and torsionally rigid shell. Various body styles are available, but these may be generally divided into Saloon and Estate styles.

Due to the design of the body, a considerable degree of protection to the driver and passengers is offered in the event of an accident. Also, body panel renewal is straightforward provided that normal bodywork repair equipment is available. During production the body-shell is treated using a special electrolytic process to assist in corrosion prevention.

2 Maintenance – bodywork and underframe

1   The general condition of a car's bodywork is the thing that significantly affects it value. Maintenance is easy but needs to be regular. Neglect, particularly after minor damage, can lead quickly to further deterioration and costly repair bills. It is important also to keep watch on those parts of the car not immediately visible, for instance the underside, inside all the wheel arches and the lower part of the engine compartment.

2   The basic maintenance routine for the bodywork is washing – preferably with a lot of water, from a hose. This will remove all the loose solids which may have stuck to the car. It is important to flush these off in such a way as to prevent grit from scratching the finish. The wheel arches and underframe need washing in the same way to remove any accumulated mud which will retain moisture and tend to encourage rust. Paradoxically enough, the best time to clean the underframe and wheel arches is in wet weather when the mud is thoroughly wet and soft. In very wet weather the underframe is usually cleaned of large accumulations automatically and this is a good time for inspection.

3   Periodically, it is a good idea to have the whole of the underframe of the car steam cleaned, engine compartment included, so that a thorough inspection can be carried out to see what minor repairs and renovations are necessary. Steam cleaning is available at many garages and is necessary for removal of the accumulation of oily grime which sometimes is allowed to become thick in certain areas. If steam cleaning facilities are not available, there are one or two excellent grease solvents available which can be brush applied. The dirt can then be simply hosed off.

4   After washing paintwork, wipe off with a chamois leather to give an unspotted clear finish. A coat of clear protective wax polish will give added protection against chemical pollutants in the air. If the paintwork sheen has dulled or oxidised, use a cleaner/polisher com-

bination to restore the brilliance of the shine. This requires a little effort, but such dulling is usually caused because regular washing has been neglected. Always check that the door and ventilator opening drain holes and pipes are completely clear so that water can be drained out. Bright work should be treated in the same way as paintwork. Windscreens and windows can be kept clear of the smeary film which often appears, by adding a little ammonia to the water. If they are scratched, a good rub with a proprietary metal polish will often clear them. Never use any form of wax or other body or chromium polish on glass.

3 Maintenance – upholstery and carpets

1   Mats and carpets should be brushed or vacuum cleaned regularly to keep them free of grit. If they are badly stained remove them from the car for scrubbing or sponging and make quite sure they are dry before refitting. Seats and interior trim panels can be kept clean by a wipe over with a damp cloth. If they do become stained (which can be more apparent on light coloured upholstery) use a little liquid detergent and a soft nail brush to scour the grime out of the grain of the material. Do not forget to keep the head lining clean in the same way as the upholstery. When using liquid cleaners inside the car do not over-wet the surfaces being cleaned. Excessive damp could get into the seams and padded interior causing stains, offensive odours or even rot. If the inside of the car gets wet accidentally it is worthwhile taking some trouble to dry it out properly, particularly where carpets are involved. *Do not leave oil or electric heaters inside the car for this purpose.*

4 Maintenance – PVC external roof covering

Under no circumstances try to clean any external PVC roof covering with detergents, caustic soaps or spirit cleaners. Plain soap and water is all that is required, with a soft brush to clean dirt that may be ingrained. Wash the covering as frequently as the rest of the car.

5 Minor body damage – repair

The photographic sequences on pages 194 and 195 illustrate the operations detailed in the following sub-sections.

Repair of minor scratches in the car's bodywork

If the scratch is very superficial, and does not penetrate to the metal of the bodywork, repair is very simple. Lightly rub the area of the scratch with a paintwork renovator, or a very fine cutting paste, to remove loose paint from the scratch and to clear the surrounding bodywork of wax polish. Rinse the area with clean water.

Apply touch-up paint to the scratch using a thin paint brush; continue to apply thin layers of paint until the surface of the paint in the scratch is level with the surrounding paintwork. Allow the new paint at least two weeks to harden: then blend it into the surrounding paintwork by rubbing the paintwork, in the scratch area, with a paintwork renovator or a very fine cutting paste. Finally, apply wax polish.

Where the scratch has penetrated right through to the metal of the bodywork, causing the metal to rust, a different repair technique is required. Remove any loose rust from the bottom of the scratch with a penknife, then apply rust inhibiting paint to prevent the formation of rust in the future. Using a rubber or nylon applicator fill the scratch with bodystopper paste. If required, this paste can be mixed with cellulose thinners to provide a very thin paste which is ideal for filling narrow scratches. Before the stopper-paste in the scratch hardens, wrap a piece of smooth cotton rag around the top of a finger. Dip the finger in cellulose thinners and then quickly sweep it across the surface of the stopper-paste in the scratch; this will ensure that the surface of the stopper-paste is slightly hollowed. The scratch can now be painted over as described earlier in this Section.

Repair of dents in the car's bodywork

When deep denting of the vehicle's bodywork has taken place, the first task is to pull the dent out, until the affected bodywork almost attains its original shape. There is little point in trying to restore the original shape completely, as the metal in the damaged area will have stretched on impact and cannot be reshaped fully to its original contour. It is better to bring the level of the dent up to a point which is about $\frac{1}{8}$ in (3 mm) below the level of the surrounding bodywork. In cases where the dent is very shallow anyway, it is not worth trying to pull it out at all. If the underside of the dent is accessible, it can be hammered out gently from behind, using a mallet with a wooden or plastic head. Whilst doing this, hold a suitable block of wood firmly against the outside of the panel to absorb the impact from the hammer blows and thus prevent a large area of the bodywork from being 'belled-out'.

Should the dent be in a section of the bodywork which has double skin or some other factor making it inaccessible from behind, a different technique is called for. Drill several small holes through the metal inside the area – particularly in the deeper section. Then screw long self-tapping screws into the holes just sufficiently for them to gain a good purchase in the metal. Now the dent can be pulled out by pulling on the protruding heads of the screws with a pair of pliers.

The next stage of the repair is the removal of the paint from the damaged area, and from an inch or so of the surrounding 'sound' bodywork. This is accomplished most easily by using a wire brush or abrasive pad on a power drill, although it can be done just as effectively by hand using sheets of abrasive paper. To complete the preparation for filling, score the surface of the bare metal with a screwdriver or the tang of a file, or alternatively, drill small holes in the affected area. This will provide a really good 'key' for the filler paste.

To complete the repair see the Section on filling and re-spraying.

Repair of rust holes or gashes in the car's bodywork

Remove all paint from the affected area and from an inch or so of the surrounding 'sound' bodywork, using an abrasive pad or a wire brush on a power drill. If these are not available a few sheets of abrasive paper will do the job just as effectively. With the paint removed you will be able to gauge the severity of the corrosion and therefore decide whether to renew the whole panel (if this is possible) or to repair the affected area. New body panels are not as expensive as most people think and it is often quicker and more satisfactory to fit a new panel than to attempt to repair large areas of corrosion.

Remove all fittings from the affected area except those which will act as a guide to the original shape of the damaged bodywork (eg headlamp shells etc). Then, using tin snips or a hacksaw blade, remove all loose metal and any other metal badly affected by corrosion. Hammer the edges of the hole inwards in order to create a slight depression for the filler paste.

Wire brush the affected area to remove the powdery rust from the surface of the remaining metal. Paint the affected area with rust inhibiting paint; if the back of the rusted area is accessible treat this also.

Before filling can take place it will be necessary to block the hole in some way. This can be achieved by the use of zinc gauze or aluminium tape.

Zinc gauze is probably the best material to use for a large hole. Cut a piece to the approximate size and shape of the hole to be filled, then position it in the hole so that its edges are below the level of the surrounding bodywork. It can be retained in position by several blobs of filler paste around its periphery.

Aluminium tape should be used for small or very narrow holes. Pull a piece off the roll and trim it to the approximate size and shape required, then pull off the backing paper (if used) and stick the tape over the hole; it can be overlapped if the thickness of one piece is insufficient. Burnish down the edges of the tape with the handle of a screwdriver or similar, to ensure that the tape is securely attached to the metal underneath.

Bodywork repairs – filling and re-spraying

Before using this Section, see the Sections on dent, deep scratch, rust holes and gash repairs.

Many types of bodyfiller are available, but generally speaking those proprietary kits which contain a tin of filler paste and a tube of resin hardener are best for this type of repair. A wide, flexible plastic or nylon applicator will be found invaluable for imparting a smooth and well contoured finish to the surface of the filler.

Mix up a little filler on a clean piece of card or board – measure the hardener carefully (follow the maker's instructions on the pack) otherwise the filler will set too rapidly or too slowly.

Using the applicator apply the filler paste to the prepared area; draw the applicator across the surface of the filler to achieve the correct contour and to level the filler surface. As soon as a contour that approximates the correct one is achieved, stop working the paste – if you carry on too long the paste will become sticky and begin to 'pick up' on the applicator. Continue to add thin layers of filler paste at twenty-minute intervals until the level of the filler is just proud of the surrounding bodywork.

Once the filler has hardened, excess can be removed using a metal plane or file. From then on, progressively finer grades of sandpaper should be used, starting with a 40 grade production paper and finishing with 400 grade wet-and-dry paper. Always wrap the abrasive paper around a flat rubber, cork, or wooden block – otherwise the surface of the filler will not be completely flat. During the smoothing of the filler surface the wet-and-dry paper should be periodically rinsed in water. This will ensure that a very smooth finish is imparted to the filler at the final stage.

At this stage the dent should be surrounded by a ring of bare metal, which in turn should be encircled by the finely 'feathered' edge of the good paintwork. Rinse the repair area with clean water, until all of the dust produced by the rubbing-down operation has gone.

Spray the whole repair area with a light coat of primer – this will show up any imperfections in the surface of the filler. Repair these imperfections with fresh filler paste or bodystopper, and once more smooth the surface with abrasive paper. If bodystopper is used, it can be mixed with cellulose thinners to form a really thin paste which is ideal for filling small holes. Repeat this spray and repair procedure until you are satisfied that the surface of the filler, and the feathered edge of the paintwork are perfect. Clean the repair area with clean water and allow to dry fully.

The repair area is now ready for final spraying. Paint spraying must be carried out in warm, dry, windless and dust free atmosphere. This condition can be created artificially if you have access to a large indoor working area, but if you are forced to work in the open, you will have to pick your day very carefully. If you are working indoors, dousing the floor in the work area with water will help to settle the dust which would otherwise be in the atmosphere. If the repair area is confined to one body panel, mask off the surrounding panels; this will help to minimise the effects of a slight mis-match in paint colours. Bodywork fittings (eg chrome strips, door handles etc) will also need to be masked off. Use genuine masking tape and several thicknesses of newspaper for the masking operations.

Before commencing to spray, agitate the aerosol can thoroughly, then spray a test area (an old tin, or similar) until the technique is mastered. Cover the repair area with a thick coat of primer; the thickness should be built up using several thin layers of paint rather than one thick one. Using 400 grade wet-and-dry paper, rub down the surface of the primer until it is really smooth. While doing this, the work area should be thoroughly doused with water, and the wet-and-

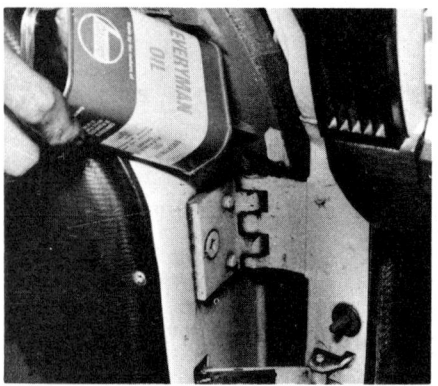
7.1 Door hinge lubrication

10.2 Removing the window winder handle

10.3 Removing the interior door handle surround

10.4a The armrest is secured by screws at the front ...

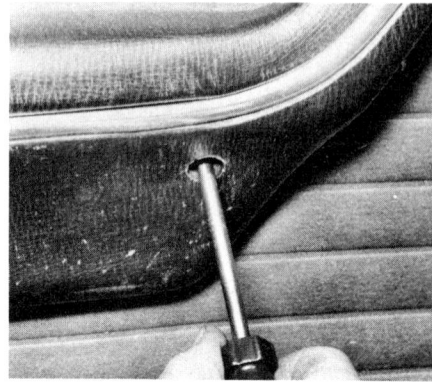
10.4b ... centre ...

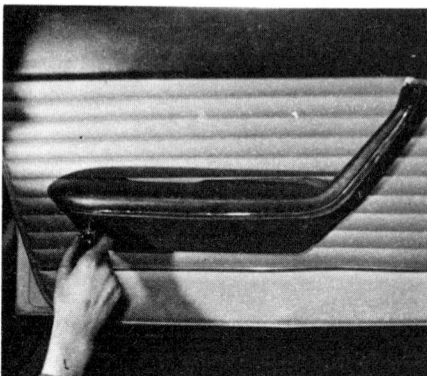
10.4c ... and rear

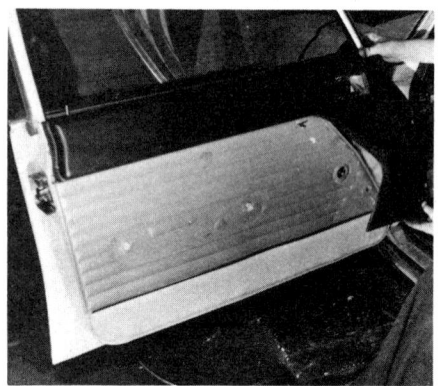
10.7 Lifting off the upper panel ...

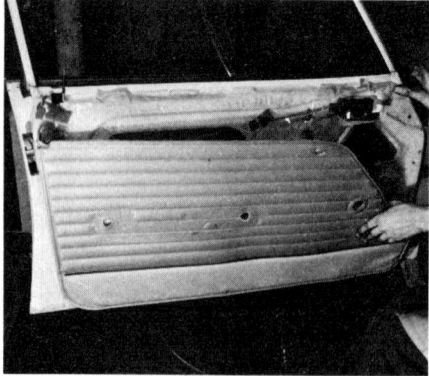
10.8 ... followed by the lower trim panel

11.2 Location of the four window winder regulator securing nuts

11.3 Window winder rollers and slide

11.4 Withdrawing the mechanism through the door aperture

dry paper periodically rinsed in water. Allow to dry before spraying on more paint.

Spray on the top coat, again building up the thickness by using several thin layers of paint. Start spraying in the centre of the repair area and then, using a circular motion, work outwards until the whole repair area and about 2 inches of the surrounding original paintwork is covered. Remove all masking material 10 to 15 minutes after spraying on the final coat of paint.

Allow the new paint at least two weeks to harden, then, using a paintwork renovator or a very fine cutting paste, blend the edges of the paint into the existing paintwork. Finally, apply wax polish.

6 Major body damage – repair

Because the body is built on the monocoque principle, major damage must be repaired by a competent body repairer with the necessary jigs and equipment.

In the event of a crash that results in buckling of body panels or damage to the roadwheels, the car must be taken to a Peugeot dealer or body repairer where the bodyshell and suspension alignment may be checked.

Bodyshell and/or suspension misalignment will cause excessive wear of the tyres, steering system and possibly transmission. The handling of the car will also be affected adversely.

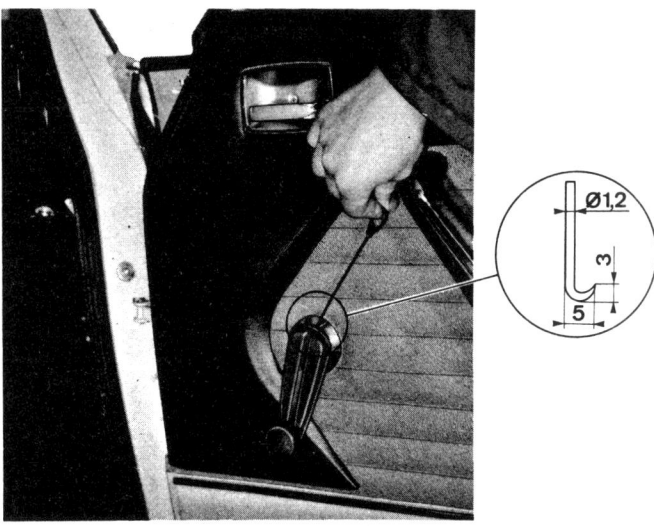

Fig. 12.1 Use of hook to remove handle retaining spring clip – dimensions in mm (Sec 10)

7 Hinges, door catches and locks – maintenance

1 Oil the hinges of the bonnet, boot lid/tailgate and doors with a drop or two of light oil periodically (photo). A good time is after the car has been washed.
2 Oil the bonnet release catch pivot pin and the safety catch pivot pin periodically.
3 Do not over-lubricate door latches and strikers. Normally a little oil on the end of the rotary pinion spindle and a thin smear of high melting point grease on the striker pinion teeth and shoe spring plunger are adequate. Make sure that before lubrication they are wiped thoroughly clean and correctly adjusted. The excessive use of ordinary grease will result, more likely, in badly stained clothing!

8 Doors – tracing rattles and rectification

1 Check first that the door is not loose at the hinges and that the latch is holding it firmly in position. Check also that the door lines up with the aperture in the body.
2 If the hinges are loose or the door is out of alignment, it will be necessary to detach it from the hinges.
3 If the latch is holding the door correctly it should be possible to press the door inwards fractionally against the rubber weatherstrip. If not, adjust the striker plate.
4 Other rattles from the door could be caused by wear or looseness in the window winder, the glass channels and sill strips, or the door handles and remote control arm; all of which are described in following Sections.

9 Front and rear doors – removal and refitting

1 Using a pencil, accurately mark the outline of the hinge relative to the door.
2 Undo and remove the two bolts securing the door arrester to the door and the bolts securing the hinge to the door. **Note**: *On some models it will be necessary to remove the door inner trim panel as described in Sections 10 and 15 to gain access to the arrester and hinge securing bolts.*
3 Carefully lift off the door and store it safely, ensuring that it is well protected with cloths or an old blanket to prevent accidental damage.
4 Refitting the door is the reverse sequence to removal. After fitting the door, carry out any necessary adjustments at the hinges or striker plates to ensure correct closure.

10 Front door trim panel – removal and refitting

1 Using a hook made from welding wire located between the window regulator handle and its thrust cap, withdraw the spring clip.
2 Note the position of the window regulator handle with the glass in the raised position and remove the handle and thrust cup (photo).
3 Remove the inner door opening control lever surround (photo).
4 Remove the armrest (photos).
5 Undo and remove the interior door locking button.
6 Disengage the clips securing the upper padded panel using a wide-bladed screwdriver.
7 Raise the upper panel and lift away (photo).
8 Again using a wide-bladed screwdriver, disengage the clips and lift away the lower trim panel (photo).
9 Refitting the lower and upper trim panels is the reverse sequence to removal.

11 Front door window winder regulator – removal and refitting

1 Refer to Section 10 and remove the front door trim panel.
2 With the window in the raised position, undo and remove the four nuts and washers securing the mechanism to the door inner panel (photo).
3 Hold the glass in the raised position, push the mechanism in and disengage the rollers from the side. To do this, work towards the rear of the mechanism (photo).
4 The mechanism may now be withdrawn through the upper aperture (photo).
5 Refitting the window regulator is the reverse sequence to removal, but it will be necessary to adjust its final fitted position, as described in the following paragraphs.
6 Check the free movement of the glass, paying particular attention to excessive play or hard spots.
7 Lower the glass and slacken the lower slide securing nut on the inner door panel. This is the bottom nut nearest to the door hinge.
8 Move the slide into contact with the bottom of the glass and tighten the nut.

12 Front door lock – removal and refitting

1 Refer to Section 10 and remove the interior trim panel.
2 Disconnect the control link at the lock end.
3 Undo and remove the three door lock securing screws.
4 Lift away the guide plate.

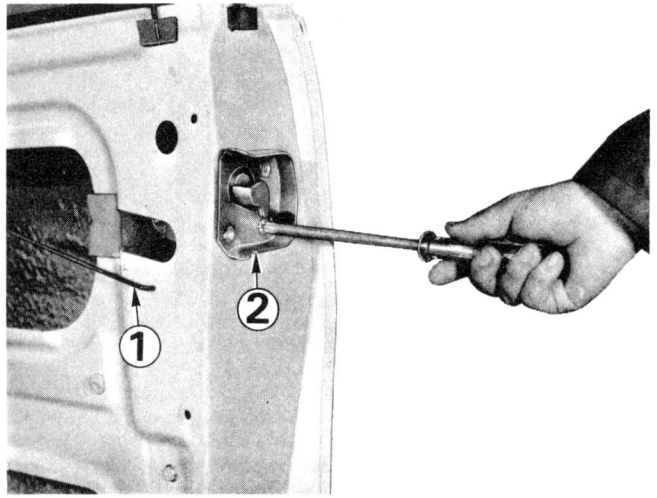

Fig. 12.2 Removal of door lock securing screws (Sec 12)

1   Control link   2   Guide plate

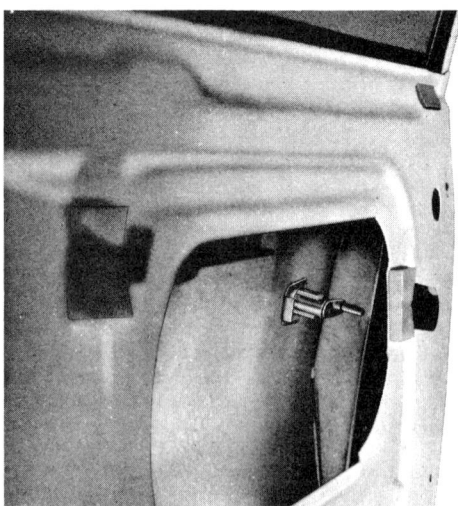

Fig. 12.3 Door outer lock (Sec 12)

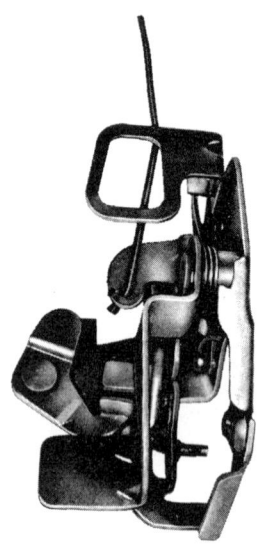

Fig. 12.4 Door lock assembly (Sec 12)

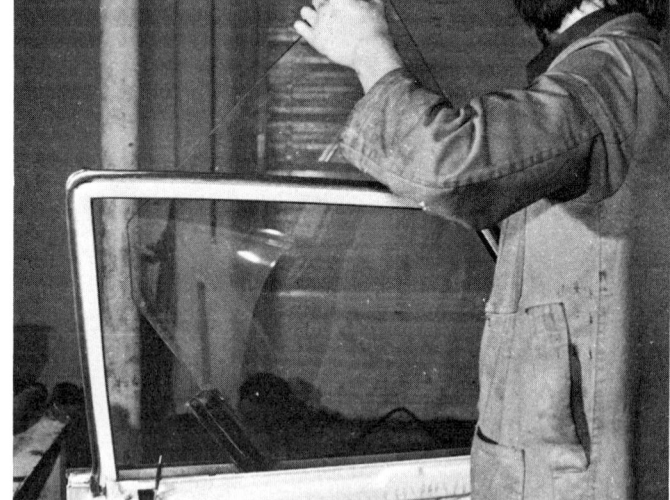

13.3 Lifting out the door window glass

5   Insert the key into the lock and slide the lock downwards until the locking crank disengages from the catch.
6   Pivot the lock around the slide support and withdraw the lock.
7   To remove the outer lock, carefully withdraw the lock stop fork and disengage in an outward manner.
8   Refitting the door lock is the reverse sequence to removal. Check the operation of the lock mechanism and the condition of all the return springs. Apply a little grease to all the pivots.

13 Front door window – removal and refitting

1   Refer to Section 11, and remove the window winder regulator.
2   With the window in the raised position, lift it towards the front so as to disengage it from its slides.
3   With the glass in this position draw it upwards and out through the outer side of the door aperture (photo).
4   Should the glass need to be renewed due to damage or other reasons, clean the glass support mounting.
5   Obtain a new rubber section and smear with a little washing-up liquid.
6   Fit the support mounting to the glass so that the extremity of the mounting is 9.5 in (242 mm) from the rear of the glass.

7   Refitting the glass and support mounting is the reverse sequence to removal.

14 Front door outer window seal – removal and refitting

1   Refer to Section 10, and remove the door trim panel.
2   Check the condition of the outer window seal, as it must not have any cracks or permanent distortion.
3   To remove the trim, insert a screwdriver between the plastic clips and the inner edges of the trim.
4   Ease the trim upwards starting at the front end.
5   Refitting the outer window seal is the reverse sequence to removal. Always fit the plastic clips to the door panel first and then push the trim into position.

15 Rear door trim panel – removal and refitting

The procedure for removal and refitting of the rear door trim panel is similar to that for the front panel. Refer to Section 10 for full information.

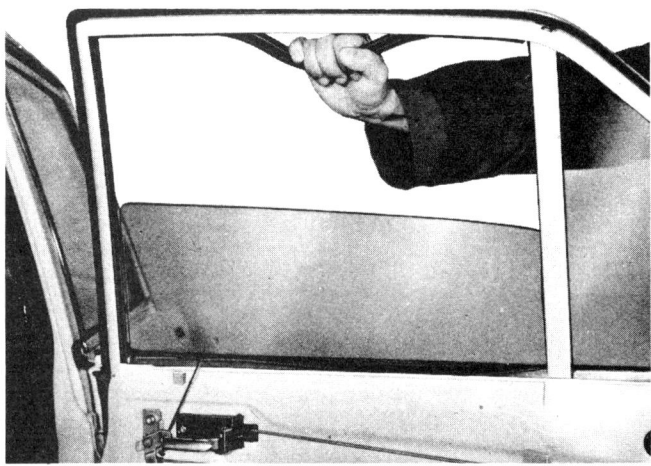

Fig. 12.5 Removal of rear upper glass slide (Sec 18)

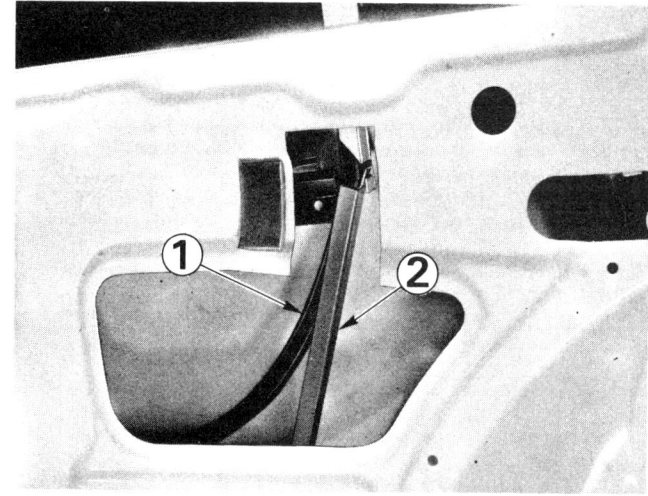

Fig. 12.6 Slide disengaged from rear support (Sec 18)

1   Slide   2   Rear support

16 Rear door window winder regulator – removal and refitting

1   Refer to Sections 15 and 10 and remove the rear door trim panel.
2   Raise the glass and hold in this position.
3   Undo and remove the four nuts and washers securing the mechanism to the door inner panel.
4   Push the mechanism inwards, then backwards until the shaft appears in the elongated hole in the interior door panel.
5   Using the handle, turn the mechanism to the maximum raised position. Remove the handle.
6   Push the mechanism inwards again and move it forwards so as to disengage the rollers from the side.
7   Withdraw the mechanism through the upper rear opening in the interior door panel.
8   Refitting the window regulator is the reverse sequence to removal. Apply a little grease to all moving parts, and before actually inserting into the door, position the quadrant to obtain a distance of 0.25 in (6 mm) between the two arms.

17 Rear door lock – removal and refitting

The procedure for removal and refitting of the rear door lock is similar to that for the front door lock. Refer to Section 12 for full information.

18 Rear door wind-up window – removal and refitting

1   Refer to Sections 15 and 10, and remove the rear door trim panel.
2   Undo and remove the three screws that secure the rear slide support.
3   Remove the upper glass slide by carefully unclipping it from the middle and working outwards.
4   Raise the glass fully and disengage the slide from the lower part of the rear support.
5   Remove the lower part of the rear slide support by pivoting it forwards, pushing the top forwards and finally disengaging the support downwards.
6   Refer to Section 16, and remove the regulator assembly.
7   Lower the glass as much as possible and then push the upper slide support forwards.
8   Remove the slide support by lifting up from the door.
9   The glass may now be removed by holding in its normal position and then lifting outwards through the door aperture.
10 Should the glass need to be renewed due to damage or other reasons, clean the glass support mounting, carefully.
11 Obtain a new rubber section and smear with a little washing-up liquid.

Fig. 12.7 Pushing upper slide support forward (Sec 18)

Fig. 12.8 Rear door fixed window removal (Sec 19)

12 Fit the support mounting to the glass so that the extremity of the mounting is 0.75 in (18 mm) from the rear of the glass.
13 Refitting the glass and support mounting is the reverse sequence to removal.

19 Rear door fixed window – removal and refitting

1   Refer to Section 18, and remove the door glass.
2   Push the fixed window towards the front of the door and withdraw the glass together with its seal.
3   Refitting the fixed window is the reverse sequence to removal.

20 Rear door outer window seal – removal and refitting

The procedure for removal and refitting of the rear door outer window seal is similar to that for the front door. Refer to Section 14 for full information.

21 Windscreen and rear screen/tailgate glass – removal and refitting

This operation is best left to specialists, as it is a job which, although easy for a specialist who is used to handling glass, can present problems for a do-it-yourself owner attempting this type of work for the first time.

22 Bonnet, boot lid and tailgate – removal and refitting

1   Accurately mark the outline of the hinges to the bonnet, boot lid or tailgate using a pencil.
2   If working on the tailgate, disconnect the electrical leads to the heated rear window and wiper/washer motor.
3   Support the tailgate with a length of wood, and disconnect the tailgate balance spring assembly or hydraulic piston from each side of the tailgate.
4   Now undo and remove the bolts securing the bonnet, boot lid or tailgate to their hinges and carefully lift off the car.
5   Refitting is the reverse sequence to removal, ensuring the hinges line up with the previously made pencil marks before fully tightening the securing bolts.

23 Bumpers – removal and refitting

1   Undo and remove the nuts and spring washers securing the bumper overriders and lift them off the bumpers.
2   Working behind the bumper or from inside the wheel arch, undo and remove the domed bolts and securing nuts that retain the bumper to the body.
3   With all the retaining bolts removed, carefully lift off the bumper.
4   Refitting the bumper is the reverse sequence to removal. Tighten all the mountings finger tight only until all the retaining bolts are in position. Make sure the bumper is central and level and then fully tighten the mountings.

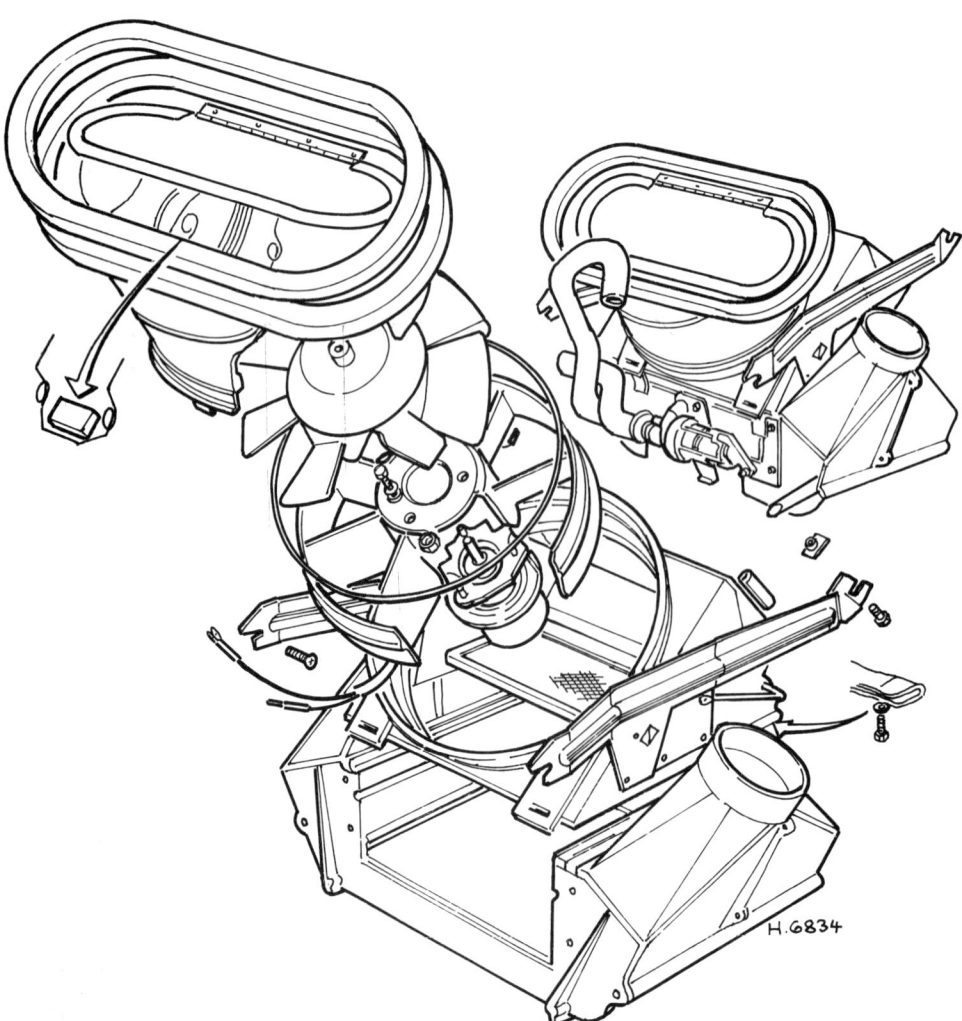

Fig. 12.9 Major components of the Sofica heater (Sec 24)

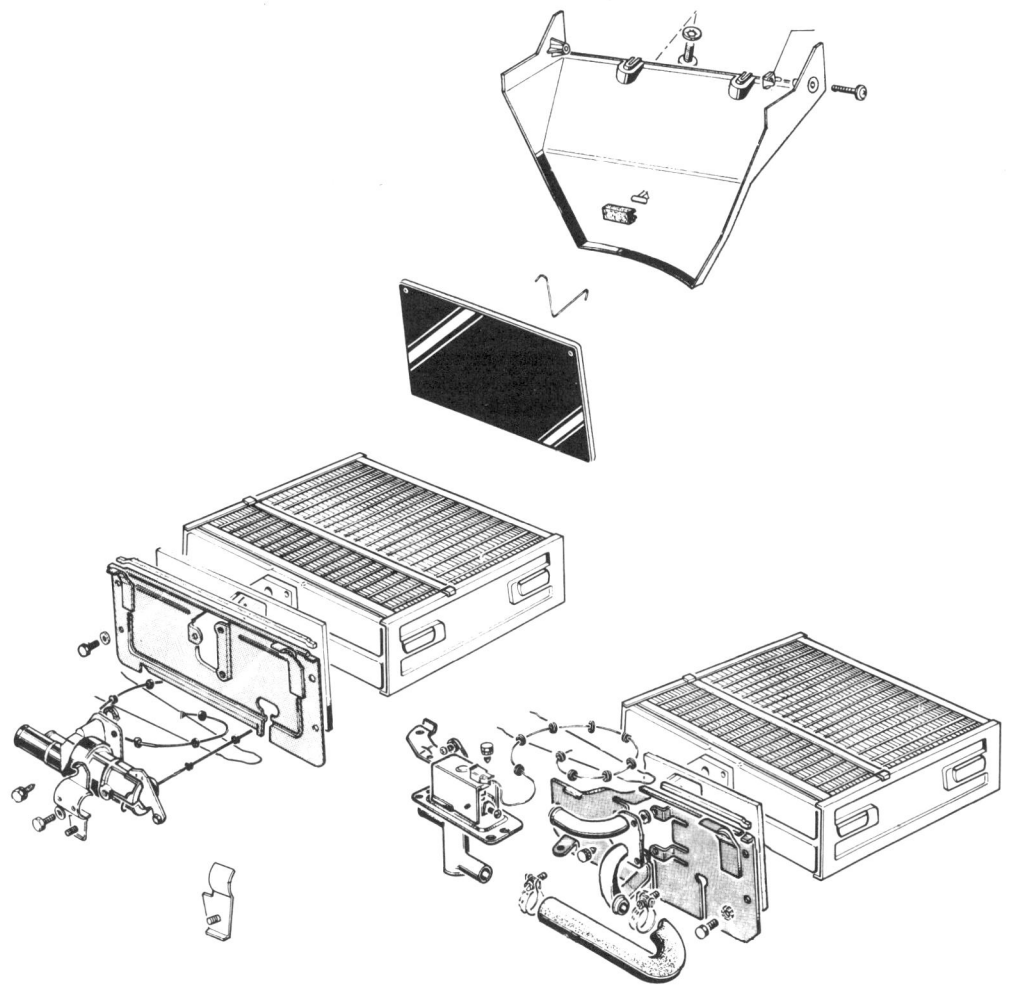

Fig. 12.10 Exploded view of heater radiator components showing alternative layouts of thermostatic control system (Sec 24)

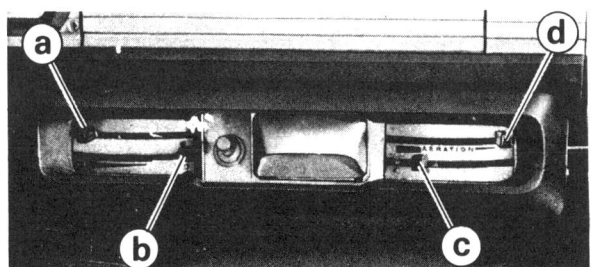

Fig. 12.11 Heater controls – Saloon models (see text for control
lever function) (Sec 24)

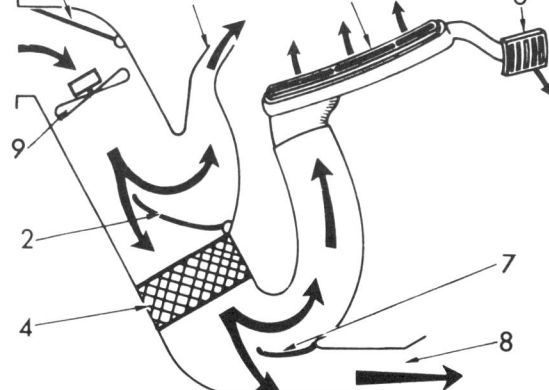

Fig. 12.12 Schematic diagram of heater system (Sec 24)

1   Air intake shutter
2   Shutter controlling airflow to 3 and 4
3   Outlet to dashboard swivelling ventilators
4   Heater radiator
5   Defrosting ducts
6   Heating duct at side of dashboard
7   Shutter controlling air output from underside of heater
8   Air outlet
9   Blower motor

24 Heating system – general description

The heater unit comprises the usual combination of blower and
radiator matrix. Two different makes of heater, the Sofica and the
Gelbon, are fitted, but these differ only in detail. Fig. 12.9 shows an
exploded view of the Sofica heater, whilst Fig. 12.10 shows details of
the radiator matrix and the thermostatic control tap associated with it.

All models covered by this manual employ the same basic heater
unit, though the ducting system varies from model to model. Fig.
12.12 gives a schematic diagram of the operation of the heater.
Referring to the numbers in the illustration, the shutter (1) controls the
admission of air to the heater, the air being circulated by the fan (9).

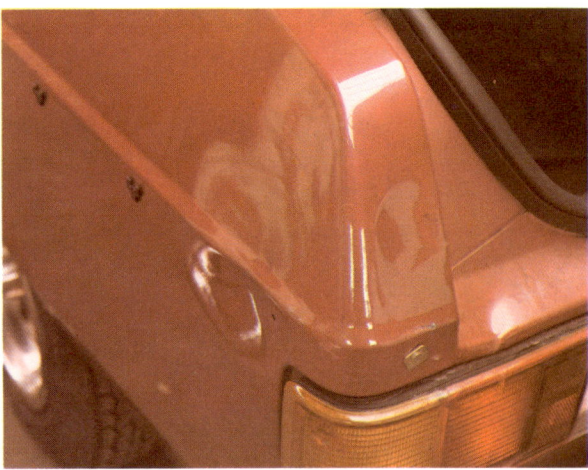

This sequence of photographs deals with the repair of the dent and scratch (above rear lamp) shown in this photo. The procedure will be similar for the repair of a hole. It should be noted that the procedures given here are simplified - more explicit instructions will be found in the text

In the case of a dent the first job - after removing surrounding trim - is to hammer out the dent where access is possible. This will minimise filling. Here, the large dent having been hammered out, the damaged area is being made slightly concave

Now all paint must be removed from the damaged area, by rubbing with coarse abrasive paper. Alternatively, a wire brush or abrasive pad can be used in a power drill. Where the repair area meets good paintwork, the edge pf the paintwork should be 'feathered', using a finer grade of abrasive paper

In the case of a hole caused by rusting, all damaged sheet-metal should be cut away before proceeding to this stage. Here, the damaged area is being treated with rust remover and inhibitor before being filled

Mix the body filler according to its manufacturer's instructions. In the case of corrosion damage, it will be necessary to block off any large holes before filling - this can be done with zinc gauze or aluminium tape. Make sure the area is absolutely clean before ...

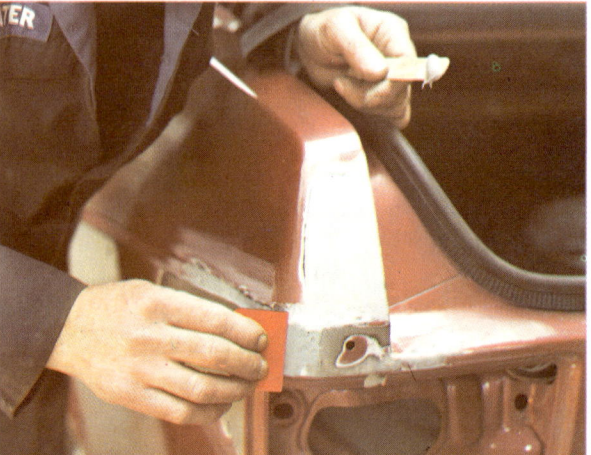

... applying the filler. Filler should be applied with a flexible applicator, as shown, for best results: the wooden spatula being used for confined areas. Apply thin layers of filler at 20-minute intervals, until the surface of the filler is slightly proud of the surrounding bodywork

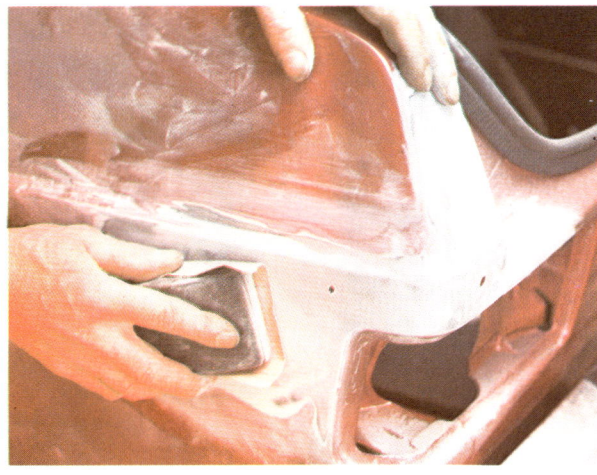

Initial shaping can be done with a Surform plane or Dreadnought file. Then, using progressively finer grades of wet-and-dry paper, wrapped around a sanding block, and copious amounts of clean water, rub-down the filler until really smooth and flat. Again, feather the edges of adjoining paintwork

The whole repair area can now be sprayed or brush-painted with primer. If spraying, ensure adjoining areas are protected from over-spray. Note that at least one-inch of the surrounding sound paintwork should be coated with primer. Primer has a 'thick' consistency, so will fill small imperfections

Again, using plenty of water, rub down the primer with a fine grade of wet-and-dry paper (400 grade is probably best) until it is really smooth and well blended into the surrounding paintwork. Any remaining imperfections can now be filled by carefully applied knifing stopper paste

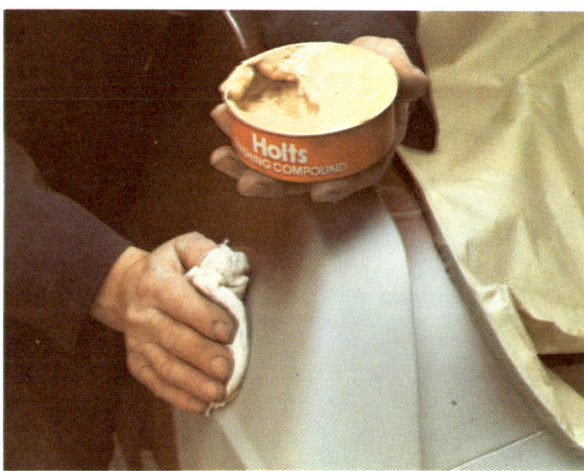

When the stopper has hardened, rub-down the repair area again before applying the final coat of primer. Before rubbing-down this last coat of primer, ensure the repair area is blemish-free - use more stopper if necessary. To ensure that the surface of the primer is really smooth use some finishing compound

The top coat can now be applied. When working out of doors, pick a dry, warm and wind-free day. Ensure surrounding areas are protected from over-spray. Agitate the aerosol thoroughly, then spray the centre of the repair area, working outwards with a circular motion. Apply the paint as several thin coats.

After a period of about two-weeks, which the paint needs to harden fully, the surface of the repaired area can be 'cut' with a mild cutting compound prior to wax polishing. When carrying out bodywork repairs, remember that the quality of the finished job is proportional to the time and effort expended

On all models except the Estate the fan speed is regulated by a thermostat. The Estate fan is operated by a simple on-off switch. The air outlet (3), which can be shut off by the flap (2), directs unheated fresh air to outlets at the sides of the dashboard. Air passing through the heater radiator matrix is warmed to a temperature depending on the water flow through the matrix (this is controlled by the thermostatic tap) and can be directed to either or both of two outlets depending on the position of the flap (7). One of these outlets goes to the defrosting louvres (5) and further small louvres at the sides of the dashboard (6), while the other one (8) is underneath the heater itself. The heater control system for Saloon models is shown in Fig. 12.11. Referring to the letters in this illustration; (a) controls the thermostatic tap on the heater radiator; (b) controls the air in-take shutter and, as it is moved further over to the left, increases the fan speed as it operates the rheostat; (c) controls flap (7) (see Fig. 12.12) shutting off outlet (8) when it is over to the left, and the defrosting system when it is over to the right. In addition to the outlets shown in Fig. 12.12 fresh air is directed to vents on either side of the dashboard positioned just below the dashboard louvres, the flow of air to these points being controlled by (a).

25 Heater – overhaul

1   Removal and dismantling of the heater is a relatively simple process. Extreme care must be taken not to damage the long thin pipe which is attached to the thermostatic regulator. This is filled with a special volatile fluid, and once the system has sprung a leak it is useless.
2   If there are signs of coolant leakage at any heater hose junction, the hose should be renewed.
3   Take the opportunity of giving the heater radiator matrix a good rinse out. When this has been done check it for leakage by filling it up with water and watching for drips or seepage.
4   On some models it is possible to renew the brushes in the blower motor. Excessive brush wear will lead to armature damage due to poor contact and excessive sparking, and brushes are much cheaper than armatures.

5   Check the bearings for excessive side play (a small amount of endplay is unimportant). Excessive bearing wear is best dealt with by renewing the motor, which will probably be in poor condition anyway if this has occurred.

26 Air conditioning system – general

1   The air conditioner optionally fitted to certain models is of a conventional type incorporating a belt-driven compressor, condenser, evaporator and allied components.
2   The refrigerant used is quite safe under normal operating conditions, but once it escapes into the atmosphere it evaporates so quickly that it will freeze the skin on contact, and displace air so quickly that suffocation can occur. In addition, when released near a naked flame or hot metal components it will produce a poisonous gas.
3   In view of the foregoing, never disconnect any part of the air conditioning system unless the system has first been discharged (evacuated) by your dealer or a qualified refrigeration engineer. It is permissible to disconnect the mountings of the compressor pump and the condenser, and to move the units within the limits of movement of their flexible hoses, as an aid to engine or radiator removal.
4   During winter months switch on the air conditioner once a week for five minutes to keep the system in good working condition.
5   Maintenance should be limited to keeping the compressor drive-belt correctly tensioned – 12.7 mm (0.5 in) deflection at the centre point between the pulleys – and occasionally checking the condition of the system hoses, pipes and connections. Keep the fins of the condenser free from flies and dirt by brushing or hosing with cold water.
6   It is advisable to check the refrigerant quantity before the summer begins. To do this, start the engine and let it run at a fast idle. Turn on the air conditioner, and after it has been running for about five minutes, observe the sight glass which should show no signs of bubbles. If bubbles are visible, have the system recharged by your dealer after he has traced the source of the leakage.

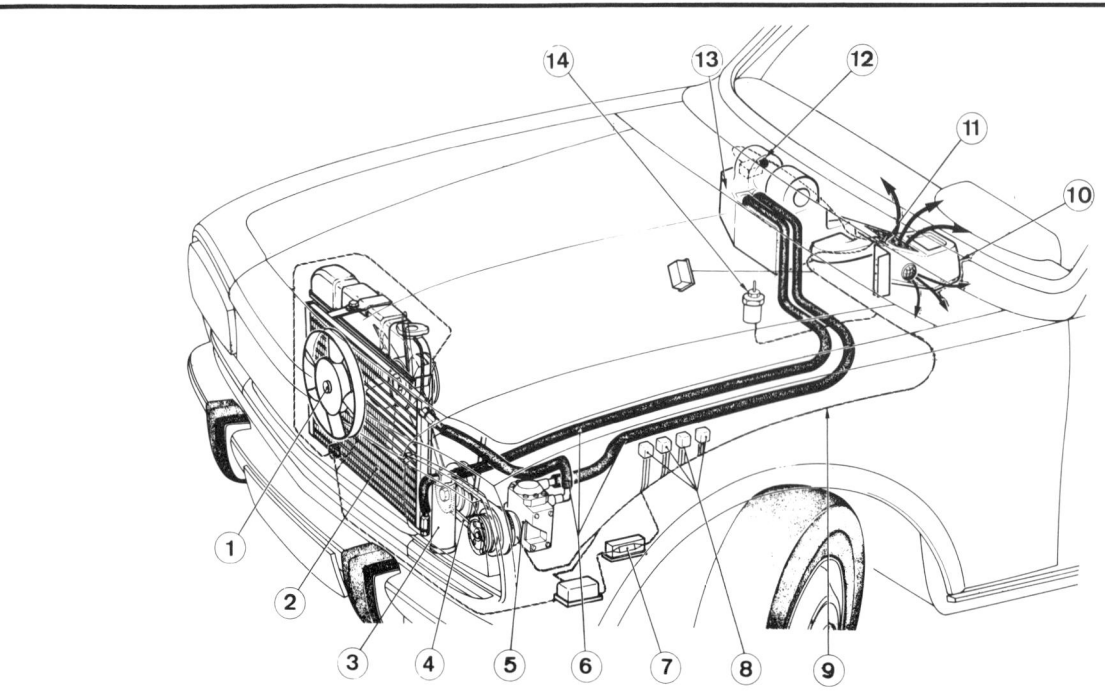

Fig. 12.13 General layout of air conditioning system (Sec 26)

1	Cooling fan	4	Drivebelt	8	Relay
2	Condenser	5	Compressor	9	Wiring harness
3	Receiver-dryer and sight	6	Hoses	10	Central console
	glass	7	Fuse	11	Fan control rheostat

12	Temperature control
13	Cold air delivery unit
14	Idle running compensator

Conversion factors

Length (distance)

Inches (in)	X	25.4	= Millimetres (mm)	X 0.039	= Inches (in)
Feet (ft)	X	0.305	= Metres (m)	X 3.281	= Feet (ft)
Miles	X	1.609	= Kilometres (km)	X 0.621	= Miles

Volume (capacity)

Cubic inches (cu in; in³)	X	16.387	= Cubic centimetres (cc; cm³)	X 0.061	= Cubic inches (cu in; in³)
Imperial pints (Imp pt)	X	0.568	= Litres (l)	X 1.76	= Imperial pints (Imp pt)
Imperial quarts (Imp qt)	X	1.137	= Litres (l)	X 0.88	= Imperial quarts (Imp qt)
Imperial quarts (Imp qt)	X	1.201	= US quarts (US qt)	X 0.833	= Imperial quarts (Imp qt)
US quarts (US qt)	X	0.946	= Litres (l)	X 1.057	= US quarts (US qt)
Imperial gallons (Imp gal)	X	4.546	= Litres (l)	X 0.22	= Imperial gallons (Imp gal)
Imperial gallons (Imp gal)	X	1.201	= US gallons (US gal)	X 0.833	= Imperial gallons (Imp gal)
US gallons (US gal)	X	3.785	= Litres (l)	X 0.264	= US gallons (US gal)

Mass (weight)

Ounces (oz)	X	28.35	= Grams (g)	X 0.035	= Ounces (oz)
Pounds (lb)	X	0.454	= Kilograms (kg)	X 2.205	= Pounds (lb)

Force

Ounces-force (ozf; oz)	X	0.278	= Newtons (N)	X 3.6	= Ounces-force (ozf; oz)
Pounds-force (lbf; lb)	X	4.448	= Newtons (N)	X 0.225	= Pounds-force (lbf; lb)
Newtons (N)	X	0.1	= Kilograms-force (kgf; kg)	X 9.81	= Newtons (N)

Pressure

Pounds-force per square inch (psi; lbf/in²; lb/in²)	X	0.070	= Kilograms-force per square centimetre (kgf/cm²; kg/cm²)	X 14.223	= Pounds-force per square inch (psi; lbf/in²; lb/in²)
Pounds-force per square inch (psi; lbf/in²; lb/in²)	X	0.068	= Atmospheres (atm)	X 14.696	= Pounds-force per square inch (psi; lbf/in²; lb/in²)
Pounds-force per square inch (psi; lbf/in²; lb/in²)	X	0.069	= Bars	X 14.5	= Pounds-force per square inch (psi; lbf/in²; lb/in²)
Pounds-force per square inch (psi; lbf/in²; lb/in²)	X	6.895	= Kilopascals (kPa)	X 0.145	= Pounds-force per square inch (psi; lbf/in²; lb/in²)
Kilopascals (kPa)	X	0.01	= Kilograms-force per square centimetre (kgf/cm²; kg/cm²)	X 98.1	= Kilopascals (kPa)

Torque (moment of force)

Pounds-force inches (lbf in; lb in)	X	1.152	= Kilograms-force centimetre (kgf cm; kg cm)	X 0.868	= Pounds-force inches (lbf in; lb in)
Pounds-force inches (lbf in; lb in)	X	0.113	= Newton metres (Nm)	X 8.85	= Pounds-force inches (lbf in; lb in)
Pounds-force inches (lbf in; lb in)	X	0.083	= Pounds-force feet (lbf ft; lb ft)	X 12	= Pounds-force inches (lbf in; lb in)
Pounds-force feet (lbf ft; lb ft)	X	0.138	= Kilograms-force metres (kgf m; kg m)	X 7.233	= Pounds-force feet (lbf ft; lb ft)
Pounds-force feet (lbf ft; lb ft)	X	1.356	= Newton metres (Nm)	X 0.738	= Pounds-force feet (lbf ft; lb ft)
Newton metres (Nm)	X	0.102	= Kilograms-force metres (kgf m; kg m)	X 9.804	= Newton metres (Nm)

Power

Horsepower (hp)	X	745.7	= Watts (W)	X 0.0013	= Horsepower (hp)

Velocity (speed)

Miles per hour (miles/hr; mph)	X	1.609	= Kilometres per hour (km/hr; kph)	X 0.621	= Miles per hour (miles/hr; mph)

Fuel consumption*

Miles per gallon, Imperial (mpg)	X	0.354	= Kilometres per litre (km/l)	X 2.825	= Miles per gallon, Imperial (mpg)
Miles per gallon, US (mpg)	X	0.425	= Kilometres per litre (km/l)	X 2.352	= Miles per gallon, US (mpg)

Temperature

Degrees Fahrenheit (°F) $= (°C \times \frac{9}{5}) + 32$

Degrees Celsius (Degrees Centigrade; °C) $= (°F - 32) \times \frac{5}{9}$

*It is common practice to convert from miles per gallon (mpg) to litres/100 kilometres (l/100km), where mpg (Imperial) x l/100 km = 282 and mpg (US) x l/100 km = 235

Index

**Printed by
Haynes Publishing Group
Sparkford Yeovil Somerset
England**